THE STUDY OF ANCIENT JUDAISM

II

THE PALESTINIAN AND BABYLONIAN TALMUDS

THE STUDY OF ANCIENT JUDAISM

II

THE PALESTINIAN AND BABYLONIAN TALMUDS

Edited by

JACOB NEUSNER

University Professor
Professor of Religious Studies
The Ungerleider Distinguished
Scholar of Judaic Studies
Brown University

KTAV PUBLISHING HOUSE, INC.
1981

Library of Congress Cataloging in Publication Data
Main entry under title:

The Study of ancient Judaism.

Includes bibliographies and indexes.
Contents: 1. Mishnah, Midrash, Siddur—2. The Palestinian and Babylonian Talmuds.
1. Judaism—History—Talmudic period, 10-425—Historiography. 2. Mishnah—Study—History. 3. Midrash—Study and teaching—History. 4. Judaism—Liturgy—Study and teaching—History. 5. Talmud Yerushalmi—Study—Bibliography. 6. Talmud—Study—Bibliography. I. Neusner, Jacob, 1932–
BM177.S76 296.1'206 81-5979
ISBN 0-87068-892-8 (v. 1) AACR2
ISBN 0-87068-893-6 (v.2)

Manufactured in the United States of America

Dedicated by the
three partners in this
project to
W. D. DAVIES
in homage

Table of Contents

Introduction ix

PART ONE

An Annotated Bibliographical Guide to the Study of the Palestinian Talmud 1

Baruch M. Bokser

PART TWO

The Babylonian Talmud 120

David Goodblatt

Introduction

These introductions to the literary evidence of earlier Rabbinic Judaism deal with the five most important types of documents: the Mishnah, the Midrashic compilations, the liturgy, and (in volume II) the two great Talmuds. The purpose is to explain the state of scholarship, with special interest in methods used for framing and answering the principal questions of systematic, critical learning in our own day: What do we know? How do we know it? Why is it important? The reader should be able to gain a fair insight into the way in which paramount masters of Jewish learning of the present generation formulate and work through their scholarly programs. For some documents the principal questions are historical; for others, exegetical; for still others, philological. All documents under discussion in these two books have been subjected to careful and reverent study for a very long time, a matter of nearly twenty centuries. Consequently, we cannot assume that the way questions now are asked must set the norm for how they will be asked in yet another generation, let alone conform to the norm for how they were asked in times past. The contrary is the case. The sole abiding fact is the document itself. What people make of it, why they want to deal with it at all, and the intellectual or religious purpose for which they do the work to begin with—these formative factors in the on-going traditions of learning require attentive specification. The purpose is to gain perspective both upon the documents under study and upon ourselves as contemporary students of them. The reward is to attain a clearer and more self-conscious understanding of what we do when we engage in what we deem to be critical and systematic learning.

To begin with, let us take note of the character of introductions to this same literature, for, as is obvious, these are not the first exercises of academic introduction. Indeed, if our generation succeeds in its labor, these books will also not be the last. For the aim of serious learning is to be made obsolete by better work done by others, both contemporaries and successors. These introductions thus stand in the context of works of introduction done long ago, and—it must be said—they take a position at variance with the prevailing definition of how the work of setting forth the earlier Rabbinic-Judaic writings should be done. As I shall explain, what is important to us as the writers of these books is the character of scholarship, the prevailing agendum of learning on the documents at hand: What do we wish to know? How do we find it out? We want to find our place in the intellectual continuum of learning, even as we hope to shape the character and direction of that tradition of learning for the future. What is important to others who also have proposed to write introductions to Talmud and midrash must now be spelled out, so that the contrast in context and purpose may be clear, the character of the present work may be understood.

Hermann L. Strack describes his *Introduction to the Talmud and Midrash* (first ed.: 1887; English translation: 1931) as "the first attempt to give objective and scientific information concerning the whole of the Talmud and to lead into the study of this literary monument. . . ." He emphasizes that his purpose is "to remove many a prejudice, whether with those who are unconditionally hostile to the Talmud or with its over-zealous admirers, and to pave the way for a more just and calm appraisal." It is worth remarking on Strack's statement of his apologetic motives in preparing his introduction. That statement shows how an introduction which simply assembles facts, as Strack's does, will be shaped by the purpose of the one who makes it, the audience he wishes to address, and the outcome he wishes to achieve. That Strack achieved his academic goals is indicated by the successive printings of his book, down to 1920, and in English as recently as 1965 (!). That he failed is, alas, equally obvious. For Strack stoutly opposed and decisively refuted the anti-Semitism of his day, so far as the Talmud presented a massive target of opportunity for anti-Semitism. No book, by itself, in the decades after Strack's death, could have prevented the extinction of German Jewry. But Strack's book cannot be said to have achieved its apologetic goal. In Germany the Talmud's fate was that of the Jews.

What is striking in Strack's design, to the eyes of a new generation approaching the labor of an introduction to the Talmud and Midrash, is the rather simple and (merely) informative approach deemed by Strack to be demanded. For Strack to introduce the Talmud is to provide factual information about the Talmud for people who are assumed to know nothing. The Talmud is not a vital document of scholarship. It does not provide the ground for vigorous debates about historical, cultural, or theological issues. There is no rigorous discourse about appropriate methods for framing and answering interesting questions pertinent to the Talmud and its age. The Talmud is a source of facts. So an introduction in like manner will present facts about that source of facts. Strack stood on the margin, between the Jews who knew the document, and the gentiles who, Strack thought, should utilize it for their own interests. So Strack told the scholarly world, meaning, the Protestant theological community of Germany, where to find what they would want to locate. There is nothing to read in Strack's book. It is as interesting as a telephone book: One looks things up and through the information one finds and makes the right connections. That is why Strack introduces the Talmud by defining principal terms; giving a generally uncritical sketch of the history of the Talmud; patiently describing the Mishnah, the tractates and their contents; treating the Palestinian and the Babylonian Talmuds by a "sketch of the history" of both. Then he addresses the matters of extra-canonical tractates, the Tosefta, the history of the Talmud's text, and then a repertoire of diverse information. There is, in addition, a full account of scholarly literature on various problems. The same procedure is carried out for the Midrashim, one by one: what are they, what are their traits. It is a compendium of information. There is no real introduction in an intellectual sense.

There is no need to repeat what Strack has done, I think, for he has done the work as well as that sort of work can be done. Merely up-dating Strack's information, on the other hand, serves no important scholarly purpose. For, as I have explained, we cannot accept as the final word Strack's definition of what an introduction should provide. His understanding of the historical and critical agendum for Talmudic and midrashic studies surely does not suffice more than a half-century after his death. Much which has happened in the field of Talmudic studies would be missed by a mere up-dating of information within Strack's organizing categories and topics. Indeed, even the need for an introduction to much of the factual matter deemed by Strack to be necessary hardly is to be gainsaid. For knowledge of the early Rabbinic literature is no longer limited to rabbinical circles. In European and American universities, not to mention the ones in the State of Israel, knowledge of the diverse writings of the ancient rabbis and appreciation for the importance of those writings for the study of history, religion, and culture of late antiquity, are commonplace. Educated people bring a different set of questions to the Talmud, whether or not they know what is in that document. What they want to know, and that to which they should be introduced, is why the Talmud is interesting and relevant to their intellectual agendum. And, on the other hand, the apologetic motive is no longer operative. If the Talmud and its "secrets" provide anti-Semites with yet another reason to hate the Jews, at this time and in this place the issue is not vividly drawn; there are now other grounds, alas, but the Talmud no longer demands an apologetic of an essentially non-academic character.

That is why we must reflect afresh on the purpose for which an introduction is constructed, the audience to be introduced to the documents under discussion, and the framework of discourse to be established for the entire enterprise. In paying tribute to Strack and in reaffirming the usefulness, down to 1920, of his classic introduction, we gain perspective on the exercise of this book, dealing with II. *The Palestinian and Babylonian Talmuds,* and of its predecessor, I. *Mishnah, Midrash, Siddur.*

What these papers propose to introduce is the state of scholarship on the literary evidence of early Rabbinic Judaism. Special emphasis is upon scholarship on the formation and history of that kind of Judaism. (Specifying that we deal with literary evidence is meant to give equal pride of place to non-literary evidence in archaeology and art, and it goes without saying that a set of introductions to the literary evidence about Judaism in late antiquity deriving from non-rabbinic and non-Jewish hands in due course will require its set of introductions as well.) The audience to whom the state of scholarship is introduced is composed of scholars and students of the history of religions in general, and the history of Judaism, in particular. Addressed are people who understand the humanistic program of studies which underlies and frames the particular issues of the history of religions, and of Judaism among them. True, a fair amount of the work is devoted to technical and not generally accessible issues of texts and language. These data are essential. They form the center of this book. But they serve a purpose central to the whole and are so arranged as to answer a range of fairly specific questions. The purpose is to describe what we know about the literary evidence of early Rabbinic Judaism, and, still more important, what we deem important to know about that evidence. Strack's repertoire of facts—names of tractates, description of contents—hardly requires repetition, since, in general, the facts are now readily in hand, if not in the mind of specialists in other documents of Judaism or in other religious literature entirely. In my *Invitation to the Talmud. A Teaching Book* (N.Y., 1973: Harper & Row), moreover, I have given outsiders a chance to enter into the kind of discourse presented by the Talmudic literature in the Mishnah, Tosefta, Palestinian Talmud, and Babylonian Talmud. There is then no need to describe what, in a small sample to be sure, is readily available.

But how working scholars view the field in which they work and define the questions they deem important—these are topics not introduced, to my knowledge, in any other place. The purpose of this book and its successor is to present a portrait of how workers in a field survey the field, to indicate what scholarship they regard as worth describing among the many works claiming attention, to show how they frame issues of description, interpretation, and reflection, within the literary framework within which they labor.

In all, the question is how they propose to set forth the state of the question of Mishnah, Midrash, Siddur, the Palestinian Talmud, and the Babylonian Talmud: What question? How answered? Why urgent? It goes without saying that a sustained effort at providing current bibliography is made. The more important works of the twentieth century on these five bodies of literature are listed. In many instances, they are carefully described and criticized. But this book is not meant to serve principally as a source of bibliography or even as a bibliographical essay. The authors of the two papers—Professors Bokser and Goodblatt—bring reflected-upon canons of critical judgment to their description and analysis of the texts for which they bear responsibility. They methodically ask a clearly defined range of questions. This is a work of reason and of argument, not merely a compilation of unused, and essentially unusable, information. To introduce is treated as an active and transitive verb: something to someone. And it is a verb with a subject, an actor, as well as an object, an "introduced," so to speak. So the book is meant to speak for a purpose, to make important points, to express judgments and to show how working scholars act upon them. Since that is the case, others who labor in the same field of study in due course will want, and will find that they have, to offer *their* introductions to the literary evidence of early Rabbinic Judaism. In so doing, they too will find it necessary to explain to themselves what they propose to introduce, to whom, and for what purpose.

The papers in these books cohere not only in the purposes just now described and in the critical perspectives implied or expressed here. They also cohere in their special interest in problems of method, in asking for definitions of fundamental categories and modes of inquiry. Simply stated, in common among us all is the concern to answer these four questions: Precisely what subject is under study? Why is this subject, rather than some other, reasonable alternative, the one chosen for study? What methods are used to answer the questions posed in a given work? Why are these methods, rather than some other, available alternatives, the ones which are chosen for answering the stated question? While we cannot claim to have provided a sustained methodological essay, the principal papers in this book do pursue an essentially methodological program. They in due course will contribute to a study of the methodology and hermeneutics of ancient Judaism.

The two papers which comprise this volume are reprinted from Wolfgang Haase, ed., *Aufstieg und Niedergang der römischen Welt. Geschichte und Kultur Roms im Spiegel der neueren Forschung. Principat.* II. 19.2. *Religion (Judentum: Palästinisches Judentum [Forts.])* (Berlin and New York, 1979: Walter De Gruyter), pp. 139–336. The two authors and editor are deeply grateful to Dr. Haase, as well as to Prof. H. Wenzel, humanities' editor for De Gruyter, for permission to reprint these papers and so to make them available to a wide audience in North America. I call attention to the concluding pages of this book, which list the contents of the three volumes of *ANRW* devoted to Judaism (II.19.1, 2, 3).

In important ways the study of the history of Judaism within the nascent field of history of religions in the Canadian and American humanities now comes of age. For one thing, sections on the history of Judaism at national academic meetings devoted to the study of religions frame issues of general concern to religion-scholars, so that in attendance are far more than a handful of specialists, Jewish pietists and devotees and gentile liberal-minded apologists for Judaism. Vigorous discussion of problems of general interest, in which the data of Judaism form the relevant set of data and examples for analysis, characterizes these discussions. Consequently, the study of the history of Judaism has found its rightful place within the academic framework in which it belongs. For another thing, scholarship on the sources of Judaism is now so shaped for the purposes of humanistic and general cultural discourse, that, as indicated earlier, there is a broad and educated audience accessible to humanistic learning on Judaism, its society, history, literature, culture, and theology. That audience consists of Jews and gentiles, scholars, clergy, and educated lay people as well. The result is that, just as diverse scholars of many specialties join in the analysis of the data of Judaism, so diverse students of many fields of study receive the results of analysis and make ample use of them. Indeed, work in the history of Judaism has become so widely known and amply diffused in the general intellectual community of the English-speaking world (as well as in the French- and German- language communities) that even the specialists and adepts of living Judaism, rabbis, theologians, ideologues, teachers and journalists, have begun not only to take note, but also to make use, of the results of critical learning for their own, entirely legitimate purposes of faith. The reason, I think, is that in the scholarly work described and explained in this book and its companion, *The Study of Ancient Judaism: Mishnah, Midrash, Siddur,* the literary evidences of early Rabbinic Judaism emerge in the light and language of contemporary academic discourse. They therefore regain that power which, to begin with, infused their creators, the power and will to speak to human issues of sanctification, to address the common cause of God's will and service.

J. N.

Providence, Rhode Island
15 Ab 5740
July 28th, 1980

An Annotated Bibliographical Guide to the Study of the Palestinian Talmud

by BARUCH M. BOKSER, Berkeley, Cal.

Contents
[Page numbers refer to pagination in the original publication.]

Abbreviations 141
Abbreviated Citations 142
Part One: I. Introduction 145
Part Two: The Text of Yerushalmi 149
   II. Title 149
   III. Printed Editions 151
   IV. Manuscripts 153
      A. The Leiden MS 153
      B. Vatican MS 155
      C. 'Yerushalmi Zera'im', and Tractate Sheq. with the Commentary of SOLOMON SIRILLO 156
      D. Other MSS 157
      E. Geniza Fragments 159
   V. Textual Notes to Yerushalmi 163
   VI. Translations 164
      A. Full Text of PT 164
      B. To Selected Portions of PT 164

Part Three: Contents and the History of the Materials Incorporated within PT 167
   VII. Scope of Yerushalmi 167
   VIII. Arrangement and Contents of Yerushalmi 168
      A. Basic Structure, Contents, and Forms 168
      B. Layout 170
      C. 'Mishnah' 171
      D. Citation and Use of Sources 173
   IX. Transferred Traditions and Pericopae and Unsmooth Flow of *sugyot* 178
      A. Transferred Material 178
      B. Examining Out-of-Place Traditions 180
      C. Additional Literature 181

X. Parallels in Midrashic Works 182
A. Issues and Guidelines 182
B. Indexes 183
C. Representative Literature 183
D. Specific Works 184
XI. Relationship between PT and BT: Mutual Material which may Differ 187
XII. Compilation of Yerushalmi 191
XIII. The Background to the Compilation of Yerushalmi 195
A. Locations of Masters 195
B. Names of Masters and Biographical Information 196
C. Reasons for the Compilation 197
D. Economic Conditions 197
E. General Historical Background 198

Part Four: Particular Guidelines for Study 199
XIV. Canons to Establish a Correct Text 199
A. Types of Mistakes 199
B. Means to Aid in Textual Reconstruction 200
XV. Language 201
A. The Nature of PT's Hebrew and Aramaic 202
B. The Greek and Latin Element 204
C. Comprehensive Dictionaries 205
D. Concordances 206
E. Grammars 206
F. Additional Bibliography 207
XVI. Terms and Fixed Usages 208
XVII. Aids to the Study of the Yerushalmi 210
A. Geography 211
B. Archaeological Materials and Realia 212
C. Inscriptions 213
D. Agricultural Matters 214
E. Legal Studies 215
F. Liturgical Works 217
G. Miscellaneous Indexes 220
XVIII. Post-Talmudic Palestinian Works 220
A. Palestinian *midrashim* 220
B. Minor Tractates: Halakhic and Ethical Monographs 221
C. 'Ma'asim LiVene Ereṣ Yisrael' = Collection or Digest Recording Court Decisions 222
D. Other Halakhic Works 223
E. 'Ḥilukim Sheben Anshe Mizraḥ UVene Ereṣ Yisrael' 224
F. Palestinian *responsa* 224
G. 'Śefer Yerushalmi' 224
XIX. Commentaries to Yerushalmi. A: To the Sixteenth Century 225
A. Introduction 225
B. The Use of Yerushalmi 225

C. Techniques of Citations and their Collection 227
D. Medieval Commentaries 229
E. Gaonic Works 231
F. North African Gaonic-Medieval Works 232
G. PT in Spain 233
H. PT in Provence 234
I. Northern France and Germany 235
J. Italy 237
K. Collections and Especially Notable Medieval Works 238

XX. Commentaries and Works on Yerushalmi. B: Sixteenth Century On. 241
A. Until the Vilna Gaon 241
B. Nineteenth and Twentieth Centuries: Traditional and Pre-Modern 244
C. Modern Works 246
D. Articles 249

Addendum 250
Index nominum 251

Abbreviations

Arak. = Arakhin
Archive = See Abbreviated Citations
A. Z. = Avodah Zarah
b. = Babylonian Talmud or Bavli; ben or bar.
B.B. = Bava Batra
Bekh. = Bekhorot
Ber. = Berakhot
Bes. = Beṣah
BIA = Bar Ilan Annual
Bik. = Bikurim
B.M. = Bava Mesi'a'
B.Q. = Bava Qamma
BT = Babylonian Talmud
Dem. = Dem'ai
EJ = Encyclopaedia Judaica. Jerusalem, 1972.
Eruv. = 'Eruvin
Git. = Giṭṭin
Hag. = Ḥagigah
Hal. = Ḥallah
Hor. = Horayot
HUCA = Hebrew Union College Annual
Hul. = Ḥullin
JE = Jewish Encyclopedia. New York, 1905, 1907.
JQR = Jewish Quarterly Review
JTSA = Jewish Theological Seminary of America
Ket. = Ketubot
Kil. = Kila'im
KS = Kirjath Sepher
M. = Mishnah
Maas. = Ma'aserot
Mak. = Makot
Meg. = Megillah
Men. = Menaḥot
MGWJ = Monatschrift für die Geschichte und Wissenschaft des Judentums

M.Q. = Mo'ed Qaṭan
MS = Manuscript
M.S. = Ma'aser Sheni
Nid. = Niddah
Orl. = 'Orlah
PAAJR = Proceedings of the American Academy for Jewish Research
Pes. = Pesaḥim
PT = Palestinian Talmud, Yerushalmi
Qid. = Qiddushin
Qod. = Qodshin
R. = Rav, Rabbi
REJ = Revue des Études Juives
R.H. = Rosh Hashanah
San. = Sanhedrin
Shab. = Shabbat
Sheq. = Sheqalim
Shev. = Shevi'it
Sot. = Soṭah
Suk. = Sukah
T. = Tosefta
Taan. = Ta'anit
Teh. = Ṭehorot
Ter. = Terumot
Tos. = Tosefta
TSJTSA = Text(s) and Studies of the Jewish Theological Seminary of America
y. = Yerushalmi, Palestinian Talmud
Yev. = Yevamot
Zer. = Zera'im
Zev. = Zevaḥim

Abbreviated Citations

The following items are repeatedly cited in the course of the paper. The first and main entry includes full bibliographical information. Thereafter the works are identified by the author's name and the date of publication. In the citation of an article in a journal, the subsequent references delete only the title of the study and are, therefore, not included here. Likewise, I do not, in general, include in the following list abbreviated, second, references within a section when the first instance includes the full bibliographical information.

ABRAMSON (1965) = SHRAGA ABRAMSON, R. Nissim Gaon. Jerusalem, 1965.

ABRAMSON (1974) = SHRAGA ABRAMSON, Inyanot BeŚifrut HaGaonim. Jerusalem, 1974.

ALBECK (1944) = CHANOCH ALBECK, Studies in the Baraita and Tosefta. Jerusalem, 1944.

ALBECK (1967) = CHANOCH ALBECK, Introduction to the Mishnah. Third ed. Jerusalem-Tel Aviv, 1967.

ALBECK (1969) = CHANOCH ALBECK, Introduction to Talmud Babli and Yerushalmi. Tel Aviv, 1969.

APTOWITZER (1938) = (A)VIGDOR APTOWITZER, Introductio ad Sefer Rabiah. Jerusalem, 1938.

Archive I (1972) = Archive of the New Dictionary of Rabbinical Literature. I. Ed. E. Y. KUTSCHER, Ramat Gan, 1972.

Archive II (1974) = Archive . . ., II. Ed. M. Z. KEDDARI, Ramat Gan, 1974.

ASSIS (1976) = MOSHE ASSIS, Parallel *sugyot* in the Jerusalem Talmud (In the Tractates: Bikkurim, Shabbath, Soṭah, Makkoth, and Niddah). (Ph. D. Dissertation, Hebrew University, 1976). Jerusalem, 1976.

Baron II—VIII = Salo Baron, A Social and Religious History of the Jews, Vols. II—VIII. New York, 1952—1958. At times cited without the date, just Baron and the volume number.

Bokser (1975) = Baruch M. Bokser, Samuel's Commentary on the Mishnah: Its Nature, Forms, and Content. I. Leiden, 1975.

Bokser, Two Traditions (1975) = Baruch M. Bokser, Two Traditions of Samuel: Evaluating Alternative Versions, Christianity, Judasim and Other Greco Roman Cults. Studies for Morton Smith at Sixty. Ed. J. Neusner. Leiden, 1975. IV, 46—55.

Epstein (1948) = Jacob N. Epstein, Introduction to the Text of the Mishnah. Jerusalem, 1948. Indexed second edition, Jerusalem, 1964.

Epstein (1957) = Jacob N. Epstein, Introduction to Tannaitic Literature. Jerusalem, 1957.

Epstein (1962) = Jacob N. Epstein, Introduction to Amoraitic Literature. Jerusalem, 1962.

Feldblum (1964) = Meyer S. Feldblum, Professor Abraham Weiss: His Approach and Contribution to Talmudic Scholarship, in: The Abraham Weiss Jubilee Volume. New York, 1964. English section, pp. 7—80.

Feldblum (1969) = Meyer S. Feldblum, Talmudic Law and Literature. Tractate Gittin. New York, 1969.

Frankel (1870) = Z. Frankel, Mavo HaYerushalmi. Breslau, 1870. Repr. Jerusalem, 1967.

Ginzberg (1909) = Louis Ginzberg, Yerushalmi Fragments from the Genizah. I. (Texts and Studies of the Jewish Theological Seminary of America, Vol. III). New York, 1909. Repr. Jerusalem, 1969.

Ginzberg, Geonica I—II (1909) = Louis Ginzberg, Geonica I—II. (TSJTSA, Vols. I—II). New York, 1909. Repr. 1968.

Ginzberg (1928—29) = Louis Ginzberg, Genizah Studies in Memory of Doctor Solomon Schechter (= Ginze Schechter). I—II. (TSJTSA, Vols. VII—VIII). New York, 1928—1929. Repr. 1969.

Ginzberg (1941) = Louis Ginzberg, Commentary on the Palestinian Talmud. 4 vols. (TSJTSA, X, XI, XII, XXI). New York, 1941, 1961. For Vol. I. 1941, Roman numerals refer to the Introduction. Those prefaced by an H = Hebrew introduction. Those without the H = English introduction.

Goodblatt (1975) = David Goodblatt, Rabbinic Instruction in Sasanian Babylonia. Leiden, 1975.

Goodblatt (1979) = David Goodblatt, The Babylonian Talmud, in: ANRW II, 19.2, pp. 257—336 (= elsewhere in this volume).

Habermann (1952) = Meir Habermann, Added chapter, 'HaTalmud HaYerushalmi', to revised ed. of Raphel Rabbinovicz, Ma'amar ʿal Hadpaśat HaTalmud. Jerusalem, 1952, pp. 203—222, 252—254.

Hirschberg (1974) = H. Z. Hirschberg, History of the Jews in North Africa. Leiden, 1974.

Hospers (1973) = J. H. Hospers, A Basic Bibliography for the Study of the Semitic Languages. I. Leiden, 1973.

Kahana (1972) = Kalman Kahana, Maśekhet Shevicjt. Ḥeqer VeʿIyun. Tel Aviv, 1972.

Kasher (1959) = Menahem M. Kasher and Jacob B. Mandelbaum, Sarei Ha-Elef. A Millenium of Hebrew Authors (500—1500). New York, 1959. Supplemented in Śefer Adam Noah. Ed. Ḥayyim Liphsitz, Jerusalem, 1970, pp. 213—299.

Kohn (1952) = P. Jacob Kohn, Thesaurus of Hebrew Halachic Literature. London, 1952.

Kutscher (1972) = See Archive I (1972) and II (1972).

Levine (1975) = Lee I. Levine, Caesarea Under Roman Rule. Leiden, 1975.

Lewin (1933) = B. M. Lewin, Monumenta Gaonica: Methiboth [Śefer Metivot]. Jerusalem, 1933. Repr. 1973.

Lewy (1895—1914) = I. Lewy, Introduction and Commentary to Talmud Yerushalmi. B.Q. I—VI. Jahresbericht des jüdisch-theologischen Seminars Fraenckel'scher Stiftung. 1895—1914. Repr. Jerusalem, 1970.

LIEBERMAN (1929) = SAUL LIEBERMAN, On the Yerushalmi. Jerusalem, 1929.
LIEBERMAN (1931) = SAUL LIEBERMAN, Talmud of Caesarea (Suppl. to Tarbiz, II). Jerusalem, 1931.
LIEBERMAN (1934) = SAUL LIEBERMAN, HaYerushalmi Kiphshuto. Jerusalem, 1934.
LIEBERMAN, TR. (1937—39) = SAUL LIEBERMAN, Tosefeth Rishonim. 4 Vols. Jerusalem, 1937—1939.
LIEBERMAN (1941) = SAUL LIEBERMAN, Greek in Jewish Palestine. N.Y., 1941, 1964².
LIEBERMAN (1947) = SAUL LIEBERMAN, Hilkhoth Ha-Yerushalmi of Rabbi Moses Ben Maimon. (TSJTSA. XIII). New York, 1947.
LIEBERMAN (1950) = SAUL LIEBERMAN, The Old Commentators of the Yerushalmi. Alexander Marx Jubilee Volume. Ed. S. LIEBERMAN, New York, 1950. Hebrew Section, pp. 287—336.
LIEBERMAN (1955ff.) = SAUL LIEBERMAN, Tosefta Ki-fshuṭah I ff. New York, 1955ff.
LIEBERMAN (1963) = SAUL LIEBERMAN, Yerushalmi Horayot. Śefer HaYovel LeRebbi Ḥanockh Albeck. Jerusalem, 1963, pp. 283—305.
LIEBERMAN, SZ (1968) = SAUL LIEBERMAN, Siphre Zutta. New York, 1968.
LIEBERMAN (1971) = SAUL LIEBERMAN, Introduction to the Leiden MS. PT Leiden MS. Cod. Scal. 3. Jerusalem, 1971. I, i—vi.

Makhon-Mishnah (1972) = Makhon HaTalmud. Mishnah. Zera'im, I. Ed. YEHOSHUA HUTNER. Jerusalem, 1973.
MARGALIOTH = See MARGULIES.
MARGULIES [or MARGALIOTH] (1960) = MORDECHAI MARGULIES [or MARGALIOTH], Midrash Wayyikra Rabbah. V: Introduction. Jerusalem, 1960.
MARGULIES [or MARGALIOTH] (1962) = MORDECHAI MARGULIES, Hilkhot Hannagid. Jerusalem, 1962.
MARGULIES [or MARGALIOTH] (1973) = MORDECHAI MARGULIES, Hilkhot Ereṣ Yisrael Min HaGenizah, Jerusalem, 1973.
MELAMED (1943) = E. Z. MELAMED, Halachic Midrashim of the Tannaim. In the Talmud Babli. Jerusalem, 1943.
MELAMED [or MELAMMED] (1973) = E. Z. MELAMED [or MELAMMED], An Introduction to Talmudic Literature. Jerusalem, 1973.

NEUSNER (1966—70) = JACOB NEUSNER, A History of the Jews of Babylonia. 5 Vols. Leiden, 1966—70.
NEUSNER (1970) = JACOB NEUSNER. Development of a Legend. Leiden, 1975.
NEUSNER, Formation (1970) = JACOB NEUSNER, Ed. Formation of the Babylonian Talmud. Leiden, 1970.
NEUSNER (1971) = JACOB NEUSNER, The Rabbinic Traditions About the Pharisees Before 70. 3 Vols. Leiden, 1971.
NEUSNER (1973) = JACOB NEUSNER, Eliezer Ben Hyrcanus. 2 Vols. Leiden, 1973.
NEUSNER, Modern Study (1973) = JACOB NEUSNER, Ed. The Modern Study of the Mishnah. Leiden, 1973.
NEUSNER, Purities (1974—1977) = JACOB NEUSNER, History of the Mishnaic Law of Purities. 22 Vols. Leiden, 1974—1977.

POZNANSKI (1907—08) = SAMUEL POZNANSKI, Inyanim Shonim HaNoge'im LiTequfat HaGeonim. HaKedem I (1907), 48—133; II (1908), 24—54, 91—109, 114—116.

RABINOVITZ (1940) = Z. W. RABINOVITZ, Sha'are Torath Eretz Israel. Jerusalem, 1940.
RATNER (1901—1917) = B. RATNER, Ahawath Zion We-Jeruscholaim. 11 Vols. Vilna, 1901—1917. Repr. in 10 Vols. Jerusalem, 1967. — Often cited by volume and publication date.

SHAKED (1964) = SHAUL SHAKED, A Tentative Bibliography of Geniza Documents. Paris and The Hague, 1964.
SIMONSOHN (1974) = SHLOMO SIMONSOHN, The Hebrew Revival Among Early Medieval European Jews. Salo Wittmayer Baron Jubilee Volume. Jerusalem, 1974. Hebrew Section. II, pp. 831—858.

SPIEGEL (1965) = S. SPIEGEL, On the Polemic of Pirqoi Ben Baboi. Harry A. Wolfson Jubilee Volume. Ed. S. LIEBERMAN. Jerusalem, 1965. Hebrew Section, pp. 243—274.

STRACK (1931) = HERMAN STRACK, Introduction to the Talmud and Midrash. Philadelphia, 1931.

SUSSMANN (1973—74) = Y. SUSSMANN, A Halakhic Inscription from the Beth-Shean Valley. Tarbiẓ 43 (1973—74), 88—158: and 'Additional Notes', Tarbiẓ 44 (1974—75), 193—195.

TCHERNOWITZ (1946—47) = CHAIM TCHERNOWITZ, Toledoth Ha-Poskim. 3 Vols. New York, 1946—47. Cited by volume and date.

TOWNER (1973) = WAYNE SIBLEY TOWNER, The Rabbinic 'Enumeration of Scriptural Examples'. Leiden, 1973.

TOWNSEND (1972) = JOHN T. TOWNSEND, Rabbinic Sources. Anti-Defamation League of B'nai B'rith. The Study of Judaism: Bibliographical Essays. New York, 1972.

UMANSKI (1952) = YOSEF UMANSKI, Ḥakhme HaTalmud. PT. Jerusalem, 1952.

URBACH (1955) = E. E. URBACH, The Tosaphists: Their History, Writings and Methods. Jerusalem, 1955.

URBACH (1963) = E. E. URBACH, Prolegomena Et Indices Continens. Sefer Arugat HaBosem of R. Abraham b. R. Azriel. Jerusalem 1963.

WEISS (1954) = ABRAHAM WEISS, The Talmud in its Development. New York, 1954.

WEISS (1957) = ABRAHAM WEISS, Court Procedure. New York, 1957.

WEISS (1962) = ABRAHAM WEISS, Studies in the Literature of the Amoraim. New York, 1962.

WEISS (1966) = ABRAHAM WEISS, Studies in the Law of the Talmud on Damages. Jerusalem-New York, 1966.

WEISS, Notes = ABRAHAM WEISS, Notes To Talmudic Pericopae. University Bar Ilan. Ramat Gan, n.d.

WEISS HALIVNI (1968, 1975) = DAVID WEISS HALIVNI, Sources and Traditions, I—II. Jerusalem, 1968, 1975.

Part One

I. Introduction

The present paper provides guidelines and a selected annotated bibliography for the study of the Yerushalmi, the *gemara* produced by Palestinian rabbis in the third to fifth centuries, C. E.*

* I cite the English titles of Hebrew books and articles where they are provided. Where a translation is lacking for an item in a clearly recognizable Israeli Hebrew journal, I generally translate the title. I transliterate the titles of the remaining works.
In several Sections, I star the more important studies.
I owe thanks to the following libraries: the University of California, at Berkeley — Doe Library, Office of Inter-Library Loan, and Robbins Collection, Boalt Law School; Graduate Theological Union, Berkeley; University of California, at Los Angeles — Research Library; and the Jewish Theological Seminary of America, New York. I also thank Profs. MENACHEM SCHMELZER and DAVID WEISS HALIVNI, of the Jewish Theological Seminary of America, Profs. JACOB NEUSNER and RICHARD SARASON, Brown University, and WOLFGANG HAASE, Tübingen, who as editor of this volume offered numerous improvements to the text. I am appreciative, as well, of the substantive improvements and corrections suggested by Profs. JACOB SUSSMANN and LEE LEVINE, Hebrew University, Jerusalem, Prof. MOSHE ASSIS, Hebrew Union College, Cincinnati, and Prof. REUVEN KIMELMAN, Brandeis University, Waltham. I am further grateful to the Committee on Research, UC Berkeley, which provided funds to cover typing and other research expenses.

1. The works and items necessary for the use and study of the text are discussed and representative books or articles cited with suggestions as to how they contribute to or differ in the analysis of a problem. Additional literature is usually cited. Full bibliographical information is provided in the first and/or main entry of a work and recurrently used items are thereafter cited by the author's name and the date of publication. An index to only these items appears at the beginning of the Guide. The format varies, as the problems and the state of the several fields greatly vary. Where there are existing bibliographies, I refer to them and refine my selection. My comments are designed to sensitize the reader to certain problems, draw attention to relevant aids and areas of investigation, and facilitate the critical use of the works and commentaries. On the other hand, in certain basic 'informational' areas a more expository format is followed. The main features of an issue are laid out and footnotes employed accordingly, although annotated lists of the literature are also provided.

My task has not been to pass judgment on every book or study. Moreover, comments generally are limited to a work's relevance to the study of y. and do not deal with its other features. As one cannot sharply distinguish between 'traditional' and 'modern' works I include both. The traditional rabbinic authorities have made important contributions to the study of the Palestinian Talmud in numerous areas in addition to exegesis. As the familiar reader knows or the unfamiliar will soon realize exegetical matters in y. are intimately tied to textual and critical concerns. While I therefore include the serious 'traditional' works and items that cite them, I add as well certain current literature because of its availability on the market. Hopefully my comments will enable one appropriately and fully to use these works.

2. My study does not stand in a vacuum. While there have been no classified, even partial, bibliographies to y., there are three works which are somewhat helpful. M. A. KASHER and J. B. MANDELBAUM, Sarei Ha-Elef, A Millenium of Hebrew Authors (500—1500) (New York, 1959), with its 'Supplement', in ḤAYYIM LIPHSHITZ, ed., Śefer Adam Noah (Jerusalem, 1970), pp. 213—229, contains various lists in which one may find items relevant to y. P. J. KOHN, Thesaurus of Hebrew Halakhic Literature (London, 1952), and JUDAH RUBENSTEIN, Quntriś HaShalem Shel Mefarshe HaYerushalmi (New York, 1949) [published as an appendix to the Shulsinger reprint of the Krotoshin edition of PT (New York, 1949)], each provides a single list of items on y. Likewise there have been several previous introductions to PT. But Z. FRANKEL's Mavo HaYerushalmi (Breslau, 1870, Repr. Jerusalem, 1967) is the only fully comprehensive study and has more or less set the agendum in the later works.*

FRANKEL pointed to the main features of y. and its history and many later writers have but varied in their emphasis, interpretation, or conclusion. Earlier ELIJAH, the Gaon of Vilna, had pointed to the proper exegetical

* For the reception accorded FRANKEL in his own day, see the review of A. GEIGER, Jüdische Zeitschrift für Wissenschaft und Leben 6 (1870), 278—306.

method to analyze y. in its own terms. I. LEWY, 1895—1914, made a methodological breakthrough in his analysis of the editing of y. and careful exegesis of B.Q. I—VI. W. BACHER in his article 'Talmud' in the Jewish Encyclopedia, Vol. 2 (New York, 1905, 1907), made an important contribution as well as excellent review of previous literature.

In the twentieth century, the rise of careful critical Talmudic scholarship, led by JACOB N. EPSTEIN, contributed to an understanding of the y. and its relationship to other bodies of sources. LOUIS GINZBERG published a huge corpus of 'Yerushalmi Fragments from the Genizah' (New York, 1909). Those and subsequently published fragments provided fairly accurate texts, free from many textual and scribal corruptions. Textual studies advanced through these publications and the growing awareness of the importance of the Leiden MS, the only MS to the complete PT and the *Vorlage* to the first printed edition, Venice, 1523.

Further publications from the Geniza indicated that Palestine was the home of creative legal and aggadic activity in the post-Talmudic period. That realization joined the emancipation or freedom from the 'traditional' preference of the BT over the PT and the former's supposed 'authenticity'. While in the nineteenth century this 'turn' may have been related to contemporary religious and intellectual issues, in the twentieth it was tied to a growing historical sophistication.

LIEBERMAN, in a series of publications, squarely faced the main issues in the study of y. He asked refined questions, sought standards in the use of tools, and demonstrated how one should and could employ careful logical evaluation of matters and not mere speculation or unbridled analysis. In 'On the Yerushalmi' (Jerusalem, 1929), he laid down the criteria for textual analysis, cataloged textual problems in the study of y., reviewed previous studies, and set out programs necessary for an adequate resolution. He further carefully analyzed the Vatican MS to 'Soṭah'. [The MS covers 'Zera'im' and 'Soṭah'.] In 'Talmud of Caesarea' (Jerusalem, 1931), he produced a systematic study [the only one to date] of the editing of one part of Yerushalmi. He, moreover provided a model how one may and should tackle such questions of higher criticism. In 'HaYerushalmi Kiphshuto: Sabbath, Erubin, Pesahim' (Jerusalem, 1934), in a 30-page introduction and 525-page application to three tractates of y., he further refined and supplemented his earlier introductory remarks. During those and subsequent years he published articles in which he focused on important methodological tools or proper uses of various materials relevant to y., e.g., liturgical poetry (*piyyuṭ*). While all of his subsequent publications illuminate PT, they formally turn away from that document — but only formally. He demonstrates that one must be sensitive to the social, cultural, and political life and linguistic milieu in Late Antiquity, especially in Palestine. Most of these articles appear in 'Greek in Jewish Palestine' (New York, 1941, 1965²), 'Hellenism in Jewish Palestine' (New York, 1950), and collected items in 'Texts and Studies' (New York, 1974). In addition, he turned to the elucidation of 'Tosefta', a corpus whose materials form one of the building blocks of y. He produced a four-volume 'Tosefeth Rishonim' (Jerusalem, 1937—39) to establish the text of 'Tosefta', and in 1955 he issued the first volumes of his monumental edition of Tosefta and comprehensive commentary, 'Tosefta Ki-Fshuṭah' (New York, 1955). There he lays out Tosefta's halakhic and aggadic teachings and modes of thought and indicates how it often forms a 'Palestinian' interpretation of matters, very frequently common to PT but not to BT. He thus enables one to have firm data in the analysis of y.'s content.

J. N. EPSTEIN as well demonstrated the careful philological analysis of texts, and systematically studied the varied knowledge of 'Mishnah' in Amoraic times and how different individuals related to it. His own 'Introduction to PT', in the form of notes, was published posthumously (Jerusalem, 1962). Finally one should mention LOUIS GINZBERG, Commentary on the Palestinian Talmud (New York, 1941—61). Along the lines of the work's subtitle, 'A Study of the Development of the Halakah and Haggadah in Palestine and Babylonia', he analyzed Ber. I—V. He included in Volume I separate long English and Hebrew 'Introductions', wherein he provides a comprehensive review of many of the features of y. and its study. That introduction has become formative in subsequent studies. H. STRACK, Introduction to Talmud and Midrash [= English translation of revised version of fifth and last German edition (Munich, 1921)] (Philadelphia, 1931, variously reprinted), had reviewed or listed the earlier (through about 1920) literature. Z. M. RABINOWITZ, Talmud, Jerusalem, EJ 15 (1972), 772—779 and especially E. Z. MELAMMED, An Introduction to Talmudic Literature (Jerusalem, 1973), review all the aforementioned and other literature. At times, MELAMMED compares the several approaches and adds independent contributions.

3. The present author draws on the above works and even where no reference is made is still often in their debt. From one perspective the paper constitutes an examination of the degree to which LIEBERMAN's program has been acted upon. In addition, however, I try to bring to bear the progress made in numerous areas required in the study of y. Moreover, writers including ABRAHAM WEISS, DAVID WEISS HALIVNI, JACOB NEUSNER, E. S. ROSENTHAL, and others have turned to literary and historical questions, and have attempted to understand rabbinic sources through the history of the materials. For example, they try to elucidate how traditions and pericopae received the shape they presently have. Formally some of these studies are not directly on y. or its problems. But naturally such studies, especially those on BT, also illuminate aspects of y. One of my tasks has been to isolate and indicate those aspects relevant and appropriate to the study of y. With new means, research may thus systematically analyze the problems raised by the earlier works. They may now be first tooled with the historical, literary and philological sophistication laid out in the works of LIEBERMAN and others, and secondly be aware of the modern scholarly agenda of the twentieth century in its study of Late Antique literature, language, religion, and history.

Scholarly circles have unfortunately paid insufficient attention to the study of y. Some interest appears in recent Israeli religious and scholarly circles which are motivated by a concern for the Jewish past in the land of

Israel, particularly in agricultural matters. They tend, though, to limit their studies to 'Zera'im' and related items. On the other hand, many individuals use PT in the study of some other discipline or in the analysis of problems external to y. Hopefully the present study which is formulated and designed to provide a perspective on the problems, issues, and literature will stimulate and facilitate further systematic study of y. and more accurate use of its materials. *

Part Two
The Text of Yerushalmi

II. Title

Sources use several terms to refer to the Yerushalmi. Palestinian circles from the post-Talmudic period refer to y. without naming the work and initially at most cite the name of a tractate. In the land of Israel, the PT undoubtedly was the 'Talmud' par excellence[1].

Elsewhere, however, a distinctive terminology was necessary. Gaonic sources use several terminologies. We find גמרא דארץ ישראל, *GMR' D'RṢ YSR'L*, "the *gemara* of the Land of Israel", or תלמוד ארץ ישראל, *TLMWD 'RṢ YSR'L*, "the Talmud of the Land of Israel". 'Halakhot Gedolot' has *TMLWD DM'RB'*, "the Talmud of the West"[2]. Rabbenu Ḥananel from

* E. S. ROSENTHAL recently uncovered a heretofore unknown Spanish MS to y. Neziqin, tractates B.Q., B.M., and B.B., and presently, as part of the Project for the Critical Editing of Amoraic Literature, of the Institute for Jewish Studies of the Hebrew University, Jerusalem, is preparing it for publication. The MS's readings are not always identical to those of the L.MS and at times it preserves a separate tradition of the y. text. See Ha'ares, January 28, 1977, p. 16, and below, IV, D. 4. An analysis of the MS is liable to confirm, disprove, or complicate various points discussed in this study, especially as to the history of the y. text, the evaluation of the L. MS, and the theories explaining the differences between y. Neziqin and the rest of the PT. The find makes clear that much work remains and new discoveries may yet appear with significant, if not potentially revolutionary, implications.

1 See E. S. ROSENTHAL, Leshonot Śofrim, in: Yuval Shy. A Jubilee Volume Dedicated to S. Y. Agnon. Ed. BARUCH KURZWEIL (Ramat Gan, 1958), p. 31, as to the practice of the scribe of Vatican MS 30 to Gn. Rabbah. We find the somewhat different unexplicit terms *TLMWD, TLMWD (LWMR) LYMDWNW RBWTYNW*, "the teaching" or "the teaching (says), our rabbis taught us." The latter formula is used to cite Amoraic, including Palestinian, traditions. See MARGULIES (1973), p. 51, fn. 3 and V. APTOWITZER, Untersuchungen zur Gaonäischen Literatur, HUCA 8—9 (1931—32), 389. Cf. Z. M. RABINOWITZ, Sepher HaMa'asim Livnei Erez Yisra'el — New Fragments, Tarbiẓ 41 (1972), 279. Cf. below, Section XVIII. C.

2 See LOUIS GINZBERG, Geonica, II: Genizah Studies (New York, 1909, Repr. 1968), index s. v. TLMWD 'RṢ YSR'L, esp. pp. 39, 142, 271, and ID., Genizah Studies, II: Geonic and

Qairawan, sometimes uses the phrase, גרסי במערבא, *GRŚY BM'RB'*, "they read in the West"[3], and R. Nissim of Qairawan, ca. 990—1062 employs a distinctive terminology, גמרא דבני מערבא, *GMR' DBNY M'RB'*, "the *gemara* of the people of the West", and only occasionally *TLMWD 'RṢ YSR'L*. At times R. Nissim names a tractate to which he appends the phrase דבני מערבא, *DBNY M'RB'*[4].

The name ירושלמי, *YRWŠLMY*, Yerushalmi, has few occurrences in Gaonic times, though it is attested. It is used commonly by Ḥananel and perhaps by R. Nissim and clearly occasionally by Alfasi and then frequently by Medieval European authorities[5]. As Jerusalem did not have an Amoraic academy, the term does not fit the historical situation of Talmudic times. BARON has aptly suggested that the term derives from a time after the Moslem conquest of Jerusalem and the subsequent reestablishment of an academy in the city[6].

Scholars have indicated that the word 'Yerushalmi' has also been used so as to refer to certain works other than the PT, a matter which I discuss below[7].

The Venice first edition, 1523—24, and its primary *Vorlage*, Leiden MS Scal. 3[8] both use the term Talmud Yerushalmi, which undoubtedly con-

Early Karaitic Halakah (New York, 1929, Repr. 1969), pp. 328, 324, 287, 335, 337, SAMUEL POZNANSKI, 'Inyanim Shonim HaNoge'im LiTequfat HaGeonim [= Variae Relating to the Gaonic Period], HaKedem, 2 (1908), 25, fn. 1, 28, and especially p. 115. J. N. EPSTEIN, Der Gaonäische Kommentar zur Ordnung — Tohoroth (Berlin, 1915), pp. 75f.; SHRAGA ABRAMSON, R. Nissim Gaon (Jerusalem, 1965), pp. 12, n. 1; 71 n. 3; 212f. Cf. B. M. LEWIN, Monumenta Gaonica: Methiboth (Jerusalem, 1933, Repr. 1973), pp. vii—x, and in general, HERMAN L. STRACK, Introduction to the Talmud and Midrash (Philadelphia, 1931), pp. 65, 265.

3 The use of the word, "in the West", undoubtedly reflects or is a continuation of BT's usage of *BM'RB 'MRY*, "In the West they say", and variations thereof, all of which serve to refer to Palestinian traditions. Cf. J. N. EPSTEIN, Introduction to Amoraitic Literature (Jerusalem, 1962), pp. 292—312.
In the several formulae, the word *GRŚY*, "read", refers to the text of *gemara*; cf. S. ABRAMSON, BeMerkazim UVaTefuṣot (Jerusalem, 1965), p. 125, and ID., 'Inyanot BeSifrut HaGaonim (Jerusalem, 1974), p. 172.

4 ABRAMSON (1965), loc. cit., and 186f., 186 n. 2, 212—213, 245, and 545f.

5 POZNANSKI (1908), p. 115; S. ASSAF, Responsa Geonica (Jerusalem, 1942), p. 41, fn. 7; ABRAMSON (1965), p. 212. For the medieval authorities, cf. e.g., the indexes to the several commentaries published in: Harry Fischel Institute Publications Section III. Rishonim. Vol. I [On Tractate Mo'ed Qaṭan] (Jerusalem, 1937); Novellae of Solomon Ben Adret to Tractate Megillah, ed. H. Z. DIMITROVSKY (New York, 1956), p. xxx; and Piskei HaRid, The Rulings of Rabbi Isaiah the Elder, I Tractates, Berakhot and Shabbat, ed. ABRAHAM WORTHEIMER and ABRAHAM LISS (Jerusalem, 1964), Introduction, p. 18. The Tosefot, according to one survey, employ the term *YRWŠLMY* 761 times, and *GMRT 'RṢ YSR'L* 305 times. See PEREZ TARSHISH, The Personalities and Books Referred to in Tosefot, ed. S. A. NEUHAUSEN (New York, 1942), pp. xvii—xviii, fns. 5 and 10.

6 SALO BARON, A Social and Religious History of the Jews, VI (New York, 1958), p. 331, n. 25. Cf., though, the use of *YRWŠLMY* to refer to Palestine in b. B. Q. 6 b [*MSS* read *YRWŠLM'H*; see R. RABBINOVICZ, Variae Lectiones in Mischname et in Talmud Babylonicum. Tractate BaBa [Kama] (Monachii, 1882, Repr. Jerusalem, New York, and Montreal,. 1960), p. 8, fn. 3] and in the Vatican MS to y. Orl. 3: 8; 63b.

7 Section XVIII. F.

8 See below Section IV. A.

tributed to or caused its subsequent popular usage. Some individuals, of course, used one of the other terms, e.g. Meiri uses תלמוד המערב, *TLMWD HM'RB*, Talmud HaMa'arav, the "Western Talmud"[9].

III. Printed Editions

This section reviews the printed editions of y. Editions that are printed along with commentaries appear in Chapter XX.

The first printed text of the whole PT, is that of DANIEL BOMBERG, Venice, 1523—24.[10] The text without any commentary covers thirty nine of the sixty three tractes of 'Mishnah'. Three of these are incomplete. As indicated below, this text is primarily based on Codex Leiden Scal. 3. All subsequent modern editions are based on the first edition, to which changes have been made, though none on the basis of other MSS.

There are several editions of individual tractates which represent a separate literary tradition. The first complete edition of BT, Venice, 1520—23, contains the text of two PT tractates, y. Sheq. and y. Horayot. As Sheq. lacks a BT tractate, y. Sheq. had been appended to M. Sheq. (1522), following a practice which goes back to Gaonic times. The text is a different type from that of the PT first edition, but it has been contaminated by BT's style and idiom. The inclusion of y. Sheq. with BT likewise accounts for the existence of several medieval commentaries to the tractate. One, the MS which includes the commentary of R. Meshullam, ed., ABRAHAM SCHREIBER, Treatise Shekalim (New York, 1954), contains a text of y. that employed MS(S) different from that used in Ven. p.e. but similar to the one in the supplement in the BT first edition[11]. A list of these MSS appear in Section IV. D.

MOSHE ASSIS is preparing a critical introduction and edition of y. Sheq. which promises systematically to trace and evaluate the readings at each stage of the text. According to his preliminary report[11a], the text of the PT first edition constitutes an eclectic text based upon the L. MS and the BT supplement. The L. MS itself suffered additions of marginal readings

[9] Cf., e. g., ADRET, DIMITROVSKY ed. (1956), ibid., and Menahem HaMeiri, Beit HaBeḥirah to Tractate Berakhot, ed. SOLOMON DAIKMAN (Jerusalem, 1965²), p. 5.

[10] A. M. HABERMANN, HaTalmud HaYerushalmi. An Added Chapter in his Reissue of Raphael Rabbinovicz, Ma'amar 'al Hadpaśat HaTalmud (Jerusalem, 1952), pp. 203—205; ABRAHAM BERLINER, Beit HaDefuś HaIvri Shel Daniel Bomberg, Ketavim Nevḥarim, II, ed. A. M. HABERMANN (Jerusalem, 1949), p. 169; P. KAHLE, Cairo Geniza (Oxford, 1959), pp. 120f.; and especially S. LIEBERMAN, Yerushalmi Horayot, Śefer HaYovel leRebbi Ḥanoh Albeck (Jerusalem, 1963), p. 286.

[11] LIEBERMAN (1963), p. 286, and LIEBERMAN, The Old Commentators of the Yerushalmi, Alexander Marx Jubilee Volume (New York, 1950), Hebrew Section, pp. 295f. and fn. 29; cf. B. RATNER, Ahawath Zion We-Jerusholaim (Vilna, Repr. Jerusalem, 1967), Sheq., pp. 1f.

[11a] MOSHE ASSIS, Concerning the History of the Text of Tractate Sheqalim. Seventh World Congress of Jewish Studies. Jerusalem, Israel, August 8, 1977.

drawn from the BT supplement and readings from another MS. The other extant MS, the Oxford MS published by SCHREIBER, is the most corrupt of all the MSS. Its value, though, is enhanced by the accompanying commentaries.

As b. Horayot lacked the commentaries of the 'Tosefot', the editor (1521) included the y. portion. This text contains important readings. SAUL LIEBERMAN, Yerushalmi Horayot, Śefer HaYovel leRebbi Ḥanoh Albeck (Jerusalem, 1963), pp. 283—305, has shown that this text represents one of the 'other' MSS upon which the Ven. p.e. of the PT purportedly is based, which, however, was not systematically used. Unfortunately each of the two locations of y. Horayot has suffered several series of corruptions by editors who unknowingly successively 'corrected' the text of one on the basis of the previous edition of the other.

y. 'Zera'im', along with that of Sheq. appears in the text and commentary of R. SOLOMON SIRILLO. This edition is discussed in Section IV. C.

Lists of editions include:

Z. FRANKEL (1870), pp. 138b—141b.
STRACK (1931), p. 83, succinct and still useful.
GINZBERG (1941), passim.
*A. M. HABERMANN, HaTalmud HaYerushalmi (Jerusalem, 1952), pp. 203—222 and ns. 252—54, describes contents of editions of the complete y. and of individual tractates and notes the relationship between each of the editions. As the editions common on today's market are reprints of earlier printings, HABERMANN's comments are useful in the evaluation of editions. The listings, with indexes, in 'Kirjath Sepher', published quarterly by Magnes Press, enables one to keep abreast of more recent editions[12].

The editions of note include Krotoschin, 1886, reprinted New York, 1948, and Jerusalem, 1969, which has a brief commentary, based upon that of the Cracow 1609 edition, to which is added corrections and an index to cross references; ZHITOMER, 1860—67, five volume edition with commentaries[13]; especially PETERKOV, 1898—1900 in eight volumes; and Vilna, 1922, with additional commentaries, in 7 volumes, reprinted New York, 1959, and Jerusalem, 1960, 1973.

A. M. LUNCZ issued five volumes of an attempted critical edition, Berakhot through Shev., Jerusalem, 1907—1919, Talmud Hierosolymitanum ad exemplar editionis principis. The text is based upon the Leiden and Vatican MSS, the MS that accompanies the commentary of SIRILLO, and some geniza fragments, and includes cross references and verse indexes, and a succinct commentary.

[12] Of course, one may also consult MENAHEM M. KASHER and JACOB B. MANDELBAUM, Sarei Ha-Elef (New York, 1959) and its 'Supplement', published in ḤAYYIM LIPHSHITZ, ed. Śefer Adam Noah (Jerusalem, 1970), pp. 213—299 [A revised edition is under preparation]; and P. JACOB KOHN, Thesaurus of Hebrew Halachic Literature (London, 1952).

[13] Useful reviews include: Z. FRANKEL, MGWJ 16 (1867), 194—198; P. RITTER, MGWJ 42 (1898), 429f.; JOSEF MIESES, MGWJ 74 (1930), 314f.

While some of the editions, especially the Krotoschin and Luncz include cogent emendations, the Venice p.e. still constitutes the best text and the only one that represents a literary tradition. Moreover, the later editions at times changed spellings and incorrectly filled in abbreviations. An offset reprint has made available the first edition; Sefarim, Berlin, 1924, and in photographic reprint, Meir and Moses Rokeah, New York, ca. 1950.

IV. Manuscripts

The present unsatisfactory state of the y. text requires the use of MSS.

A. The Leiden MS

1. Description and Evaluation. The Leiden Codex Scal. 3, finished in 1334, is the only MS to the complete PT as now extant in print. That is, it contains the text of all portions of y. printed in the Venice first edition. One finds on the margins and the spaces between the lines additions and 'corrections', while in the text itself crossed out or erased and rewritten words and letters. These changes ostensibly are to 'correct' the text, to fill in perceived *lacunae*, to present a reading from a different MS, or to offer a logical connection between two passages. A few corrections are by the same hand as that of the scribe, some of which are introduced by the letters נ״ל, N″L, or נ״א, N″A, the abbreviations for נראה לי, NR'H LY, "it seems to me", and נוסח אחר, *NWŚḤ 'ḤR*, "an alternative reading", but most of the changes are made by a second or even a third hand.

I. Zvi Feintuch, The Mishna of the MS Leiden of the Palestinian Talmud, Tarbiẓ 45 (1976), I—II, 178—212, a careful and systematic evaluation of the Mishnah in the L. MS and the practices of the MS's scribe. The scribe often — but not always — copied the Mishnah from Mishnah MS De Rossi 138, Parma.

Schiller-Szinessy, VeHemmah BaKetuvim, Occasional Notices of Hebrew Manuscripts. No. 1: Description of the Leyden MS of the Palestinian Talmud (Cambridge, 1878). Cf. Lieberman (1971), fns. 10 and 12.

Frankel (1870), p. 143a.

S. Lieberman, HaYerushalmi Kiphshuto (Jerusalem, 1934), pp. xv—xvi, xx—xxi.

J. N. Epstein, Introduction to Amoraitic Literature (Jerusalem, 1962), pp. 326—327.

Mishnah. Zera'im, I. ed. Yehoshua Hutner (Makhon HaTalmud: Jerusalem, 1972), p. 72, provides a comprehensive recent description of the MS.

Baruch Bokser, Samuel's Commentary on the Mishnah (Leiden, 1975), pp. 45, fn. 109; 60, fn. 151; especially 135, fns. 402, 403; and 143, fn. 427, contains examples of 'corrections' entered in the MS.

Schiller-Szinessy (1878), especially, pp. 14, 15, J. N. Epstein[14], Mediqduqe Yerushalmi, I: Leiden MS, Tarbiẓ 5 (1934), 257-272, and 6a (1934), 38—55, and Lieberman (1934), pp. 15—16, and (1963), proved that the L. MS provided the basis for the Venice first edition. Lieberman (1963) showed that, contrary to the colophon, that edition was not systematically based upon three additional MSS, but rather upon just this single one[15]. That is, the copy editor only occasionally consulted a different MS.

Lieberman, Introduction, Palestinian Talmud, Leiden MS, Cod. Scal. 3 (Kedem: Jerusalem, 1971), I, i—vi, reviews the previous evaluations of the L. MS and Ven. p.e. and emphasizes several points with additional examples. The original scribe of the L. MS performed a careful exact work. The emendations which he did on the basis of his own reasoning and which he entered into the text were items blatant to the eye or glaringly necessary and, where verification is possible, are often confirmed. The very few instances of mistakes produce only an insignificant loss. In addition, this scribe often left difficult readings and added, as well, some marginal notes. On the other hand, the copy editor of the Venice p.e. was an unqualified faker whose emendations corrupted the text and often introduced superficially smooth readings which go undetected unless one methodically and carefully employs the L. MS[16]. As already indicated, he did not systematically check other MSS.

E. Z. Melammed, An Introduction to Talmudic Literature (Jerusalem, 1973), pp. 508—512.

2. Editions and Use of the Leiden MS. The Leiden MS was recently reprinted in a less than fully adequate facsimile edition, Palestinian Talmud, Leiden MS, Cod. Scal. 3. I—IV (Kedem Publishing: Jerusalem, 1971), with an introduction by Saul Lieberman[17]. This edition inadequately reproduces

[14] Cf. especially p. 257, fn. 1. Epstein demonstrates that the text of the L. MS contains correct readings, which were corrupted by the Ven. p. e.'s copy editor. Some are emendations of letters and words and others are mistakes in the process of editing or printing; cf. Lieberman (1934), p. xi. Cf. Epstein (1962), p. 337, and Ginzberg (1941), p. H: xxxiii—xxxv, and E. Z. Melammed, An Introduction to Talmudic Literature (Jerusalem, 1973), pp. 508ff. Frankel, Notizen, MGWJ 6 (1857), 398—400, and (1870), 55a and 141b—143a had seen a relationship between the L. MS and Ven. p. e. but he did not correctly evaluate it. He did point to some systematic changes made by the Ven. p. e., for example, it regularly fills in the abbreviations which appear in the MS.

[15] While even Liebermann had earlier considered the Ven. p. e. an eclectic text, he had emphasized the importance of the readings in the L. MS. Cf. Saul Lieberman, On the Yerushalmi (Jerusalem, 1929), pp. 46—47, and Id., More on the L. MS, Tarbiẓ 20 (1950) [= J. N. Epstein Jubilee Volume], 107—117. The relationship between the L. MS and Ven. p. e. emerges from any careful comparison of the various readings. Cf. Bokser (1975), pp. 26, fn. 55; 29, fn. 61; 47, fn. 117; 49, fn. 123; 51, fn. 127; 78, fn. 210; 90, fn. 250; 101, fn. 280; 103, fn. 286; 117, fn. 333; 134, fn. 396; 143, fn. 429; 148, fn. 449; 151, fn. 461; and especially, 126, fn. 362, 363, 365.

[16] Lieberman (1934), p. xvi indicates that the relative number of corruptions varies in each tractate, e. g., few in 'Nezikin', and many in Pes.

[17] The facsimile was originally published in two volumes under the imprint of Makor Publishing Ltd., Jerusalem, but its copies, under suit, were withdrawn and it then

the marginal notes; some are made illegible and some, in handling, are not at all reproduced. Moreover, at times, the text itself is illegible. See P. SJ. VAN KONINGSVELD and A. VAN DER HEIDE, The Pirated Edition of the Leyden Talmud Jerushalmi, Studia Rosenthaliana 8 (1974), 131--137. A new and better edition is being prepared by the firm of ROSENKILDE and BAGGER.

Additional works which employ or discuss the L. MS include:

ISAAK LEVY, Der Achte Abschnitt aus dem Tractate 'Sabbath' [ch. 7(8), 10d—11c]. Inaugural-Dissertation der philosophischen Facultät der Kaiser Wilhelms-Universität Strassburg (Breslau, 1891).

I. LEWY, Jerushalmi B.Q. I—VI, Jahresbericht des jüdisch-theologischen Seminars, 1895—1919, Repr. as Mavo UPerush LeTalmud Yerushalmi (Jerusalem, 1970), Ch. V.

B. RATNER, Ahawath Zion We-Jeruscholaim, I—XI (Vilna, 1901—1917, Repr. in 10 vols., Jerusalem, 1967), where available selectively cited readings from L. MS. but did not explain them. See LIEBERMAN (1934), xvi and 397f., and below.

M. SACHS, Diqduqe Śoferim LeTalmud HaYerushalmi: Maśekhet Berakhot (Jerusalem, 1943).

J. N. EPSTEIN, all his works, but especially (1962), 'Notes and Explanations to Chapters of Talmud (Pes. I—II, B.M. X., B.B. I—III)', pp. 147—268, and ID., 'Diqduqe Yerushalmi', pp. 335—606 (supplemented by E. Z. MELAMMED), a full, but not exhaustive, comparison of readings in Ven. p.e. and L. MS. EPSTEIN's notes run through 'Zera'im'.

Additional articles by LIEBERMAN, see XX. C.

EDWARD A. GOLDMAN, A Critical Edition of Palestinian Talmud Tractate Rosh HaShanah, [in 4 installments:] HUCA 46—49 (1975—78), provides a 'critical' text that employs the L. MS and geniza fragments. Though Part One discusses the L. MS, it fails to mention and take into account LIEBERMAN's articles.

The editions and commentaries of LUNCZ, Berakhot-Shev.; LIEBERMAN (1934), Shab., Eruv., Pes., and n.b., p. 526, Ber. I; GINZBERG, Ber. I—V; SHELOMOH GOREN, HaYerushalmi HaMeforash (Jerusalem, 1961), Ber. I—V (see Section XX. B); ISRAEL FRANCUS, Talmud Yerushalmi, Maśekhet Beṣah (New York, 1967); YEHUDAH FELIKS' editions of chapters on agricultural materials. See XVII. D, and DAVID WEISS HALIVNI, Sources and Traditions, I—II (Orders Nasihim and Mo'ed, from Yoma to Hagiga), (Jerusalem, 1968, 1975).

B. Vatican MS

1. Talmud Yerushalmi. Codex Vatican 133 (Vat. Ebr. 133), Introduction by SAUL LIEBERMAN (= reprint of 'On the Yerushalmi', 1929). Page

appeared, in four volumes, under the name of Kedem Publs., which thus became the publisher of record.

concordance index to the Venice edition by A. P. SHERRY (Jerusalem, 1971). The MS, whose suggested origin is placed at the thirteenth century, contains tractates 'Soṭah' and the Order of 'Zera'im', less 'Bik'. The MS contains many scribal errors though apparently it is based upon a good underlying MS tradition which preserves many fine readings, orthographically, linguistically, and content-wise.

The MS's readings often accord with the citations of y. found in 'Tosefot', cf. LIEBERMAN (1929), p. 54.

2. Study of the MS:

L. GINZBERG, Yerushalmi Fragments from the Genizah (New York, 1909, Repr. Makor: Jerusalem, 1969, and Hildesheim and New York, 1970), appendix, pp. 347—372, presents selected variants, at times inaccurately, copied, from Vat. MS. Cf. GINZBERG (1941), p. lxv.

LIEBERMAN (1929), presents a general study of the MS and its role in an overall textual analysis of y., and a listing with explanatory notes of variants to Sot. Cf. especially pp. 46f. and 53f.

GINZBERG (1941), p. H: xxxv.

EPSTEIN (1962), especially 326—327, notations in the MS for abbreviated pericopae.

SHAMMA FRIEDMAN, Conservative Judaism 26 (1972), 92—94, a fine review of the Makor reprint and a description of the MS in general.

Makhon-Mishnah, I (1972), p. 73, describes the MS.

MELAMMED (1973), pp. 512—514, describes the MS.

ZVI MEIR RABINOVITZ, New Genizah Fragments of the PT, Henoch Yalon Memorial Volume [= Bar Ilan Department Researches, II]. Ed. E. Y. KUTSCHER, et al. (Bar Ilan University, Ramat Gan and Kirjath Sepher, Jerusalem, 1974), p. 500, concerning good readings preserved in the MS.

Y. SUSSMANN, A Halakhic Inscription from the Beth-Shean Valley, Tarbiẓ 43 (1973—74), 107f., fn. 110.

Commentaries and editions that employed the Vat. MS include: LUNCZ (1907—1919), Ber.-Shev.; GINZBERG (1941—61), Ber. I—V; and S. GOREN, (1961), Ber. I—V.

C. 'Yerushalmi Zera'im', and Tractate Sheq. with the Commentary of SOLOMON SIRILLO.

1. The work is found in British Museum MSS 403, 404, and 405 = Or. 2822, 2823, 2824, and in part, in Paris, Bibliotheque Nationale, Supplement Hebreu 1389.

The MSS to the y. text and commentary come from the sixteenth century. According to SUSSMANN (1973—74), p. 108, fn. 110, while the texts of the commentary may represent a first (Paris MS) and a second edition (Brit. Mus.), the y. texts do not substantively vary, excluding mechanical scribal errors.

The text of y. preserves some valuable readings. Often, however, interpolations or 'corrections' were introduced on the basis of BT, *midrashim*, or early rabbinic commentaries. Therefore, one must carefully evaluate the readings. LIEBERMAN (1943), p. xv, however, points out that one can rely upon a reading where in his commentary SIRILLO states that he found it in "exact texts". The readings are particularly valuable as they may derive from MSS and not the Venice 1523 edition of y., a work that did not appear until after SIRILLO had already started his commentary. Only later did he make us of that edition. See LIEBERMAN (1950), pp. 301—302. M. LEHMANN, in an edition of tractate 'Berakhot', 'Meir Netiv' (Mainz, 1875), suggests that volume III of the British Museum MSS, on Hal., Orl., and Bik., is written by SIRILLO himself; cf. Makhon-Mishnah I (1972), p. 74, fn. 9. LEHMANN and G. MARGOLIOUTH, Catalogue of the Hebrew and Samaritan Manuscripts in the British Museum (London, 1905, Repr. 1965), II, 55, suggest that the other two volumes, I—II, were written by a scribe and SIRILLO reviewed and annotated it.

2. The MS has been published:

LEHMANN, Meir Netiv (Mainz, 1875). Tractate 'Berakhot'. Repr. along with Tractate 'Pe'ah' in Vilna ed. of y.

ḤAYYIM YOSEF DINGLAS, ed. of individual tractates of 'Zera'im', including 'Berakhot', I—IX (Jerusalem, 1934—1967). This is a far from perfect edition; cf. KALMAN KAHANA, Maśekhet Shevi'it, Ḥeqer VeIyun I (Bene Brak, 1972), pp. 11f., and SUSSMANN (1973—74), p. 108, fn. 110.

EPHRAIM ZE'EV GERBOZ, ed. to y. Sheq. (Jerusalem, 1958).

KALMAN KAHANA, I—II (1972—73) printed anew from the British Museum MS SIRILLO's text and commentary to y. Shev.

3. Discussion of the text and commentary:

Introductions to edition by LEHMANN (1875), DINGLAS (1934—67), and KAHANA (1972).

MARGOLIOUTH (1905), pp. 54—56.

*LIEBERMAN (1929), p. 47; (1934), p. xv; and (1950), pp. 301—302.

GINZBERG (1941), p. H: cxvii.

*Makhon-Mishnah I (1972), pp. 73—75, excellent remarks.

EJ 14, 1618—1619, s.v. SIRILLO.

*SUSSMANN (1973—74), p. 108, fn. 110.

BOKSER (1975), p. 148, fn. 450, presents an example of an interpolation added into the text.

D. Other MSS

1. As indicated above, y. Sheq. was included with many BT editions. Thus, it is found in Munich Cod. Hebr. 95, written in 1343, reprinted by HERMAN L. STRACK, Der Babylonische Talmud nach der einzigen vollstän-

digen Handschrift München Codex Hebraicus 95 mittels Facsimile-Lichtdrucks vervielfältigt, mit Inhaltsangaben für jede Seite u. einer Einl. versehen (Repr. Sefer: Jerusalem, 1971, I, 218—227). As this formed the basis of RAPHAELO RABINOVICZ's invaluable 'Variae Lectiones', he dealt with y. Sheq., 'Tract. Megillah Et Shekalim' (Munich, 1887, Repr. New York, 1960).

In addition, a text of y. is found in the MS with the commentary of R. Meshullam, ed. ABRAHAM SCHREIBER, Treatise Shekalim (New York, 1954). The y. text, which is somewhat corrupted, is similar to the one in the printed BT's supplement ed. Cf. LIEBERMAN (1950), pp. 295—96, and SCHREIBER's introduction. As to the commentary, see below, Section XIX.I. For the text with SIRILLO, see above, Section C. MOSHE ASSIS's forthcoming critical edition (1979?) will provide a full description of the MSS. See above, Section III, and fn. 11a.

2. ZVI MEIR RABINOVITZ, ed., Qeta' Shel Mishnah ViYerushalmi Shevi'it, Bar Ilan Annual, Studies in Judaica and Humanities, II (= Samuel Bialoblocki Memorial Volume), (Jerusalem, 1964), pp. 125—133. RABINOVITZ provides an introduction and notes to this ca. fourteenth century Yemenite MS to Shev. VII. According to SUSSMANN, however, the fragment actually derives from the Geniza and its continuation is in the Cambridge Library.

3. A. H. FREIMANN, A Fragment of Jerushalmi Baba Kama, Tarbiz 6 (1934), 56—63. This fragment of Vatican MS (Vat. Ebr. 530), "not later than fourteenth century", is to B.Q. 2 : 4, 3a[14]—3 : 4, 3c[53]. The text is somewhat carelessly copied, though it contains some good readings and preserves Palestinian orthography; cf. LIEBERMAN (1934), p. xv. It confirms some of the emendations suggested by I. LEWY (1895—1914, Repr. 1970).

The edition includes an introduction and brief notes; Supplementary Comments by S. LIEBERMAN; and an appendix on one pericope by J. N. EPSTEIN, To 'A Fragment of Jerushalmi Baba Kama', pp. 64—65.

4. E. S. ROSENTHAL. Escorial G-1-3, Spanish MS to y. Neziqin, from middle of B.Q. Ch. III to middle of B.B. 9 : 4, written on the side of a MS to b. B.Q. — B.B. The MS has fewer corruptions than Ashkenazi (European) texts of PT and far fewer textual lacunae than the L. MS. Furthermore, it more accurately preserves Galilean Hebrew and Aramaic. It may serve to explain corrupt texts and evaluate previously proposed emendations. It basically confirms LIEBERMAN's thesis as to the distinct nature and Caesarean origin of Neziqin. But it does not represent a single y. tradition. On the one hand, the readings generally are the same as those of the L. MS and Venice first edition, and its terminology, style, and idioms usually are distinct from those of the rest of PT and characteristic of Caesarea. But, on the other hand, the MS at times lacks the terminology and spelling supposedly distinct to y. Neziqin. Preliminary Report of E. S. ROSENTHAL, Concerning the New MS to PT Neziqin, Seventh World Congress of Jewish Studies, Jerusalem, Israel, August 8, 1977. See also footnote *, at the end of Section I.

5. MOSHE ASSIS, A Fragment of y. Sanhedrin, Tarbiz 46 (1977), 29—90, 326—329. The text covers y. San. 5:1, 22c, l. 42 to 6:9, 23c, l. 47. Besides

the introduction and extensive notes, SAUL LIEBERMAN adds important additional comments, 'On the New Fragments of the Palestinian Talmud', ibid., 91—97.

E. Geniza Fragments

These fragments originally found in the so called Cairo Geniza are presently dispersed in libraries throughout the world. One may find an introduction and bibliographical information to the collections in S. D. GOITEIN, A Mediterranean Society, I (Berkeley and Los Angeles, 1967), pp. 1—28, and especially, Involvement in Geniza Research, in: Religion in a Religious Age, ed. S. D. GOITEIN (Association for Jewish Studies, Ktav: New York, 1974), pp. 139f; Article, Genizah Cairo, EJ 16, 1323—44; and MORDECHAI A. FRIEDMAN, 'Introduction', in his forthcoming 'Marriage and Marriage Traditions in Palestinian Tradition as Reflected in the Documents of the Cairo Geniza' (The School of Jewish Studies, Tel Aviv University, 1979). See also SHAUL SHAKED, A Tentative Bibliography of Geniza Documents (Paris and The Hague, 1964).

The fragments constitute brief selections of y. and are not all of the same quality, provenance and date, though scholars have usually dated them to ca. tenth century. SUSSMANN (1973—74), pp. 155f., fn. 497, has questioned this assignment. He believes that the fragments, despite their universally recognized importance, have not been systematically and methodically analyzed as to their date, and may, in fact, come from an earlier period. See below, for ALLONI's edition of fragments. Whether or not he is correct in his suggestion, the fragments deserve further systematic attention. This is especially so since LIEBERMAN's revelation (1963), that the Venice p.e. basically represents the reading of one and not four MSS. This is not to say that earlier scholars have not recognized the importance of these fragments. They have, cf. LIEBERMAN (1934), pp. 14f. and GINZBERG (1951), pp. H: xxxvi—xl. They noted that the fragments accurately preserve Palestinian orthography and assumedly, as well, textual readings, for the texts could not have been revised by European scribes familiar with the more 'popular' and 'authoritative' Babylonian traditions. See below, Section XV. A.

While many fragments have been published, many others have not. These include items from Dropsie College, Philadelphia [see Makhon-Mishnah, I (1972), p. 76 and B. HALPER, Descriptive Catalogue of Genizah Fragments in Philadelphia (Philadelphia, 1924), p. 45, no. 82, y. Dem. 2:1, 22d$^{15-30}$ and l.^{64}—23a^{4}], and (only) a few brief pieces from the Jewish Theological Seminary of America, as I am informed. Forthcoming editions are promised by Makor Publishers, Jerusalem, by ABRAHAM I. KATSH, Mosad HaRav Kook, Jerusalem, and comprehensive, separate, corpora by YAAQOV SUSSMANN, Jerusalem, and by ELIEZER HOROWITZ, Yeshiva University, New York. The more recent editions have included facsimiles, and accordingly at times republish items that had previously appeared. Thus, fragments once published may have appeared a second time or may do so in the future. Therefore, to facilitate identification I include in the following list of published items, the individual fragment's number in its respective collection.

1. Talmudical Fragments in the Bodleian Library, S. SCHECHTER and A. SINGER, ed. (Cambridge, 1896, Repr. Makor: Jerusalem, 1971). Fragments to Ber. $4b^{18-59}$ and $6b^{25-60}$. Description and introduction, p. 6; text, pp. 27–28. Published by LOUIS GINZBERG, in his 'Yerushalmi Fragments' (1909). See next item. Several mistakes in copying are corrected by GINZBERG (1941), I, 238, fn. 8.

2. L. GINZBERG, Yerushalmi Fragments from the Genizah, Vol. I (All published) (= Text and Studies of JTSA) (New York, 1909, Repr. Makor: Jerusalem, 1969, and Hildesheim and New York, 1970).

Fragments to all parts of y. from 'Taylor-Schechter Collection' in Cambridge University Library; Bodleian Library; and from private hands with two supplements, I: 'Extracts from y. found in first edition of Yalqut Shimeoni, Salonica, 1526–27', pp. 309–343; and II: 'Selected variants to Zera'im from Vat. MS number 133', pp. 347–372.

Some texts are incorrectly transcribed. See, e.g., SAUL LIEBERMAN Siphre Zutta (New York, 1968), p. 105 fn. 73, and GINZBERG (1941), I, 238, fn. 8.

On Supplement I, see ARTHUR B. HYMAN, The Sources of the Yalkut Shimeoni, I (Jerusalem, 1974), pp. xxiv–xxv.

Several sections, pp. 29–36, 152–153, 183–184, 230, are not actual y. texts but rather part of a medieval collection which is based upon the y. and which incorporates additions from BT and later sources. See LIEBERMAN (1934), xxv; V. APTOWITZER, Introductio ad Sefer Rabiah (Jerusalem, 1938), p. 276; and EPSTEIN, Ma'asim Livne Ereṣ Yisrael, Tarbiz 1b (1930), 37; and SAUL LIEBERMAN, ed. Hilkhot HaYerushalmi (The Laws of the Palestinian Talmud) of Rabbi Moses Ben Maimon (Text and Studies of JTSA. Vol. XIII) (New York, 1947), preface p. 3. Pp. 29–36 in GINZBERG are part of a book of decisions to be attributed to Maimonides. LIEBERMAN presents a photographic reproduction, and more accurate transcription and thorough annotation of the fragment. See below, and cp. B. Z. BENEDICT, KS 27 (1952), p. 329.

EPSTEIN (1962), p. 327 lists scribal notations for deletions of pericopae.

3. LOUIS GINZBERG, Genizah Studies. In Memory of Doctor Solomon Schechter (= Ginze Schechter), I. Midrash and Haggadah (= Texts and Studies of JTSA, Vol. VII) (New York, 1928, Repr. Hermon Press: New York, 1969).

a. 'Qiṣur Hagadot HaYerushalmi', Abbreviation of y. aggadic material, from the order of Mo'ed., pp. 387–429. Dropsie MS, HALPER, 85.

See LIEBERMAN (1934), p. xxv; EPSTEIN (1930), p. 37; and APTOWITZER (1938), p. 276, who believes that through p. 422 the text is part of 'Śefer Yerushalmi', the medieval compilation based on PT with additions.

b. 'Sheloshah Seride HaYerushalmi', pp. 430—448.
Ber. 7 : 1, 11a—7 : 4, 11c[29].
Shab. 6 : 9, 8d—7 : 1, 9b[1].
Pes. 4 : 9, 31b[34]—5 : 1, 31d[6] and 6 : 1, 33a[20–51].

All are from ADLER, JTS, 1493.

4. J. N. EPSTEIN, LiSeride HaYerushalmi, Tarbiẓ 3 (1932), 99.

a. A. Z. Ch. II, 41d[37]—42a[7]; ch. III, 42c[2 from bottom] to 42d[34] = pp. 15—20. Ant. 16.

b. Abbreviated Ket. Ch. I, 25c[3 from bottom] — ch. VIII, 32b[34] = pp. 21—26. T.S.F. 17 7a. Cf. LIEBERMAN (1934), p. xxvi.

The passage constitutes explanations glossed into a text. LIEBERMAN (1947), preface p. 3, believes the text is part of Maimonides' work. He presents a photographic reproduction, transcription, and annotated text. See above, on GINZBERG's Yerushalmi Fragments (1909).

c. Hal. Chs. I—IV = pp. 121—136. Ant. 309.

d. Ber. Ch. VIII, 12c = pp. 237—239. Ant. 42.

e. Shab. Ch. XV, 15a—ch. XVI, 15c; ch. XX, 17c—d = pp. 240—245. Ant. 324.

See LIEBERMAN (1934), p. 144.

f. A. Z. Ch. V, 44d—45a = pp. 246—248. Ant. 999.

The several fragments are published with brief textual notes and introductory remarks, especially pp. 15—16 and 121—123, and a supplement on one pericope, pp. 134—136.

5. SOLOMON WIEDER, Qeta' Yerushalmi, Tarbiẓ 18 (1949), 129—136. San. end and Mak. 1 : 1—4; 2 : 7—13 : end. Hungarian Academy of Sciences, Budapest (Kaufmann collection), number 594.

Besides the introduction and notes, EPSTEIN, pp. 136—137, adds a supplementary comment on the importance of the fragment. Of note, the fragment proves that a y. passage existed to Mak. Ch. III and thus confirms the reconstruction of LIEBERMAN (1947), pp. 67—68.

6. D. S. LOEWINGER, Seridim Ḥadashim, MiYerushalmi Peśaḥim Pereq 5, 6, 7, Alexander Marx Jubilee Volume (New York, 1950), Hebrew Section, pp. 237—283. Pes. Chs. V—VII. Hungarian Academy of Sciences, Kaufmann Collection.

LOEWINGER provides a brief introduction, slight notes, and an appendix by S. LIEBERMAN, 'LaSeridim HaḤadashim', pp. 284—86. With this new data, LIEBERMAN evaluates the printed edition, readings in MSS, and previously proposed emendations.

7. NEHEMYA ALLONI, Geniza Fragments of Rabbinic Literature, Mishna Talmud, and Midrash with Palestinian vocalization (Jerusalem: Makor, 1973), presents fragments from eight-ninth century, with a careful description and listing (with some misprints) of each fragment, pp. 35—44, 91—93 and full facsimiles, pp. 42—77.

a. Pes. 10 : 2, 37c[13]—10 : 9, 37d[end]. T.S. 16/328.

b. Taan. 4 : 11, 69c[43]—end.
c. Mashqin 1 : 1, 80a[15]—3 : 1, 81d[9].
} T.S. 12/186—188.

These items were previously published by C. Taylor, Cairo Genizah Palimpsests (Cambridge, 1900), facsimiles III—VIII, and Ginzberg, Yerushalmi Fragments (1909), pp. 191—98.

d. B.Q. 4 : 10, $5a^{15}$—9 : 5, $6d^{5}$. Ms. Georg. c. 1 [2672] and T.S. 12/183, 741.

These were previously published by Ginzberg (1909), pp. 242, 244, 249—250; and P. Qurqovsuv, Zapisok Vostocnie (Pressburg, 1898), pp. 185—205, and analyzed by R. Ratner, HaMelitz (St. Petersburg, 1899), nos. 56, 61, 65, 68, and 72.

e. Shevu. 1: 9,$33c^{12-24}$ [ls. 12—17 = San. 7: 1, $23c^{41-46}$], 1: 9,$33b^{58}$—$33c^{7}$ [= San. 7: 1, $27c^{-5}$—d^{10}]. T.S. 12/749. Alloni incorrectly identified these fragments and labelled them on the basis of their San. parallel. Accordingly, he mistakenly claimed that ls. 17—24 of the first one was otherwise unattested in texts of y. Ginzberg (1909), pp. 266—267, though, previously published these fragments and correctly labelled them. Prof. Sussmann, to whom I owe the above observations, has an additional as yet unpublished fragment to the remaining portion of y. Shevu.

f. Shevu. 1 : 1, $32c^{1}$—d^{43}. T.S. 12/748.

g. A. Z. 2 : 9, $41d^{29}$—$42a^{7}$.
7 : 2, 42c—$42d^{34}$. } Ant. 165.

These fragments were previously published by Epstein, Tarbiẓ 3 (1932), 16—20.

8. Israel Francus, Talmud Yerushalmi, Maśekhet Beṣah (New York, 1967), pp. 259—260. Paris III A35.

In an addendum, Francus describes the fragment and compares it to other readings. The fragment is to be fully published by Eliezer Horowitz.

9. Zvi Meir Rabinovitz, New Genizah Fragments of the PT, Henoch Yalon Memorial Volume, ed. E. Y. Kutscher, et al. (Bar Ilan University, Ramat Gan and Kirjath Sepher, Jerusalem, 1974) (= Bar Ilan Department Researches, II), pp. 499—511, presents introduction, text of fragments from the Cambridge Taylor Schechter Collection, and notes.

a. Ber. 3 : 4, 6c. NS 329/661.

b. Ber. 3 : 5, 6d. 329/608.

c. Shab. 12 : 3, 13c. 329/578.

d. Qid. 3 : 1, 63c; 3 : 2, 63d; 3 : 3, 64a. NS 171/1.

10. E. A. Goldman, A Critical Edition of Palestinian Talmud Tractate Rosh HaShanah, [in 4 installments:] HUCA 46—49 (1973—78), presents facsimiles of several fragments and fresh transcription and citation of fragments to y. R.H. and to pericopae elsewhere in y. which parallel R.H. Items to Chapter One are:

a. R.H. Ch. 1. T.S.F. 17.9.13.16.24.

b. M.Q. 3: 7. T.S.F. 17.16.

c. Sheq. 3: 1. T.S.F. 17.24.

Ginzberg (1909), 140—147, 152—153, 205^{2-10}, 126^{25-20} and 127^{2-18}, previously published these fragments.

11. S. ABRAMSON, Qeta' Genizah MiYerushalmi Shabbat Pereq Hamaṣni'a, Kobez Al Yad 8 (18) (Jerusalem, 1976), pp. 1—13.

Shab. 10: 2, 12c[5]—10: 3, 12c[30]; 10: 5, 12c[39]—10: 7, 12d[5]. Cambridge fragment without exact box identification.

ABRAMSON provides an introduction, pp. 3—9, to the transcribed and annotated fragments, pp. 10—13.

12. Shev. VII. See Section D. 2. above. According to SUSSMANN this text is a Geniza fragment the second half of which is in the Cambridge Library.

V. Textual Notes to Yerushalmi

The following items focus on the literary history of the text and demonstrate the uses of lower textual criticism which employs MSS. Further works may be found among the commentaries and exegetical articles, presented below in Section XX. C.

1. B. RATNER, Ahawath Zion We-Jerusholaim. 12 vols. (Vilna, 1901—1917, Repr. Jerusalem, 1967), covers Ber. and the Orders of 'Zera'im' and 'Mo'ed', less tractate 'Eruv'.

RATNER realized that early authorities (Rishonim) may have had different literary traditions of y. and he therefore provided citations from these works. At times he adds his own comments. He based the work on the Venice first edition and where available employed Geniza fragments or MSS. Thus once it had appeared he was able to consult GINZBERG's 'Yerushalmi Fragments' (1909). A colleague supplied him with some variants from the Leiden MS.

While the work is enormously helpful, one cannot totally rely on it. He generally gives the early citations only when they diverge from the present text and not where they coincide and therefore confirm it. Moreover, he does not supply the full citations and often fails carefully to isolate the citation of y. from explanatory glosses. Accordingly, one must recheck the sources he lists. Further, RATNER's citations may be inaccurate in that he relied upon later editions of the Rishonim, whose texts are often corrupted, indeed 'corrected' on the basis of the supposed correct text of y. Today one can use first or critical editions of these volumes which are now being published. See below, on Commentaries, Chs. XIX—XX. Finally, RATNER overvalued readings in y. editions that appeared after the Venice first edition. He thought they were based on different MSS. On the other hand, he undervalued the L. MS; cf. 'Introduction' to Ber. A separate issue, which I discuss below, in Section XIX. C, is how to evaluate differences that clearly emerge from the citations, viz., do they represent variants, paraphrases, etc.

The reviews of individual volumes often constitute separate studies. These include: W. BACHER, REJ 43 (1901): 310—317; 46 (1903): 154—159; 50 (1905): 140—144; 52 (1906): 311—314; 53 (1907): 277—280; 57 (1909):

308—311; 60 (1911): 151—154; 62 (1912): 157—159; and 64 (1912): 315—317. S. BUBER, Maaśef 1 (5662) [= 1902], B: 48—62; HaMelitz (1903), #87, 88, 92, 113, 117, 121, 124, 125, 127. S. POZNANSKI, HaṢefirah (1903), #68, 70—72, (1905), #24, (1917), #11, 12; HaOlam (1907), #14; Hed Hazman (1909), #284, 287; HaIvri (5671) [= 1911], #14, 15. V. APTOWITZER, MGWJ 52 (1908): 307—316, 54 (1910): 160—172, 287—288, 417—419, 60 (1916): 107—109.

2. Virtually all the works of SAUL LIEBERMAN, especially: 'Emendations in Jerushalmi' A—F, in Tarbiẓ: A: 2,i (1930), 106—114 (to which cf. EPSTEIN, ibid., pp. 241—243); B: 2, ii (1930), 235—240; a note to A and B: 2, iii (1931), 380; C: 3 (1932), 205—212; D: 337—339; E: 452—457 [to which cf. 4 (1933), 293]; F: 4 (1933), 377—79; and F.b: 5 (1933), 97—110 [to which cf. 6 (1935), 111]. ID., The Uzziahu Inscription and the Torah of the Ancients, Tarbiẓ 4 (1933), 292—293. ID., Jerushalmi Miscellanies, Tarbiẓ 6 (1935), 24—35 (to which cf. EPSTEIN, ibid. pp. 236—37).

3. J. N. EPSTEIN, Jerushalmian Miscellanies, Tarbiẓ 6 (1935), 236—37. ID., Some Varia Lectiones in Jerushalmi, I: The Leiden MS, Tarbiẓ 5 (1934), 257—272, and 6 (1934), 38—55. Note, pp. 39—46 focus on the Ven. p.e.'s copy editor's mistakes in names, first, of masters and their titles and, secondly, of places. ID., Talmudical Miscellanies, Tarbiẓ 3 (1931), 110—111.

VI. Translations

A. Full Text of PT

1. French translation: M. SCHWAB, Le Talmud de Jérusalem. 11 vols. (Paris, 1871, Repr. 1932—33), a generally unreliable rendering.

2. German translation of aggadic portions: AUG. WÜNSCHE, Der Jerusalemische Talmud in seinen haggadischen Bestandtheilen übertragen (Zürich, 1880, Repr. Hildesheim, 1967), with a brief introduction, pp. iii—viii.

B. To Selected Portions of PT

1. Latin translation to twenty tractates: B. UGOLINO, Thesaurus Antiquitatum Sacrarum, Vols. 17—30 (Venice, 1755—65). The texts and translations of *gemara* include: Maas, M.S., Hal., Orl., Bik, in Vol. 20 (1757); Pes., in Vol. 17 (1755); Yoma, Sheq., Suk., R.H., Bes., Tan., Meg., Hag., M.Q., in Vol. 18 (1755); Sot., Ket., Qid., in Vol. 30 (1765); and San., Mak., in Vol. 25 (1762).

2. Ber., in English translation:

a. M. SCHWAB, The Talmud of Jerusalem I: Berakhoth (London, 1886, Repr. N.Y. 1969).

b. Ch. Eight, in English: Jacob Neusner, Invitation to the Talmud. A Teaching Book (N.Y., 1973). Besides the translation, which is based on a corrected text, this work includes an introduction to the Yerushalmi and the chapter, and a full commentary on the content and the literary traits of the materials.

3. Bik. The Jerusalem Talmud (Talmud Yerushalmi) Bikkurim. Text, translation, introduction, and commentary, by Joseph Rabbinowitz (London, 1975).

4. Shab., Ch. Seven (Eight), in German: Isaak Levy, Der achte Abschnitt aus dem Traktate 'Sabbath'. Inaugural-Dissertation der philosophischen Facultät der Kaiser Wilhelms-Universität Strassburg 1891 (Breslau, n.d.). The translation includes some notes.

5. Suk., in German translation: Charles Horowitz, Der Palästinische Talmud. Sukkah. Die Felshütte. Bonner Orientalistische Studien (Bonn, 1963). The introduction, pp. 7—13, focuses on motifs and institutions of the tractate and of the holiday of Sukkot. The text, pp. 14—100, contains brief notes.

6. Taan., in English translation: A. W. Greenup, Taanith From the Palestinian Talmud (London, 1918, 1921). The work lacks an introduction to the translation and tractate and contains only very brief explanatory notes to the text and references to parallels.

7. Ned., in German translation: Charles Horowitz, Der Palästinische Talmud. Nedarim (Düsseldorf-Benrath, 1957). This work has a one page preface, and brief notes on the bottom of the translation. They are based upon commentaries in the Krotoschin and Vilna editions, and on parallels, and focus, first, on variants and their importance and, secondly, on the exegesis of difficult passages.

8. B.M., Ch. Three, in English translation. A. Ehrman, ed. The Talmud with English Translation and Commentary (El-Am: Jerusalem, 1965). This work contains an introduction and a modern, though less than fully critical, long commentary and notes. To date, of the several portions published only one part includes a text of y., B.M. 3 : 1, 8b—3 : 9, 9b.

Part Three
Contents and the History of the Materials Incorporated within PT

VII. Scope of Yerushalmi

1. The Venice first edition covers four orders of 'Mishnah' and only several folios in the fifth, of Nid. Traditional authorities and modern scholars have discussed whether this represents the full y. or whether some

part(s) have not been preserved. This includes individual passages; pericopae; the last chapters in three tractates, Mak. 3, Sab. 21—24, Nid. 4—10; and the tractates in 'Qodshin' and 'Ṭehorot'.

There are three possible solutions:

a. The portion was lost at the time of printing or writing of L. MS, or at some earlier, post-Talmudic time.

b. Incomplete compilation. Material other than that extant was never redacted.

c. Further material as unedited sources or in some pre-edited stage never existed.

2. The evidence consists of:

a. Supposed citations by medieval authorities of passages now non-extant or in non-extant portions of y. Cf. the sources and literature listed under 'citations', Section XIX. C.

References to y. may not actually refer to PT, but rather to some midrashic work, qabbalistic tract, or medieval compendium-anthology of y. that consists of material with additions from BT and Gaonic sources, the 'Śefer Yerushalmi'; cf. below, Section XVIII. F. While all the citations cannot be discounted, FRANKEL (1870), pp. 45a—49a, already indicated that a citation in a medieval commentary, even if correctly interpreted, only proves that the authority knew the individual Palestinian tradition and not the whole section or tractate in which the passage supposedly appears.

b. The presence of abbreviated or deleted or whole pericopae that parallel material elsewhere in y. These are scribal deletions; cf. LIEBERMAN (1929), pp. 12—13, 39, and (1949), p. xv. There are also *sugyot* which apparently originate in the missing y. portions (of Shab. and Nid.) and whose extant versions should thus constitute "parallel transferred pericopae". See MOSHE ASSIS, Parallel *sugyot* in the Jerusalem Talmud (In the Tractates: Bikkurim, Shabbath, Soṭah, Makkoth, and Niddah) (Ph. D. Dissertation, Hebrew University, 1976) (Jerusalem, 1976), especially pp. 102, 105—112, 145, 151—157, and Section IX. A. below.

c. Evidence of MSS and geniza fragments. They cover only the already published portions, with the exeception of Mak. Ch. 3, which LIEBERMAN (1947), pp. 67f., had already reconstructed on the basis of parallel *sugyot* elsewhere in y. and of testimonies in medieval authorities. The fragment to Shab. Ch. 20 end, indicates that already at the time of the writing of that fragment the latter chapters of Shab. were missing; EPSTEIN, Tarbiẓ 3 (1931), 245.

d. Fragments of a Palestinian halakhic work on themes contained in the non-extant y. portion, y. Hul.; MORDECHAI MARGULIES [= MARGALIOTH], Hilkhot Ereṣ Yisrael Min HaGenizah (Jerusalem, 1973). Both positions can claim support from this item. It proves that these subjects were studied and therefore assumably preserved in y. Alternatively, as these materials were found in a practical compendium, there was no need for a y. tractate. Cp. LIEBERMAN (1931) and ID., A Few Words on the Book by Julian The Architect of Ascalon 'The Laws of Palestine and its Customs', Tarbiẓ 40 (1971), 409–417.

e. Material on Qod. and Ṭeh. attributed to Palestinians which appears elsewhere in extant portions of y. or in BT.

f. Assumptions of whether or not Palestinians would have studied and taught certain materials, those supposedly halakhicly relevant or practical.

Concerning nos. d–f:

The fact that materials were studied does not logically yield the conclusion that there was an edited y. Indeed BT refers to Palestinian traditions which are appropriate to extant tractates of y. but which are not found there; cf. below, Section XI. 3. Thus y. did not incorporate all traditions. In addition, there existed in Palestine different compilations of materials and *gemarot*; cf. LIEBERMAN (1931) and SZ (1968); GINZBERG (1941), pp. xxxix and H: cxvf. Therefore, one cannot speak of y. in monolithic terms.

g. Publications, supposedly from a lost MS, of an edition of y. Qodshin (Hul., Bekh., Zev., Arak.), 1907–09, which today, however, is recognized as a forgery. See, e.g., B. Z. BACHER, Talmud Yerushalmi 'al Maśekhet Ḥullin UMaśekhet Bekhorot, HaKedem 1 (1907), 20–40, 70–85; V. APTOWITZER, MGWJ 52 (1908), 316–317, 435–436, 625f.; and 54 (1910), 564–570; and HABERMANN (1952), pp. 204 and 253; and SHMUEL HAKOHEN WEINGARTEN, Sinai 32, vol. 62 (1968), 281–287.

h. Supposed testimony by Pirqoi ben Baboi, beginning of ninth century, that Palestinians lack laws of 'Sheḥiṭah' and have forgotten the Orders of 'Qodshin' and 'Ṭehorot'. Pirqoi's testimony, however, is not fully reliable due to his propagandist motives to deemphasize Palestinian tradition, especially in the area of laws of 'Ṭerefah'. See SHALOM SPIEGEL, On the Polemic of Pirqoi Ben Baboi, Harry Wolfson Jubilee Volume (Jerusalem, 1965), Hebrew Section, pp. 243–274, esp. 253–260, MARGULIES (1973), esp. pp. 102–104, and SHLOMO SIMONSOHN, The Hebrew Revival Among Early Medieval European Jews, Salo Baron Jubilee Volume (Jerusalem, 1974), pp. 843–845; and DAVID GOODBLATT, Rabbinic Instruction in Sasanian Babylonia (Leiden 1975), p. 15.

3. Tentative consensus:

The missing chapters in Mak. Shab. and Nid. existed. As to 'Qodshin' and 'Ṭehorot' there is no firm agreement.

4. Literature:

*FRANKEL (1870), pp. 45a–49a, 144a.

MORITZ STEINSCHNEIDER, Handschriften-Verzeichnisse der Königlichen Bibliothek zu Berlin, II: 1 (Berlin, 1878), p. 65.

Z. W. RABINOVITZ, Some Comments on y. Qodshin, Yerushalayim 7 (1907), 177–179; and ID., Sha'are Torath Eretz Israel (Jerusalem, 1940), pp. 128, 222, 308, 351, 590.

RATNER, Orlah (1971), p. 225.

GINZBERG (1929) II, 560; and (1941), pp. li and H: cxiv—vi.

*LIEBERMAN (1929), pp. 12—13, 39—43 (1947), pp. 67f.

*STRACK (1931[5]), pp. 66—69, 266.

CH. ALBECK, Introduction, Bereschit Rabba (Jerusalem, 1965[2]).

*EPSTEIN (1962), pp. 330—334.

*SHALOM SPIEGEL, On the Polemic of Pirqoi Ben Baboi, Harry Wolfson Jubilee Volume (Jerusalem, 1965), pp. 253—260.

*JACOB SUSSMANN, Śugyot Bavliot LiŚedarim Zera'im UṬehorot (unpublished Ph.D. dissertation Hebrew University, Jerusalem, 1969), pp. 1—13 [in press: Israeli Academy of Sciences].

MELAMMED (1973), pp. 509—512.

VIII. Arrangement and Contents of Yerushalmi

A. Basic Structure, Contents, and Forms

The *gemara* in y., as in b., basically is structured around 'Mishnah'. One may describe the contents in terms of their formal traits or of their function. *Gemara* consists of: materials formulated as glosses, e.g., to 'Mishnah' or some other teaching or text; autonomous statements; *baraitot*; disputes; debates; questions; answers; lists; biblical exegeses; songs; laments; prayers; stories; and narrative *aggadah*. Items may be unassigned, or attributed to a master, prefaced or unprefaced by the name of a tradent or list of tradents.

The materials serve to: comment upon and analyze the text and content of 'Mishnah' and related sources; present independent teachings and discussion thereon; attack or defend interpretations or statements; cite sources; compare or associate a principle in one text or interpretation with that of another found elsewhere; present cases, stories, and aggadic materials.

Most of the literature deal with a self-defined selection of sources and thus do not cover all the data. Moreover, as generally they do not fully or at all analyze an item's occurrence in y., for comparative purposes I include some works on non-y. sources.

*FRANKEL (1870), pp. 49a—51b, on aggadic materials; 36a—40a, 53b, on attributive formulae that mention a tradent.

*SHMUEL VALDBERG, Śefer Darkhe HaShinuyin (Lemberg, 1870, Repr. Jerusalem, 1970), classifies and analyzes, with lists of instances, methods used in exegesis and expounding of verses.

S. SEKLES, The Poetry of the Talmud (New York, 1880), hardly exhaustive but suggestive.

*LIEBERMAN (1931), pp. 84—108, attributive formulae of traditions in y. Neziqin; ID., Greek in Jewish Palestine (New York, 1941, 1965[2]), p. 110.

GINZBERG (1941), pp. H: lxxxi—lxxxii.

*JULIUS GREENSTONE, Popular Proverbs in the Jerusalem Talmud, Essays in Honor of the Very Rev. Dr. J. Hertz, ed. I. EPSTEIN, et al. (London, 1943), pp. 187—201.

ABRAHAM WEISS, The Babylonian Talmud as a Literary Unit (New York, 1943), and ID., Studies in the Literature of the Amoraim (New York, 1962), for which see DAVID GOODBLATT, Abraham Weiss: The Search for Literary Forms, in: The Formation of the Babylonian Talmud, ed. J. NEUSNER (Leiden, 1970), pp. 95—103.

DOV NOY, HaŚipur Ha'Amami VeTalmud U VaMidrash (Jerusalem, 1960), on folk narratives and stories.

*JOSEPH HEINEMANN, Prayer in the Period of the Tannaim and the Amoraim—Its Nature and Patterns (Hebrew), (Jerusalem, 1964). English revised edition (Berlin, 1977).

*JACOB NEUSNER, Development of a Legend (Leiden, 1970); ID., The Rabbinic Traditions About the Pharisees Before 70, 3 vols. (Leiden, 1971); ID., Eliezer Ben Hyrcanus, 2 vols. (Leiden, 1973); ID., A History of the Mishnaic Law of Purities, I—III: Kelim (Leiden, 1974); IV—V: Ohalot (Leiden, 1975); VI—VIII: Negaim (Leiden, 1975), present systematic study, classification, and analysis of literary forms, patterns, and structures.

*AARON MIRSKY, HaShirah HaIvrit BiTequfat HaTalmud, Yerushalayim, Shenaton LeDivre Śifrut VeHaGut, ed. GEDALIAH ALGOSHE (Jerusalem, 1966), II: 161—179, a suggestive study on literary characteristics and forms of songs and poetry.

*D. BEN-AMOS, Narrative Forms in the Haggadah: Structural Analysis, Ph. D. Dissertation, Indiana University, 1967 (University Microfilms, Ann Arbor, 1967, 1975), includes an excellent review of previous treatments of *aggadah*, careful analyses of the traits of legends, tall tale, fable, exemplum, and riddling tale, and a full bibliography.

BENJAMIN DEVRIES, Meḥqarim BiŚifrut HaTalmud (Jerusalem, 1968), pp. 284—289, and 290—300, on literary dimensions and types of *aggadah*.

J. FLORSHEIM, Rav Hisda as Exegetor of Tannaitic Sources, Tarbiẓ 40 (1971), 24—48.

WAYNE SIBLEY TOWNER, The Rabbinic Enumeration of Scriptural Examples (Leiden, 1973). This excellent study includes a discussion and bibliography of earlier works on rabbinic literary patterns.

*MELAMMED (1973), pp. 275—296, 312—317, and his forthcoming book, 'The Halakhic Midrashim in the Palestinian Talmud'.

*BOKSER (1975), by type, formulation, and use analyzes and classifies traditions and attributive formulae of Samuel, some of which appear in y.

JOSEPH HEINEMANN and JAKOB J. PETUCHOWSKI, Literature of the Synagogue (New York, 1975), introductions and selections of prayer and poetry in both Talmuds and in early liturgy, laments, and sermons. Many examples are from y.

*GARY G. PORTON, The Legal Traditions of Rabbi Ishmael. I: The Earlier Legal Traditions (Leiden, 1976).

*WILLIAM S. GREEN, The Traditions of Joshua ben Hananiah. I: The Earlier Legal Traditions (Leiden, 1979).

GOODBLATT (1979), IV. 1: b. ζ and IV. 2.

There are various practical reasons to consider the nature and uses of formulations and patterns. Below, in Section IX. B, I shall discuss the application to exegesis, especially where two or more versions of an item may exist. One should note that the several literary genres may be reflected in variations in grammatical forms. For example, texts of prayers, songs, and public or formal declarations may employ different grammatical forms and usages from passages of colloquial materials. While this has been demonstrated for the BT, it undoubtedly applies, as well, to the PT; SHAMMA FRIEDMAN, Three Studies in Babylonian Grammar, Tarbiẓ 43 (1973—74), 58—69.

As to terms, structured phrasings, and fixed bridging language, all of which may provide or determine the strucutre of a whole pericope, see below, Chapter XVI.

B. Layout

1. Some scholars have tried to describe the layout of the materials. Many have compared y.'s *gemara* to that of b. and have made the obvious observation that PT is briefer, usually with shorter and elliptical or less clear discussions, more to the point and simpler in explaining 'Mishnah' or discussing a tradition. I review the import of these phenomena in the sections on the editing of the text and the role of the scribes, Sections IX and XII. At this point let me say only that much of the greater expansive nature of b. *gemara* unbpubtedly comes from the end of the Amoraic period and more so from the Saboraic activity, a process which y. lacked. Cf. ASSIS (1976), pp. 7f.

The only systematic study of the structure is LIEBERMAN, Talmud of Caesarea (1931), in which he compares the structure of y. 'Neziqin' to that of the rest of y. To my knowledge all other general comments, whatever their merits, are part of research in progress or are not based on a comprehensive and careful study of the data. Moreover, in the formulation of their comments, many works do not sufficiently take into account the diversity of *gemara*, which is the product of different circles. Cf. LIEBERMAN (1931), pp. 23—25; GINZBERG (1941), p. H: lxxxi; and MELAMMED (1973), pp. 566—567.

Clearly y., like b., presents materials along certain lines. These include:

a. Explanations of 'Mishnah', analyses thereof, and independent teachings related to the theme of 'Mishnah'. LIEBERMAN (1934), p. 215 notes, PT first offers or establishes the reading or simple sense of 'Mishnah' . . ., or cites a *baraita*, and then analyzes and discusses the first part of the text.

b. Series of comments, statements, adages or incidents formally related, one of which is relevant to the context. E.g., *gemara* may contain a series of items attributed to the same master. See FRANKEL (1870), pp. 39a—b, 49a—51b; EPSTEIN, Tarbiẓ 3 (1931), 122; GINZBERG (1941), p. H: lxxvii; and MELAMMED (1973), pp. 565—566, and cp. R. EDELMANN, Some Remarks on the Literary Aspect of the Talmud and Midrashim in their Relation to Hellenistic Civilization, Third World Congress of Jewish Studies, Synopses of Lectures Section: Talmud and Rabbinics (Jerusalem, 1961), pp. IV, 1—7; and A. WEISS (1962).

c. Repetition of a pericope from elsewhere. *Gemara* on the basis of a tangential reference in a pericope elsewhere may include that whole pericope in the referred-to location. Cf. FRANKEL (1870) and LIEBERMAN (1947), pp. 67f. Below I discuss transferred pericopae and to what degree this phenomenon derives from the editors or scribes of the text.

Finally, one should note that Aramaic and Hebrew within y. tend consistently to be used for different purposes. Traditions generally appear in Hebrew while discussions and narratives employ Aramaic. Cf. JULIUS GREENSTONE (1943), esp. p. 187, fn. 2, who indicates that proverbs in contrast to *aggadah* employs Hebrew twice as frequently as Aramaic; E. MARGALIYOT, Ivrit Ve'aramit BaTalmud U VaMidrash, Leshonenu 27—28 (1963—64), 20—33; and MELAMMED (1973), pp. 315—317.

2. Additional literature on the above items include:

FRANKEL (1870), pp. 18b—40a, 47, provides the basic description, though his evaluation does not sufficiently take into account the literary nature of the materials and he unconsciously adopts the Jewish Enlightenment's apologetic that the b. is too long-winded and convoluted.

LEWIN, Methiboth (1933), pp. x—xii.

A. WEISS, The Literary Development of the Babylonian Talmud, 2 vols. (Warsaw, 1937, 1939); (1943); and (1962). Cf. SHAMAI KANTER, Abraham Weiss: Source Criticism, in: NEUSNER, Formation (1970), p. 89.

*ABRAHAM GOLDBERG, The Sources and Development of the Sugya in the Babylonian Talmud, Tarbiẓ 32 (1962—63), 143—152.

B. DEVRIES, Mavo Kelali LeŚifrut HaTalmudit (Tel Aviv, 1966), pp. 108—110.

DAVID WEISS HALIVNI (1968, 1975), passim and for comparative purposes, II: 'Introduction'.

BOKSER (1975), pp. 21—26, 145—157. As to the location of a b. tradition within a y. pericope, see pp. 77—80, and fn. 216; 97—101; and 117—120.

C. 'Mishnah'

1. J. N. EPSTEIN, Introduction to the Text of Mishnah (Jerusalem, 1964²), provides a definitive treatment of most matters concerning 'Mishnah', including the text of 'Mishnah' and how later authorities perceived that work. The work is outstanding in both conception of the problem, use of all examples of a phenomenon, analysis, bibliographical comments, laying

out of issues, and usually his conclusions. The relevant portions are pp. 160—508, 673—726, 771—946. See Baruch M. Bokser, Jacob N. Epstein's 'Introduction to the Text of the Mishnah', in: The Modern Study of the Mishnah, ed. J. Neusner (Leiden, 1973), pp. 13—36.

2. PT originally was one continuous text, without chapter, tractate and *halakhah* 'division'. These are later additions; cf. Lieberman (1929), pp. 11—12; (1934), pp. xxviii—xxix and 238, fn. 1. Later arrangers of y. included certain internal lemmas of 'Mishnah'. Thus the 'Mishnah' presented in the y. MSS or editions and most lemma-citations of 'Mishnah' do not represent the 'Mishnah' used by the Palestinian masters. The passages or citations are added by scribes, who in the process may have placed them in the wrong location. Moreover, the order of *gemara* or its sources may have differed from that of 'Mishnah''s, but scribes arranged the Amoraic material according to 'Mishnah''s order.

Additional literature includes:

Y. H. Shor, Mishnayot in Talmud Yerushalmi and Bavli, HeḤaluṣ 6 (1862), 32—47.

Epstein, Fragments, Tarbiẓ 3 (1932), pp. 121f.; Id., HaMada' HaTalmudi Uṣerakhov, Proceeding of the Academy of Jewish Studies 2 (Jerusalem, 1935), pp. 5—7; and (1962), pp. 604—606.

Rabinovitz (1940), p. 636.

Melech Schachter, The Babylonian and Jerusalem Mishnah: Textually Compared (Jerusalem, 1959) is inexact, unreliable, and conceptually poor.

*Melammed (1973), pp. 535—543.

Solomon Zeitlin, HaMishnah SheBiYerushalmi VeHaMishnah SheBeBavli, in: Zer li-Gevurot [= Zalman Shazar Jubilee Volume], ed. B. Z. Luria (Jerusalem, 1973), pp. 539—548.

Feintuch, Tarbiẓ 45 (1976), I—II, 178—212.

S. Abramson, As to Two Terms Used to Cite Mishnah, Sinai 40 (79) (1977), 211—228, especially 228.

3. No single reading or text of 'Mishnah' existed in Amoraic times. Rather masters may have had different recensions and variant individual readings, on the basis of which they taught. Epstein traces how early Amoraim had a 'reliable' text of 'Mishnah', yet taught independent of 'Mishnah'. On the other hand, the later Amoraim read 'Mishnah''s text with greater freedom but tried to base their teachings on it. Reciters or later scribes may alter a text of 'Mishnah' to accord with a given interpretation. Epstein, moreover, historically and philologically classifies modes and terminologies used in citing, explaining, questioning, and ostensibly emending 'Mishnah'.

See also:

Frankel (1870), pp. 19a—22a, described many of the phenomena. Epstein besides producing a more systematic and analytical treatment evaluated the assumptions in the study and reformulated the questions.

HANOCH ALBECK, Nuśḥaot BaMishnah Shel Ha'Amoraim, Zvi Chajes Memorial Volume (Vienna, 1933), pp. 1—28.

GINZBERG (1941), pp. H: li—lvi.

LIEBERMAN, SZ (1968).

WEISS HALIVNI (1968 and 1975).

MELAMMED (1973), pp. 535—548.

D. Citation and Use of Sources

1. Y. contains items which ostensibly represent a 'source', i.e., materials which employ some type of a structure, the pattern for which does not depend upon the present context, and which ostensibly represent a teaching from an earlier period. Technically this could include many of the items which I earlier listed under the 'forms' or 'formulations' of the materials, but I presently refer only to *baraitot* and texts of midrashic exegesis.

The major methodological problem in the study of any supposed 'source', whether a *baraita* or even a sermon, is: Does the material represent true 'sources' used or incorporated by the spokesperson-tradent or editor of the pericope or of the PT? Alternatively, is it a literary way in which to arrange and transmit material produced by the one who cited it or edited the pericope? Unfortunately, to my knowledge this issue, in terms of Amoraic material, has not been squarely faced. Cf. DAVID GOODBLATT, Abraham Weiss: The Search for Literary Forms, in: J. NEUSNER, Formation (1970), pp. 96—103, and especially ID. (1979), IV. 1: a, c. Clearly, however, individual material did circulate outside the framework of *gemara*. We find them, whether or not in an earlier or later recension or version, in other literary sources, e.g., 'Tosefta' and 'Bereshit Rabbah', and possibly even in a halakhic mosaic inscription on the pavement of a Beth Shean synagogue. Cf. SUSSMANN (1973—74), and ID., The Boundaries of Eretz-Israel, Tarbiẓ 45 (1976), II—III, 213—257; SAUL LIEBERMAN, The Halakhic Inscription from the Bet-Shean Valley, Tarbiẓ 45 (1976), IV, 54—63, 331; and below, Chapter X, on the *Midrashim*. Cf. Z. SAFRAI, Immanuel 8 (1978), 48—57.

Such texts thus existed; in fact it is the only way to account for the history of materials which appear e. g., in Tos., a 'Midrash Halakhah', and in one or more *baraitot*. But we do not know if every instance of such a text represents a 'source' or a conventional way in which to formulate and present materials. On the other hand, if the text pre-existed outside its present context, irrespective of any revisions, it may include material in addition to or even some that is inconsistent with that which is needed in the present instance. This accords with LIEBERMAN's observation (1934), p. 216, that y. may cite a biblical verse, 'Mishnah', or *baraita* as a metaphoric-idiomatic usage, for such texts were fixed in the mouths of the Amoraim. One must, accordingly, not confuse the issue of form with that of source and must carefully examine each item.

2. Indexes. The reference index in the Krotoschin edition of y. is superior to that in the other editions.

Z. BACHER, Baraitot beTalmud Yerushalmi, Yerushalayim 10 (1913), 59—82, a classified list, with comments, of *baraitot* cited in y.

MICHAEL HIGGER, Oṣar HaBaraitot, 10 vols. (New York, 1938—48), comprehensive, classified collection of *baraitot* in both *gemarot.* He consistently employs MSS and citations of medieval authorities and indicates all the item's versions which appear elsewhere. Vol. 10 includes a page index to *gemara.*

*E. Z. MELAMMED, Halakhic Midrashim in the Talmud. II: Halakhic Midrashim in the Talmud Yerushalmi (Jerusalem, in preparation). A comprehensive classified study. Cf. MELAMMED (1973), pp. 275—296, 312—317, for the tentative results and classifications.

3. Technique of 'citing'. Scholars and commentators describe the ways in which items are cited and the terminologies that are used; they discuss the texts' 'origins' and how they relate to 'Mishnah', *baraitot,* and to other extant versions or corpora of the materials, and they try to account for variations.

I deal here with the modes by which the items are cited, and in the next section with the relationship of a source in y. to its analogue elsewhere.

On the citations of 'Mishnah', see also above, Section C. Of note, differences did not always exist between the modes of citation of 'Mishnah' and *baraita.* A sharp conceptual difference between corpora stems from the latter part of the Amoraic period. Then Rabbi's 'Mishnah' became the 'Mishnah' with a capital M. See EPSTEIN (1948, 1964^2) and LIEBERMAN, SZ (1968).

Y. contains fixed terminologies that mark something as a *baraita,* a Tannaitic source, i. e., deriving from a 'known' collection of *baraitot,* or to be more accurate, some type of worked over text.

The classification and usages of such words may be found in:

*HIGGER (1938—48). Besides the full listings, there are introductions.

CHANOCH ALBECK, Studies in the Baraita and Tosefta (Jerusalem, 1944, 1969), examines *baraitot* with the several types of attributive formulae, assigned and unassigned; ID., Introduction to the Talmud, Babli and Yerushalmi (Jerusalem, 1969), Ch. III, esp. pp. 19—43.

*EPSTEIN (1948, 1964^2), systematically classifies the items used for 'Mishnah' and *baraitot.* In ID., Introduction to Tannaitic Literature (Jerusalem-Tel Aviv, 1957), pp. 499—746, he focuses on items that correlate with texts in the Tannaitic Midrashim. On p. 501, he refers to the earlier literature.

*MELAMMED (1973), pp. 275—296 and 312—317.

The following phenomena are of note:

a. PT may digest a 'Mishnah', hint at it, and scribes later filled in the rest, and, at times, did so incorrectly; see FRANKEL (1870), pp. 36a—40a;

LIEBERMAN (1934), p. 157; and BOKSER (1975), pp. 101f., fn. 280. This likewise occurred with *baraitot*. Thus LIEBERMAN points out that y. may identify an item with the phrase, ——מתניתא דר׳, *MTNYT' DR'*————————, "the teaching is that of R. ————————," and the scribes filled in the referent, ——אמר דר׳ . . . , *DR'*——————————*'MR*, . . . "For R. ———— said". But they may have erred in this identification.

The fact that originally y. did not always include the citation of the source and that the tendency later was to fill it in would preclude wholesale adoption of RABINOVITZ (1940), pp. 88, fn. 1; 237; 360, who holds that *baraitot* may have been deleted. One thus must evaluate the type and purpose of each citation.

b. PT may paraphrase a *baraita* which, therefore, may not be in its original language; EPSTEIN (1962), p. 254.

c. PT may cite the beginning of a text and refer to its end, and do so even without including, וכו׳, *WKW*, "etc."

d. PT may abbreviate a *baraita*; MELAMMED (1973), pp. 580f.

e. A text may employ some linguistic peculiarities in presenting materials. Thus a, ו, *W*, may represent, הוא, *HW'*, "he" or "that is"; cf. LIEBERMAN, Tarbiẓ 4 (1933), p. 377; BOKSER (1975), p. 27, fn. 56. (The reference to the pages in the article by KUTSCHER should read p. 1602 and not p. 1595.)

A separate issue is, what constitutes a *baraita* or 'true' Tannaitic material? The question responds to the following data:

a. Y. often cites a *baraita* without an introductory term. Writers discuss whether such terms were originally lacking or whether they were subsequently deleted. See LIEBERMAN (1934), pp. 192, 410; and EPSTEIN (1957), pp. 253—255.

b. An Amoraic tradition may be identical to an item in a Tannaitic corpus or to a text in BT, represented as a *baraita*. See EPSTEIN (1957), pp. 253—255; NEUSNER (1973); MELAMMED (1973), pp. 294—296. The Amora may thus represent the teaching as a 'tradition', and not as a 'source'. On the other hand, the individual's contribution may consist in the citation of a given 'source' in a specific context or by the choice of one *baraita* and the rejection of another. See BOKSER (1975), pp. 6—7, and passim.

c. Y. may also introduce disputes or individual teachings of early Amoraim with, תני, *TNY*, "teaches", a term 'normally' associated with a *baraita*, e. g., *TNY ŠMW'L*, "Samuel teaches". See LIEBERMAN (1931), p. 64, fn. 124, and SZ (1968), p. 127; HIGGER (1938—48), esp. Vols. I and IV; RABINOVITZ (1940), p. 68; ALBECK (1944), pp. 15—48; EPSTEIN (1948, 1964²), pp. 212—216; GOODBLATT (1975), pp. 77—80, 200—201.

4. The relationship between different versions of *baraitot*. As already indicated, a *baraita* cited in y. may elsewhere have parallels or analogous versions. Commentators and scholars have noticed and tried to account for the variations between the several versions. Too much of the analysis, however, has been prejudiced by a desire to prove or disprove that *gemara*, taken as a monolithic construct, knew or did not know a given

document, also taken as a construct. While evidence may at times support a general conclusion, in fact one can speak of only individual pericopae of a Tannaitic source and of individual *sugyot*. This accords with the existence of different oral reciters who were the depository for the 'sources' and who, when appropriate, would cite individual materials. Moreover, even *sugyot* may be composed of different parts, each of which comes from different circles. See LIEBERMAN (1931), pp. 22—24; GINZBERG (1941), pp. H: lxxx—lxxxi; EPSTEIN (1962), pp. 275—276; ABRAHAM WEISS, Studies in the Literature of the Amoraim (New York, 1962), pp. 166—175, — to which see MEYER FELDBLUM, Professor Abraham Weiss: His Approach and Contribution to Talmudic Scholarship, The Abraham Weiss Jubilee Volume (New York, 1964), English Section, pp. 69—71; and MEYER FELDBLUM, Talmudic Law and Literature: Tractate Gittin (New York, 1969), p. 32; and cp. EJ. s. v. baraita.

In addition, some writers speculate as to the lack, in *gemara*, of a reference to a *baraita* from 'Tosefta' and argue that the failure to cite the source indicates that the document was not known and, therefore, not yet composed. But, as indicated above, the purpose and context of the Amoraic comment and the way in which it circulated may, at times, have made it inappropriate to cite the *baraita*; BOKSER (1975), pp. 6f. Cf. WEISS HALIVNI (1968), p. 295, fn. 6; (1975), pp. 86, 159f., 163f. Moreover, the proposition assumes that everything known was recorded and compiled in *gemara* and that nothing was ever left as a mere allusion—something known to be otherwise, as already indicated; see LIEBERMAN (1947), p. 68, fn. 18.

As to variations, differences between *baraitot* or a *baraita* and passage in a corpus, e. g., 'Tosefta', may reflect divergent attitudes originating in different circles. See LIEBERMAN (1934), pp. 17, 18f.; NEUSNER, Pharisees (1971); Eliezer (1973); and Purities (1974—77), passim. Furthermore, different circles may have had different readings in Tos. A particular *baraita* may accord with such a divergent reading, one that may be preserved in one of the MSS of Tos. See GINZBERG (1941), pp. H: lvi—lxiii; LIEBERMAN, TK (1955ff.), passim and esp. I, 'Introduction', 2—5, 20, and WEISS HALIVNI (1968, 1975), passim,

Recent linguistic and historical studies indicate that one must consider *baraitot* as a separate stratum of materials and not one 'identical' with that of Tannaitic collections. The former employ a separate stratum of Middle Hebrew, which differs from that in 'Mishnah' and 'Tosefta'. In addition, the one who cited the *baraita*, a later Amoraic authority, or the editor of the pericope may gloss the text with explanatory comments, revise it to fit redactional considerations or Palestinian conceptions, or simply to follow a different pattern or structure. Sustained analysis may indicate how these revisions systematically introduce new conceptions into a text or associate new themes with a given-master. Therefore, these *baraitot* must primarily represent 'Amoraic' material. They constitute what an Amora thought, or what was represented as the view of a tannaitic master, or what was considered important to so represent.

Additional literature:

FRANKEL (1870), pp. 22a—28a.

M. S. ZUCKERMANDEL, Tosefta Mishnah und Boraitha (Frankfurt, 1908—1910), includes an index by tractate and page. See H. MALTER, A Talmudic Problem and Proposed Solutions, JQR 2 (1911—12), 75—95.

BOAZ COHEN, Mishnah and Tosefta Shabbat (New York, 1935).

*LIEBERMAN, TR (1938), II: viii—xv; (1947), p. 22, n. 5; TK (1955ff.), passim, esp. I: ii—v, xiv—xxii, III: xiii—xiv, IV: xi—xxiv, V: xiii. See entry ROSENTHAL.

HIGGER (1938—48); and ID., A Yerushalmi View of the Authorship of the Tosefta, PAAJR 11 (1941), 43—46.

RABINOVITZ (1940), pp. 19, 73, 86f., 217, 229, esp. 380f., 482.

ALBECK (1944), pp. 60—185, esp. 89—138; and (1969), esp. pp. 51—78 and 102—143. ALBECK's works contain much useful analysis and do distinguish between our extant text and the item in *gemara* referred to under the same name. But they are flawed by his overly monolithic view of matters and insufficient literary and critical approach. See GARY G. PORTON, Ḥanokh Albeck on the Mishnah, in: The Modern Study of the Mishnah, ed. J. NEUSNER (Leiden, 1975), pp. 209—224; S. C. REIF, Review, Journal of Semitic Studies 19 (1974), 112—117; and ABRAHAM GOLDBERG, Review, KS 47 (1971), 9—19.

EPSTEIN (1948), pp. 1—165, 404—508, 950—970.

A. WEISS (1962), pp. 153—168; 166ff.; and ID., Meḥqarim BaTalmud (Jerusalem, 1975), p. 33, focuses on independent revisions of *baraitot* by separate circles.

ELIEZER ROSENTHAL, HaMoreh, PAAJR (1963), Hebrew, pp. 1—71, esp. 52—57. He reconstructs LIEBERMAN's view on 'Tosefta' and its relationship to y. and summarizes previous views on the matter.

*WEISS HALIVNI (1968, 1975), passim. See Index, s. v. *baraita*.

*NEUSNER, Development (1970), esp. pp. 83—86, 110—111, 133—142, 154—158; Pharisees (1971); Eliezer (1973), esp. II: 236; Purities (1974—77). Besides examining sources for variations in names, details, context, and applying form and tradition criticism, he demonstrates the differences between strata.

DEVRIES, Meḥqarim BeŚifrut HaTalmud (Jerusalem, 1968), pp. 148—160.

FELDBLUM (1969), p. 32.

*TOWNER (1973), passim.

*JOSEPH HEINEMANN, Aggadah and Its Development [Hebrew] (Jerusalem, 1974), esp. 17—47, on divergent versions of aggadic texts.

*MENAḤEM MORESHET, Further Study of the Language of the Hebrew Bārāytot in the Babylonian and Palestinian Talmudim, Archive of the New Dictionary of Rabbinic Literature, II (Ramat-Gan, 1974), pp. English viii—ix, and Hebrew 31—73, esp. 56—73.

BARUCH BOKSER, Two Traditions of Samuel, in: Christianity, Judaism, and Other Greco-Roman Cults, Studies for Morton Smith at Sixty, Part IV, ed. J. NEUSNER (Leiden, 1975), pp. 46—47.

E. E. HALEVY, HaAggadah HaHiśtorit-Biographit (Tel Aviv, 1975), e.g., pp. 129—130.

*GOODBLATT (1979), IV. 1 : a, c.

In the analysis of a *baraita* one cannot automatically conclude that a text which ostensibly serves to support or correspond to an immediately preceding Amoraic tradition represents the view of that master or even constitutes material known during his lifetime. Such texts may be introduced by the notation כהדא דתני, *KHD' DTNY*, "Like this it was taught". A later authority may have cited the text and not the author of the tradition, who in fact may even dispute it. See RABINOVITZ (1940), p. 467; G. ALON, Tarbiẓ 12 (1940), 91, 95; and WEISS HALIVNI (1975), p. 540, fn. 7.

IX. Transferred Traditions and Pericopae and Unsmooth Flow of sugyot

A. Transferred Material

1. One finds in y. traditions or complete pericopae which do not seem to fit in their present context. The referrents may be unclear or they may not relate to the preceding or following materials. Moreover one finds in two, three, or four locations analogous traditions or pericopae which show no or slight variations or which present the material in different arrangement. According to ASSIS (1976), p. 1, there are close to one thousand such *sugyot*. These repetitions are the result of transference. The process whereby one duplicates or adapts a tradition or pericope from elsewhere theoretically can occur at several stages in the history of *gemara*; certain types undoubtedly occurred prior to the final compilation of the text and others clearly afterwards, by scribes.

While scholars agree when certain types happened, they disagree as to others. Part of the argument centers on the appropriateness of a comparison with a similar phenomenon of transference found in other texts, e.g., 'Genesis Rabba', 'Sifra', and 'Bavli'.

2. A reciter, tradent or editor of a pericope may apply a comment or tradition to a new context. He may adapt the item's language so as to be appropriate to the issue as formulated in the new context or he may not fully reformulate the material. One may recognize this type of transference when one comes across analogous or identical items which seem to have originated in two separate contexts, or when one notices that the idiom or technical language does not exactly fit in one context.

The more recent literature, which list the earlier studies and traditional authorities who noticed this phenomenon, include:

EPSTEIN (1948), (1957), (1962).

A. WEISS, Court Procedure (New York, 1957), pp. 24, 58—61, 85, 94, 163—165; (1962); ID., Notes to Talmudic Pericopae (Bar Ilan, n.d.), pp. 215--217, esp. fn. 45.

B. DEVRIES, Literary Transfer as a Factor in the Development of Talmudic Law, Bar Ilan Annual I (1963), 156—164, esp. 163f.

WEISS HALIVNI (1968, 1975).

ALBECK (1968), pp. 452—545; 557—576; 657f.; esp. 496—504; 558—560; 657; and cf. 492, fn. 77; 514f.

BOKSER, Two Traditions of Samuel (1975); and (1975), p. 76, fn. 208, and 92, fn. 255.

SHRAGA ABRAMSON, Baale Tosefot ʿal HaTorah (Jerusalem, 1975), pp. 27—43.

3. But the type of transference in y. that creates the greatest problems are those where whole pericopae are repeated and which appear as foreign matter. FRANKEL (1870) and others focused on these materials and LIEBERMAN (1929), (1931), (1933), and (1934) critically analyzed them. EPSTEIN, Tarbiẓ 3 (1932) and (1962), summarized in MELAMMED (1973), also dealt with them. EPSTEIN believes that these items were transferred not only by the earlier scribes but also by the compilers of y. LIEBERMAN holds that they are the results of scribes. See now ASSIS (1976)'s evaluation of the problem and his comprehensive analysis of the phenomenon. See also WEISS HALIVNI (1968, 1975), esp. II: 144, fn. 1; 166, fn. 3; 262, fn. 10; 714, fn. 11; BOKSER (1975), pp. 85—88.

A pericope which contains a tangential reference to a text elsewhere may be transferred to that other context. But this process created problems. As the tradition may not properly fit the context or a whole pericope may not originate in its present location, one must not impose an interpretation upon the item to fit the new context.

The transferences might occur in several stages. Once material was transferred from one place to the second, other material originally from the second place might be transferred to the first. Each of the two locations may thus contain primary and secondary material. At times a reading in a Geniza fragment which lacks the 'second' transference may confirm the process. See BOKSER (1975), p. 126, fn. 362, for an instance where the Gaon ELIJAH of Vilna, in one passage, made such a suggestion, which is confirmed by a Geniza fragment. In general, see ASSIS (1976), passim.

The transferred pericope may have been placed into the wrong location. Where a scribe placed the material in the 'correct' place, he may have juxtaposed disputing *sugyot* deriving from different *yeshivot* and circles. Naturally the inconsistencies create exegetical problems as items may thus not only lack transitional bridging language but may even externally appear to form a single *sugya*.

A scribe may have deleted one or more of the occurrences of the pericopae, as he relied on one of the other instances. But he may delete the original instance. Naturally where the transferred pericope had been incorrectly placed, the deletion of the original instance creates problems.

The MSS and Geniza fragments indicate that at times the scribes made a notation גרש, כו׳, *GRS* or *KW*ʿ, to the effect that material is deleted. The latter term means 'etc.' LIEBERMAN and EPSTEIN differ as to the meaning of the former. LIEBERMAN renders the former as "abbreviated", while EPSTEIN as "[we] learned"; LIEBERMAN (1929), pp. 12—13; and ID., Tarbiẓ 5 (1933), 107—110; and EPSTEIN (1962), pp. 324—330; see MELAMMED (1973), pp. 578—579. E. S. ROSENTHAL, Leshonot Śofrim, in: Yuval Shy, ed. B. KURZWEIL (Ramat Gan, 1958), pp. 294—297, on the other hand argues that this term means "in extenso". Cp. BOKSER, AJSReview 4 (1979).

Subsequent to the deletion, later scribes may have filled in the missing portion and have done so incorrectly. They may have filled in material above or below the proper place and thereby included irrelevant lines. Alternatively, they may have started after the beginning or end before the conclusion of the whole passage and thereby included insufficient material. On the other hand, scribes, relying on the portion preserved before the deletion, may have filled in the deleted sections from a text which has a similar beginning but a different ending, and thus may have supplied the wrong text. EPSTEIN's claim that the scribes would have filled in only on the basis of MSS seems to constitute only an assumption and one which does not sufficiently take into consideration the textual nature of *gemara* and actual scribal practices. See EPSTEIN, Tarbiẓ 3 (1932), 123, fn. 6; (1962), pp. 324—332, and MELAMMED (1973), pp. 580f.

LIEBERMAN proves that one must not automatically conclude that all variations between analogous pericopae are the results of only scribal corruptions. The differences may represent different stages or circles in the redaction of common materials. He demonstrates how the brevity and curtness in 'Neziqin' derive from its earlier compilation and not from deletions of portions found in the parallels elsewhere; LIEBERMAN (1931) and ID., SZ (1968), esp. pp. 125—136. Cf. GOODBLATT (1979), IV. 1:6. g.

B. Examining Out-of-Place Traditions

One has to determine what constitutes the relevant portion of the text. One must isolate each unit of the *sugya* and not impose concepts or issues from one part into the next. One must interpret the passage on the basis of its own content, see if its references are clear and its language appropriate. Where more than one instance is extant one separately examines each part of the pericope. Where 'parallels' do not exist, one must consider if language inappropriate in the present setting makes sense in another one. Where the pericope comments on 'Mishnah', the possibilities are fewer and one can easily employ a concordance to check key terms or matters mentioned in the passage. A similar procedure is necessary for pericopae that do not comment on 'Mishnah'. The forthcoming edition of KOSOVSKY's 'Concordance to the Palestinian Talmud' will facilitate this.

A further aid is that of form criticism. Certain comments may employ a fixed or stereotyped formulation recurrently used for particular purposes. Thus a B- prefix introducing a brief tradition which for comprehension depends upon some other passage serves to comment and gloss a previous text like 'Mishnah'. See BOKSER (1975), pp. 97—101. Once one notices the presence of the form, one can lift the clause out of its context and relate it to its actual referent. Likewise is the case with fixed terminologies, which introduce a structured pericope. Furthermore, the chronology of the masters may be helpful in determining the relationship of the parts of a *sugya*. Finally, one must realize that y. often lacks answers to a question. As a result the material following a question may constitute a separate pericope. See the Sections on Forms and Terminology, VIII, A; and XVI.

One should also consider that the referent to a passage may not be the immediately preceding matter. The referent may have been deleted or interrupted. For the former one must search for the missing deleted pericope or text. In the latter, one must examine the passage penultima to the difficult text. The contiguous text, whether the result of an incorrectly placed transference or inclusion of a marginal addition, may be an interpolation. See LIEBERMAN (1929); (1934), pp. xxv—xxvii, especially p. 27; EPSTEIN, Śefer Ma'asim, Tarbiẓ 1 (1930), 38; A. WEISS, Notes, pp. 44, 46, 127, 217; y. Shev. 1 : 2, 33b, Śefer Nir, loc. cit., and BOKSER (1975), pp. 74—77 and cp. 97—101, especially fn. 275; cp. RABINOVITZ (1940), pp. 88, 237, and 360. See above on the L. MS, to which add RABINOVITZ (1940), p. 28, and A. WEISS, Studies in the Law of the Talmud on Damages (New York, 1966), pp. 67f.

Moreover, as indicated in an earlier section, *gemara* may include an incorrectly filled-in reference; Section VIII. D. See below on interpolations into y. made from post-Talmudic texts.

Thus in examining a text one must be open to the several possibilities and consider if one occurred. See now the additional criteria set out and exemplified in ASSIS (1976). Other guidelines and tools are presented in the following sections.

C. Additional Literature

FRANKEL (1870), pp. 36b—40a, 136—139b.

LEWY (1895—1914), Introduction.

I. H. HALEVY, Dorot HaRishonim II: Amoraic Period (Frankfurt a.M., 1901. Repr. Jerusalem, 1967), pp. 529—536.

S. HOROWITZ, Analecten, MGWJ 45 (1901), 310, 314—322, adds examples of transference to those in FRANKEL.

W. BACHER, Talmud, Jewish Encyclopedia, 12, 6—7, lists of repeated pericopae.

LIEBERMAN (1929), pp. 112—113; (1931), pp. vii, 23f., 26; ID., Miscellanies, Tarbiẓ 5 (1933), 107—110; (1934), pp. xv, 28, fn. 1, 29, 83, 120, 238—239, fn. 1, 479, 523.

EPSTEIN, Additional Fragments, Tarbiẓ 3 (1932), 122—123, 134—136; (1962), pp. 276—279, 322—330.

GINZBERG (1941), pp. H: lxviii—lxxxii.

E. S. ROSENTHAL, Leshonot Śoferim, in: Yuval Shy. A Jubilee Volume Dedicated to S. Y. Agnon, ed. BARUCH KURZWEIL (Ramat Gan, 1958), pp. 293—324.

WEISS HALIVNI (1968, 1975), esp. II: 144, fn. 1; 166, fn. 3; 262, fn. 10; 714, fn. 11.

FELDBLUM (1969), pp. English, 11; Hebrew, 37—41.

MELAMMED (1973), pp. 575—581.

ISRAEL FRANCUS, Additions and Parallels in TB Bava Qamma VII, BIA 12 (1974), pp. ix, 43—63, and the literature cited there, especially S. FRIEDMAN and B. Z. BENEDICT, on transferred pericopae in b.

BOKSER (1975), pp. 76, fn. 208; 85—88; 122—125.

X. Parallels in Midrashic Works

A. Issues and Guidelines

Earlier, under 'Sources', I dealt with items that had parallels in halakhic *midrashim*. Here I consider materials which may have word-for-word parallels of whole pericopae in works nearly contemporaneous or subsequent to the compilation of y., e. g., 'Genesis Rabba'.

Scholars have analyzed the relationship between the y. passages and the parallels in the midrashic works, have tried to account for the variations and have argued the merits of three different propositions: (1) one source knew the other; (2) they both drew from a mutual source; (3) some early version or recension of the one used an early recension or version of the other. Furthermore, some scholars distinguish between the halakhic and aggadic portions in their assertions as to the existence of a 'mutual source' and the rejection of direct borrowing. Some have argued that the midrashic, aggadic materials in y. in toto derive from a midrashic work or source from which the y. editors transposed them into the y. This assumes the unlikely assumption that the aggadic materials do not have an organic place within the y.

One may use the midrashic works and the analogous versions or parallels to (1) establish the reading of a text, which is corrupted in y.; (2) clarify the sequence of the y. text on the basic of the structure in the *midrash*; (3) throw light, in general, on the Palestinian tradition, realia and practices, items which are common to y. and the Palestinian *midrashim*.

Two factors necessitate caution in the use of these materials:

1. Some items in the *midrash*, e. g., Gn. R., may not be integral to the text but additions added into it. Cf. DAVID DAUBE, Collaboration with Tyranny in Jewish and Roman Law (Oxford, 1965), whose insightful comments are partially flawed by his reliance on a scribal interpolation in Gn. R. See THEODOR-ALBECK ed., III, 1184, fn. 5.

2. The *midrash* may have used the passage and adapted and restructured it according to its own purposes. In the process it may add explanatory comments and fill in elliptical or unspecified details. These comments are useful as they serve as commentary to the pericope. But, on the other hand, they may not represent the original meaning of the passage or the one in its context in y.

Thus, as indicated with *baraitot*, one must consider the effect of the history of the tradition. TOWNER has demonstrated the process of standardizing and regularizing a midrashic pattern and how the later use of a text contemporizes the biblical evidence. TOWNER (1973), pp. 124—126; 209—211; cf. 197, 202. See also NEUSNER (1970—77).

B. Indexes

Where y. uses a biblical verse, one should examine the appropriate *midrash* to see if the *midrash* to the work includes the passage. The index in the Krotoschin edition provides a guide to many of the parallels. A. HYMAN, Torah haKetuvah VeHameśurah, 3 vols. (Tel Aviv, 1936, 1965[2]), is an index to biblical verses in rabbinic literature. In addition, there is an index at the end of Yefeh Mareh, Venice, 1590 commentary and edition to y. *aggadot*.

C. Representative Literature

Items on specific works appear in the appropriate entry below.

FRANKEL (1870), pp. 51b—53b.

BACHER, Talmud, JE, p. 7.

LIEBERMAN (1931), p. vii; (1934), p. xviii, fn. 1; and SZ (1968), p. 130.

L. ZUNZ, HaDrashot BeYisrael, revised. H. ALBECK (Jerusalem, 1957).

M. MARGULIES, Midrash Vayikra Rabbah, V (Jerusalem, 1960), pp. xvii—xxxi.

EPSTEIN (1962), pp. 287—290.

MYRON BIALIK LERNER, The Book of Ruth in Aggadic Literature and Midrash Ruth Rabba, 3 vols. (Ph. D. dissertation, Hebrew University, Jerusalem, 1971), I: 118—131.

MELAMMED (1973), pp. 573—575.

J. HEINEMANN, Aggadah and Its Development (Jerusalem, 1974).

SUSSMANN (1974—75), pp. 127, 141—143 and ID., Tarbiẓ 45 (1976), 218—257, especially 226—227, 252—254.

SAUL LIEBERMAN, On Persecution of the Jewish Religion, Salo Wittmayer Baron Jubilee Volume (Jerusalem, 1974), Hebrew pp. 213—246, demonstrates how to evaluate revisions in aggadic materials.

Z. M. RABINOVITZ, Ginze Midrash (Tel Aviv, 1976), contains fragments to many *midrashim*. See index for specific parallels to y.

D. Specific Works

I include bibliographical items which directly relate to use of y. Additional items may be found in entries in EJ; TOWNSEND, Rabbinic Source, in: Study of Judaism, Bibliographical Essays, Anti-Defamation League (New York, 1972), pp. 37—43; and STRACK (1931).

1. 'Genesis Rabba'.

M. LERNER, Anlage des Bereschith Rabbah und seine Quellen, Magazin für die Wissenschaft des Judentums 7—8 (1880—81) [Reprinted separately: Berlin, 1882], especially 8 (1881), 40—48, 92—107, 130—131.

Ed. J. THEODOR and CH. ALBECK, Bereschit Rabba (Berlin, 1903—1939; Repr. with corrections, Jerusalem, 1965). In the 'Introduction', Vol. III, 66—84, ALBECK discusses the relationship between y. and Gn. R. Pp. 75—84 contain a list of y. materials, arranged in sequence in *gemara*.

See also: LIEBERMAN (1929), p. 39; and SZ (1968), pp. 129—130.

MARGULIES (1960).

EPSTEIN (1962), pp. 287—290, who lists earlier literature. He holds that the y. of Gn. R., like y. 'Neziqin' [sic!] are distinct recensions of y., each different from the extant y. They stem from different *yeshivot*, i. e., places, and not different times.

M. SOKOLOFF, Introduction and index to Midrash Bereshet Rabba, MS Vat. Ebr. 30 (Jerusalem, 1971).

Midrash Bereshet Rabba, Codex Vatican 60 (Jerusalem, 1972).

J. HEINEMANN, Structure and Divisions of Midrash Genesis Rabbah, BIA 9 (1971), 279—289.

LEWIS BARTH, An Analysis of Vatican 30 (Cinn., 1973), esp. pp. 60—65 and fn. 68.

M. D. HERR, Genesis Rabahb, EJ 7, 399—402.

BOKSER, Two Traditions (1975); and AJSReview 4 (1979).

2. Lev. R.

Critical edition, commentary, and indexes by M. MARGULIES, 5 vols. (Jerusalem, 1953—60), esp. V: xxvii—xxxiii.

ALBECK, Midrash Vayiqra Rabba, Louis Ginzberg Jubilee Volume (New York, 1945), Hebrew pp. 25—43.

HEINEMANN, Parshot BeVayiqra Rabbah Shemeqorotehen Mefuqpaqot, Tarbiẓ 37 (1968), 339—354; ID., Profile of a Midrash: The Art of Composition in Leviticus Rabba, Journal of the American Academy of Religion 39 (1971), 141—150, and an expanded version, ID., HaŚifrut 24 (1971), 808—834. ID., Leviticus Rabbah, EJ 15, 152—154.

3. Dt. R.

SAUL LIEBERMAN, Midrash Debarim Rabbah (Jerusalem, 1964²), Introduction, especially pp. xv—xvii, re use of PT: at times it, like Tanḥumma, summarizes y.

M. D. HERR, Deuteronomy Rabba, EJ 5, 1584—1586.

4. Lam. R.

See LIEBERMAN (1934), p. xii.

5. 'Ruth Rabba'.

Edition, notes, and indexes: LERNER (Jerusalem, 1971). Y. used one of the earlier recensions of R. R. in one of its later editorial stages.

6. Midrash Tehillim

Edition, S. BUBER (Vilna, 1891), Introduction, I: xi—xiii, discusses and lists some 117 sources that ostensibly derive from y.

Engl. transl. with notes: W. BRAUDE, The Midrash on Psalms, 2 vols. (New Haven, 1959), I: xxv—xxxi, reviews the literature on the work.

Forthcoming comprehensive critical edition: SHMUEL LEITER.

7. 'Pesiqta'

Edition, MEIR FRIEDMANN (Vienna, 1880, Tel Aviv, 1963), a fine commentary, but does not sufficiently consider how 'Pesiqta' adapts the materials.

Translation and notes: W. BRAUDE, Pesikta Rabbati, 2 vols. (New Haven, 1968). The introduction, pp. 1—33, reviews the earlier literature, MSS, and editions. The Parma MS and the Prague edition are vital.

M. ZUCKER, Teguvot Littenu'at 'Avele Ṣiyyon haQara'im BaŚifrut HaRabbanit, Albeck Jubilee Volume (Jerusalem, 1963), pp. 378—385, demonstrates the ninth-century date for the work. In the passage examined and throughout the work a careful reading indicates that the *midrash* reflects a definite point of view and restructures and adapts y. material for its own purposes.

'Pesikta Rabbati', EJ, s. v.

A new critical edition is under preparation by NORMAN COHEN, at Hebrew Union College.

8. 'Pesikta DeRav Kahana'

Critical edition with indexes: B. MANDELBAUM, 2 vols. (New York, 1962).

A. GOLDBERG, Review, KS 43 (1968), 69—79.

Translation and notes: W. BRAUDE and I. KAPSTEIN, Pesiḳta de Rabb Kahana (Philadelphia, 1975), with Introduction and indexes.

9. 'Midrash Shir HaShirim'

Edition, L. GRUENHUT, Midrash Shir HaSchirim (Jerusalem, 1897), Introduction, pp. 19f. discusses the large number of materials parallel to y.

B. M. LERNER, Review, KS 48 (1973), 543—549.

10. 'Yelamdenu Midrashim'

GINZBERG, Genizah Studies (1928), I: 36.

LIEBERMAN (1934), p. 36; ID., Midrash Debarim Rabbah (Jerusalem, 1964[2]), Introduction.

Midrash Tanḥuma, ed. S. BUBER (Levuv and Vilna, Repr. Jerusalem, 1964), Introduction, pp. 5—6.

E. URBACH, Seride Tanḥuma-Yelamdenu, Qoveṣ 'al Yod 16 (1967), 1—54.

Tanḥuma-Yelamdenu, EJ 15, 794—796.

YAAQOV ADLER, Midrash Tanḥuma, Vatican MS 44, in: Kobez Al Yad 8 (18) (Jerusalem, 1976), 15—75, describes the MS and compares its readings to those of the printed edition.

11. 'Midrash Shmuel'

Edition S. BUBER (Vilna, 1925[2]), Introduction, pp. 5—6.

12. 'Avot De R. Nathan'

Ed. SOLOMON SCHECHTER (Vienna, 1887; New York, 1945, 1967[2]).

JUDAH GOLDIN, The Two Versions of Abot DeRabbi Nathan, HUCA 14 (1946), 97—120, demonstrates systematic conceptual adapting of the material; ID., The Fathers According to Rabbi Nathan (New Haven, 1955; New York, 1974). Introduction, translation, notes, and indexes.

ANTHONY SALDARINI, The Fathers According to Rabbi Nathan, Version B (Leiden, 1975). Introduction, translation, notes, and indexes.

XI. Relationship between PT and BT: Mutual Material which may Differ

1. Each *gemara* contains traditions attributed to masters of both Palestine and Babylonia. At times *gemara* may present a whole pericope from the other land. Some traditions or pericopae may be found in both y. and b.; others, though, appear in only one *gemara*, and at times that work is not the one from the master's native land. PT or BT may even specify that a matter comes from 'there' or the 'West', i. e., represents a 'Palestinian' or Babylonian tradition, but the 'native' document lacks that source.

Where both b. and y. contain an item, they may vary in attribution, formulation, context, emphasis, or language. Thus one *gemara* may present a tradition as a statement, while, the other does so as an incident.

Traditional commentators and modern writers have tried to account for the existence of material from the other land and for the variations between common items. The standard explanation focused on the possibility that one *gemara* had seen the completed, or incompleted, work from the other land, a view no longer held. See EPSTEIN (1962), pp. 290—292, and YEQUTIEL GREENWALD, HaRa'u MeŚadre HaBavli et HaYerushalmi? (New York, 1954).

2. FRANKEL (1870), pp. 40a—45a, suggested that on the basis of the 'travelers' who went back and forth between Babylonia and the Land of Israel one can account for the 'foreign' materials. Subsequent scholarship has variously defined the role of these individuals who transmitted traditions between the two countries. Clearly they were not 'official' emissaries (whatever the term 'official' might mean): *Gemara* often indicates that some masters were displeased at their departure. Moreover, many apparently left for economic purposes, as to participate in the silk trade. See NEUSNER, History of the Jews in Babylonia (Leiden, 1969²), I, 94—99; and MOSHE BEER, The Babylonian Amoraim (Ramat Gan, 1974), pp. 158f., 180—191. The part played by the travelers accords with what we know as to how oral reciters in general served to circulate traditions. See, e. g., LIEBERMAN, SZ (1968), pp. 130f. The main travelers include: Ulla, Dimi, and R. Abin, from Israel to Babylonia; and Eleazar, Asi, and Ze'ira, and the return of Dimi, from Babylonia to Israel .

Certain terms, in particular, are used in these contexts: BT uses phrases with the word, **במערבא**, *BM'RB'*, "in the West", e. g., . . . **הכא . . . במערבא**, *HK'* . . . *BM'RB'*. . . , "Here . . . [it is said], in the West . . ."; **בעו במערבא**, **הוו במערבא**, **מחכו עליה במערבא**, *B'W BM'RB'*, *HWW BM 'RB'*, *MḤKW 'LH BM'RB'*, "They asked in the West," "They discussed in the West", "They laughed concerning it in the West"; and **במערבא מתני/ו**, *BM'RB' MTNY/W*, "They taught in the West"; and **כי אתא**, *KY 'T'*, "When came". In PT one finds **תמן אמרין**, *TMN 'MRYN*, "There they say"; **רבנן דתמן**, *RBNN DTMN*, "Rabbis of there"; or a phrase with the word, **תמן**, *TMN*, "there". For full entries, see C. J. KASOWSKI, Thesaurus Talmudis (Jerusalem, 1954),6, 3047—3050, 30, 1033—1035; YOSEF UMANSKI, Ḥakhme Ha Talmud: Yerushalmi (Jerusalem, 1952), pp. 132, 148. See EPSTEIN (1962), 292—322, who lists and analyzes the usages. See as well TIBOR H. STERN, Composition of the Talmud (New York, 1959), for an uncritical but not unuseful lengthy treatment; LIEBERMAN (1931), pp. 8f, 17; and WEISS HALIVNI (1968), p. 497 and (1975), p. 273, fn. 26.

3. The variations have been explained by the following factors:

a. Mistakes: Transmitters or editors made mistakes which corrupted the materials; FRANKEL (1870), and I. H. WEISS, Dor Dor VeDorshov III (Berlin, 1924), p. 237.

b. Post-compilation corruptions: Scribes through their mistakes produced the corruptions in the text.

c. Transmission and formation: The process of citing and using the tradition yielded variations. This involved: The tradent, the one who cited the item in a specific context, or the editor of a pericope may have adapted it to fit the issue at hand or have revised the tradition on the basis of an interpretation given to it. The differences, as LIEBERMAN emphasizes, may reflect the presence of different sources. The two versions may come from different circles or academies, a fact that accounts for many of the differences between two similar items that are found in different locations in the same *gemara*. See LIEBERMAN (1931), p. viii; ID. (1968), pp. 130f; and A. GOLDBERG, R. Ze'ira and Babylonian Custom in Palestine, Tarbiẓ 36 (1967), 319—341; WEISS HALIVNI (1968, 1975); ALBECK (1969), pp. 559f., and the additional literature, below.

These variations were facilitated by prior differences between: readings or interpretations of mutual sources (*mishnayot* or *baraitot*); overall positions or approaches on a matter through which a tradition is perceived and explained; social, economic, political, and natural realia; language and usage in Middle Hebrew and Aramaic. See above on 'Mishnah' in y., Section VIII. C, and LIEBERMAN (1934), pp. xiii—xiv, ID. (1955ff.), passim; GINZBERG (1941), pp. H: lii—lxxiv; ABBA BENDAVID, Biblical Hebrew and Mishnaic Hebrew (Tel Aviv, 1967), pp. 171—222; WEISS HALIVNI (1968, 1975), e. g., I, 151; S. ABRAMSON, On the Hebrew in the Babylonian Talmud, and M. MORESHET, Further Studies of the Language of the Hebrew Bārāytot in the Babylonian and Palestinian Talmudim, both in: Archive 2 (1974), 9—15, 31—73, and the literature cited there, and English pp. v, viii.

The nature of the compilation itself may have produced differences. BT, and not PT, went through a process which worked over materials and placed them in an expanded literary context. Much of this activity is associated with the anonymous Saboraic masters in Babylonia. As a result, y. items often appear more 'pristine'. See GOLDBERG (1962—63); WEISS HALIVNI (1975), Introduction; BOKSER (1975), p. 236; EPSTEIN (1962), pp. 273—274; and especially S. FRIEDMAN, Glosses and Additions to TB Bava Qamma vii, Tarbiẓ 40 (1971), 418f, and fn. 1, and the literature cited there.

Cf. A. WEISS (1962), pp. 15—23, and (1975), pp. 8—15, and index, s. v. PT, and FELDBLUM (1964), p. 43, and especially GOODBLATT (1979), IV, 1: b. π, 3: c; and S. FRIEDMAN, TSJTSA 1 (1977), 275—441.

The compilation process which also entailed the selection of teachings from certain circles and the rejection of those from others may further account for the lack, in y., of a 'Palestinian' tradition, cited in b. The missing item may derive from a circle or academy whose materials were not included within y. See LIEBERMAN (1931); A. WEISS, as cited in FELDBLUM (1964), p. 43; ALBECK, Bereschit Rabba (Jerusalem, 1965[2]), III, Introduction; and EPSTEIN (1962). This partially explains why b. contains many traditions attributed to Palestinians which deal with M. Ṭehorot while y. lacks a *gemara* on this order. Moreover, even if the items come from the same 'circles', one cannot automatically assume that everything known was included within the compilation of y. See Section XII. 3, on Compilation of y.

4. Additional literature, besides items entered under variations in Baraitot, Section VIII, 4, includes:

Y. H. S., Talmud HaYerushalmi VeTalmud HaBavli, HeḤalutz 6 (1862), pp. 47—55.

ABRAHAM KROCHMAL, Yerushalayim HaBenuyah (Lemberg, 1867, Repr. Jerusalem, 1971), pp. 6—10.

FRANKEL (1870), pp. 40a—45a.

I. H. WEISS, Dor Dor VeDorshov III (Vienne, 1871—92, Repr. Berlin, 1924).

RATNER, HaMelitz (St. Petersburg, 1899), nos. 55, 72, 201, 208, 212, 214, 215, 219, 220, 234, 236, 238, 240—242, 244—246, 248, 251, and (1900), nos. 82, 83, 85, 118—120, 128, 198—203.

HALEVY (1901), II, 289—293, 297—298; 327—332; 384—391; 455—473; 526—536, 571—573.

Z. W. RABINOVITZ, Yerushalayim 10 (1913), 233—254; ID. (1940), p. 519.

W. BACHER, Tradition und Tradenten in den Schulen Palästinas und Babyloniens (Leipzig, 1914, Repr. Berlin, 1966), esp. pp. 506—523 — long, though incomplete, classified lists by master and tradent, including travelers, of occurrences of traditions in *gemara*.

A. S. RABINOVITZ, Yerushalayim 13 (1916), 286—292.

A. WEISS (1939), pp. 132ff.; (1943), pp. 169ff.; (1954), pp. 136ff.

GINZBERG (1941), pp. H: xlvii—lxxxiii.

Z. H. CHAJES, Students Guide Through the Talmud, trans. and ed. JACOB SCHACHTER (London, 1952, Repr., New York, 1960), pp. 233f., 258ff, 265—270, a comprehensive analytical but not critical study.

DOV NOY, HaŚipur Ha'Amami VaTalmud UvaMidrash (Jerusalem, 1960), e.g., pp. 9, 76, demonstrates how different stories may contain the same motif or similar stories may express different motifs. (Therefore, one must not level differences between diverse versions of an item without asking whether or not the motifs vary. On the other hand, an appreciation of the formal structure and traits of given items may enable one to isolate conflations, additions, or interpolations); and ID., The Jewish Versions of the 'Animal Languages' Folktale (AT 670) — A Typological-Structural Study, Scripta Hierosolymitana 22 (1971), 171—208.

B. DEVRIES, Review of ABRAHAM WEISS (1962), KS 39 (1964), 197—200, which should be read in the light of WEISS HALIVNI (1968, 1975).

STEINSALTZ, Links Between Babylonia and the Land of Israel, Talpioth 9 (1964), 294—306. Cp. M. BEER (1974) [below].

*NEUSNER, History of the Jews in Babylonia, 5 vols. (Leiden, 1966—1970), passim, esp. II, 129, 144—145; III, 218—220 — see b. Ber. 24b; and IV, 389.

FELDBLUM (1969).

*A. GOLDBERG, Review of ALBECK (1969), KS 47 (1971), 9—19.

*ISRAEL FRANCUS, The Original Readings of Three Talmudic Discussions, Tarbiẓ 38 (1969), 338—353, compares b. and y. *sugyot*; ID., Clarification and Explanation in Talmud, Sinai 36 (72) (1971), 32—45, and 37 (73) (1973), 24—49 [= *sugyot* in Ket.]; ID., The Meaning of the Verb PRṬ in Leshon Hakhamim, Sinai 38 (74) (1974), 178—182; ID., Textual Readings and Explanations of the Sugya in TB Yoma 82a [and y. Yoma 8:3, 45a], Tarbiẓ 43 (1973—74), 34—45; and ID., TSJTSA 1 (1977).

*S. KANTER, I. H. Weiss and J. S. ZURI, in: Formation, ed. NEUSNER (1970), pp. 11—19, analysis of the methods of those named.

*ZWI MOSHE DOR, The Teachings of Eretz Israel in Babylon [sic] (Tel Aviv, 1971) [= Bar Ilan Research Monographs 10], on the role of the travelers; they made deliberate changes to harmonize Palestinian *halakhah* with halakhic principles that had crystallized in Babylonian circles. The work includes an index to y. passages and references to other literature.

J. FRAENKEL, Bible Verses quoted in Tales of the Sages, Scripta Hierosolymitana 22 (1971), 100—123, while on BT, the literary analysis is also suggestive for PT.

M. D. HERR, The Historical Significance of the Dialogues between Jewish Sages and Roman Dignitaries, Scripta Hierosolymitana 22 (1971), 123—150, includes dialogues found in y.

Z. KAGAN, Divergent Tendencies and their Literary Moulding in the Aggadah, Scripta Hierosolymitana 22 (1971), 151—170, from a literary point of view suggestive as to y.

*S. SAFRAI, Tales of the Sages in the Palestinian Tradition and the Babylonian Talmud, Scripta Hierosolymitana 22 (1971), 209—232, while he claims that divergent and variant episodes contain a historical core, he squarely faces the presence of the variations.

*ROBERT GOLDENBERG, The Deposition of Rabban Gamaliel II, An Examination of the Sources, Journal of Jewish Studies 23 (1972), 167—190.

*M. BEER, Nehote, EJ 12, 942—943, and (1974), p. 43, fn. 75.

*J. FRAENKEL, Ha Gufa Qashya — Internal Contradictions in Talmudic Literature, Tarbiẓ 42 (1973), 266—301, esp. 288—291, examines how divergent formulations of mutual sources in BT and PT affected the interpretations of *gemara* and the structures of pericopae, and how b. and y. differently formulate certain types of analyses and questions.

*MELAMMED (1973), pp. 597—604, on differences between BT and PT, pp. 442—451, on the travelers. Cf. pp. 461—478.

WILLIAM S. GREEN, The Talmudic Historians: N. Krochmal, H. Graetz, I. H. Weiss, and Z. Jawitz, in: Modern Study, ed. NEUSNER (1973), pp. 107—108, and 114—118, relevant comments on the methods of certain historians.

*LEE LEVINE, Caesarea Under Roman Rule (Leiden, 1975), pp. 89—92, 96, on travelers who come to Caesarea, the city's economic attraction for Babylonians, and the transmission by Caesareans of Palestinian traditions to Babylonia.

S. FRIEDMAN, Qiddushin BeMilvah, Sinai 39 (76) (1975), 47—76, an example of the comparison of b. and y. pericopae.

JACOB N. EPHRATI, Another Meaning of NWH-N'WH, Archive 2 (1974), pp. 16—23.

*BOKSER (1975), pp. 125—128, 219—220, 224—225, 235, on the role of travelers, and ID., Two Traditions (1975).

*WEISS HALIVNI (1975), pp. 253, fn. 4**, 364, fn. 4, 416, fn. 2*.

AMINOAH NOAH, Redaction of the Tractate Qiddushin in the Babylonian Talmud (Tel Aviv, 1977), extensively compares the PT to the BT.

*HENRY A. FISCHEL, Essays in Greco-Roman and Related Talmudic-Midrashic Literature (New York, 1977), and the bibliography there, on literary forms or dimensions which may account for divergent presentation of similar items and varied treatment of the same event or personage. Thus one should not attempt to level differing accounts in order to isolate the 'historical' original.

DAVID ROSENTHAL, Pirqa De'Abbaye (TB Rosh Ha'Shana II), Tarbiẓ 46 (1977), III, 97—109, analyzes an "early [Babylonan] 'Talmud' similar to the Yerushalmi."

BARUCH M. BOKSER, Minor for a Zimun (y. Ber. 7:2, 11c) and Recensions of Yerushalmi, AJSReview 4 (1979), demonstrates how y. may revise a Babylonian tradition to fit its context.

GOODBLATT (1979), IV. 1: a, c, on Palestinian materials in BT.

XII. Compilation of Yerushalmi

1. Classical and modern writers have focused upon the formation of y., an understanding of which is necessary for any study of the work. The scholars take into account the following external (a—b) and internal (c—e) factors:

a. Gaonic and medieval authorities claim that b. knew and rejected y. and its traditions. This statement, however, testifies only to Babylonian propaganda for the supremacy and halakhic preference of BT. See GINZBERG

(1941), pp. H: lxxxiii—vi; MELAMMED (1973), pp. 556—558, and the literature cited in Section XIX. A, especially TWERSKY.

b. Certain post-Talmudic authorities, e.g., Maimonides, attributed y.'s composition to R. Yoḥanan, a second-generation Palestinian Amora. See GERSON COHEN, The Book of Tradition by Abraham ibn Daud (New York, 1967), p. 122, n. to line 18.

c. The present disordered arrangement of the text indicates the absence of any real editing. But this absolute judgment imposes standards based upon the literary character of the b. A refined statement (see paragraph 2) describes the particular nature of the disarray. PT's pericopae are generally briefer and less developed than those of BT. PT's pericopae often run into each other and lack transitional terms and are often out of place.

d. The date indicated, first, by incidents mentioned or not mentioned in y. and, secondly, by the names and number of masters correlated with their chronologies, a point which KROCHMAL (1867), pp. 14—30, had already emphasized. The references end in the fourth century.

e. Evidence of other recensions of y. These include: BT references to supposed Palestinian material not found in our y.; parallels in Gn. R. which do not totally fit the extant y. text.These variations or references may refer to different recensions of y. As to Gn. R.'s references, however, see above Section X. A. In addition, y. in one location, at times, refers to something elsewhere in y. but that reference is not found in the appropriate, supposedly original, place. The reference and the place to which referred apparently come from different recensions. The former's version of the latter location contained the 'missing' citation.

2. The ostensible glaring disarray is such that one writer, YONAH ELIJAH VIEZNER, Givat Yerushalayim, Suppl. to HaShaḥar 2 (Vienne, 1871), was led to claim that the extant y. represents the product of an eighth- or ninth-century incompetent faker, who without understanding collected and combined matter from b. and other sources. This position and the one by HALEVY (1901), II, 528f., that y. is completely unedited, are contradicted by the realization that there existed separate Palestinian traditions which do not agree with those of BT (see above, Sections I. 3. and XI), and by the presence of a certain order within *sugyot* and chapters; LIEBERMAN (1931); GINZBERG (1941); EPSTEIN (1962). Rather, the issue is, What was the nature of the composition and why does it differ from that of BT? In the previous section I partially dealt with the latter problem. I thus turn to a reconstruction of the compilation.

3. FRANKEL suggested a three-stage compilation: (a) Sages orally recited and memorized questions and answers or in lecture notes briefly hinted at them. (b) Individual masters filled out such notes or traditions and edited discrete tractates. Since various individuals independently were active, at times more than one work was produced on the same tractate. (c) In Tiberias the individual tractates were collected and the material therefrom combined. As a result, *gemara* incorporated inconsistent materials from different treatments of the same portions of 'Mishnah'.

Scholars agree that y. contains *sugyot* from different circles or academies and that the bulk of y. received final compilation in Tiberias. See e.g., Z. W. Rabinovitz, Yerushalayim 8 (1909), 331—334; Lieberman (1931), p. 9, (1934), pp. xii, 471; Epstein (1962); Feldblum (1964), p. 43; and Sussmann (1973—74), pp. 142, 143, and fn. 394. They have varied, however, as to the reconstruction of the process and the nature of y. B.Q, B.M., and B.B., together called 'Neziqin'.

Lewy (1895—1914), esp. Introduction, pp. 15, 22, n. 1, proved the distinctive nature of 'Neziqin' and suggested that it represents a separate recension. In the process, he indicated how b. and y. contain different versions of the same material.

Lieberman (1931), basing himself on choice of terminology and vocabulary, style, realia, named masters, and differences in construction and content of its pericopae in comparison to those in other tractates, proved that 'Neziqin''s distinctive character reflects a composition earlier (ca. 350) than that of other tractates (ca. 400) and one completed in Caesarea. See Herman Blumberg, Saul Lieberman on the Talmud of Caesarea, in: Formation, ed. Neusner (1970), pp. 114—124. 'Neziqin' is brief, as it represents brief and insufficiently organized and worked over notes (prepared perhaps for judges), in contrast to those of the rest of y., where they were more fully spelled out and expanded. Lieberman goes on to provide a general description of the y. editing. The editor reconstructed notes of students and academies, out of which a later editor selected materials to be in the wider work. The latter also placed pericopae in appropriate places and deleted items inconsistent with views of Palestinian academies. Scribes later further transferred pericopae or disarranged pericopae.

Epstein (1962) [posthumously published] represents Epstein as arguing that, while 'Neziqin' uses Caesarean *gemara*, it does so like *gemarot* of other tractates. It thus represents a different but not chronologically earlier recension of y. and not a Caesarean *gemara*.

Lieberman, SZ (1968), esp. pp. 130f., and Id., A Few Words by Julian the Architect of Ascalon, The Laws of Palestine and its Customs, Tarbiẓ 40 (1971), pp. 409—417, rebuts Epstein's arguments. See also Lee Levine (1975), pp. 63f., 86—106; Bokser, AJS Review 4 (1979), focuses on a recension of y. which is found in Gen. R. and which predates the one in PT; and especially Goodblatt (1979), IV. 3: a, b, for a possible analogue in redaction of 5½ BT tractates vis-à-vis the rest of BT.

4. Further points include:

The anonymous parts of 'Neziqin' come from Caesarea, while those elsewhere in y. ostensibly derive from Tiberias.

Though y. represents a compilation of expanded reconstructured notes, it still is briefer than b. As indicated in Section XI. 3, this is due to the fact that y. lacked the later Amoraic-Saboraic enrichment and literary expansion. Moreover, as Lieberman indicates, the out-of-place pericopae are those items that have parallels elsewhere in y. and which scribes inexactly transferred. Scribes also brought disorder by incorrectly adding scribal, marginal notations. Moreover, some of the lack of order is due to the later editors or scribes who had a sequence in their 'Mishnah' different from that assumed in the materials and who rearranged the latter to fit the former. Cf. ASSIS (1976), pp. 7f.

Finally, the attribution of editing to Yoḥanan is not a problem. Some writers accept and reinterpret it: The reference refers to a different Yoḥanan or to something associated with Yoḥanan, e.g., his academy: or it implies that he provided only the basic rubric for *gemara*. Alternatively, the attribution is rejected.

5. Additional bibliography:

KROCHMAL (1867), pp. 10—30.
*FRANKEL (1870).

YONAH ELIAHU VIEZNER, Givat Yerushalayim = Suppl. HaShaḥar 2 (Vienna, 1871), covers many of the main features of y. But he sees the text as it is and assumes that b. and y. are a unit, and not compilations of transmitted traditions, and that they and other sources should present a monolithic picture, without variations and differences.

I. H. WEISS, Dor Dor VeDorshov III (Vienna, 1883, Repr. Berlin, 1924), p. 105.

B. RATNER, HaMelitz (St. Petersburg, 1889), nos, 55, 72, 201, 208, 212, 214, 215, 219, 220, 234, 236, 238, 240—242, 244—246, 248, 251; and (1900), nos. 82, 83, 85, 118—120, 128, 198—203.

*BACHER, JE, 13, 5, re relationship of anonymous parts to those assigned.

*Z. W. RABINOVITZ, Yerushalayim 8 (1909), 331—352, and (1940), pp. 61f. and 311, on editing of y. and its location in Tiberias, indicated by ways in which it refers to places and realia of the city. Cf. HIRSCHORN's note, Yerushalayim 9 (1911), 186.

*LIEBERMAN (1931), pp. 5—6.
*GINZBERG (1941), p. H: lxxxiii.

STERN (1959); while he covers many of the problems, he misrepresents FRANKEL and is uncritical from a literary and historical perspective; e.g., for pp. 41—43, re b. Hag. 10a, see 'Diqduqe Śoferim to Hag.', p. 27, n. 3.

*EPSTEIN (1962), pp. 233—279.

M. A. TENENBLATT, Peraqim Ḥadoshim LeToldot Ereṣ Yisrael UBavel BiTqufat HaTalmud (Tel Aviv, 1966); an industrious work marred by an uncritical approach and unfounded assumptions.

*MELAMMED (1973), pp. 555—568.
*WEISS HALIVNI (1968, 1975).

Y. FLORSHEIM, On the Editing of the Palestinian Talmud, Sinai 40 (79) (1976), 30—43.

See also Chapters VII, IX, XVIII.

XIII. The Background to the Compilation of Yerushalmi

A. Locations of Masters

Palestinian masters resided and taught in different locations. Their major centers include: Tiberias, the main center, Sepphoris, Caesarea, and the 'South'. For the last item, only masters from Lud are specified. There, a center existed through the beginning of the Amoraic period. In addition, archaeologists have found a lintel inscription from the Golan that refers to a Bet Midrash, a place of study, בית מדרש, *BYT MDRŠ*.

The literature includes:

Frankel (1870), pp. 3b—6b.

*W. Bacher, Zur Geschichte der Schulen Palästina's im 3. und 4. Jahrhundert, MGWJ 43 (1899); Id., Die Gelehrten von Caesarea, MGWJ 45 (1901), 298—310.

S. Zuri, Toldot Darkhe HaLimmud Bishivot Darom, Galil, Sura, VeNeharde'a (Jerusalem, 1914); Id., R. Yose bar Hanina MeQiśrin [of Caesarea] (Jerusalem, 1926).

*Lieberman (1931), especially re Caesarea, p. 9; Id., SZ (1968), pp. 92—94, 122—124, and fn. 173.

Benjamin Mazar, Beth She'arim, Report on the Excavations, 1936—1940 [= I] [Hebrew edition] (Jerusalem, 1957²), pp. 15—20. [English edition, Jerusalem, 1973].

Ephraim E. Urbach, The Sages: Their Concepts and Beliefs (Jerusalem, Hebrew edition, 1969. English edition, 1975), Chapter Sixteen.

*Dan Orman, Jewish Inscriptions from Dabura in the Golan, Tarbiẓ 40 (1971), 399—408.

Nahman Avigad, Beth She'arim, Vol. 3, The Archaeological Excavations 1953—1958 (Jerusalem, 1971), pp. 1—6.

*Moshe Beer, Academies in Babylonia and Erez Israel, EJ 2, 199—205.

M. Avi-Yonah, et al., Sepphoris, EJ, 14, 1177—1178; Id., Tiberias, EJ 15, 1130—1135.

*Melammed (1973), pp. 503—507.

*Sussmann (1973—74), pp. 88f., concerning places of rabbinic instruction in the Beth Shean area.

*Levine (1975), especially pp. 61—106, note 86—97, and fns. 497—523, presents a comprehensive discussion and bibliography on rabbinic circles and institutions in Caesarea and elsewhere.

*Goodblatt (1975), while focuses on Babylonia provides methodological criteria by which to evaluate the earlier studies and critical guidelines for any inquiry. The work includes a rich bibliography.

REUVEN KIMELMAN, R. Yoḥanan of Tiberias. Aspects of the Social and Religious History of Third Century Palestine. (Unpublished Ph. D. dissertation, Yale University, New Haven, 1977).

See also the literature listed under 'General Historical Background', below, and the additional entries in EJ, s.v. name of the place.

B. Names of Masters and Bibliographical Information

*FRANKEL (1870), pp. 54b—132a.

BENJAMIN W. BACHER, Die Agada der Babylonischen Amoräer (Strassburg, 1878); ID., Die Agada der Tannaiten, 2 vols. (Strassburg, 1890), Hebrew edition, Agadot HaTannaim (Jerusalem, 1920, 1922[2]); ID., Die Agada der Palästinensischen Amoräer, 3 vols. (Strassburg, 1892—1899), Hebrew edition, Aggadot Amorae Ereṣ Yisrael, 4 vols. (Tel Aviv, 1925—28); = a series of collections of sources attributed to or about different masters subdivided according to subjects, with notes; and (1901).

*AARON HYMAN, Toldot Tannaim Veamoraim, 3 vols. (London, 1909, Repr. Jerusalem, 1964).

ZURI, R. Yose bar Hanina MeQiśrin (Jerusalem, 1926).

*UMANSKY (1952), page index to instances where a name appears in y.

*LIEBERMAN (1931), pp. 6—7, 18, masters' names and their spelling; 84—108, a list of all attributive formulae in 'Neziqin' and the location of each instance.

*EPSTEIN, Tarbiẓ 6 (1934), 39ff.; (1948, 1964[2]), the second edition includes an index, pp. 1297—1302; (1957); (1962).

RABINOVITZ (1940), especially p. 261 and index, pp. 633—636.

MORDECHAI MARGALIOTH, Encyclopedia of Talmudic and Geonic Literature (Tel Aviv, 1961).

ALBECK (1969), pp. 144—170, 451, 611—622, which must carefully be used, as it does not distinguish between types of sources.

SAMUEL LACHS, R. Abbahu and the Minim, JQR 60 (1970), 197—212.

*MELAMMED (1973), pp. 626—644.

M. BEER, The Babylonian Amoraim (Tel Aviv, 1974), pp. 362—364, on the number of masters. Cf. BARUCH BOKSER, Review, Newsletter, Association for Jewish Studies, 17 (June, 1976), pp. 19, 22.

BOKSER (1975).

*BENIAMIN KOSOVSKY, Otzar Leshon HaTalmud, Yerushalmi (Jerusalem, in press).

LEE LEVINE, R. Abbahu of Caesarea, Christianity, Judaism, and Other Greco-Roman Cults, ed. J. NEUSNER (Leiden, 1975), IV, 56—76, this and LACHS are examples of two recent biographical treatments.

See also ZURI and KIMELMAN, in Section A, and JE and EJ, s.v. name of the individual master for articles with bibliographies.

C. Reasons for the Compilation

Many writers supply the standard reason of 'necessity' to account for the writing down of y. Due to persecution and oppression, the editors of y. worked to preserve 'Torah' from being forgotten. This, as well, explains the supposed disarray of the y. text; in haste the editors did not have an opportunity to orderly arrange the materials. See FRANKEL (1870), pp. 2a—3b, and SUSSMANN (1973—74), pp. 154f. and fn. 494. Two assumptions prompt this 'reason'. The first is the need to find an adequate reason for the writing down of the 'oral' Torah — which assumably would not otherwise have been put into writing (sic!). Further, this approach assumes that Palestine lacked an unbroken tradition of teaching; it thus reflects the gaonic propaganda that Palestine suffered persecutions, a fact which accounts for its 'inferior' Talmud. See Sections VII. 2 and XIX. A. Both of these considerations, however, are not cogent. Moreover, LIEBERMAN denies that in the third and fourth centuries Palestinian Jewry suffered religious persecution and rebelled against the Roman Empire. There was only one insignificant insurrection on the part of Sepphorean Jews; otherwise there was only the general oppression of taxes, which Jews shared with other provincials; SAUL LIEBERMAN, Palestine in the Third and Fourth Centuries, JQR 36 (1946), 329—370; 37 (1946—47), 31—54, and especially 423—424; a popular version of which appears in ID., 'Jewish Life in Eretz Yisrael As Reflected in the Palestinian Talmud', Israel: Its Role in Civilization, ed. MOSHE DAVIS (New York, 1956), pp. 82—91, both reprinted in SAUL LIEBERMAN, Texts and Studies (New York, 1974), pp. 112—189; and BARON IV (Jerusalem, 1954), pp. 234—245. Cf. BARON, II, 295f. and 425, fn. 2, and S. D. GOITEIN, Mediterranean Society II (Berkeley, 1971), p. 197. See JACOB NEUSNER, History IV (1969), 27—35, and the literature cited there, especially pp. 32f.; and S. SIMONSOHN (1974), pp. 831—858, especially 842—846. At this point, we thus do not have an adequate explanation why y. was compiled when it was.

See further literature under 'General Historical Background'.

D. Economic Conditions

F. M. HEICHELHEIM, Roman Syria, in: Economic Survey of Ancient Rome, IV, ed. TENNEY FRANK (Baltimore, 1948), pp. 121—257.

A. KINDLER, ed., Proceedings, International Numismatic Convention. The Pattern of Monetary Development in Phoenicia and Palestine in Antiquity (Jerusalem, 1967), includes various papers on numismatics and economic conditions.

DANIEL SPERBER, Roman Palestine 200—400. Money and Prices (= Bar Ilan Studies in Near Eastern Language and Culture), (Ramat Gan, 1974), especially the Introduction, pp. 15ff., for a review of previous research and their methods. From a textual point of view, this is an excellent work;

see pp. 20f., re Palestinian and Babylonian reinterpretations and revisions of earlier traditions.

LEVINE (1975), especially pp. 48—56 and 68—70.

See Section XVII. B.

E. General Historical Background

I. H. WEISS, Dor Dor VeDorshov III (Vienna, 1883; Repr. Berlin, 1924).

H. GRAETZ, Geschichte der Juden, II[4] (Leipzig, 1897—1911). Hebrew edition, Divre Yime Yisra'el, with additional notes by S. P. RABINOWITZ, II (Warsaw, 1907).

*HALEVY (1901), on the basis of sources critically evaluates often superficial treatments by earlier 'more modern' historians.

A. BUECHLER, The Political and Social Leaders of the Jewish Community of Sepphorus in the Second and Third Century (Oxford, 1909); ID., Studies in Jewish History (London, 1956).

*JEAN JUSTER, Les Juifs dans l'Empire romain, 2 vols. (Paris, 1914). See now R. A. RABELLO, Israel Law Review 11 (1976), 216—287, 391—414, 563—590.

A. S. RABINOWITZ, Attitude of Palestinian Masters to Babylonians, Yerushalayim 13 (1919), 286—292.

ZE'EV JAVITZ, Śefer Toldot Yisra'el, VI—VIII (Tel Aviv, 1934—1935).

*SAMUEL KLEIN, Śefer HaYishuv I (Jerusalem, 1939), a collection of archaeological and literary references to places in Palestine. See S. LIEBERMAN, Review, Sinai, vol. 3, no. 5—6 (30—31) (1939), 462—468. Revisions and additions to entries are appearing in 'Sinai'; e.g., TUVIAH KAHANA, Meqomot Yishuv BeEreṣ Yisrael BaTalmudim UBaMidrashim, Sinai 76 (1975), 134—147.

*SAUL LIEBERMAN, The Martyrs of Caesarea, Annuaire de l'Institute de Philologie et d'Histoire Orientales et Slaves (1939—44), pp. 395—446; ID., Roman Legal Institutions in Early Rabbinics and in the Acta Martyrum, JQR 35 (1944), 1—55, reprinted in Texts and Studies (1974), pp. 57—111.

*GEDALIAH ALON, Toldot HaYehudim BeEreṣ Yisrael Bitqufat HaMishnah VeHaTalmud, 2 vols. (Tel Aviv, 1953, 1955; 1967[4], 1961[2]) [English edition under preparation]; ID., Studies in Jewish History [Hebrew], 2 vols. (Tel Aviv, 1958; I[2], 1967). — More sophisticated studies than earlier works and well indexed, though the 'Toldot', especially volume II, does not represent a finished statement but posthumously published lecture notes.

*MICHAEL AVI-YONAH, In the Days of Rome and Byzantium (Hebrew edition: Jerusalem, 1962, 1970[4]; German edition: [= Studia Judaica, II] Berlin, 1962; English revised edition: [as 'Jews of Palestine'] London 1976).

NEUSNER (1966—1970).

M. A. TENENBLATT, Peraqim Ḥadashim LeToldot Ereṣ Yisrael UBavel BiTqufat HaTalmud (Tel Aviv, 1966), an industrious but uncritical work shaped by incorrect assumptions.

W. GOTTLIEB, A Messianic Movement in the Third Century as Reflected in the Teachings of R. Johanan and his School at Tiberias, Essays Presented to Chief Rabbi Israel Brodie, ed. H. J. ZIMMELS, et al. (London, 1967), Hebrew volume, pp. 79—105.

*BENJAMIN MAZAR, M. AVI YONAH, et al., ed., Encyclopaedia of Archaeological Excavations in the Holy Land, Hebrew edition, 2 vols. (Jerusalem, 1970), English revised edition, 4 vols. (1975ff.).

MOSHE BEER, Who are the RWBYN [y. Hal. 4 : 4, 60a] ?, Sinai 35 (68) (1971), 144—152, and ID., On the Leaders of the Jews in Sepphoris in the Third Century, Sinai 38 (74) (1974), 133—138.

ISRAEL KONOVIṢ, Ma'arakhot Tannaim VeAmoraim: Amoraim (Jerusalem, 1973ff.), a thematically arranged collection of Talmudic sources on individual masters. The texts are completely unreliable.

Y. BRAND, Beit She'arim and the Nabateans, Sinai 38 (74) (1974), 139—160.

LEE LEVINE (1975); ID., Roman Caesarea (An Archaeological-Topographical Study), Qedem, Monographs of the Institute of Archaeology, 2 (Jerusalem, 1975).

E. M. SMALLWOOD, The Jews Under Roman Rule from Pompey to Diocletian (Leiden, 1976).

See also entries throughout this Chapter, in Chapter XVII, below, and in GOODBLATT (1979), V. 4: a.

Part Four
Particular Guidelines for Study

XIV. Canons to Establish a Correct Text

A. Types of Mistakes

The text of y., as indicated above in Sections III; IV, A; IX. A, B; and XII. 1, has suffered corruptions by scribes, a fact already recognized by medieval rabbinic authorities. See also GOODBLATT (1979), II. 1 and 5. This fact relates to the lack of an unbroken exegetical tradition, and as a result many portions have been incorrectly explained. FRANKEL (1870), pp. 36a—40a, 136a—138b, focused attention to many of the phenomena and noted that once we are familiar with the usual type of mistakes or what was liable to happen, we can develop procedures to correct readings and offer emendations. LIEBERMAN (1929), (1934) critically analyzed, catalogued and documented the several types, dividing them into (a) standard corruptions that affect any text and (b) those particularly characteristic to y. He did this to set standards for the corrections so that one does not rely just on logic and the context.

(a) Standard corruptions include: 1, exchange of orthographically similar letters; 2, combining two letters into one; 3, division of one letter into two; 4, combining two words into one; 5, division of one word into two; 6, metathesis; 7, homoioteleuton; 8, corruption of foreign words; 9, marginal additions entered into the incorrect place; 10, abbreviations and short forms of words erroneously expanded, especially in the editions subsequent to the Venice first edition, which often incorrectly spelled out words. See especially Louis Ginzberg, Some Abbreviations Unrecognized or Misunderstood in the Text of the Jerusalem Talmud, Jewish Theological Seminary of America, Students' Annual (New York, 1914), pp. 138—148.

The second category (b) includes: 1, clauses which have to be inverted; 2, incorrect notation of references to and lemmas of 'Mishnah', see Section VIII. C; 3, presence of 'foreign' items in the text, which do not relate to what precedes or to what follows. Lieberman subdivides this: a, mistakes in boundaries of copied and filled in pericopae; b, scribal mechanical citations; c, mistaken transfers from elsewhere which were not erased. In addition, there are remnants of deleted sections and scribal abbreviations for a deleted middle of a passage, the whole of which is paralleled elsewhere. See above, Section IX. A.

In (1934), pp. xii, xvi—xix, Lieberman adds the following items: 1, incorrect erasures, where the copy editor of a text did not understand the passage or falsely thought there was an apparent duplication; 2, printing mistakes; and 3, general revision of Palestinian orthography or spelling on the basis of that commonly used in the time of scribe; 4, combination of two readings, both of which may be correct: one popular and one literary usage.

See also Ginzberg (1941), pp. H: xvii—xxv, and Melammed (1973), pp. 582—594, for further examples, and variations. The several works by Lieberman and Epstein contain many discrete examples of scribal corruptions. See Chapter V.

B. Means to Aid in Textual Reconstruction

1. Fully use parallels in Talmudic literature. With great care one should use the parallel *sugyot*, for as Lieberman warns, the two versions may make up contradictory *sugyot*, deriving from different circles. See, e. g., Lieberman (1931), pp. 2—7. A definitive cross index is still lacking. See above, Sections VIII. D; IX. A; X. A; XI.

2. Readings from MSS. The Geniza fragments are important for they are 'purer' and went through fewer scribal hands. One must rely on the MSS, especially the Leiden MS. See above for a description of these MSS and the guidelines for their use, Chapter IV,

3. Witnesses in medieval authorities and works. With the lack of early commentaries and early witnesses directly to the text, one must fully employ the citations in early authorities, whether in their commentaries on

BT or other works, and the analogous pericopae in midrashic works and other collections. RATNER, 11 vols. (Vilna, 1901—1917), had comprehensively initiated this approach, though his work is incomplete and not totally reliable; see Section XIX. C. Accordingly it is still necessary to collate the readings. To do so, one must know how the medieval authorities had access to y., what type of texts they had, and their methods of citation. See Chapter XIX.

The medieval works contain three types of materials: readings, explanations usually based upon some tradition the authority had received or heard, and filled in lacunae of the text. LIEBERMAN (1929), p. 39, reviews previous attempted collations and the necessary standards required. See GINZBERG (1941), pp. H: xxvi—xxxii, and Section XIX. C.

LIEBERMAN himself provides examples of how one may systematically employ these methods: (1934), and (1947), in which he reconstructs the third chapter of Mak., which found confirmation in a subsequently published Geniza fragment. See also GINZBERG (1941), pp. H: xxv—xxxii, and Sections V, and XX. C.

4. Language of y. Moreover, one must realize the distinctive style and terminology of y. and its usage of Hebrew. See Chapters XV and XVI.

See above, Section IX. B, for suggestions by which to uncover the presence of material out of place in a *sugya* and steps by which to evaluate an unsmooth text.

XV. Language

FRANKEL (1870), chapter Two, esp. 8b—11a, had recognized and described various linguistic peculiarities of the Hebrew and Aramaic in y. These include the fact that the Hebrew and Aramaic differ from those of BT; interchange of certain letters; deletion of certain initial letters; and aspects of orthography. The scientific study of these matters, though, was done in the twentieth century by H. YALON, S. MORAG, J. N. EPSTEIN, E. KUTSCHER, and S. LIEBERMAN who, in particular, tied the textual study of y. with that of its language.

As KUTSCHER, in Archive of the New Hebrew Dictionary of Rabbinical Literature 1 and 2 (Ramat Gan, 1972, 1974), and KUTSCHER and RABIN, in Current Trends in Linguistics 6 (1970), review the history of the research, the characteristics, both strengths and weaknesses, of earlier studies, works, and tools, the major problems, and the ways in which to make use of dialects and languages related to Hebrew and Aramaic, I shall basically confine my remarks to the Hebrew and Aramaic in y. and shall cite the main works. For the dictionaries and grammars of and research relevant in Christian Palestinian Aramaic, Samaritan Aramaic, Syriac, Mandaic, Akkadian, Iranian languages and such, see KUTSCHER and RABIN, and LIEBERMAN (1934), pp. xiii, xviii—xix. For all matters, see the excellent bibliography of DAVID GOODBLATT, The Languages of Rabbinic Literature, in: Understanding Rabbinic Judaism, ed. JACOB NEUSNER (New York, 1974), pp. 396—402, and the somewhat different J. H. HOSPERS, A Basic Bibliography for the Study of the Semitic Languages, I (Leiden, 1973). See also GOODBLATT (1979), III, for literature and an excellent analysis of the state of scholarship.

A. The Nature of PT's Hebrew and Aramaic

1. Hebrew. The Hebrew used and found in y. is part of Middle (or Mishnaic) Hebrew, which exhibits significant differences from that of Biblical Hebrew and later or Medieval and Modern Hebrew. It was a spoken language in the time of the first century. In post-Talmudic times, however, scribes tended, in general, to biblicize the usages found in Talmudic documents and, for those works from Palestine, tended to Babylonianize the forms. The careful study of MSS that preserve the early readings, comparative Semitics, and the like, has enabled scholars in this century to set out the developments and stages of Hebrew. Further research has demonstrated that the Hebrew in y. is to be separately classified from that of 'Mishnah' and 'Tosefta' and thus designated as MH^2.

M. H. SEGAL, Mishnaic Hebrew and Its Relation to Biblical Hebrew and to Aramaic, JQR, O.S. 20 (1907—08), 647—737.

E. BEN YEHUDAH, Thesaurus Totius Hebraitatis, Prolegomena (Jerusalem, 1940, Repr. London and New York, 1960), pp. 83—254.

*E. KUTSCHER, Leshon Ḥazal, Henoch Yalon Jubilee Volume (Jerusalem, 1963), pp. 246—280; ID., The Present State of Research into Mishnaic Hebrew. Some Problems of the Lexicography of Mishnaic Hebrew and Its Comparison with Biblical Hebrew, Archive 1 (1972), pp. 3—82, English summary, iii—xxvii, a revision and expansion of ID., Mittelhebräisch und Jüdisch-Aramäisch im Neuen Köhler—Baumgartner, Festschrift W. Baumgartner (= Suppl. to Vetus Testamentum, 16) (Leiden, 1967), pp. 168—175; ID., Hebrew, Language Mishnaic, EJ 16, 1590—1607, 1659.

H. L. GINSBERG, New Light on Tannaitic Jewry, The Jewish Expression, ed. J. GOLDIN (New York, 1970, and New Haven, 1976), pp. 109—118.

*CHAIM RABIN, Hebrew, Current Trends in Linguistics 6 (1970), pp. 304—346.

*MOSHEH BAR-ASHER, ed., Qoveṣ Maamarim BeLashon Ḥazal (Hebrew University: Jerusalem, 1972), a collection of all the important articles through 1972, many with corrections, and an index; includes KUTSCHER (1963) and MICHAEL SOKOLOFF, HaIvrit Shel Bereshet Rabbah Vat. MS. 30, pp. 257—301, republished from Leshonenu 33 (1965), 25—42, 135—142, 270—279, which isolated the second strata of Middle Hebrew.

M. MORESHET, New and Revived Verbs in the Bārāytot of the Babylonian Talmud, Archive 1 (1972), pp. 117—162, English summary, xxxvi—

xxxix; Id., The Language of the Bārāytot in the Babylonian Talmud is not MH[1], Henoch Yalon Memorial Volume, ed. E. Y. Kutscher et al. (Ramat Gan, 1974), pp. xxi—xxii, 275—314, and Archive 2 (1974).

2. a. Aramaic. Galilean Aramaic, as well, has been studied on the basis of uncontaminated texts. Its place within Western Aramaic is clear, though scholars do not all agree as to the sequence and nature of the several dialects.

The following literature includes rich bibliographies:

*Kutscher, Studies in Galilean Aramaic, Tarbiẓ 21 (1950), 192—205; 22 (1951), 53—63, 185—192 (English translation with additional notes and bibliography, Bar Ilan Studies in Near Eastern Languages and Culture, 1976), the pioneering study; Id., Aramaic, Current Trends in Linguistics 6 (1970), pp. 347—412, an excellent bibliographical survey of the field and its problems; Id., Aramaic, EJ, 3, pp. 259—287, an excellent exposition and summary, with rich bibliography; Id., Some Problems in the Lexicography of the Jewish Aramaic Dialects, Archive 2 (1974), Hebrew translation of part two of Id., Mittelhebräisch und Jüdisch-Aramäisch im Neuen Köhler-Baumgartner, Festschrift W. Baumgartner (Leiden, 1967), pp. 168—175.

Paul Kahle, Cairo Geniza (Oxford, 1959), pp. 200—208, especially 203—205.

*Jonas Greenfield, Standard Literary Aramaic, Actes du Premier Congres International De Linguistique Sémitique et Chamito-Sémitique, Paris 16—19, juillet, 1969, réums par André Caquot et David Cohen (Paris, 1974), pp. 280—289.

Barry Levy, A Grammar of the Neofiti Targum (Leiden, in press), Introduction.

b) Use of Targum: The Targumim may provide help as to the definition of a word or usage. See Chaim Joshua Kasowski, Theasurus Aquilae [= Onqelos] Versionis (Jerusalem, 1940).

For the relevant literature, see Kutscher, Archive 1 and 2 (1972, 1974); Bernard Grossfeld, A Bibliography of Targum Literature, I—II (Cincinnati, 1972, 1977), and the Review of Joseph A. Fitzmyer, JBL 93 (1974), 135—136; Goodblatt (1974) and Hospers (1973); and the recent studies by Abraham Tal (Rosenthal), Ms. Neophyti 1: The Palestinian Targum to the Pentatuech, Israel Oriental Studies 4 (1974), 31ff., on the Aramaic, and Id., The Language of the Targum of the Former Prophets and Its Position within the Aramaic Dialects (Texts and Studies in Hebrew Language and Related Subjects, ed. Aron Dotan, Vol. 1) (Tel Aviv, 1975), which concludes that the language under study is close to that of PT.

Moreover, y. at times cites a Targumic rendering of a verse. See M. Kasher, Torah Shelemah XXIV (Jerusalem, 1974), pp. 143—154, for a collection and analysis of the instances. (The volume is devoted to a study of the several Targumim and their characteristics.)

B. The Greek and Latin Element

FRANKEL (1870) and others had noticed the large amount of Greek in y. LIEBERMAN's works show how scribes who did not understand the words often corrupted them, a fact that further makes vital the use of MSS.

According to LIEBERMAN, Hellenism in Jewish Palestine (New York, 1950), p. 3:

"Almost every foreign word and phrase have their «*raison d'etre*» in rabbinic literature... all Greek phrases in rabbinic literature are quotations. If a common Greek word is employed by the rabbis only very rarely, whereas they generally use its Aramaic equivalent, some reason must lie behind the rabbinic choice of a Greek term in a particular case."

'Neziqin', in particular, is rich in Greek usage and often uses words in a sense different from that of the rest of rabbinic literature; LIEBERMAN (1931), pp. 13—16, SZ (1968), p. 132, fn. 27.

As to Latin, Palestinian rabbis did not know Latin except for military and judicial terms and names of objects imported from Latin speaking countries, words that usually also were in Syriac and later Greek; LIEBERMAN (1950), p. 17.

S. KRAUSS, Griechische und lateinische Lehnwörter in Talmud, Midrasch und Targum, 2 vols. (Berlin, 1898—99), indicates, whatever the merits of each entry, the large number of Greek and Latin words. See LIEBERMAN (1941), p. 9, and (1950), p. 3; KUTSCHER, Archive 1,2 (1972, 1974), H. ROSEN, Palestinian Koine in Rabbinic Illustration, JSS 8 (1963), 55—72; and D. SPERBER, cited below. The work is highly useful for references to all instances of each entry known to the author and his collaborators.

SAUL LIEBERMAN, virtually all of his works, especially: Greek in Jewish Palestine (New York, 1941, 1965²); ID. Hellenism in Jewish Palestine (New York, 1950) — see the reviews of (1941), listed on p. 210, reprinted in (1965²), pp. 194f. [especially that of G. ALON, reprinted in his 'Studies in Jewish History', II (Tel Aviv, 1958), pp. 248—277]; TK Iff. (New York, 1955ff.), which includes indexes to foreign words; his collected articles, in 'Texts and Studies' (1974), especially his comments, pp. 1f. (= Esser Millin, in: Eshkoloth (Jerusalem, 1959)] and 59f. [= Roman Legal Institutions, JQR, N.S. 35 (1944), 1—2], that we must make use of Greek sources from Palestine, the coastal area, and Egypt, in particular the works written in popular Greek; and his carefully argued 'How Much Greek in Jewish Palestine', pp. 216—234 [= in: Biblical and Other Studies, ed. A. ALTMANN (Cambridge, 1962), pp. 123—141], wherein he evaluates previous research.

BARON II, 299—300.

J. N. SEVENSTER, Do You Know Greek? (Leiden, 1968), with long bibliography, surveys the sources by which to evaluate the knowledge and use of Greek in various social strata. See the reviews of B. LIFSHITZ. KS 44

(1969), 379—385, whose comments are important, in general; and of D. SPERBER, Leshonenu 34 (1970), 225—227 — while SEVENSTER focuses on the first century, his remarks are (also) relevant to a later period, for many of his literary sources come from a later period, and statements therein even if attributed to an individual from an earlier period may actually reflect the language of the time in which the work was edited or composed.

B. GROSS, To the Etymology of ŠBWRYN (collection of water), Leshonenu 32 (1968), 279—297.

S. SIMONSOHN (1974), pp. 832—834.

D. SPERBER, Greek and Latin Words in Rabbinic Literature, BIA 14—15 (1977), 9—60.

The especially useful Greek dictionaries include:

Hesychius Alexandrinus. Lexicon post IOANNEM ALBERTUM rec. M. SCHMIDT, ed., 5 vols. (Jena, 1858—68, 1966); rec. et emend. K. LATTE, 3 vols. (Kopenhagen, 1953—1966). See LIEBERMAN, SZ (1968), p, 66, fn. 242, and the references cited there.

E. A. SOPHOCLES, Greek Lexicon of the Roman and Byzantine Periods (Cambridge, 1914).

JAMES HOPE MOULTON and GEORGE MILLIGAN, The Vocabulary of the Greek Testament (London, 1930; Grand Rapids, 1974).

WALTER BAUER, WILLIAM F. ARNDT, and F. WILBER GINGRICH, A Greek English Lexicon of the New Testament and Other Early Christian Literature (Chicago and Cambridge, 1957).

C. Comprehensive Dictionaries

KUTSCHER, Archive 1 (1972), pp. 3ff., reviews the dictionaries and related specialized works, cites important reviews, and notes the weaknesses and strengths and thus provides guidelines by which to use the works. As indicated above, I include only the highly important items and secondary literature. For the rest, see KUTSCHER and RABIN (1970).

JACOB LEVY, Wörterbuch über die Talmudim und Midraschim, 4 vols. (Leipzig, 1876—1889, Berlin and Vienna, 1924², Repr. Darmstadt, 1963). The second edition contains additions by HEINRICH L. FLEISCHER and LAZARUS GOLDSCHMIDT.

ALEXANDER KOHUT, et al., The Aruch Completum of Nathan b. Yeḥiel, ca. 1030—1106, Italy, an expanded critical version in 8 vols. (Vilna, 1878—1892, 1926², Repr. New York, 1957, Jerusalem, 1971). The original work is important for its citations of y., under alphabetical entries. Vol. VIII includes indexes, to y., pp. 100—104. A very important supplement-volume, with notes on Iranian words, by B. GEIGER, appeared, Additamenta ad Librum Aruch Completum, ed. SAMUEL KRAUSS, et al. (= Vol. IX), (Vienna, 1937, Repr. New York, 1957, Jerusalem, 1971). See KRAUSS' introduction and the bibliographical references, iv, n. 1, and LIEBERMAN'S Review, KS 14 (1937), 218—228. In general, see BARON VII, 29—32, and

231—232, and especially S. ABRAMSON, On the Aruḳ of R. Nathan, Leshonenu 36 (1972), 122—149; 37 (1973), 26—42, 253—269; 38 (1973—74), 91—117, which analyzes the nature of the work, including the Talmudic texts that it used; e. g., Aruch on the basis of the explanatory sources that it employed may contain different readings of *gemara*. Note, pp. 114—117, an index to entries discussed; and ABRAMSON's additional notes, in his collected articles, Inyanot BeŚifrut HaGaonim (Jerusalem, 1974), pp. 420—421.

I. LOEW, Die Flora der Juden, 4 vols. (Vienna, 1924—34); ID., Fauna und Mineralien der Juden (Hildesheim, 1969), excellent works.

MARCUS JASTROW, A Dictionary of the Targumim, the Talmud Babli and Yerushalmi, and the Midrashic Literature, 2 vols. (New York, 1903, in 1 vol., New York, Berlin, 1926, various subsequent reprints), weak on derivations.

BENJAMIN MAZAR, MOSHE SCHWAB, B. LIFSHITZ, and NAHMAN AVIGAD, Beth She'arim, 3 vols. (Jerusalem, 1957—71), with indexes, is an important source for Hebrew, Aramaic, and Greek inscriptions.

WALTER BAUMGARTNER, B. HARTMANN, and E. Y. KUTSCHER, Hebräisches und Aramäisches Lexicon zum Alten Testament I (Leiden, 1967), KUTSCHER's additions are important.

For collections of inscriptions, see Section XVII. C.

D. Concordances

BENIAMIN KOSOVSKY, Thesaurus to Talmud Yerushalmi, though already finished, has not yet appeared. For earlier attempts, see PAUL KAHLE, Cairo Geniza (Oxford, 1959²), pp. 203—204. Meanwhile the several other concordances to Palestinian texts are highly useful:

CHAIM JOSHUA KOSOWSKI, Thesaurus Thosephthae, 6 vols. (Jerusalem, 1932—1961).

CHAYIM YEHOSHUA KOSOVSKY, Thesaurus Mishnae, corrected edition, 4 vols. (Jerusalem, 1956—60).

BENIAMIN KOSOVSKY, Otzar Leshon HaTanna'im: Concordantiae Verborum Mechilta D' Rabbi Ismael, 4 vols. (Jerusalem, 1965—66); ID., Thesauris Sifra, 4 vols. (Jerusalem, 1967—69); ID., Thesaurus Sifrei, 5 vols. (Jerusalem, 1971—74).

E. Grammars

There are no completely satisfactory grammars. See KUTSCHER, Archive 1 and 2 (1972, 1974).

GUSTAF DALMAN, Grammatik des Jüdisch-Palästinischen Aramäisch (Leipzig, 1905, Repr. Darmstadt, 1960), KUTSCHER: "outdated".

J. T. MARSCHALL, ed. J. BARTON TURNER, Manual of the Aramaic Language of the Palestinian Talmud (Leiden, 1929).

H. Odeberg, The Aramaic Portions of Bereshit Rabba. II Short Grammar of Galilean Aramaic (Lund, 1939), Kutscher: "good for syntax".

W. B. Stevenson, Grammar of Palestinian Jewish Aramaic, 2nd ed. by J. A. Emerton (Oxford, 1962²), Kutscher, "of little significance".

*E. Y. Kutscher, 'Aramaic', and 'Hebrew Language, Mishnaic', EJ 3, 270—274, and 16, 1590—1607, include descriptions of the languages.

F. Additional Bibliography

Moses Schlesinger, Das Aramäische Verbum im Jerusalemischen Talmud, Magazin für die Wissenschaft des Judentums 16 (1899), 1—9.

*Saul Lieberman, virtually all of his works, especially (1929), (1931), 1ff.; (1934); TR (1937—1939); and TK (1955ff.), which includes long indexes to linguistic and lexicographical comments, though not to all of them. N. B. Introductions, vols. I, III, VI, VIII; and Texts and Studies (1974). See M. Z. Kaddari, Grammatical Notes on Saul Lieberman's Tosefta Kifshutah (Zera'im), Archive 1 (1972), pp. 163—173, xl; and Baruch Bokser, Review, Newsletter, Association for Jewish Studies, 12 (November, 1974), pp. 18—19. Lieberman notes that variations in language in different *sugyot* may reflect their different location and time of origin; (1931), pp. 1—2, 16; (1934), pp. xi—xiii.

Jacob N. Epstein, virtually all of his works, especially (1948, 1964²), pp. 1007—1269. See the bibliography to his works, S. Abramson, Tarbiẓ 20 (1950), pp. 7—16. See Shimon Sharvit, Studies in the Lexicography and Grammar of Mishnaic Hebrew. Based on the 'Introductions of J. N. Epstein', Archives 2 (1974), pp. 112—124, xv—xvi.

Henoch Yalon, virtually all of his works. See the bibliographies, S. Esh, Henoch Yalon, Bibliography, 1922—1963, Henoch Yalon Jubilee Volume (Jerusalem, 1963), pp. 37—50, to be supplemented by Raphael Weiss, Bibliography, 1963—1970, Henoch Yalon Memorial Volume, ed. E. Y. Kutscher, et al. (Ramat Gan, 1974), pp. 1—7. The following three works include much of his important research: Id., Bulletin of Hebrew Language Studies, Wahrman Books, 1963² (corrected reissue, bound together of Jerusalem, 1937—1943); Id., Mavo Leniqud Hamishnah [Introduction to the Vocalization of the Mishna] (Jerusalem, 1964); and especially Id., Studies in the Hebrew Language (Jerusalem, 1971), collected, corrected articles with detailed indexes to words, grammar, and subject.

Rabinovitz (1940), p. 308.

Simḥa Assaf, Tequfat HaGeonim VeŚifrutah (Jerusalem, 1955), p. 172, on the languages of Palestine after the completion of y.

Abba Bendavid, Biblical Hebrew and Mishnaic Hebrew Compared, I—II (Tel Aviv, 1967, 1971), points to many changes in usage, grammar, and style. While his individual examples are not always correct, and he insufficiently systematically employed MSS and weighed alternative explanations, he points to many important phenomena and includes useful indexes. See Review, JOSHUA BLAU, KS 44 (1969), 29—35; 46 (1971), 424—428.

M. SOKOLOFF, Introduction, to Midrash Bereshit Rabba MS. Vat. Ebr. 30 (Makor: Jerusalem, 1971).

JAMES BARR, Linguistic Literature, Hebrew, EJ 16, 1352—1401.

RABINOWITZ, Tarbiẓ 41 (1972), 276, re Yerushalmi spelling.

Archive 1, 2 (1972, 1974), the remaining articles not previously cited.

MELAMMED (1973), pp. 605—620.

SUSSMANN (1973—74), pp. 138f., 139, 146—152, discusses an inscription of a Talmudic text, some of which is based on y. and which linguistically cannot have been revised, and surveys its spelling, forms, and vocabulary.

S. FRIEDMAN, Three Studies in Babylonian Aramaic Grammar, Tarbiẓ 43 (1973—74), 58—69, while on BT undoubtedly also applies to PT: variations in linguistic and grammatical forms may be due to differences in the literary genre of materials.

SHLOMO SIMONSOHN (1974), an excellent critical survey, with bibliography, of the languages of Palestine.

N. B. Indexes to Leshonenu 1—25, 1929—1961 (1967), and Israel Exploration Journal 1—10, 1950—1960, in 11 (1961), 261—264, and 11—20, 1961—1970, in 26 (1976), 271—288, include indexes to words.

XVI. Terms and Fixed Usages

Y. employs a distinctive style, including patterned phrasings and specific terminologies, usages, and words. Aspects of the style and some of the usages are unique to y. while others are found in Palestinian literature in general, and still others have parallels or analogues in Babylonian sources. SIRILLO, in his 'Introduction', Part Two, published in his 'Commentary to Berakhot', ed. DINGLAS (Jerusalem, 1967), pp. 7—8, already focused on such terms as well as the names of masters in y.

The 'unsmooth' nature of the y. often entails the lack of a term. For example, y. may not contain a term joining sentences or indicating the relationship between two items. See above, Section IX. A. But on the other hand, the presence of a fixed usage may provide a guide to the structure of an ostensibly confused pericope or whole *sugya*.

Various studies have examined the usages of many phrases and terms but a full and exhaustive study of all the relevant items is lacking. Hopefully, the forthcoming concordance to PT will facilitate such a study.

Primary tools to elucidate the fixed language and usage include familiarity with: (a) Palestinian Aramaic and Hebrew, for which see above, Section XV. A; (b) orthographic practices whereby a letter, e. g., *aleph*, א, ', is deleted, or two words are combined, or one is separated into two component parts; and (c) the recurrent patterns in which the words appear.

Methodological guidelines include:

One must not superimpose the Babylonian conception of a term onto its y. parallel or analogue. See e. g., EPSTEIN (1948), pp. 245, 262, and BOKSER (1975), p. 130, fn. 380.

Within y. one must not superimpose one specific usage onto each instance. The terminology may vary in different locations, as pericopae may derive from different circles or places. This is especially so as to 'Neziqin': LIEBERMAN (1931), pp. vii—viii, pp. 1, 6, 7—9, 16, 17. Moreover, the referent or connotation of an item in one place may differ from that elsewhere. Thus, אית אמרין, *'YT 'MRYN*, in 'Neziqin', refers to a Tiberian teaching; LIEBERMAN (1931), p. 17.

A term may often make up the second half of a balanced phrasing. I. e., the word or term is in balance to one in a preceding passage or clause: LIEBERMAN (1934), pp. 17, 254, 453; NEUSNER, Pharisees (1971), and Purities (1974—1977).

A pericope's editor may revise a term in a comment or tradition so as to fit it into its present context. For example, he may replace 'here' in a comment where it originally referred to the location of the spokesperson and where that place differs from that of the place of the editing of the pericope; LIEBERMAN, SZ (1968), p. 131, fn. 22.

Where a term introduces a citation and thereby ostensibly bridges it with a preceding Amoraic statement with which it is compared, the term and citation may be later and or unconnected to the Amoraic tradition; WEISS HALIVNI (1975), p. 540f., fn. 7 and the references there, and BOKSER (1975), p. 95, fn. 263; and 101—102, fn. 280. See above, Section VIII. D, for further related items.

FRANKEL (1870), pp. 13a—17a and chapter Two, focuses on and classifies different usages, in particular patterned phrasing to introduce citations or structured phrases and clauses, and terms. While very useful, the lists are inexhaustive and at times inexact; LIEBERMAN (1929), pp. 47—49. Of note, many of FRANKEL's entries, in abbreviated and at times inexact form, were reprinted in y. Vilna ed., volume one, 'Zera'im'; LIEBERMAN (1929), p. 45.

WILHELM BACHER, Die Exegetische Terminologie der jüdischen Traditionsliteratur, 2 vols. (Leipzig, 1899, Repr. in one vol., Darmstadt, 1965), in Hebrew translation, by A. S. RABINOVITZ, Erchē Midrash, 2 vols. [I = Tannaim; II = Amoraim] (Tel Aviv, 1933, Repr. Jerusalem: Carmiel, 1970²), is very important, especially as it differentiates between Palestinian and Babylonian usages; ID., Die Ausdrücke mit denen die Tradition bezeichnet wird, JQR, O. S. 20 (1907—08), 572—596; ID., Tradition und Tradenten in den Schulen Palästinas und Babyloniens (Leipzig, 1914, Repr. Berlin, 1966), while quite useful is marred. See JACOB LAUTERBACH, Bacher's Tradition and Traditionists in the Schools of Palestine and Babylonia, JQR, N. S. 8 (1917), 105—112; the work does not note the significance and usage of each item; the entries are not aptly selected (inexhaustive, lacking significant entries and important instances of included items). LAUTERBACH's article contains important notes on usages.

LIEBERMAN (1929), (1931), (1934), and various articles. Moreover, TK (1955ff.), is replete with notes on y. style and terminology, many of which are indexed, in vols. II, V, VIII, under subject or words. As (1934) lacks an index, I include the following selected items (partial list):

לית כאן . . . אית כאן. *LYT K'N . . . 'YT K'N*, p. 65.

מן, מאן. *MN, M'N* (*mān*) = מה, *mah*, pp. 76, 288.

סלקת מתניתא. *ŚLQT MTNYT'*, p. 80. Cf. HY (1948), p. 68 = 'Mishnah', the matter, is finished; henceforth a new topic.

כך אנו אומרים?, *KK 'NW 'WMRYM*, pp. 178—179.

ר' — — הורי כההן תנייא., *R — — HWRY KHHN TNYY'*, p. 228.

ר' מסתכל ביה., *R MŚTKL BYH*, = in anger, p. 289, and fn. 2.

ומה ופליג., *WHM WPLYG*, p. 316 = A question reacting against 'Mishnah', *baraita*, or an Amora.

חוץ מדעתי., *ḤWṢ MD'TY* = שלא מדעת, *ŠL' MD'T*, p. 497.

See also (1950), pp. 290—292, on כן אנו אמרין (כן אני אומר) *KN 'NW 'MRYN* (*KN 'NY 'WMR*), which is a question.

EPSTEIN, many of his articles. See bibliography, Tarbiẓ 20 (1950). Note, esp. ID., The One Who Taught This Did Not Teach This, Tarbiẓ 7 (1936), pp. 143ff.; (1948, 1964[2]), the second edition includes a highly useful index; (1954), (1962).

RABINOVITZ (1940). See index, p. 637.

WEISS HALIVNI (1968, 1975), see index. E. g., I: 299, fn. 1, and 360, fn. 11.

'Mafteḥot' [Indexes] to Leshonenu, Vols. 1—25, 1924—1961 (Jerusalem, 1967).

*MELAMMED (1973), pp. 605—625, esp. 620—625, a long annotated list of usages.

MARGALIOTH (1973), contains a list of Palestinian forms and terms in the Post-Talmudic documents therein published, pp. 23—25, 57—60, 98, 100.

BOKSER (1975), pp. 101—102, fn. 280; 102—105, esp. fn. 289; 133—135, and fns. 380, 393; 135, fn. 400; 144—145; 187—215.

GOODBLATT (1975), an exemplary critical study, demonstrates the necessity and method to distinguish between y. and b. usages. While primarily on BT, it focuses on y. usages of educational institutions and how b. uses fixed language for Palestinian items, e. g., p. 136.

XVII. Aids to the Study of the Yerushalmi

This chapter deals with several subjects and bodies of materials which may greatly illuminate y. They include: geography, archaeology and realia;

inscriptions; history of agriculture; legal studies; and liturgical works. The degree of completeness for each unit varies. The purpose is to bring to the reader's attention the particular area and indicate its importance and relevance to the study of y. Additional items may be found in STRACK (1931), pp. 183—198; MIELZINER (1968), pp. 403—410, 415; EJ, index; and GOODBLATT (1979), V, and Chapter XIII, above.

A. Geography

ADOLPH NEUBAUER, La Géographie du Talmud (Paris, 1968), see the criticisms by ROMANOFF (1935—36), p. 150 (= 4), cited below.

YEḤIEL ṢEVI HIRSCHENSON, Sheva Ḥakhmot (Lemberg, 1883), a helpful dictionary-encyclopedia to places and persons, with notes as to textual variants.

HIRSH HILDESHEIMER, Beiträge zur Geographie Palästinas (Berlin, 1886), Hebrew translation in: Studies in the Geography of Eretz Israel (Jerusalem, 1965).

*Estori ha Parḥi, Kaftor UPeraḥ, ed. A. M. LUNCZ (Jerusalem, 1897³, Repr. Israel, n. d. [1976?]), critical edition of a thirteenth-century work on geographic and agricultural laws and realia of Palestine. A less adequate edition is Caftor wa-pherach (Berlin, 1852, Repr. Jerusalem, 1959).

SOLOMON J. L. RAPPAPORT, Erek Millin, 2 vols. (Warsaw, 1914—, Repr. Jerusalem, 1970).

ISRAEL S. HOROWITZ, Palestine and the Adjacent Countries (Vienna, 1923, Repr. Jerusalem, 1970,) covers geographical names.

SAMUEL KLEIN, Das Tannaitische Grenzverzeichnis Palaestinas, HUCA 5 (1928), 197—259, Hebrew translation in Studies in the Geography of Eretz Israel (Jerusalem, 1955); ID., Ereṣ Yehudah (Tel Aviv, 1939), includes an index of places and subjects; ID., Ereṣ HaGalil (Jerusalem, 1946). KLEIN's works cite and discuss the texts that mention and describe geographical places.

*PAUL ROMANOFF, Onomasticon of Palestine, PAAJR 7 (1936), 147—227, reprinted with preface, errata, and index (New York, 1937); an exemplary study with attempted complete collection of sources and use of MSS and early editions of texts, including Geniza fragments to y. Note his review of earlier works, pp. 149—150.

*MICHAEL AVI-YONAH, Historical Geography of Ereṣ Yisrael [Hebrew] (Jerusalem, 1951²); ID., The Holy Land. From the Persian to the Arab Conquest. A Historical Geography (Grand Rapids, 1966).

MOSHE KOCHAVI, ed., Judah, Samaria, and the Golan. Archaeological Survey (Archaeological Survey of Israel, ed. A. BIRAN, et al. I), (Jerusalem, 1972).

SUSSMANN (1973—74), and Tarbiẓ 45 (1976), 213—252.

B. Archaeological Materials and Realia

*Samuel Krauss, Talmudische Archäologie, 3 vols. (Leipzig, 1910—12), with indexes, and Hebrew edition, Qadmoniyot HaTalmud, I, i—ii, II, i—ii (Berlin-Wien, n. d. and 1923, Tel Aviv, 1929, 1945). While Krauss' method of analysis may need improvement, the work contains a very useful collection of rabbinic and extra-rabbinic sources and discussion; Id., Paraś VeRomi BaTalmud UVamidrashim (Jerusalem, 1948).

Gustaf Hermann Dalman, Arbeit und Sitte in Palästina, 7 vols. in 8 (Gütersloh, 1928—1942, Repr. Hildesheim, 1964).

S. Yeivin, ed., Trade, Industry, and Crafts in Ancient Palestine (= Library of Palestinology of the Jewish Palestine Exploration Society IX/X), (Jerusalem, 1937).

Baron II, 299—307.

*Yehoshua Brand, Ceramics in Talmudic Literature (Jerusalem, 1953), an excellent study and discussion of rabbinic, archaeological, and classical sources; Id., LeOr Nerot Ḥereś 'Atiqin, Sinai 73 (1973), 163—167.

Erwin R. Goodenough, Jewish Symbols in Greco-Roman Period, 13 vols. (Princeton, 1953—1965). Note the list of reviews, 13, 229—230.

Mazar, et al., Beth She'arim, 3 vols. (Jerusalem, 1956—71), contains numerous items of Palestinian realia.

R. J. Forbes, Studies in Ancient Technology, 9 vols. (Leiden, 1964—1972).

Yigael Yadin, ed., Judean Desert Studies: The Finds from the Bar Kokhba Period in the "Cave of Letters" (Jerusalem, Hebrew edition: 1963, English edition: 1963). The finds also throw light on third through sixth-century matters.

*Mazar, ed., Encyclopaedia of Archaeological Excavations in the Holy Land (Jerusalem, Hebrew 2 vol. edition, 1970, 4 vol. English edition: 1974ff.), includes individual entries with pictures of the sites.

*Eleanor K. Vogel, Bibliography of Holy Land Sites, HUCA 42 (1971), 1—96.

*Eric M. Meyers, Jewish Ossuaries: Reburial and Rebirth, Biblica et Orientalia, No. 24 (Rome,19 71). Id., The Use of Archaeology in Understanding Rabbinic Materials, in: Texts and Responses. Studies Presented to Nahum N. Glatzer, ed. Michael A. Fishbane and Paul R. Flohr (Leiden, 1975), pp. 28—41. These excellent studies demonstrate how archaeology can help in the interpretation of Palestinian rabbinic sources.

Moshe Kochavi, ed., Judah, Samaria, and the Golan, Archaeological Survey (= Archaeological Survey of Israel, ed. A. Biran, et al., I), (Jerusalem, 1972).

Shmuel Safrai, The Synagogues South of Mt. Judah, Immanuel 3 (1973—74), 44—50.

Arye Ben-David, Talmudische Ökonomie. Die Wirtschaft des jüdischen Palästina zur Zeit der Mischna und des Talmud 1 (Hildesheim und New York, 1974).

C. Inscriptions

Inscriptions in Hebrew, Aramaic, and Greek may shed light on geographical, economic, cultural, political, and textual matters. In general see the excellent bibliographies in EMIL SCHÜRER, The History of the Jewish People in the Age of Jesus Christ. New English Version I, by GEZA VERMES and FERGUS MILLAR (Edinburgh, 1973), pp. 11—16, and, in particular, in CASSUTO—SALZMANN, Hebrew Inscriptions of the End of the Second Temple Period, in: A. M. RABELLO, ed., Studies in Judaism. Jubilee Volume Presented to David Kotlar (Tel Aviv, 1975), pp. 123—144, and the 'Index to Newly Published Documents and Inscriptions' in Israel Exploration Journal 11—20, 1961—1970, printed in 26 (1976), 271—288; and Chapter XV.

S. KRAUSS, et al., SeferHaYishuv, I, i (Jerusalem, 1939).

B. MAZAR, et al., Beith She'arim, 3 vols. (Jerusalem, 1956—71).

H. DONNER, W. RÖLLIG, Kanaanäische und Aramäische Inschriften, 3 vols., 2nd ed. (Wiesbaden, [2]1966—69).

BARUCH LIFSHITZ, Prolegomenon, to Ktav reprint of JEAN B. FREY, Corpus Inscriptionum Judaicarum, 2 vols. [Rome, 1936—52] (New York, 1970).

E. KUTSCHER, Aramaic, EJ 3, 267—270; 283—287.

HOSPERS (1973), especially pp. 319—321.

JOSEPH NAVEH, Corpus of Synagogue Inscriptions (Jerusalem: Israel Exploration Society, in press).

Recent inscriptions include:

An 'En Gedi Inscription: various interpretations thereof in Tarbiẓ 40 (1970), especially that of Saul LIEBERMAN, A Preliminary Remark to the Inscription of 'En Gedi', pp. 24—26, who uses the inscription to throw light on a y. passage.

A. DOTAN, The Secret in the Synagogue Inscription of 'En Gedi, Leshonenu 36 (1971), 211—217, which overly accepts the historicity of Pirqoi ben Baboi's propaganda concerning the historical events in the Holy Land.

DAN ORMAN, Jewish Inscription from Dabura in the Golan, Tarbiẓ 40 (1971), 399—408.

SUSSMANN (1973—74), and ID., Additional Notes, Tarbiẓ 44 (1974—75), 193—195, and Tarbiẓ 45 (1975—76), II—III, 213—257.

FANNO VITTO, Ancient Synagogue At Rehov, Atiqot. Hebrew Series 7 (1974), 100—104, 17*—18*.

LIEBERMAN, Tarbiẓ 45 (1975—76), IV, 53—63, 331.

ELISHA QIMRON, Some Comments to the Tel Reḥov Inscriptions, Tarbiẓ 45 (1975—76), X, 154—156.

Z. SAFRAI, Immanuel 8 (1978), 48—57.

D. Agricultural Matters

Many texts deal with agricultural matters or otherwise require the knowledge of these materials. For general bibliographies, see YEHUDA FELIKS, Mixed Sowing, Breeding, and Grafting (Tel Aviv, 1967) and K. D. WHITE, Bibliography of Roman Agriculture (England, n.d.), a classified detailed index.

The following literature either deals with ancient agriculture in general or in part, or else tries to relate those concerns to Talmudic texts:

*I. LOEW, Aramäische Pflanzennamen (Leipzig, 1881); ID., Die Flora der Juden I—IV, in 5 vols. (Vienna, 1924—34, Repr., in 4 vols., Hildesheim, 1967).

*A. M. LUNCZ, ed. of Estori HaParḥi, Kaftor UPeraḥ (Jerusalem, 1897[3]), a comprehensive collection and study of sources on agricultural matters.

*S. KRAUSS (1910—12) and (1923, 1929, 1945). (See under B, above).

*JULIUS PREUSS, Biblisch-Talmudische Medizin (Berlin, 1911, Repr. London, 1969, and New York, 1970; English ed., New York, 1978).

*A. S. HIRSCHBERG, HaṢemer UPishtah BiTqufat HaMishnah VeHa-Talmud (Jerusalem, 1912).

DALMAN (1928—42). (See under B, above).

*LIEBERMAN, TK Iff. (1955ff.), especially vols. I—II, with an index to flora.

YEHUDAH FELIKS, Plant World of the Bible (Tel Aviv, 1957); *ID., Agriculture in Palestine in the Period of the Mishna and Talmud (Jerusalem, 1963), a systematic study of all facets, with indexes; ID., Rice in Rabbinic Literature, BIA 1 (1963), 177—189; ID., Graft Hybredization of Trees and Vegetables, BIA 3 (1965), 25—45; ID., Mixed Sowing, Breeding, and Grafting (Tel Aviv, 1967), a botanic commentary to Kil. I—II; ID., The Prohibition of Ploughing in the Summer Preceding the Seventh Year, BIA 9 (1972) [= Memorial to H. M. Shapiro, ed. H. Z. HIRSCHBERG (Ramat Gan, 1972], 142—220, and xvii—xviii; ID., Go and Seed in the Seventh Year Because of Arnona, Sinai 37 (1973), 235—249; ID., Pereq Zeraʿim, in: MORDECHAI MARGALIOTH, Hilkhot Ereṣ Yisrael Min HaGenizah (Jerusalem, 1973); ID., The Fifteenth of Shevat, Tarbiẓ 46 (1977), 181—211.

URIAH FELDMAN, Ṣamhe HaMishna (Tel Aviv, n.d.).

FORBES (1964—1972), especially vols. 2, 3, 5. (See under Section B.)

*MICHAEL ZOHARY, Flora Palaestina, 3 vols. (Jerusalem, 1966—75).

*K. D. WHITE, Agricultural Implements of the Roman World (Cambridge, 1967); and ID., Roman Farming (Ithaca, 1970), an excellent introduction and study, with a survey of the ancient literary sources. Although it does not employ Talmudic sources, it throws considerable light on them.

ARMAS SALONEN, Agricultura Mesopotamica (Helsinki, 1968).

ISAAC GILAT, As to the Applicability of the Laws of Ploughing and Seeding and other Labors in the Seventh Year, Sinai 36 (70) (1972), 200—210.

M. E. Kislev, Ḥitta and Kussemet, Notes on Their Interpretation, Leshonenu 37 (1973), 83—95; 242—252, an excellent study.
Sussmann (1973—74).

E. Legal Studies

The knowledge of the legal background of a matter is a prerequisite to the understanding of a text. Naturally, one must not impose a supposed reconstruction of the legal history onto the text, but rather base that reconstruction on the text itself. This is especially so for y. where texts, even analogous ones, may derive from different and disputing circles. Scholars have made different sorts of studies, and have successfully clarified through comparative investigations many oblique matters. They have drawn on the Greek papyrological materials from the Eastern Mediterranean and Egypt, Roman, Syriac, Aramaic, Akkadian, and Biblical materials. See Baron II (1952), pp. 299—302, and Shamma Friedman's Review of Ze'ev Falk, Mavo L'Dine Yisrael, Conservative Judaism 25 (1971), 85—88.

Many studies in 'Jewish Law', however, have not realized the import of historical-literary critical research. Rather they tend to accept attributions at face value, insufficiently to distinguish between the strata of sources, and inadequately to take account of different versions of the same source. See Bernard Jackson, Introduction, Essays in Jewish and Comparative Legal History (Leiden, 1976). For a specific example, the matter of *prozbul*, see Gulak, History of Jewish Law, Talmudic Period I: Law of Obligation and Its Guarantees (Jerusalem, 1939), pp. 31—52, and Menachem Elon, Lien, EJ 11, 227—237, whose pictures of the developments must be reassessed in light of Neusner, Pharisees (1971), I—III; Weiss Halivni (1968), pp. 225—227; and E. Halevy, HaAggadah HaHiśṭorit-Biographit (Tel Aviv, 1975), pp. 129—130; cf. Bokser (1975), pp. 80—85.

Thus it is vital to pay attention to the date in which conceptual modes emerged and to avoid an anachronistic projection back as if the concepts or principles existed throughout all periods. This is especially so as far as the classification of laws; see, e.g., Yitzhak D. Gilat, From Biblical Severity to Rabbinic Injunction, Benjamin DeVries Memorial Volume, ed. Z. M. Melammed (Jerusalem, 1968), pp. 84—93. Accordingly, one must consider the literary history of the text and the history of the traditions contained therein when one employs the various studies.

Nahum Rakover, A Bibliography of Jewish Law (Jerusalem, 1975), presents a classified and comprehensive listing of Hebrew items. See also Baron II (1952), 299—302.

Major and representative works include:

Asher Gulak, Yeśode HaMishpat HaIvri, 4 vols. (Berlin, 1922, Repr. in 2 vols., Tel Aviv, 1967²); Id., σύμφωνον in Betrothal According to the Jerusalem Talmud, Tarbiẓ 5 (1934), 126—133; *Id., Das Urkundenwesen im Talmud (Jerusalem, 1935); *ID., History of Jewish Law, Talmudic Period I: Law of Obligation and Its Guarantees [Hebrew] (Jerusalem, 1939).

JACOB J. RABINOWITZ, Jewish Law, Its Influence on the Development of Legal Institutions (New York, 1956).

*REUVEN YARON, Gifts in Contemplation of Death in Jewish and Roman Law (Oxford, 1960), a careful historical study.

SHALOM ALBECK, General Principles of the Law of Tort in the Talmud [Hebrew] (Tel Aviv, 1965), focuses on B.Q. This and his many articles deal with legal theory and principles, especially in civil matters, e.g., ID., Davar Shlo' Ba' Le'olam, Sinai 38 (1974), 97–119. ID., Dine Mamonot BeTalmud (Tel Aviv, 1976).

BEZALEL PORTEN, Archives from Elephantine (Berkeley, 1968), contains much useful material concerning the nature of documents and procedures used in their writing.

*BOAZ COHEN, Jewish and Roman Law: A Comparative Study, 2 vols. (New York, 1966), a collection of various articles previously published in many different places, with an introduction surveying earlier literature, and comprehensive indexes.

*AARON KIRSCHENBAUM, Self-Incrimination in Jewish Law (New York, 1970).

Dine Israel, An Annual of Jewish Law and Israeli Family Law, ed. ZE'EV W. FALK and AARON KIRSCHENBAUM Iff. (Tel Aviv, 1970ff.).

S. LIEBERMAN, A Few Words on the Book by Julian the Architect of Ascalon 'The Laws of Palestine and its Customs', Tarbiẓ 40 (1971), 409–417.

BERNARD JACKSON, Theft in Early Jewish Law (Oxford, 1972), with rich bibliography.

MENACHEM ELON, Ha-Mishpat Ha-Ivri, 3 vols. (Jerusalem, 1973), a voluminous work which, however, does not sufficiently take into account the critical matters mentioned above. Too often it deals with items as they were perceived in the post-Talmudic times; ID., ed., The Principles of Jewish Law (Jerusalem, 1975), a separate publication of the 'Jewish Law' material from the Encyclopaedia Judaica, with indexes.

NEUSNER, Purities (1974–1977), though on Mishnaic materials provides examples of careful historical study of the law.

YOCHANAN MUFFS, Joy and Love as Metaphorical Expressions of Willingness and Spontaneity in Cuneiform, Ancient Hebrew, and Related Literatures, in: Christianity, Judaism, and Other Greco-Roman Cults. Srudies for Morton Smith at Sixty, ed. J. NEUSNER (Leiden, 1975), III, 1–36, especially 1–9, which surveys the field.

MORDECHAI FRIEDMAN, Marriage and Marriage Tradition in Palestinian Tradition as Reflected in Documents of the Cairo Geniza (Tel Aviv, 1979), with bibliography, throws much light on marriage laws and the scribal procedures for documents.

F. Liturgical Works

This section deals with *piyyuṭ* (early liturgical poetry) and other liturgical works.

1. In the study of y. one may make use of early *piyyuṭ* and liturgical texts from Palestine or from lands which drew on Palestinian tradition. They employ biblical, halakhic and aggadic motifs, the themes of which were often coordinated with special Sabbaths or biblical readings. Such works are a continuation of a genre that has roots in Talmudic times; see LIEBERMAN, SZ (1968), pp. 104, 115—116, especially fn. 128, and A. MIRSKY, The Origin of Liturgical Poetry, Studies of the Research Institute for Hebrew Poetry in Jerusalem 7 (1958), 1—129. These works thus form an important resource for liturgical and festival motifs and ideas, midrashic notions, as well as lexicographical and linguistic data. LIEBERMAN, Ḥazanut Yannai, Sinai 9 (22) (1939), 221—250, especially 245—250, demonstrated with numerous examples the importance of these poems for the study of y. Moreover, often an unclear y. passage has been interpreted on the basis of b., especially where the text related to ritual and liturgical matters. Some scholars at times have speculated that a y. text has been doctored to fit a Babylonian tradition. When the matter is employed or reflected in a *piyyuṭ*, we have a reliable text which cannot have been revised and on the basis of which we may evaluate the issue. For examples, see first, LIEBERMAN, TK (1955) I, 322, especially fn. 13 and 360; Z. M. RABINOWITZ, Halakha and Aggada in the Liturgical Poetry of Yannai (Tel Aviv, 1965), pp. 164, fn. 22; and BOKSER (1975), p. 90, fn. 249; and, secondly, LIEBERMAN, TK I (1955), 32—33, on abbreviated forms of the 'Tefillah'. See also the reference to a universal messianic judgement, y. Ber. 4: 3, 8a, as indicated by K. KOHLER, The Origin and Composition of the Eighteen Benedictions, in: Contributions to the Scientific Study of the Liturgy, ed. J. J. PETUCHOWSKI (New York, 1970), pp. 65—66 [= HUCA 1 (1924)], and confirmed by A. M. HABERMANN, Tefillot Me'en Shemoneh Esreh (Berlin, 1933), p. 46, ls. 4—5.

Scholars have employed the liturgical texts; see especially RABINOVITZ (1965). While they agree that the materials stand within the Palestinian tradition and are exegetically important, they differ as to the date of the early liturgical poets (e.g., LIEBERMAN: fourth century) and whether they directly used the y. and several *midrashim* or drew on those traditions through some other medium or earlier versions of the works. Thus scholars differ whether or not the authors of the *piyyuṭim* cited from a finished or arranged y. Moreover, it has been cogently suggested that the poets would not have examined a written text of y. or such. Rather they would have cited motifs from memory. Naturally this point is important in the evaluation of slight differences between the parallels in *piyyuṭim* and y. In addition, one must note that the poets may have combined several motifs.

A summary of the various positions and lists of sources and literature may be found in EZRA FLEISHER, Piyyut, EJ 13, 573—602; and ID., Shirat

HaQodesh HaIvrit Bime HaBenayim (Jerusalem, 1975). See also references in SHAKED (1964).

2. An important area related to *piyyuṭ* is the history of prayer, its patterns, and practices, JOSEPH HEINEMANN, Prayer in the Period of the Tannaim and Amoraim: Its Forms and Structure (Hebrew: Jerusalem, 1966²; English revised edition: Berlin, 1976), has shown, first, the necessity to recognize the fluidity of prayer-texts and the fallacy of maintaining prior conceptions as to what makes up the required text, and, secondly, how one may use form criticism to understand many aspects of the prayers. Several post-Talmudic works, liturgical halakhic compendia on prayer, like 'Tractate Soferim', ed. M. HIGGER (New York, 1937, Repr. Jerusalem, 1970), and early prayer books provide important information on these matters. These materials and the relevant bibliography are reviewed in ISḤAQ (ISMAR) ELBOGEN, HaTefillah BeYisrael, A Hebrew Revised and Expanded Edition, by YEHOSHUA AMIR, J. HEINEMANN, H. SCHIRMANN, et al. (Tel Aviv, 1972), which includes, as well, important chapters on the triennial cycles, pp. 117ff., and *piyyuṭ*, pp. 210—291.

3. Additional important and representative items on both *piyyuṭ* and prayer include:

ABRAHAM I. SCHECHTER, Studies in Jewish Liturgy (Phil., 1930), especially 21—79, on the 'Palestinian rite', suggested criteria to identify it, its place in certain works, and its role in Italy and elsewhere.

*ABRAHAM M. HABERMANN, Tefillot Me'en Shemoneḥ Esreh (Berlin, 1933), texts of the *tefillah* in the form of a *piyyuṭ* and a discussion of this genre; ID., Poetry as a Preserver of Forgotten Words and Meanings, P'raqim, ed. E. S. ROSENTHAL, 1 (Jerusalem, 1967—68), 29—35.

*LIEBERMAN (1934), xxi—xxii, on *piyyuṭ* for spelling, usage, exegesis, and readings.

*M. ZULAI, Piyyuṭe Yannai (Berlin, 1938), an important corpus; ID., Linguistic Matters in the Piyyuṭ of Yannai (Hebrew), Studies of the Research Institute for Hebrew Poetry 6 (1946), 161—248.

*JACOB MANN, The Bible as Read and Preached in the Old Synagogue I (Cincinnati, 1940, Repr. Jerusalem, 1970), II (Cincinnati, 1966), Ktav Repr. of Volume I, with Prolegomenon, by BEN ZION WACHOLDER (New York, 1971), especially xx—xxix, xxxvii, which must be carefully used. MANN's work on the Palestinian tradition of the reading of the 'Torah' and the prophetic portions and related laws and customs provides a key to understand many *midrashim* and *piyyuṭim*.

RABINOWITZ (1940), pp. 10—12, 15, 19, 20, 150, 174, 197, 357, 394, on ritual and liturgical matters.

ISRAEL DAVIDSON, et al., Siddur R. Saadja Gaon (Jerusalem, 1941, 1970³), an important early prayer book with notes.

*J. SCHIRMANN, Hebrew Liturgical Poetry and Christian Hymnology, JQR 44 (1953), 123—161, an important study reviewing the evidence for an early date for the beginnings of *piyyuṭ*.

*RABINOWITZ (1965), especially p. 65 (on the ways in which Yannai used materials), and pp. 252—262 (on PT), to which cp. B. Z. WACHOLDER, Prolegomenon, Ktav Reprint of JACOB MANN, The Bible as Read and Preached in the Old Synagogue I [Cincinnati, 1940] (New York, 1971), p. xlix, fn. 64; ID., Interpretation and Sources of Kerovot Yanai, BIA 4—5 (1967), 138—159.

AARON MIRSKY, Reshit HaPiyyuṭ (Jerusalem, 1965); ID., Definitions of Poetry Among Anonymous Liturgical Poets, P'raqim, ed. E. S. ROSENTHAL, 1 (Jerusalem, 1967—68), 109—113; ID., From Midraš to Piyyuṭ to Jewish Poetry, Leshonenu 32 (1968), 129—139, on the early history of *piyyuṭ*; ID., Śegulot HaPiyyuṭ Shel Yose be Yose, Yerushlayim, Shenaton LeDivre Śifrut Ve'Amanut, 3—4 (1970), 345—362.

*JOSEPH HEINEMANN, An Ancient Piyyuṭ Pattern, BIA 4—5 (1967), 132—137; ID., The Triennial Lectionary Cycle, JJS 19 (1968), 41f.

EZRA FLEISHER, Maḥzor Piyyuṭ Mitokh Qedushta LeYom Qippur Ha-Meyuḥeset LeYose be Yose, Kobez al Yad 7 (17), (Jerusalem, 1968), 1—80, especially 1—5 and 14—15; ID., Studies in Piyyuṭ and Medieval Hebrew Poetry, Tarbiẓ 39 (1969), 19—38, how *piyyuṭ* may throw light on y. and Palestinian practices; and ID., Studies in the Problems Relating to the Liturgical Function of the Types of Early Piyyuṭ, Tarbiẓ 50 (1970), 41—63, suggests a relative late date for *piyyuṭ*, post fifth century. Somewhat overly accepts Pirqoi's propaganda. Cf. SARASON (1978), below.

JACOB J. PETUCHOWSKI, Contributions to the Scientific Study of Jewish Liturgy (New York, 1950), a collection of important articles by various writers, and an introduction which reviews the field; ID., Theology and Poetry (London, in press), includes translations and commentary to many *piyyuṭim*.

ESTHER GOLDENBERG, Hebrew Language, Language of Piyyut, EJ 16, 1609—1612, 1660.

E. S. ROSENTHAL, Two Comments, Tarbiẓ 41 (1972), 450.

DANIEL GOLDSCHMIDT, Liturgy, EJ 11, 392—402, especially 395—396; ID., Seder R. Amram Gaon (Jerusalem, 1972), a critical edition of the first extant prayerbook. See below, Section XIX. E.

Y. TOBI, About the Tradition of Mishnaic and Talmudic Hebrew in Medieval Hebrew Poetry, Leshonenu 37 (1973), 137—155.

Y. ROZABI, On the Mishnaic Language Tradition in Spanish Hebrew Poetry, Leshonenu 37 (1973), 311—312.

*SHLOMO SIMONSOHN (1974), 831—888, especially p. 841, reviews the present scholarship as to the date and origin of *piyyuṭ*.

JOSEPH HEINEMANN and JAKOB J. PETUCHOWSKI, Literature of the Synagogue (New York, 1975), includes numerous examples, in English translation, of prayers and *piyyuṭ* from both Talmuds and early liturgical works, and introductions. PETUCHOWSKI, in particular, discusses the evidence as to the origin of *piyyuṭ* and the ways in which modern scholars deal with it.

*RICHARD SARASON, On the Use of Method in the Modern Study of Jewish Liturgy, in: Approaches to Ancient Judaism, ed. WILLIAM S.

GREEN [= Brown Studies in Judaism, I] (Missoula: Scholars Press, 1977), an important critical review and history of scholarchip, which pays attention to the assumptions that guide the various studies.

Of note, J. SCHIRMANN annually publishes in KS a bibliography on *piyyuṭ*.

G. Miscellaneous Indexes

Aphorism: ABRAHAM ISAAC DZIUBAS, Milin DeYerushalmi (Jerusalem, 1970), non-exhaustive alphabetical index to aphorisms, proverbs, etc. in y.

AARON HYMAN, Oṣar Divre Ḥakhamin UPitgamehem (Tel Aviv, 1956[3]), alphabetical index to idioms in y. and other rabbinic works. See the review (to an earlier edition) of JUDAH FRIES-HOREB, KS 11 (1934), 14, which raises methodological problems in the anthologizing of idioms.

Biblical verses: *AARON HYMAN, Torah HaKetuvah Vehameśurah, 3 vols. (Tel Aviv, 1936—38, Repr. 1965), an index of citations of biblical verses in rabbinic literature.

Index to PT from BT: 'Yefeh Enayim', in back of Romm, Vilna editions of b. See below Section XX. B, s.v. 'Yellin' and 'Kanevski'.

YEHOSHUA HESCHEL ELI ZEEV of Vilna, Ṣion Yehoshua (Vilna, 1869, Repr. Jerusalem, 1970).

Halakhic authorities: ISAAC ARIELE, 'Enayim LeMishpat, III (Jerusalem, 1966). An index to halakhic cross references, supplements and corrections to the 'Ein Mishpat' index in printed editions of y.

XVIII. Post-Talmudic Palestinian Works

There are various works composed or compiled in Ereṣ Yisrael from late or post-Talmudic times and which throw light on the text or content of PT. Somewhat like *piyyuṭ*, they thus represent primary data, though, of course interpretations and practices may have changed since the time of the PT. In general, see ASSAF (1955), pp. 172—179; BARON VI (1958), pp. 62—65; MARGALIOTH (1973), Introduction, pp. 1—16, and passim.

A. Palestinian *midrashim*

As indicated above, these *midrashim* may provide analogues of different versions of materials incorporated in y. From a different perspective, however, they constitute an exegetical resource. For example, they may rework or paraphrase a tradition on the basis of a given interpretation, substitute an unclear word with one which is more common, or preserve the original reading of a text, which in y. has been corrupted. In addition, a *midrash*'s rearrangement of a *sugya* may throw light on its sequence [as already indicated by FRANKEL (1870)] and the setting in which it is used may make clear a referent or content. For these items, see above, Chapter X, and JOHN T. TOWNSEND, Rabbinic Sources, The Study of Judaism, Bibliographical Essays (Anti-Defamation League of B'nai B'rith: New York, 1972), pp. 68—72.

B. Minor Tractates: Halakhic and Ethical Monographs

There is a genre of juridical and ethical collections from Palestine which generally summarize the existing laws in special areas. These non-Talmudic tractates are published in the printed editions of BT, at the end of the order of 'Neziqin'. M. HIGGER provided critical editions, some with English translations. A. COHEN, et al., The Minor Tractates of the Talmud (London, 1965), are not fully critical editions.

Each work varies in its date, nature, and use of y. and/or Palestinian traditions. While some of the material may be based on Talmudic sources, each work is edited after the y. Despite the invariable expansions and developments of the materials, the works serve as a guide to Palestinian practices and traditions, which may enable one to free oneself from superimposing BT's understanding and concepts onto y. At times, moreover, the materials may closely parallel PT sources. HIGGER in his introductions cites all parallel and analogous texts from y.

a) Avot deRabbi Nathan. See above, Section X. D.

b. Treatise Semaḥot (N.Y., 1931, Repr. Jerusalem, 1970—71) on mourning. DOV ZLOTNICK, The Tractate Mourning with a Hebrew text vocalized by E. Y. KUTSCHER (New Haven, 1966), provides a fine English translation, introduction, and notes. Cf. ERIC MEYERS, cited in Section XVII. B.

c) Kallah and Kallah Rabbati (New York, 1936, Repr. Jerusalem, 1970—71).

d) Derekh Ereṣ (New York, 1935, Repr. Jerusalem, 1970), on etiquette.

e) Maśekhtot Zeirot: Yirat Ḥet; Derekh Ereṣ Ze'ira; 'Arayot; Pereq Ma'sim; Pereq Shalom; Pereq Gadol HaShalom (New York, 1928, Repr. Jerusalem, 1970), on various ethical matters.

f) Seven Minor Tractates (Qeṭanot): Sefer Torah; Mezuzah; Tefillin; Ẓiẓit; 'Abadim; Kutim; Gerim; and Treatise Soferim II (New York, 1930, Repr. Jerusalem, 1971).

g) Śoferim (New York, 1937, Repr. Jerusalem, 1970), on scribal and liturgical practices.

Additional bibliography besides KASHER (1959), and EJ, includes:

ASSAF (1955), p. 174.
BARON VI (1958), pp. 62 and 354f.
DEVRIES, Studies in Talmud (Jerusalem, 1968), pp. 259—262.
TOWNSEND (1972), pp. 62—64.

C. 'Ma'asim LiVene Ereṣ Yisrael' = Collection or Digest Recording Court Decisions

The 'Ma'asim' constitute various fragments of Palestinian halakhic works, initially published in Tarbiẓ, by B. LEWIN, 1 (1930), 97—101; 2 (1931), 25f., J. N. EPSTEIN, 1 (1930), 33—42, 143—45; 2 (1931), 319—327, and J. MANN, 1 (1930), 1—14. These were collected and reprinted in: 'Śefer HaMa'asim LiVene Ereṣ Yisrael' (Tel Aviv, 1971). An additional fragment was simultaneously published by Z. M. RABINOWITZ, Sepher HaMa'asim Livnei Ereṣ Yisra'el — New Fragments, Tarbiẓ 41 (1972), 272—305, and English summary, ii—iii, and by MORDECHAI MARGALIOTH (1973), pp. ii—vii, and 39—55, which includes facsimiles. One should consult both of the editions, as the text and footnotes may vary, as well as the study of MORDECHAI FRIEDMANN, Shene Qeta'im MeŚefer HaMa'asim LiVene Yisrael, Sinai 38 (1974), 14—36.

The characteristics of each fragment vary. Apparently, each does not come from the same period. Some represent or are quite close to the original 'Ma'asim', others are abbreviated reworkings of earlier items. They originate clearly at least from the end of the Byzantine period, while the reworkings perhaps from the eight or ninth centuries.

While the texts are somewhat corrupt and the materials therein often, though not always, presented or recorded in an unclear or garbled order, they are very important for the study of y. They indicate the existence of creative legal activity in Palestine in the post-Talmudic period (Byzantine and later), and the acceptance and use of PT in Palestine; much of the materials deal with practical life-matters. See RABINOWITZ (1972), pp. 280f, and MARGALIOTH (1973), pp. 2—4. Moreover, the fragments provide witness to many y. texts and exegetical keys to both terminology and passages. See besides the notes of the editors of the texts, SAUL LIEBERMAN, LeMa'asim LiVene Ereṣ Yisrael, Tarbiẓ 1 (1930), 137—139; ID., Śefer HaMa'asim — Śefer HaPeśaqim, Tarbiẓ 2 (1931), 377—379; ID., Al HaMa'asim LiVene Ereṣ Yisrael, Ginze Kedem 5 (1934), 177—185; ID., Concerning Sepher HaMa'-'asim, Tarbiẓ 42 (1972—73), 90—96; and M. FRIEDMAN (1974). The fragments published by RABINOWITZ (1972) and MARGALIOTH (1973) contain, appended to several of the *peśaqim* (decisions), a lenghty selection from *gemara*, mainly from y. 'Yevamot', 'Ketubot', and 'Qiddushim'. FRIEDMAN (1974) places the materials in the context of the history of the relevant legal issues; re pp. 32—36, cf. BOKSER (1975), pp. 110—115.

Familiarity with the 'Śefer Ma'asim' is also important due to its use in Babylonia where it constituted a source for Palestinian traditions; traces thereof may be found in 'Halakhot Gedolot' (see below, Section XIX. E), 'Responsa', and other works. See EPSTEIN, Tarbiẓ 1 (1930), 36, and RABINOWITZ (1972), pp. 275, 278. The isolation of the 'original source' thus better enables one to evaluate the y. references in these Babylonian works.

Reference to y. is found, in part, in EPSTEIN, Tarbiẓ 1 (1930), 33, and with a brief description, in MARGALIOTH (1973), Introduction, pp. 5—7.

The only full index to the y. passages is in MARGALIOTH (1973), pp. 209—210.

Additional bibliography includes:

B. M. LEWIN, Sepher Methiboth (Jerusalem, 1933, Repr. 1973), p. xi.

M. MARGALIOTH/MARGULIES, MaSheu ʿal Śifrut HaHalakhah HaEreṣ Yisraelit BiTequfat HaGeonim, World Congress of Jewish Studies I, Jerusalem, 1947 (Jerusalem, 1952), pp. 255—258; ID. (1973), Introduction, pp. 2—7.

ASSAF (1955), p. 175.

BARON VI (1958), pp. 64—65, 355f.

D. Other Halakhic Works

Several different items including a new edition of 'Hilkhot Ṭerefot Mishel Ereṣ Yisrael', all with introductions and notes are found in MARGALIOTH (1973). Each item reflects Palestinian usages, language, laws, and thus to various degrees illuminates y.

The items deal with ritual slaughter; lists and texts of blessings and other household documents of family matters; family laws; copy of a Palestinian *geṭ*; fragments of laws in a Palestinian Siddur; an agricultural work from various sources — prepared by YEHUDAH FELIKS — that deals with times and duration of seeding, pregnation, and flowering of plants, trees, and animals.

Two indexes facilitate access to y. To the agricultural work: pp. 199—200, to the whole book: pp. 209—210. On the earlier literature see EPSTEIN, Tarbiẓ 2 (1931), 308—320; and ASSAF (1955), p. 175.

E. 'Ḥilukim Sheben Anshe Mizraḥ UVene Ereṣ Yisrael'

This work originates from the beginning of the Gaonic period, ca. eighth century. It consists of a list of fifty-five differences in customs between Babylonians and Palestinians. It enables one to clarify many Palestinian practices and concepts.

Two critical editions exist:

M. MARGULIES [= MARGALIOTH], The Differences Between Babylonian and Palestinian Jews (Jerusalem, 1937), the fullest complete edition with comprehensive introduction, notes, and commentary. MARGULIES dates the work ca. 700; on import for y., see, e. g., pp. 91—94.

B. M. LEWIN, Otzar Hilluf Minhagim Ben Bene Ereṣ Yisrael UVen Bene Bavel (Jerusalem, 1942, Repr. Jerusalem, 1974).

See also ASSAF (1955), p. 179; and ISRAEL SCHEPANSKY, Eretz-Israel in the Respona Literature (Jerusalem, 1966), pp. 50ff.

F. Palestinian *responsa*

Responsa from Palestinian authorities which use the y. text or reflect its conceptions are not extant from the early period (seventh century) and only in few numbers from later. Previously, scholars have attributed this to the fact of Babylonian hegemony such that throughout the Caliphate questions were directed to the Babylonian authorities. Some of the items are preserved in European collections; see ASSAF (1955), pp. 173—174, and others in the 'Genizah'. The 'Ma'asim' works indicate that *responsa* were made for use in Palestine and they apparently were not otherwise preserved.

MARGALIOTH (1973), Introduction, pp. 11—13, contains a full list of publications, and comments on the degree to which an item uses y. See also GINZBERG, Geonica I (1909), pp. 90—98.

G. 'Śefer Yerushalmi'

'Śefer Yerushalmi' consists of portions of PT in sequence with chapter and *halakhah* divisions combined with passages from BT and Gaonic additions.

Some unknown authority compiled the work in Palestine after Gaonic teachings spread in the land, ca. eighth century; cf. MARGALIOTH (1973), Introduction.

Various Gaonic and European scholars used the work as if citing y. APTOWITZER reconstructed the work and EPSTEIN, Tarbiẓ 1b (1930), 37, identified various geniza fragments as remnants of the compilation.

Scholars differ as to the relationship of this work and the 'Śefer Ma'asim', and whether Geonim took material from 'Śefer Yerushalmi' or from 'Śefer Ma'asim'.

Literature includes:

B. RATNER (1901—1917), especially Taan., pp. 115—120. See LIEBERMAN's list of references (1929), p. 39.

GINZBERG, Genizah Fragments (1909), pp. 29—36, 152—153; 183—184, 230; ID., Ginze Schechter (1928), I, 390—422. See above, Section IV. E.

AVIGDOR APTOWITZER, Unechte Jeruschalmizitate, MGWJ 55 (1911), 419—425; ID., Untersuchungen zur Gaonäischen Literatur, HUCA 8—9 (1931—32), 418—421; and Mavo (1938), pp. 275—276.

LIEBERMAN (1934), p. xxv; and (1947), Preface and Introduction.

URBACH (1955), p. 551, and fn. 69.

See also above, Chapter II.

Desideratum

What is needed is a comprehensive index to y. passages and topics for each of the above works. The topic index will help, for the y. passage relevant to the text may not immediately be clear. The student of y. though may be able to make the connection. In the interim, the following two works may be helpful:

ISRAEL SCHEPANSKY, Eretz-Israel in the Responsa Literature. I: The Period of the Geonim and the Rishonim (Jerusalem, 1966), an excellent thematically arranged collection of sources with the editor's footnotes. The texts, however, are not critically analyzed to determine if an item constitutes an actual Palestinian practice or something merely attributed to them by non-Palestinians.

YAAQOV GALIŚ, Minhage Ereṣ Yisrael (Jerusalem, 1968), while it focuses on later ‘accepted’ Palestinian rituals and customs, as it is arranged by subject matter it provides much useful information on many points.

XIX. Commentaries to Yerushalmi. A: To the Sixteenth Century

A. Introduction

As indicated above, the lack of extant early commentaries to y. and, therefore, a full exegetical tradition to the text, requires one to rely on various sorts of works that in passing comment on y. I first deal with those items, commentaries and works from the middle ages (Chapter XIX), and then turn to the actual commmentaries to PT, which generally come from the sixteenth century and on (Chapter XX. A—B), and finally I survey contemporary works on the y. or works which are relevant to its study (Chapter XX. C). See GOODBLATT (1979), II, 3 and 5 and IV, 2, for further introduction to these materials and problems in their use in text criticism and exegesis.

B. The Use of Yerushalmi

Many medieval commentaries to BT and autonomous halakhic and aggadic treatises and codes contain references to y. along with explanations. To make use of the materials one must consider first how and why and to what degree PT was used by the various authorities and the role of the citation or reference. For example, the purpose of an explanation along with a citation may be to support an exegetical or halakhic position and may therefore affect that interpretation; it thus may not represent the simple rendering of y. Alternatively, where the citation is not accompanied by an explicit explanation, one may isolate the implied explanation on the basis of its use. Accordingly, I briefly review the literature which deals with this topic. Secondly, it is important to isolate the technique of citations, viz., what constitutes an actual citation and whether it derives from a y. text or from some intermediate source. I therefore focus on this subject, as well.

1. I. Twersky, Rabad of Posquieres (Harvard Semitic Series, XVIII) (Cambridge, 1962), pp. 104, 107—108, 172, 206—213, 241, 242, 245, presents an excellent comprehensive review of the status and significance of the Yerushalmi in Gaonic and later medieval rabbinic writings. See also Lieberman (1950), pp. 287—289; M. Margalioth, Hilkhot HaNagid (Jerusalem, 1962), Introduction, and Melammed (1973), pp. 515—525.

Traditional authorities through the middle ages and many modern scholars have deemphasized the role and use of the y. As remnants of this attitude may still be found in current works and commentaries, I point to several of the suggested explanations. Some may have actually contributed to the imperfect knowledge, while others may be the result of a prior religious prejudice favoring or accepting the BT as the authoritative halakhic source. The factors include: the supposed inferiority of y., viz. its unedited and unfinished nature; its supposed lack of authority even in Palestine, i. e., the now proven incorrect assumption as to the lack of post-Talmudic Palestinian creativity; the justification that the BT is more inclusive, i. e., the BT is edited after the PT. This assumes the "law follows the last authority" and that the later authority — BT — must have known and selected the valid portions of the earlier, y., or if y.'s logic was correct BT would have grasped and mentioned it. See Twersky; Tchernowitz, Toldot HaPosqim I (New York, 1946), pp. 29—38; Ginzberg (1941), pp. H: xliv—xlv; and Poznanski, HaKedem 1 (1907), 133, 135—148; 2 (1908), 24—54, 114—116; and Spiegel (1965), pp. 243—273; Abramson (1965), p. 550; and Goodblatt (1979), I, end.

2. I now provide guidelines as to the actual use of y.

Babylonian Gaonic authorities, especially in the early period, only briefly and infrequently used the PT. PT initially was widely studied, naturally, in the Holy Land, as proven by the 'Sefer Ma'asim', in Egypt, in North Africa and Southern Italy, though as a result of strong opposition by Babylonian Gaonim the BT received priority. Undoubtedly the success of the b. was greatly enhanced by the fact of the Central Abbasid Caliphate whereby ecumenical law and authority, for all Jewry within the Caliphate, was centralized in Bagdad. Moreover, y. was extensively used in Spain, especially in Provence, and Franco-Germany, particularly from the twelfth century on. In fourteenth and fifteenth century Europe, its use declined. For the later period, see below, Section XX. A.

3. Additional literature includes:

Frankel (1870).

Ratner, HaMelitz (St. Petersburg, 1899), nos. 201, 208, 212, 214, 215, 219, 229, 238, 240—242, 244—246, 248, 251; and (1900), nos. 82, 83, 85, 118—120, 198—203. Id. (1901), preface to 'Berakhot', pp. iv and vi.

*Lewin (1933), pp. xxxix—xlv, on spread of y. and critique of Aptowitzer.

Mordechai Margalioth, Halachoth Kezuboth (Jerusalem, 1942) Introduction, pp. 15, 16; *(1973), pp. 2, 8—16, 102—104.

GINZBERG (1941), pp. xli—l; H: lxxxv, lxxxviii—xc, c—ciii.

TCHERNOWITZ, 3 vols.(1946—47).

B. Z. BENEDICT, On the History of the Torah Centre in Provence, Tarbiz 22 (1951), 85—109, especially p. 93 and fn. 76, "PT studied for its own sake".

*EPHRAIM E. URBACH, The Tosaphists: Their History, Writings and Methods (Jerusalem, 1955), especially pp. 543ff.

*BARON VI (1958), especially pp. 24—26; 330f., fns. 24f.; 346, fn. 57.

H. J. ZIMMELS, Ashkenazim and Sephardim (London, 1958), especially pp. 150—151.

SPIEGEL (1965).

ABRAMSON (1965), pp. 312—313.

S. D. GOITEIN, A Mediterranean Society (1967ff.), especially I, 53, re the tenth century foundation of Qayrawan's academy; ID., Jewish Society and Institutions under Islam, Journal of World History 11 (1968), pp. 170—184 [Reprinted as, Jewish Society Through the Ages, ed. H. BEN-SASSON (New York, 1922)].

ABRAHAM SCHREIBER, ed., Responsa of the Sages of Provence (Jerusalem, 1967), list, p. xxiv, and n. b., p. 433.

HIRSCHBERG (1974), pp. 322—323, 338f.

Specific bibliography for particular individuals appears below.

4. In all the lands and periods where BT was given preference authorities widely used PT to explain a Bavli passage or adjudicate between two explanations of a matter of law. Theoretically the authorities professed the superiority of BT, i.e., not to follow PT when it contradicted BT, a classic statement of which was enunciated by R. Hai Gaon, and then many twelfth-thirteenth century scholars. As a result, masters, especially in Provence, often reinterpreted the PT on the basis of the BT so as not to reject the PT. But they might in fact be swayed by the PT. They in particular did this when certain factors drove them to find a solution differing from that of the plain sense of the BT, e. g., the need to justify a custom. Those who differed with them might then criticize them with the standard charge of relying on the PT. The uses included explanations of words, phrases, or entire passages.

To judge on the basis of the formulation of the extant materials, with very few exceptions, y. did not constitute a subject of independent study. Rather masters explained it when it was cited in the course of an exposition of BT. Thus for the study of y. one must examine relevant parallel or analogous pericopae in b. and consult the commentaries or works thereon and the halakhnic monographs or codes which cite sources from b.

C. Techniques of Citations and Their Collection

Traditional authorities through the ages (see below) as well as modern writers have recognized the importance of employing y. citations found in earlier works. The uses of such citations have basically fallen in two categories. First, individuals have tried to isolate no longer extant portions of y. This assumes that the earlier authorities had texts of y. more complete than the later ones. In Sections VII and XIV. B, I dealt with this literature. See CHAJES, Imre Binah, p. 2; and A. EPSTEIN, Z. W. RABINOWITZ, and S. BUBER, Yerushalayim 7 (1907), 147—179, 229—278. Similarly these citations have been used to fill in *lacunae* in a text. Secondly, writers have sought to establish the correct reading of a text and its explanation; usually the earlier authorities employed exegetical traditions and not mere speculation. RATNER's work represents a serious attempt to gather these citations and explanations. LIEBERMAN (1929), pp. 46f, in his review of these efforts, as indicated above, points to their conceptual flaws. Even RATNER while very useful is marred as well as incomplete. See LIEBERMAN, p. 39, for a list of references in which RATNER discusses the nature of these citations.

LIEBERMAN (1929), pp. 36—46, and (1934), pp. xxiii—xxiv, raised the appropriate methodological questions and suggested guidelines as to what actually constitutes a citation and explanation. I first lay out LIEBERMAN's programmatic principles and then provide a breakdown, drawing as well on individual studies. Unfortunately, to my knowledge a comprehensive systematic examination has not yet been published. [MELAMMED (1973), pp. 515—525, is somewhat helpful.]

The task is threefold. One must determine each authority's characteristic method of citation, his access to y., and the effect of the genre of the work on its citations. An individual may cite exactly, or in a non-exact manner. The latter includes: paraphrase with expansion; digest of content; changed formulation; imposition of one's own style or that more common in the rest of y. [as for pericopae in 'Neziqin'; (1931), p. 2, fn. 1]; brief slice, deleting material irrelevant to the point at hand. But LIEBERMAN notes that even the abridged citation may be helpful so as to reconstruct a text and its meaning, if not the wording, or to choose one of several readings. Below I draw on many of LIEBERMAN's descriptions of individual characteristics.

Secondly, LIEBERMAN focuses on whether or not an individual directly took from y. Earlier other scholars, in particular APTOWITZER, had discussed part of the problem in terms of the circulation of the 'Śefer Yerushalmi' compilation. See Sections II and XVIII. F. LIEBERMAN, though, is concerned whether an individual cites on the basis of a predecessor and not the y. directly. This applies, at times, to even those who frequently cite y. (e. g., Rabiah, Ramban, and Rashba) and who may have employed original texts of y. [See also (1934), pp. 9—8, 89]. This particularly holds for a student who may cite the reading and explanation of his master.

LIEBERMAN likewise points out that two versions or editions of the same work do not represent two separate testimonies (e. g., 'Kol Bo' and 'Orḥot Ḥayyim'), and, further, where different authorities used the same MSS their readings, naturally, constitute only one testimony.

Thirdly, the genre of a work may tend to shape the characteristic types of citations. Codes cite exactly where wording affects *halakhah,* commentaries retrieve explanations of *sugyot,* expounders and moralizers employ aggadic and midrashic materials.

LIEBERMAN turns to the related problem of identifying an actual reference. First, portions of or a whole reference may be to another source ('Śefer Yerushalmi', known to Germans; *Midrash* or Gaonic work; compendia-collections based on PT, like 'Śefer Ma'asim'). He supports CHAJES' observation that an unannotated citation to y. without identifying the tractate and the rest of the pericope may tend to represent a *midrash* or *peśiqta.* Secondly, a reference may constitute a glossed explanation added to the citation. See also (1934), p. 35, fn. 1, and ID., Yemenite Midrashim (Jerusalem, 1940, 1970²), pp. 35—39; and J. N. EPSTEIN, Tarbiẓ 1 (1930), 36—38, and fn. 2, who studies several citation-terminologies, and who suggests a logical criterion by which to isolate non-PT material: "an item not in extant y., and inappropriate on the basis of language and content, and elsewhere attributed to Geonim. Of course, a corruption in the text may have yielded the supposed mention of y". On the other hand, misattributions may occur in reverse. An authority may attribute a y. citation to 'Tosefta'; LIEBERMAN, Tashlum Tosefta (Jerusalem, 1970²), pp. 19, 46—51 (cf. p. 30, fn. 1), 65—66.

D. Medieval Commentaries

1. In the next section I focus on the more important individual commentaries and works and their characteristics. Once a history of rabbinism and medieval Jewish intellectual history is written, we may have a sophisticated comprehensive discussion. Several different sorts of such a study are being undertaken in different locations: Ph. D. dissertations under the guidance of ISADORE TWERSKY, at Harvard, and under E. URBACH and others at the Hebrew University, Jerusalem, and a comprehensive project by HAIM Z. DIMITROVSKY, Jewish Theological Seminary, New York.

2. In the interim the following may be helpful:

P. JACOB KOHN, Thesaurus of Hebrew Halakhic Literature (London, 1952), a comprehensive list, especially useful for items written after 1500, which are not covered in the next work.

M. A. KASHER and J. B. MANDELBAUM, Sarei Ha-Elef. A Millenium of Hebrew Authors (500—1500) (New York, 1959), an excellent guide which includes some references to modern scholarly literature, and its 'Supplement', ID., Quntreś Hashlamah Leśefer Sarei Ha-Elef, in: Śefer Zikaron Adam Noaḥ Baron, ed. ḤAYYIM LIPHSHITZ, et al. (Jerusalem, 1970), pp. 213—299 (a revised edition is under preparation).

Makhon HaTalmud, Yad Harav Herzog, Editions of Mishnah Zera'im (Jerusalem, 1972); ID., b. Ketubot, I (Jerusalem, 1972), contain lists of early authorities, imprintings, and extant MSS.

ARON FREIMANN and M. SCHMELZER, Union Catalog of Hebrew Manuscripts and Their Location, 2 vols. (New York, 1964—73), is a collated index of MSS found in libraries throughout the world.

*N. RAKOVER, A Bibliography of Jewish Law (Jerusalem, 1975), includes an index to Hebrew studies specifically on individual rabbinic figures and their works.

3. The following studies are especially helpful:

APTOWITZER (1938).

*GINZBERG (1941).

TCHERNOWITZ (1946—47).

B. Z. BENEDICT, numerous articles, published in KS, Sinai, Tarbiẓ, and Torah SheBe'al Peh.

*URBACH (1955).

*BARON VI (1958), whose notes on these matters are excellent. Besides listing publications, it virtually takes account of all previous literature.

SHAKED (1964), highly useful for editions and reviews of Gaonic material.

*MELAMMED (1973), pp. 515—525, an excellent concise survey that focuses on the use of y.

*EJ articles, many of which I have examined, generally include listing of editions and a summary of scholarly literature.

*I. TA-SHMAH, Ḥiddushei ha-Rishonim — their Order of Publication, KS 50 (1975), 325—336.

4. In my lists below I attempt to confine my comments to introductory remarks concerning a group of works, list the more important individuals and some of their key works, and very selectively refer to the literature which deals with the use of y., the appropriate secondary works and editions. Where a reference to y. is in the analogous pericope in b., access is easy. Most of the recent editions of 'Rishonim' include an index to works 'cited', wherein, if appropriate, are listed y. references. This is especially true of the fine series of critical editions under preparation by Makhon HaTalmud (Yad Harav Herzog) and Mosad HaRav Kook.

5. *Responsa* Literature: The *Responsa* literature which includes many references to y. is being indexed by the Israeli Institute for Jewish Law. Several volumes have so far appeared. These include: M. ELON, ed., Responsa of R. Asher b. Yeḥiel (Jerusalem, 1965), and ID., Responsa of R. Yom Tov Avraham Ashbili and R. Yehudah b. Asher (Jerusalem, 1973). See M. ELON, Responsa and Indices and the Institute for Research in Jewish Law, Proceedings of the Fifth World Congress of Jewish Studies, Jerusalem, 1969, Division V (Jerusalem, 1973), pp. English, 67, and Hebrew, 69—77, on the items completed and under preparation or planned. As to a bibliography of Responsa in addition to KASHER and KOHN, BOAZ COHEN, Quntraś HaTeshuvot (Budapest, 1930, Repr. Jerusalem, 1970) is still useful.

I heavily draw on LIEBERMAN's publications. It should be assumed that the items in subsections 2—3, especially the starred ones, include relevant information and I therefore usually do not cite them in the following sections.

E. Gaonic Works

1. POZNANSKI, HaKedem 1 (1907), 136—142, 143, and 2 (1908), 24—40, reviews earlier positions on the use of y., and conveniently lists and evaluates citations of y. in the 'Sheiltot' of Aḥai of Shabḥa, an eighth century homiletical legal-juridical work, 'Seder R. Amram Gaon', 'Halakhot Gedolot', and *Responsa*.

B. M. LEWIN, Oṣar HaGaonim, 13 vols., Berakhot — B.M. (last volume incomplete) (Haifa and Jerusalem, 1938—1943), and ḤAYYIM TAUBES, Oṣar HaGaonim to Sanhedrin (Jerusalem, 1966), presents the Gaonic materials arranged according to the sequence of the b., and is therefore quite useful.

To fully make use of the Gaonic works, besides covering materials not previously used, one should bring up to date the references in POZNANSKI and LEWIN and TAUBES with the literature subsequently published and employ the more recent improved or critical editions of the books.

Concerning, in particular, the Gaonic works, scholars have evaluated the supposed citations. Additional comprehensive literature includes: GINZBERG, Geonica (1909), and ASSAF (1955). See also Y. H. S., HeḤalus 5 (1860), 31—54 (Repr. Jerusalem, 1972), on Gaonic use of y. to explain 'Mishnah' contra b.

2. Individual works:

'Sheiltot': Editions with indexes, ISAIAH BERLIN, 3 vols. (Jerusalem, 1961, Repr. of Vilna), and S. K. MIRSKY, 5 vols. (Jerusalem, 1959—66, 1977), and B. Z. WACHOLDER's Review, JQR, N.S. 53 (1963), 257—61, Geniza fragments (which constitute full and uninterpolated versions), Tarbiẓ 6, 7, 10, 13; EPSTEIN, Tarbiẓ 6 (1935), 460 ff; A. N. Z. ROTH, Gaonic Writings from the Kaufmann Collection, Sura 2 (1955—56), 283f; ABRAMSON (1974), pp. 9—23, 317, 389, 398f.; and cf. A. KAMINKA, Al Divre HaSheiltot DeRAḥai VeYiḥuśan LiYerushalmi, HaKedem 2 (1908), 20—23.

Śeder R. Amran Gaon, ed. DANIEL GOLDSCHMIDT (Jerusalem, 1971); Review, G. L. ORMAN, KS 47 (1972), 361ff.

Halakhot Peśuqot: Śefer Halachot Peśuqot, attributed to R. Jehudai Gaon of the eighth century, ed. S. SASOON (Jerusalem, 1950, Makor Repr. with facsimile, 1969). Cf. p. 14.

Śefer Halakhot Peśuqot O Hilkhot Re'U, ed. A. L. SCHLOSSBERG (Paris, 1886, Repr. Jerusalem, 1967) — a Palestinian Hebrew translation of the previous work. See MARGALIOTH (1973), p. 14; SAMUEL MOREL, edition and study (unpublished Ph. D. dissertation, Jewish Theological Seminary of America).

Halakhot Gedolot, J. HILDESHEIMER, ed. (Berlin, 1888—1892), pp. 10—11, index to y. New edition in press; Vol. I, by EZRIEL HILDESHEIMER (Jerusalem, 1972), who challenges accepted consensus on the relationship of this work to previous two times. See also LEWIN (1933) and A. N. Z. ROTH, Gaonic Writings, Sura 2 (1955—56), 280—283.

*Halakhot Qeṣuvot [Adjudicated Laws], ed. MORDECHAI MARGALIOTH (Jerusalem, 1942), ninth century work that extensively draws on Palestinian customs and 'Sefer Ma'asim'.

F. North African Gaonic-Medieval Works

In general see HIRSCHBERG (1974).

*Śefer Metivot: Monumenta Gaonica, Methoboth to Mo'ed, Nashim, and Neziqin, to which is appended Śepher Hefez to Mo'ed, Nashim, Neziqin, and Qodashim, ed. B. M. LEWIN (Jerusalem, 1933, Repr. 1973), with notes by SAUL LIEBERMAN, pp. 44—45, 53—55, 115—118, 138—140, a tenth century work most likely from Qairawan, which mediates between Palestinian and Babylonian materials. Arranged in sequence of BT, it abbreviates b. pericopae and focuses on practical law, cites analogous PT pericopae which dispute, supplement, or explicate its law. The work is vital for textual readings and interpretations of y. as it directly lifts pericopae from y. and introduces them usually with the term *GYRŚT YRWŠLMY*, "the reading of the Yerushalmi", or anonymously. Often where b. and y. contain varying formulations of a tradition, the work cites it in y.'s version.

This treatise served as a prototype for several subsequent works, including, probably, 'Śefer Ḥefeṣ', as well as a possible source for indirect citations of y. found in various Rishonim. LEWIN, pp. 134—135, in sequence of PT, collected many citations of y. which employ the Metivot's characteristic formula, *GYRŚ' YRWŠLMY*.

See Review by S. ASSAF, KS 11 (1934), 161—166; V. APTOWITZER, Śefer Ḥefetz and Śefer M'thiboth, Tarbiẓ 4 (1933), 127—152; LIEBERMAN (1934), p. 120, and (1950), pp. 287f.; GINZBERG (1941), p. H: xci; *SAMUEL LOEWINGER, Qeta'im Ḥadashim MeŚefer Metivot, in: S. LOEWINGER, Genizah Publications in Memory of David Kaufmann (Budapest, 1949, Repr. Jerusalem, 1971), pp. 42—58, and the literature cited there; and MARGALIOTH (1962), pp. 9—11, 18—19.

R. Ḥananel (tenth century). PT is very frequently cited often to decide a *halakhah* in Ḥananel's running commentary-paraphrase of b., and these citations were used by many European scholars including the Tosafists. See B. RATNER, HaMelitz (1899), nos. 208, 212, 214, 215, 219, 220, especially 234; TCHERNOWITZ (1947), II, 4; and ABRAHAM Y. FRIEZLER, Yaḥaso shel Rabenu Ḥananel LiYerushalmi BePherush LeVabli, Niv HaMidrashiyah (1972—1973), pp. 126—134; and cf. MELAMMED (1943), pp. 65—66, 81.

R. Nissim (eleventh century). ABRAMSON (1965), who critically published and analyzed Nissim's works, indicates his great use of y., especially in the

'Megilat Śetarim', which provided or became a 'source' for y. for many later scholars (e.g., Alfasi, Aruch of Nathan, R. Tam). ABRAMSON collects and analyzes their citations, pp. 214—244. Nissim uses the introductory phrase *GMR' DBNY M'RB'*, "*Gemara* of the children of the West", and, occasionally, *TLMWD 'RṢ YSR'L*, "Talmud of the Land of Israel". See pp. iv—v, xxxvii, 12, 17—19, 186, 338f., and also LIEBERMAN (1947), p. xiv. Cf. MELAMMED (1943), pp. 66f, 81.

Isaac Alfasi (b. ca. 1013) Halakhot, frequently cites y., according to ABRAMSON, many of which are from R. Nissim, to explain BT or to derive laws not found in BT. He rejects explicit PT for an implication of the BT. As Alfasi became the main text of study in Spain, his citations were used by many other authorities; LIEBERMAN (1934), p. 267. See TCHERNOWITZ I (1946), pp. 140—149; B. Z. BENEDICT, Books and Fragments on Alfasi and his Method, KS 28 (1952), 210—232, and especially ID., R. Ephraim's Śefer HaTashlum on Alfasi, KS 26 (1950), 322—338, fn. 28; ABRAMSON (1965), pp. 214—222 [cf. RATNER, references under 'R. Ḥananel', to which add nos. 238, 240—242]. YAAQOV SPIEGEL, On the Identity of the Commentary Nemuqe Yosef on Rif's Halakhot, Sinai 37 (72) (1973), 222—227; MARGALIOTH (1973), pp. 40—43; and the very important SHAMMA FRIEDMAN, Introduction, to Halakhot Rabbati of R. Isaac Alfasi MS. JTSA Rab. 692, . . . Facsimile (Jerusalem, 1974), who reviews existings MSS, previous printed editions, their characteristics, and relevant scholarly literature.

Maimonides (Moses b. Maimon, Ramban). Maimonides widely used y. in several works, including the 'Commentary on Mishnah'; 'Śefer Miṣvot'; 'Mishneh Torah', and *Responsa*, while he practically makes it a subject of study in its own right in the Laws of the Palestinian Talmud, ed. SAUL LIEBERMAN (New York, 1947). LIEBERMAN's introduction, esp. pp. v, xv, and notes, in particular to the portion on Ketubot, demonstrate the work's importance for PT's elucidations. As to B. Z. BENEDICT's review, KS 27 (1952), 329—349, cf. BARON VI (1958), p. 370, fn. 100. See also TCHERNOWITZ I (1946), pp. 220—221, on his independent use of y., even as an equal authority to b.; MELAMMED (1973), pp. 522. Cf. H. Y. EHRENREICH, Ozar Hachaim 11 (1935), 152—164, and on the important new edition of the Commentary to the Mishnah, ed. YOSEF QAFIH, 7 vols. (Jerusalem, 1963—1968), see J. BLAU's incisive reviews, Leshonenu 30 (1966), 54—60; 31 (1967), 235—239; 32 (1968), 399—401; 35 (1970), 75—78, which indicates that while QAFIH's work is highly competent, he does not sufficiently use reference works, especially dictionaries, and, at times, is inaccurate when dealing with variant readings.

G. PT in Spain

MARGALIOTH (1962) reviews the role of y. in Spain.

Palestinian *gemara* and customs had first recognizable influence in the generation prior to that of Shmuel HaNagid. Shmuel HaNagid was the first to use y. His 'Hilkhata Gibarata', partially reconstructed by MARGALIOTH, has some twenty citations of y. (listed p. xiii), some of which are explained, and includes other matters based upon Palestinian customs. The work follows 'Metivot''s pattern and supplements BT decisions with related y. passages and Gaonic materials. According to MARGALIOTH, Shmuel learned y. from his master, R. Ḥanokh who (so MARGALIOTH) came from Italy. Shmuel set an example for Spanish scholars to employ independent judgement by comparing and evaluating sources. Remnants and the influence of his work may be found in those of Iṣḥaq ibn Giat; Judah of Barcelona, Śefer HaItim [see also his 'Book of Documents', ed. HALBERSTAM (Berlin, 1898, Repr. Jerusalem, 1967)]; Avraham b. Isaac Av Bet Din of Narbona, d. 1158 (Śefer HaEshqol, a collection of laws and customs, which fairly accurately preserves material from its sources); and Naḥmanides. See MARGALIOTH (1962), esp. pp. 13, 18f., 21f., 37—51; ABRAMSON (1965), pp. 227—231.

Solomon ben Adret of Barcelona (Rashba): Often cites y., especially in Piśqe Ḥallah (On laws of Ḥallah), ed. ISAKHAR D. BERGMAN (Jerusalem, 1970). Of note, the standard printed editions of *novellae* and *responsa* are abridged. Exemplary critical editions: H. ZALMON DIMITROVSKY, Novellae to Megillah (New York, 1956); ID., Rosh Hashanah (New York, 1961), ID., Responsa, 10 vols. (Jerusalem, in press). His citations often served as the source for Ritba and Meiri; LIEBERMAN (1934), p. 281. DIMITROVSKY (1956) traces how in general various medieval authorities cite from each other. See DIMITROVSKY (in press), vol. 10.

Yom Tob Ashbili: Often cites PT from Rashba; LIEBERMAN (1934), p. 281. In general he cites earlier authorities and then adds his own explanation. *Novellae* to any tractate, may contain passages from many locations, M. Y. BLAU, Commentary of . . . to B.B. (New York, 1954), II, 636—637. Mosad HaRav Kook, Jerusalem, is publishing a critical edition of this important commentary (1974).

Joseph HaLevi ibn Migas: ISRAEL TA-SHMAH, The Literary Work of. . ., KS 46 (1970—71), 136—153, 541—553, 47 (1972), 318—322.

Isaac ibn Giat: In 'Hilkhot Kelulot', he critically uses y.'s analogues to b. A remnant, on most of Mo'ed, arranged by subject, is in 'Sha're Simḥah', ed. ISḤAQ BAMBERGER (Fürth, 1861—62, Repr. Israel?, n.d.); MARGALIOTH (1962), pp. 37—40.

Naḥmanides: He clearly cites PT. On his methodology, see S. ABRAMSON, Kelale HaTalmud BeDivre HaRamban (Jerusalem, 1971), and cf. (1965), p. 233. A critical edition is in progress; ID., Makhon HaTalmud I (Jerusalem, 1970ff.).

H. PT in Provence

On the rabbinic and intellectual climate, see I. TWERSKY, Aspects of the Social and Cultural History of Provencal Jewry, Journal of World History 11 (1968) [Reprinted as Jewish Society Through the Ages, ed. H. BEN-

SASSON (New York, 1972)], pp. 185–207, and the literature cited there, especially TWERSKY (1962); and BENEDICT, LeToledotaw shel Merkaz HaTorah BeProvence, Tarbiẓ 22 (1951), 85–109; to which add ID., Contributions to a Compendium of Provence Jewish Scholars, KS 27 (1951), 237–248, 392.

R. Abraham b. David (Rabad) of Posquiers. In his commentaries to 'Sifra' and 'Mishnah' and glosses to 'Mishneh Torah', he extensively uses PT, compares its readings with other versions, and explains words, phrases, or entire passages; TWERSKY (1962), pp. 104, 107–108, 211. His pupil, R. Isaac Hakohen, apparently wrote the first commentary to y., now lost. See LIEBERMAN (1950), pp. 289–292.

Isaac b. Abba Maari: Śefer HaIttur (Repr. Jerusalem, 1970), frequently cites y., compares analogous though differing *sugyot* within y. LEWIN (1933), pp. xx, xxiii, isolates sixty citations from Metivot. See LIEBERMAN (1931), p. vii; ID., 'Addenda' to D. S. LOEWINGER's Article, Genizah Publications... Kaufmann 1 (1949), pp. 59–61.

R. Menaḥem HaMe'iri of Perpignan (d. ca. 1315): Beit HaBeḥirah, frequently cites y., at times from another authority, including Rashba; LIEBERMAN (1934), pp. 231, 281. He employs two introductory terminologies: *TLMWD HM'RB*, "the Western Talmud", which is not necessarily an exact quotation and, therefore, must be carefully evaluated, and, at times, *WNWŚḤ DBRYHM*, "and the reading of their words", or *BLŠWN ZH*, "in this language", which are used for exact citations in the original language and style; so ABRAHAM SCHREIBER [SOFER], Beit HaBeḥirah Maśekhet Avodah Zarah (Jerusalem, 1965²), p. x, and to Ketubot (Jerusalem, 1947), pp. xviii–xix. See S. MIRSKY, R. Menachem Hameiri. His Life, Teachings, and Works, Talpioth IV, 1–2 (1943), 42–90.

I. Northern France and Germany

Rashi (1040–1105): His several works, especially the commentary to BT, contain references to y., explicit and non-explicit, which some but not all scholars have identified with actual and direct citations from y. M. HIGGER, The Yerushalmi Quotations in Rashi, Rashi Anniversary Volume (New York, 1941), pp. 119–217, presents a long list in order of their occurrence in the respective works, with notes as to parallels. See also YOSEF HALEV, Yerushalayim 7 (1907), 370–376, citations to y. 'Temurah'; I. BROMBERG, Rashi and the Yerushalmi, Sinai 7–8, 11–12 (94–99) (1945), 62–72, 193–199, 277–290, and 17 (210) (1954), 165–169, 240–244; and especially URBACH (1955), p. 545, and fn. 33; DAVID WEISS HALIVNI, Al Rashi VeHa-Yerushalmi, HaDoar Year 34, vol. 35, no. 24 (April 29, 1955) (1585), pp. 473–474; BARON VI (1958), 346, fn. 57; and JONAH FRAENKEL, Darko Shel Rashi Beferusho LaTalmud HaBavli (Jerusalem, 1975). There are several compendia of rituals, customs, and liturgy attributed to Rashi and which come from his circle of students. They contain various citations of y.; e.g., 'Śiddur Rashi', 'Śepher HaPardeś', and 'Maḥzor Vitry'.

URBACH (1955), especially pp. 543ff, contra GINZBERG and APTOWITZER demonstrates the not infrequent use of y. among Franco-German Tosafists, led by R. Meir, R. Tam, and Rabiah. Important are not only the commentaries published in the editions of *gemara*, but also those in separate volumes. URBACH traces the presence and uses of y. in the various works. These include: to support an interpretation or to explain and analyze a b. pericope, in the process of which the y. may be explained. The Tosefists generally rely on BT to explain PT; the German ones tend to harmonize b. and y. to remove conflicts, while the French authorities often admit the conflicts. As to texts of y., they often had an incomplete corpus, or did not have the work at hand and cited from memory. They generally do not contain quotations to non-extant portions of y. though their references to y., at times, refer to Palestinian *Midrash-aggadah*. Particular use of y. is found in the works of Samson from Sens, especially his commentary to 'M. Zera'im' in which he systematically cites and explains the appropriate y. pericopae [see Section K], and in Yehudah b. Qalonymous (see below). See also URBACH, Sefer Arugat HaBosem of R. Abraham b. R. Azriel, IV, Introduction (Jerusalem, 1963), p. 157, 230—234, and the exemplary study of JOSE FAUR, Tosefot HaRosh LeMaśekhet Berakhot, PAAJR 33 (1965), 41—65.

Eliezer b. Nathan (RAbN) of Mainz: Even HaEzer, 2 vols. (Prague, 1610, Repr. N.Y., 1958), frequently cites y. and at times is a source for his grandson, Rabiah; LIEBERMAN (1934), pp. 395, 405, and TCHERNOWITZ II (1947), 46.

Eliezer b. Yoel HaLevi (mid 12th century): 'Śefer Rabiah', in two editions, V. APTOWITZER, incomplete critical edition with separate 'Introductio ad Sefer Rabiah' (Jerusalem, 1938), and second, revised reissued and completed edition by ELIJAH PRISMAN et al., 4 vols. (Jerusalem, 1965), with introduction. He very frequently cites y. and tries to harmonize it with BT; TCHERNOWITZ (1947), p. 54. APTOWITZER (1938), pp. 90, 93—95, 275—277, 468—472, traces the use of y. and employment of actual PT to several tractates and of 'Śefer Yerushalmi', a compilation that included PT and other materials. Thus part of the latter's references to y. may actually derive from such an addition. Moreover, he may present only the content and not the exact wording of y., and he may cite, as well, from Naḥmanides, or may call 'Tosefta', 'Yerushalmi'. See LIEBERMAN (1934), p. 151, 206—207, 405, 420.

Its citations of y. are significant in their own right and because the work served as the source for many authorities including Isaac b. Moses of Vienna, author of 'Or Zarua', MahRam of Routenberg, R. Asher (Rosh), Mordechai, author of 'Hagahot Maimoniot', and Jacob Asheri. On the use in Mordechai see LIEBERMAN (1934), pp. 412—413, and JOEL ROTH and MEIR RABBINOWITZ, Unpublished Ph.D. dissertations, JTSA, critical editions, with introduction, of Mordechai.

The first part of the work, in sequence of BT, presents and evaluates explanations of predecessors and comments in halakhic codes. The second part is made up of decisions and *responsa*. Thus one may consult BT in sequence for analogues to b. pericopae in addition to APTOWITZER's index (1938), pp. 468—472 (which also serves for the second edition, I—III, which maintains the same pagination). The new material in Vol. IV, which remains unindexed, concerns family law. Cf. LIEBERMAN (1934), p. 151; URBACH (1955); (1963), p. 157; ABRAMSON (1965), pp. 545f.

Eleazar b. Judah: 'Śefer Roqeaḥ' uses 'Śefer Yerushalmi'; LIEBERMAN (1929), pp. 36f., APTOWITZER (1938), p. 277, and URBACH (1955), p. 327, fn. 40. His 'Ma'aseh Roqeaḥ' abridges citations; LIEBERMAN (1934), p. 523, and URBACH (1955), pp. 331—334, especially as to the authorship.

Isaac b. Moses of Vienna (13th century): 'Or Zarua', a rearrangement of *gemara* by topic, constitutes an excellent source for y. citations and explanations. Isaac presents an exact citation of the portion which he needed, and often adds explanatory glosses. The work is in 4 vols. (Zhitomir, 1862, and Jerusalem, 1888—1890, Repr. in 2 vols., with additional fragment, New York, n.d.). See LIEBERMAN (1929), pp. 23f.; (1934), pp. 219, 282; and URBACH (1955), pp. 359—370.

Abraham b. R. Azriel: 'Sefer Arugot HaBosem' [Commentary on 'Piyyuṭim'], ed. by E. E. URBACH, 4 vols. (Jerusalem, 1939—1963), employs y., of which he had two texts; (1963), pp. 157, 230—234.

Moses of Quzy (13th century): 'Śefer Miṣvot Gadol', gives content of y., at times with explanations; LIEBERMAN (1929), pp. 23f.

Yehudah BeRebi Qalonymous of Spires: Yiḥuse Tannaim VeAmoraim', ed. YEHUDAH LEB HAKOHEN MAIMON (Jerusalem, 1963), an alphabetical biographical encyclopaedia that cites comments attributed to individual Talmudic rabbis, often from y. He had different texts (MSS) of y., many of which differ from the extant text. He also adds explanations of others or of his own. See pp. xvii, xxix, and URBACH (1955).

R. Meshullam: Commentary on 'Treatise Shekalim', ed. A. SCHREIBER (New York, 1954), thirteenth century. See Section IV.D; especially SCHREIBER's introduction, and LIEBERMAN (1950), pp. 295—297. E. URBACH, KS 31 (1956), 325—328 disputes the attribution and assigns the work to an earlier Tosefist.

A Disciple of R. Samuel Ben R. Sheneur of Evreux: Commentary on 'Treatise Shekalim', ed. A. SCHREIBER (New York, 1954). See LIEBERMAN (1950), pp. 298—300, and URBACH, op. cit.

Unidentified Commentary to y. Shev. Ch. VII. Unpublished JTSA MS, ADLER 3033, pp. 7—8. See S. ABRAMSON, On the 'Aruḳ of R. Naṭan, Leshonenu 36 (1972), 124.

J. Italy

Isaiah the Elder, of Terani, thirteenth century, and the Younger, fourteenth: Rulings of .... Critical edition, Makhon HaTalmud, Iff. (Jerusalem, 1964ff.).

K. Collections and Especially Notable Medieval Works

Here I include (1) Collections or Compilations and (2) Works which heavily draw on y. in particular areas, chiefly 'Zera'im'.

1. Collections, Compilations, and Medieval *midrashim*.

Shimeon HaDarshon (13th century): 'Yalqut Shimoni', the largest extant collection of Talmudic-Midrashic sources arranged on the Bible. It contains 199 references in the text and 256 in a special 'addendum', *quntraś*, which appears only in the first edition, in the collections of JELLINEK and EISENSTEIN, and in GINZBERG (1909); ARTHUR B. HYMAN, Meqorot Yalqut Shemeoni, 2 vols. (Jerusalem, 1974, 1975), I, x, xxv. HYMAN contains indexes to y. passages. LIEBERMAN, e.g., (1934), demonstrates the importance of the 'Yalqut' to the study of y. He, however, also notes that at times it did not directly use y., but rather an anthology-collection of y. *aggadot*, like that published in GINZBERG, Genizah Studies (1928), pp. 390ff. Further, we may learn from LIEBERMAN's comments concerning 'Śifre Zutta', SZ (1968), pp. 79f., that while 'Yalqut' does not add anything in the source's style, it apparently, at times, independently replaced and changed an unusual usage with a more common word or deleted difficult words that do not change the content. Moreover, MELAMMED (1943), pp. 68—70, 81f., points out in the process of citation and placement of the sources, 'Yalqut' may make some 'slight' changes or rearrangements. HYMAN reviews the editions and MSS of 'Yalqut'. Of note, the later editions are somewhat corrupt and the citations have often been 'corrected' on the basis of the printed editions of the cited work. LIEBERMAN, SZ (1968), p. 120, fn. 149, notes that the phenomenon earlier demonstrated, as cited above, is especially true in the printed editions. It is therefore important to use the first edition, Salonica, 1501, 1506—07 (Repr. Jerusalem, 1968, 1973), and an Oxford MS, both of which are employed in a new critical edition, ed. HYMAN, LERRER, SHILONE, Iff. (Jerusalem, 1973ff.). See also MORDECHAI MARGULIES [MARGALIOTH], Midrash HaGgadol on the Pentateuch, Genesis (Jerusalem, 1947, 1957²), p. 6, and AARON GREENBAUM, Sinai 76 (1975), 120—133, especially 121, 132.

R. David b. R. Amram of Eden, Midrash HaGgadol, to 'Genesis', ed. M. MARGULIES [MARGALIOTH] (Jerusalem, 1947, 1967²); to 'Exodus', ed. M. MARGULIES [MARGALIOTH] (Jerusalem, 1947, 1967²); to 'Leviticus', ed. E. N. RABINOWITZ (New York, 1932), and ed. STEINSALTZ (Jerusalem, 1976); to 'Numbers', ed. Z. M. RABINOWITZ (Jerusalem, 1967); to 'Deuteronomy', ed. SOLOMON FISCH (Jerusalem, 1972). This fourteenth-century Yemenite midrashic compilation lifts from various sources materials associated with biblical verses and arranges them according to the sequence in the Pentateuch. Occasionally it draws on y. The author combines, rearranges, adds, deletes, and glosses explanations. One must thus carefully examine his references. In particular, he freely constructs the formal arrangement and combination of the sources, formulates materials on the basis of Maimonides, though according to MARGALIOTH, to 'Exodus',

p. 6, he does not change the text of the citation. LIEBERMAN, SZ (1968), p. 79, agrees that difficult words are not replaced or corrupted. On the other hand, Z. M. RABINOWITZ, to 'Numbers', p. xi, found that he changed y. readings, revised them according to b. Aramaic, terminology, forms of names of scholars, language and style, as well as glossed explanations and interpolated at the end or cut off in the middle. Cf. MELAMMED (1943), pp. 70f. See LIEBERMAN, Yemenite Midrashim (Jerusalem, 1940, 1970[2]), p. 6, and especially MOSHE ZUCKER, Pentateuchal Exegeses of Saadia Gaon and Samuel ben Chofni Incorporated into the Midrash HaGadol, Abraham Weiss Jubilee Volume (New York, 1964), Hebrew Section, pp. 461—462, and fn. 4. On the authorship, see RABINOWITZ to 'Numbers', p. v, fn. 1.

R. Israel ibn al-Nakawa, Menorat Ha-Maor, 4 vols., ed. H. G. ENELOW (New York, 1929—32, Repr. Jerusalem, 1972), an ethical-aggadic compilation. Vol. 4, index, s.v. Talmud, Yerushalmi, lists entries by tractates.

The Mishnah of Rabbi Eliezer or the Midrash of Thirty-Two Hermeneutic Rules, ed. H. G. ENELOW (New York, 1933, Repr. Jerusalem, 1970), a collection of exegetical canons composed by Shmuel b. Ḥofni, a late Suran Gaon. See BARON VI (1958), 406, and especially M. ZUCKER, PAAJR 25 (1956), Hebrew pp. 1ff., pp. 20f. on ENELOW's edition, and fn. 6, there, on the complete free use and alteration of sources. The numerous references to y. are indexed on pp. 390 and 394.

R. Machir bar Abba Mari, Yalqut Makhiri, a ca. fourteenth century collection of talmudic and midrashic sources, to Isaiah, ed. Y. SPIRA (Berlin, 1894), on Proverbs [chs. 18—31], ed. L. GRUENHUT (Jerusalem, 1902), reprinted together (Jerusalem, 1964); on Psalms, ed. S. BUBER (Berdychev, 1899, Repr. Jerusalem, 1964); on Twelve Minor Prophets, ed. ALBERT W. GREENUP, 2 vols. (London, 1909—13, Repr. Jerusalem, 1967); and additions to Proverbs (parts of chs. 2, 3, 14), ed. ISAAC BERDEHAV (Jerusalem, 1927), and to Hosea (1 : 1—14 : 1), ed. A.W. GREENUP, JQR, N.S. 15 (1924—25), 141—212, both republished together as 'Supplement (Hashlamah)' to Hosea and Proverbs (Jerusalem, 1968). Its literal citations of sources are extremely important for textual readings. Wherever a y. pericope contains a verse in toto it is likely to be cited in the 'Yalqut'. Of note, the edition to Proverbs, p.v., contains a list of y. passages. See H. ALBECK, in L. ZUNZ, supplemented Hebrew translation, HaDrashot BeYisrael (Jerusalem, 1954), p. 415, n. 45; GREENUP's Introduction to 'Zephania, Haggai, and Malachi' (London, 1913), and to the Hosea additions, pp. 141—145; LIEBERMAN (1934), p. 72; and MARGALIOTH, Midrash HaGgadol to Genesis (Jerusalem, 1947, 1967[2]), pp. vi—vii.

R. Samuel be Nissin from Senuth (12th century), Majan-Gannim, Commentary on Job, ed. SOLOMON BUBER (Berlin, 1889, Repr. Jerusalem, 1970), cites many expositions and materials from y. and is thus like a *midrash* on Job, pp. xii—xiv. Wherever y. uses a verse from Job it is thus worth consulting the Commentary, ad loc.

Batei Midrashot, ed. SHLOMO AHARON WERTHEIMER and ABRAHAM JOSEPH WERTHEIMER (Jerusalem, 1968[2]), a collection of various medieval brief *midrashim*, many of which cite y.; index II, 535. See J. TOWNSEND, Minor Midrashim, in: Anti-Defamation League of B'nai B'rith, Bibliographical Essays in Medieval Jewish Studies: The Study of Judaism, II (New York, 1976).

R. Moseh HaDarshon, Midrash Beresit Rabbati, ed. CHANOCH ALBECK (Jerusalem, 1940, Repr. 1967), various citations, though not exact: combined passages, added items, or only presented the content, p. xxi.

2. Other Especially Notable Works:

Raymond Martini, Pugio Fidei, adversus Mauros et Judaeos (JOHANNES BENEDICTUS CARPZOVUS: Lipsia, 1687, Repr. Gregg, 1967 [1968]), a medieval polemic against Judaism, cites y. passages with Latin translation. See SAUL LIEBERMAN, Shkiin (Jerusalem, 1939, 1970²), pp. 76—77, a list of references, "though they have little value as to the reading of the y." and 89; ID., Texts and Studies (1974), pp. 285—300, especially pp. 293 and 294 [reprinted from Historia Judaica 5 (1943), 88—102, 95—96]; YIṢḤAQ BAER, Hamidrashim Hamezuyafim shel Raymondus Martini UMeqomom Bamilḥemet HaDat shel Yeme HaBenayim, in: Studies in Memory of Asher Gulak and Samuel Klein (Jerusalem, 1942), pp. 28—49, who discusses the passages; and for further literature, REUVEN BONFIL, The Nature of Judaism in Raymundus Martini's *Pugio Fidei*, Tarbiẓ 40 (1971), 360—375, especially pp. 360f., fn. 3, 5. See now C. MERHAVYA, The Hebrew Versions of Pugio Fidei in the Sainte Geneviene MS, KS 51 (1976), 283—288.

Several commentaries to 'M. Zera'im' heavily draw from y. 'Zera'im', as the tractates lack a Babylonian *gemara*. See TWERSKY (1962), pp.107—109; CHANOCH ALBECK, Introduction to the Mishna (1967³), pp. 245—249; and JOEL H. ZAIMAN, The Traditional Study of the Mishnah, in: The Modern Study of the Mishnah, ed JACOB NEUSNER (Leiden, 1973), pp. 5—6; and APTOWITZER (1938), to the named individuals. These include:

Isaac b. Malkiṣedeq of Siponto (first half of 12th century), in his 'Commentary to Mishnah Zera'im', contains numerous citations of y., which many later authorities, e.g., Rashi, Sens, and Meiri, used. He tends to emend his citations. See LIEBERMAN, Tosefeth Rishonim IV (Jerusalem, 1939), pp. xviii—xxi, and ID. (1955), II, 803, fn. 1. Critical annotated edition: NISSAN SACHS (Jerusalem: Yad HaRav Herzog, 1975), based on MSS (Oxford, 392, London OR 6712, but not a third one, JTSA 1304). It was previously available to the end of Bik., in Venice 1522 edition of BT, and to all tractates, in Vilna Romm edition. See the introduction for a list of previous (partial) critical editions; KALMAN KAHANA, ed., Maśekhet Shevi'it, Ḥeqer VeIyyun (Bene Brak, 1972), pp. ii—iii; and especially ISAAC GOTTLIEB, Perush HRYBMṢ, Sinai 39 (77) (1975), 98—109, especially 105f., which demonstrates the importance of evaluating his citations of y. Cf. URBACH (1955), pp. 253f., and BOKSER (1975), passim.

Samson b. Abraham of Sens (ca. 1150—1230), one of the Tosafists. In his 'Commentary to M. Zera'im', in b. editions since Venice, 1522, he presents virtually an analytical commentary on the y. portions that deal with M. He systematically cites and then explains all relevant y. material and compares a *sugya* with its analogues or parallels elsewhere in y. and in b., and its sources with *baraitot* in 'Tosefta' and other works. He, however, does not always exactly cite a source. He employed more than one text of y. and on the basis of an alternative reading, parallel pericopae, and analysis, corrected the text of y. See LIEBERMAN, Tosefeth Rishonim IV (Jerusalem, 1939), pp. xvi—xvii; URBACH (1955), pp. 248, 250f., 253; and KAHANA (1972), pp. i, iii—ix, xii, who emphasized the importance of MS Paris Sorbonne Hebr. 362, which he publishes on Shevicjt, and which is the basis for a new edition, in progress, at Yad HaRav Herzog.

Asher b. Yeḥiel (1250—1328), in his Commentary to M. Zera'im, cites y. The work was first published, in part, in Amsterdam, 1715 ed. of BT, and, in full, Śefer Pi Shenayyim (Altona, 1735) which was reprinted (Bene Brak, 1966/67) with variants from MSS.

Elijah of London (13th century), Commentary to M. Zera'im and Decisions, published in 'The Writings of Rabbi Elijah of London', ed. M. Y. S. SACKS (Jerusalem, 1956), is interspersed with references from y.

XX. Commentaries and Works on Yerushalmi. B: Sixteenth Century On

A. Until the Vilna Gaon

I review both actual commentaries to y. and other works which regularly contain comments or citations of y. FRANKEL (1870), GINZBERG (1941), and MELAMMED (1973), pp. 525—534 (which is most useful when it adds material not found in GINZBERG), review the individuals and provide some characteristics of their work. Editions are listed in: STRACK (1931), pp. 83 and 149; JUDAH RUBINSTEIN, Quntraś HaShalem shel Mefarshe HaYerushalmi [A Complete List (whith author index) of Commentaries to Yerushalmi], (New York, 1949) [published as a supplement to SHULSINGER: New York, 1949, one volume edition of 'Talmud Yerushalmi'] — while not complete, includes most works, among which are items which only tangentially deal with or explain sections of y.; and KOHN (1952). LIEBERMAN (1934), Introduction, and especially (1950) provide a systematic analysis of the important works, those preserved as well as non-extant. As I need not duplicate their efforts, I assume those references and confine myself to a few comments and only cite one of the above for specific critical observations.

YOSEF CORCOS, Commentary on Maimonides' Mishneh Torah, Śefer Zera'im, frequently cites and analyzes y. passages. The commentary appeared in Izmir, 1757, in the SHULSINGER edition of 'Mishneh Torah' (New York, 1957), and in sections, in DINGLAS' edition of SOLOMON SIRILLO (Jerusalem, 1934—67).

Y'AQOV IBN HABIV (ca. 1460—1510), Ein Y'aqov (first ed., Salonica, 1516—1522, with many subsequent editions, some with various commentaries), a collection of *aggadot* from BT and some from PT. According to LIEBERMAN (1950), p. 312, fn. 152, he did not employ MSS of y. LIEBERMAN (1934), xxvii—xxviii, 21, 71, 72, notes that it yet preserves some good readings, though those in the present published editions are corrupt so that one cannot recognize the early text. Moreover, it used an antholog-compendium of *midrash-aggadah* and not necessarily (always ?) the PT itself. Cf. GINZBERG (1941), p. H: cviii.

SOLOMON SIRILLO, Commentary to y. Zera'im and Sheqalim (ca. 1530), "one of the best commentaries to y." See LIEBERMAN (1950), pp. 301—302, and above, Section IV.C, for editions and the remaining literature.

YOSEF QARO, Commentary, Kesef Mishneh, to Maimonides' 'Mishneh Torah', cites y., especially on 'Zera'im', and had various y. MSS; LIEBERMAN (1950), p. 313, fn. 157.

MOSEH PIZANTI (1514—1573), 'Commentary to y. Zera'im', only extant in citations in his other work, 'Ner Miṣvah' (Constantinople, 1567) and citations of others; LIEBERMAN (1950), 302—303.

ELEAZAR AZIKRI (1553—1600, Safed), 'Commentary to y. Berakhot', in: Zhitomire, 1860, ed. of PT and reprints; to 'Beṣah', in: ISRAEL FRANCUS, ed. and intro., Talmud Yerushalmi: Maśekhet Beṣah (New York, 1967); and to y. 'Pe'ah', 'Demai', 'Terumot', and 'Pesaḥim', only extant in citations of 'Melekhet Shlomo' of SOLOMON AEDENI. LIEBERMAN (1934), pp. xxvii, 410, and (1950), pp. 304—313, provides a full introduction, which FRANCUS (1967) reproduces with additions, pp. 42—43, as well as a careful analysis of the commentary's characteristics, pp. 53—61.

SAMUEL YAFEH ASHKENAZI, Yefeh Mareh (Venice, 1590), collection of aggadic portions of y. with an extensive commentary. See M. BENAYAHU, R. Samuel Yaffe Ashkenazi and Other Commentators of Midrash Rabba, Tarbiẓ 42 (1973), 419—460, especially 428—430, 444—452, a survey of the various later editions, and excellent observations on the work's characteristics. ASHKENAZI did not employ MSS to PT; LIEBERMAN (1950), pp. 312, fn. 152, 317. Cf. GINZBERG (1941), p. H: cviii. The portion on 'Zera'im' was repeatedly and separately republished, e.g., as 'Aggadot Yerushalmi' (Vilna, 1863), as 'Sefer Ein Yaaqov', ed. ISRAEL SHAPIRO [Warsaw, 1898, Repr. in 'Yerushalmi Zera'im', (Jerusalem, 1972)], and as '(Kol) Aggadot Yerushalmi' (Jerusalem, 1899, Repr. 1964—65). See BENAYAHU, pp. 429f.

SOLOMON AEDENI, 'Melekhet Shelomo', in Venice Romm edition of 'Mishnah' and its reprints. See A. MARX, The Romm Mishnah, JQR 2 (1911—12), 266—270, especially 267—270. The author often cites y. with explanations of 'Rishonim' or of his own, and uses MSS of y. whose variants he notes; LIEBERMAN (1934), pp. xxvii, 128, 129, 155, 367; SZ (1968), p. 100. In general, see E. Z. MELAMMED, Melekhet Shelomo of R. Shelomoh Aedeni, Sinai, vol. 22 (year 44), #5—6 (267—268) (1959), 346—363; and ALBECK (1967), p. 252. KAHANA (1972), p. iii, fn. 6, points to his 'Notes to Śeder Zera'im', a Brit. Mus. MS OR. 5014; see G. MARGALIOUTH, Catalogue of the Hebrew and Samaritan Manuscripts in the British Museum II (London, 1905, 1965), pp. 65—66.

DAVID DARSHAN, author of a brief commentary published in Crocow (1610) edition of y. See LIEBERMAN (1934), p. viii, fn. 1, and especially MELAMMED (1973), pp. 527f.

JOSHUA BENVENISTI (1590?—1665?), Shedeh Yehoshua, A "diffusive and discursive" commentary to I, 'Zera'im' (Ber., 'Peah', 'Hallah, Orlah', 'Bikkurim'), (Constantinople, 1662), reprinted in: Yerushalmi Zera'im (Jerusalem, 1972), II—IV, 'Mo'ed', 'Nashim', and 'Neziqin', parts (Constantinople, 1749), abridged reprint to 'Neziqin', in: Hashlamah LiYerushalmi (= Supplement Volume to Vilna Romm edition, and reprints). See GINZBERG (1941), pp. H: cvxiii—cxix and especially EJ 4: 561f., for a concise description of the commentary's characteristics. The author had only the MS with commentary of SIRILLO; LIEBERMAN (1950), pp. 312, fn. 152, 317.

ELIJAH BEN LOEB FOULDA OF WIZNICIA (Poland, ca. 1650/60—1720), author of an edition with a terse commentary along with separate more lengthy selected notes to y. ,'Zera'im' and Sheq. (Amsterdam, 1710, Repr. Jerusalem, 1971), and B. Q., B. M., and B. B. (Offenbach and Frankfurt, 1725, 1742, Repr. in: HaShlamah LiYerushalmi, Supplement to Romm ed.). GINZBERG (1941), pp. H: cxxi—cxxiii, and especially JACOB HABERMAN, s.v., EJ 6, 648, provide concise descriptions of the work's characteristics. It greatly influenced the study of y. in Germany. LIEBERMAN (1950), pp. 317—318, proves that he did not make use of MSS. His emendations, rather, are based on his own reason, speculation, and readings and interpretations in earlier commentaries, including JOSHUA BENVENISTI.

DAVID OPPENHEIM, of Bohemia (1664—1736), marginal notes to y. (and Foulda), published in Vilna Romm ed.

DAVID FRANKEL of Berlin (1707—1762), author of one of the two basic commentaries to y. (see M. MARGALIOTH, next item), to tractates not covered by Foulda (plus Sheq.), 'Qorban HaEdah', a running commentary that elucidates the text, and 'Shire Qorban', *novellae* reconciling contradiction in *gemara*, textual emendations, with some attention to historical problems, both published in Dessau, 1742, and Berlin, 1757, 1760—62. 'Mo'ed' and 'Nashim' reprinted in Zhitomire ed. and to which 'Neziqin' was added in the Romm Vilna ed. See GINZBERG (1941), p. H: cxxiv, and especially MELAMMED (1973), pp. 528f., and ALEXANDER ALTMANN, Moses Mendelssohn (University, Alabama, and Philadelphia, 1973), pp. 12—13, 180, and fn. 31.

MOSES MARGALIOTH (d. 1780), Pene Moshe, a running commentary, and Mareh HaPannim, additions; in part, Amsterdam and Leghorn, 1754 and 1770, and in full, Zhitomire and subsequent editions. This basic commentary to the entire y. includes textual emendations, draws on spectrum of Talmudic literature, especially 'Tosefta', though at times still follows the practice of introducing b. concepts and issues. The commentaries of FRANKEL and MARGALIOTH provide the pattern for all subsequent work: GINZBERG (1941), pp.lvi—lvii, H: cxxxiv—cxxxv; LIEBERMAN (1934), p. vii, (1950), pp. 318f., and MELAMMED (1973), pp. 529—530.

ELIJAH, Gaon of Vilna (GRA), produced vital explanations and notes to PT; he interprets a text in its own terms and frequently offers incisive emendations. They are preserved or embedded in his works and those of his students. These include (1) 'Commentary to Shulḥan Arukh', published from an autographed MS; systematically cites y.; (2) 'Shenot Eliyahu', to 'M. Zera'im', published in his lifetime (and variously republished, including Romm 'Mishnah'); (3) 'Commentary to y. Zera'im', in Vilna ed., 1926, in two versions (produced by students); (4) 'Emendations and notes to Śeder Zera'im'; (5) embedded in ISRAEL OF SHKLOV, Taklin Ḥadtin, 'Commentary to y. Sheq'. (Minsk, 1812); (6), cited in ISRAEL OF SHKLOV, Pe'at HaShulḥan (Safed, 1834), from which Ridbaz (in Romm ed. of y.) at times quotes. See GINZBERG (1941), pp. lvii—lx, H: cxxv—cxxx; TCHERNOWITZ III (1947), pp. 212—216; and especially KALMAN KAHANA, LeḤeqer Be'ure HaGRA LiYerushalmi ULeTosefta (Tel Aviv, 1957), esp. pp. 9f., 32—44, and 54—61, which focuses on the texts used by the GRA, MSS and texts used in the printing of his commentaries, and the relationships between different works and editions; and YEHUDAH LEIB MAIMON, Toldot HaGRA (Jerusalem, 1970), especially pp. 176—200 and 252; and SIMEON KOHEN, R. Yosef Qaro, ed. IṢḤAQ RAFAEL (Jerusalem, 1969), pp. 258—290, on the 'Commentary to the Shulḥan Arukh'. Cf. I. JOEL, A Collection of Hebrew MSS from the Romm Press, KS 13 (1937), 520f., on texts and MSS used in the printed editions; and JACOB DINSTAG, R. Elijah of Vilna — Bibliographical List, Talpiot 4 (1959).

B. Nineteenth and Twentieth Centuries: Traditional and Pre-Modern

I now turn to works from the nineteenth and twentieth centuries. The bibliographical lists and works earlier cited also deal with these materials and accordingly I cite only important or representative works or those for which I wish to indicate important secondary literature. I further have expanded my criterion for works published since the nineteen-fifties, as they are not included in the several bibliographies. I separately treat those items which systematically employ MSS or other 'modern scientific' methods, C. This is an arbitrary criterion, for many of the 'traditional' works are highly sophisticated. The former items, however, consciously and systematically make use of the results of the latter group, usually respond to different series of exegetical and historical questions, and, therefore, differently perceive their task and method.

*HIRSCH MENDEL PINELIS, Darkhah Shel Torah (Vienne, 1861, Repr. Jerusalem, n. d. [1968?]), series of critical analyses of *gemara*. See WEISS HALIVNI (1968), p. xii, fn. 2, and JOEL GEREBOFF, Hirsch Mendel Pineles: The First Critical Exegete, The Modern Study of the Mishnah, ed. J. NEUSNER (Leiden, 1973), pp. 90—104.

*MEIR MARIM of Kobrin (d. 1873), Śefer Nir, Zera'im (Warsaw, 1875, Repr. with Foulda, Jerusalem, 1971); ID., Mo'ed (Vilna, 1890), excellent incisive commentary, which is aware of the deplacement of materials within the text. Often, though, it is overly elliptical while suggesting several alternative explanations. See LIEBERMAN (1934), pp. vii, and e. g., 11, fn. 1, 53, 66, 76, 82, 157, 229f., 297; and GINZBERG (1941), p. cxxxi.

DOB BERISH ASHKENAZI, Shaare Yerushalmi (Warsaw, 1866).

*JOSHUA ISAAK SHAPIRO of Slonim (1801—1873), Noam Yerushalmi, 4 vols. (Vilna, 1863 and 1869, Repr. in 2 vols., Jerusalem, 1968), excursive and lengthy commentary that often contains insightful comments. It compares b. and y. *sugyot*, points out differences, and refers to relevant pericopae elsewhere in both b. and y. See LIEBERMAN (1934), pp. viii, 80f. It is digested in EFRAYIM DOV HAKOHEN LOF in Gilyone Efrayim, in Vilna ed.

A. KROCHMAL, Yerushalayim HaBenuyah (Lemberg, 1867, Repr. Jerusalem, 1971), on selected passages of y. Ber. to San. with an introduction on the date of y.'s compilation.

ZECHARIAH FRANKEL, Ahavat Ṣion, Talmud Yerushalmi, I: Ber. and Pe'ah (Vienne, 1874, Repr. Jerusalem, 1971); II: Demai (Breslau, 1875), to republished Venice, p. e. text, he adds a brief commentary, with occasional longer notes.

JACOB DAVID of Slotz, 'Perush HaRidbaz', in Vilna Romm ed., contains illuminating explanations, especially on 'Zera'im' and tractate 'Yevamot'; LIEBERMAN (1934), p. viii.

JOSEF H. DUENNER, Commentaries (Hagahot) (Frankfurt am Main, 1897—1923); critical commentary, especially as to flow of materials, and their placement within *gemara*, though insufficiently used 'Rishonim'; WEISS HALIVNI (1968), p. xii, fn. 13.

*ARYEH LEIB YELLIN, 'Yefeh Enayim', published in back of Romm, Vilna b., cites y. and often critically analyzes y. pericopae relevant to b. See LIEBERMAN (1934), p. 226, and RIVKA ZISKIND, Rabbi Aryeh Loeb Yellin Author of 'Yefeh Einayim' (Jerusalem, 1973), especially pp. 21, fn. 30, 63—103, 114—118. For supplements see KANEVSKI, below.

M. S. SIVITZ, Śefer Mashbiaḥ (Jerusalem, 1913, and St. Louis, 1918, Jerusalem, 1929[3]) includes a commentary and a list of words and terms peculiar to y. See RABINOVITZ (1940), pp. 629—634.

*JOSEPH ENGEL, Giljonei HaSchass [on b. and y. Zer.-Neziqin] (Vienne, 1924, and 1929, Repr., n. p., n. d. [Israel, 1972?], and on y. 'Zera'im', in: Yerushalmi Zera'im [Jerusalem, 1972]), of great importance, especially for references to other passages in y. and b. which throw light on a given pericope, and for its citation of medieval authorities.

*ḤAYYIM DAICHES, Netivot Yerushalayim, to 'Neziqin', 3 vols. (Vilna, 1900, London, 1926—27), to y. 'Neziqin', combines depth, erudition, critical sense, and resource to 'Rishonim'; LIEBERMAN (1934), p. vii.

*'Hashlamah LiYerushalmi' (Romm: Vilna, 1928), reprint of numerous important commentaries, variously republished, including as 'Shiṭah Mequbeṣet al Yerushalmi' (Jerusalem, 1971).

DOV MALACHI ENGLENDER, Zehav Ha'Areṣ, I: Ber. Pe'ah, Dem. (Jerusalem, 1944), San. Shev., Mak. (Jerusalem, 1960), lucid explanations of many selected passages, draws on 'Rishonim' and pays attention to the readings of y. upon which their comments are based, and takes account of the peculiar language of y.

SAMUEL ISAAC HILLMANN, Or HaYashar, I: Zer. and Mo'ed; II: Nashim and Neziqin (Jerusalem, 1947 and 1948).

Mayyim Efrayim (Boston, 1951).

MORDECHAI SAVITSKY, Mareh Esh (Brooklyn, 1956), on 'Sheqalim'.

JOSEPH ROSEN, Ṣafnat Paneaḥ, 3 vols. (Jerusalem, 1959, 1962), on 'Neziqin'.

ḤAYIM KANEVSKI, Tashlum Yefeh Enayim, in: El HaMekorot edition of Vilna Babylonian Talmud (Tel Aviv, 1959), and with additions and corrections in ḤAYIM KANEVSKI, Siaḥ HaSadeh (Bene Brak, 1969), pp. 45a—59b.

SHELOMOH GOREN, HaYerushalmi HaMeforosh Berakhot (Jerusalem, 1961), projected as a critical edition based on MSS, Geniza fragments, collation of 'Rishonim', and other works with a new commentary. It heavily draws on GINZBERG (1941, 1961) and LIEBERMAN (1947) and (1955) without however giving proper credit. (And this is so even where GINZBERG errs.) The commentary does not capture Palestinian usage, and still has a tendency to introduce concerns not inherent in the text. Moreover, he lets 'Rishonim' set the exegetical alternatives; A. GOLDBERG, KS 38 (1963), 195—202. On the other hand, at times his comments are of interest and his apparatus helpful, but hardly definitive. His arrangement, though, is an attempt at providing a manageable format for the relevant materials.

ARYEH POMERANCHIK, Torat Zera'im (Tel Aviv, 196?), *novellae* to y. 'Zera'im'.

YOSEF SEVI AARONSON, ed., Maśekhet Sheqalim min Talmud Yerushalmi VeHaTosefta (Jerusalem, 1964); ID., Pe'ah, Dem., Kil., Shev. (Jerusalem, 1972,) includes various commentaries and the editor's running comments based upon earlier authorities.

ISRAEL FAJGENBAUM, Śefer Yad VeShem, II: y. Pe'ah, Shevi'it (Petaḥ Tikvah, 1966), *novellae* and notes.

MOSHEH LEITER, Beshuleh Gilyone (Jerusalem, 1967), 724 pp. of brief, and occasionally long, notes to y.

ELIYAHU SCHLESINGER, Yad Eliyahu, I: Yerushalmi-Zera'im (Jerusalem, 1971), especially useful for references to similar phrases and usages elsewhere in *gemara*.

ABRAHAM KARLITZ, Ḥazon Ish. Zera'im (Bene Brak, 1973), on Dem., Kel., Shev., Maas., and Orl.

C. Modern Works

I herein include those who consciously employ critical analysis. Aspects of these methods appear in items above or other works, e. g., in different ways, GRA, DUENNUR, PINELIS, and MEIR MARIM. But the following works have tried to take account of the ways in which y. is put together, the history of its text, as well as to some degree general historical and philological considerations, and, at times, literary matters. Where a work still lacks or insufficiently treats one of these matters, the sensitized reader may appropriately revise it. Unfortunately, however, the exegetical and other comments are done in passing, left embedded within the commentary, or are within an article on individual passages. Thus other than brief comments, e. g., the quite different remarks by GINZBERG (1941), pp. H: lxx—lxxx, FRANCUS, Talmud Yerushalmi, Maśekhet Beṣah (New York, 1967), Introduction, and M. S. FELDBLUM. Talmudic Law and Literature, Tractate Gittin (New York, 1969), pp. 37—42, a study to date has not undertaken historical-literary analysis so as to describe systematically and fully the contents of a y. tractate as a whole. NEUSNER, Purities (1974—77), on a different genre of materials, provides one model of what such a commentary could be like. See also he comments by GOODBLATT (1979), IV. 1: c and V. 2, the last two paragraphs.

I do not include the various works which from a specific perspective or discipline, whether, e. g., history, agriculture, or liturgy, explain or deal with y. The items in Chapter XVII provide examples of these approaches. See, as well, Chapters XIII, XIV, and XVIII.

A. M. LUNCZ, Talmud Hieroselymitanum Ad Exemplarin Editiones Principis, I—V (Jerusalem, 1907—1919), text and commentary to y. Ber.-Shev. See Ch. III, above.

ISRAEL LEWY, Commentary to B. Q. I—VI, Jahresbericht des jüdisch-theologischen Seminars (1895—1914, Repr. Jerusalem, 1970), an example of what a critical work can be. See above, Section XII. 3, and E. URBACH, Zechariah Frankel, Israel Lewy, Saul Horowitz, Three Professors of Talmud of the Breslau Seminary, in: Das Breslauer Seminar, The Breslau Seminary, Memorial Volume, ed. G. KISCH (Tübingen, 1963), pp. 177—182.

B. RATNER, Ahawath Zion We-Jerusholaim, 12 vols. (Vilna, 1901—1917, Repr. Jerusalem, 1967), on Ber., Zer.-Mo'ed (less Eruv.), in addition to textual notes includes explanations and comments. See above, Ch. IV. A, and V. 1, and note the list of review-studies by W. BACHER, S. BUBER, S. POZNANSKI, and V. APTOWITZER.

ḤAYYIM HELLER, Concerning a Cross-Reference Index to Yerushalmi, in: Festschrift zum siebzigsten Geburtstage David Hoffmanns, ed. S. EPPENSTEIN (Berlin, 1924), Hebrew section, pp. 55—66; ID., HaM'alot Leshlomon. A Cross-Index and Notes to y. Ter., in: Festschrift zum Vierzigjährigen Amtsjubiläum Dr. Salomon Carlebach, ed. MORITZ STERN (Berlin, 1910), Hebrew section, pp. 246—249. [Reprinted together as 'Shene Quntreśim (Berlin, 1929).]

Z. W. RABINOVITZ (1940), with indexes, incisive notes, comments, and emendations to all of y., employs both early rabbinic works and modern scientific literature available to him, focuses on usage and style of y., and deals with issues stemming from the composition of the text. See the comprehensive review, G. ALON, Tarbiẓ 12 (1940), 88—95.

J. N. EPSTEIN, virtually all his works, especially (1948, 1964²) (1957), and (1962), and, e. g., ID., Owni ('WNY—'NTYKRYS), (y. Git. 4, 46a), Tarbiẓ 8 (1937), 316—318. See the indexed bibliography in Tarbiẓ 20 (1950) — "The father of the study of careful Talmudic scholarship", LIEBERMAN, SZ (1968), p. 135.

GINZBERG, 4 vols. (1941—1961), a voluminous commentary ostensibly to y. Ber. chs. I—V, which analyzes each item in terms of its history in rabbinic literature. It cites medieval authorities and readings from MSS and geniza fragments, pays close attention to y.'s style and terminology, and is invaluable for textual and exegetical purposes. The exposition, though, lacks discipline and systematic arrangement and the comments, at times, have a slight tendency to introduce novel interpretations. One should systematically compare the material to that contained in LIEBERMAN, TK I (1955), on 'Berakhot', which explicitly or without so indicating clarifies, or disagrees, with GINZBERG, or explicitly confirms his suggestions. Moreover, HEINEMANN's research undermines certain aspects of GINZBERG's attempted historical analysis of liturgical matters. See the reviews of A. WEISS, Jewish Social Studies 5 (1943), 70—73, and A. GOLDBERG, KS 38 (1963), 195—202, and MELAMMED (1973), pp. 533f. For his other works, see the 'Bibliography', Louis Ginzberg Jubilee Volume, ed. S. LIEBERMAN, et al. (New York, 1945), English section, pp. 19—47.

SAUL LIEBERMAN, virtually all his works, especially (1934), a commentary along his programatic lines to y. Shab., Eruv., and Pes. [cf. H. Y. EHRENREICH, Ozar Hachaim 11 (1935), 85—86, 90—91, 175], (1947) to Ber. and Ket., in which his notes to Maimonides' text actually constitute a commentary in their own right; ID., Tosefeth Rishonim 4 vols. (Jerusalem, 1937—39), to the whole of Tosefta, and TK Iff. (1955ff.) (presently, I—VIII, through the end of 'Nashim'), on which he analyzes practically every y. passage which cites or relates to 'Tosefta'. The indexes to y. passages and usages, vols. II, V, VII, VIII refer to only a fraction of the entries. 'Tosefta' may provide the key to the interpretation of y. as the former often reflects the tradition or approach of Palestine, vis-à-vis that of Babylonia; pp. I: xx, xxi, V: xvii; to which cp. III: xiv. For his other works, see the bibliography, T. PRESCHEL, Dr. Saul Lieberman and his Contribution to Jewish Scholarship, reprint from Hadoar 43, no. 23 (New York 1963); to which add (items not earlier cited): ID., Forgotten Meanings, Tarbiẓ 23 (1967—68), 89—102, and ID., Interpretations in Mishna, Tarbiẓ 40 (1970), 9—17. See now the supplementary bibliography, in: Hadoar 56, no. 15 (2459) (February 11, 1977), 229—231.

A. WEISS, in his books and articles systematically focuses on numerous tractates and pericopae, compares b. and y. *sugyot* and raises historical literary questions, though he does not always sufficiently employ MSS. For a complete listing of his works, see BENJAMIN WEISS, Annotated Bibliography of the Writings of Dr. Abraham Weiss, Abraham Weiss Jubilee

Volume (New York, 1964), Hebrew section, pp. 5—11, to be supplemented by ID., Meḥqarim BeTalmud (Jerusalem, 1975), pp. 252f. Note in particular the book of collected articles, ID., Notes to Bavli and Yerushalmi Pericopae (Ramat Gan, n. d., 196?).

JACOB BANIEL (Berliner), An Arithmetical Subject in Jerushalmi (y. Shab. 7:1, 9a), Tarbiẓ 15 (1943), 65—70.

S. ABRAMSON, Jerushalmi Shebuoth VI. 2, Tarbiẓ 16 (1944), 53.

HARRY M. ORLINSKY, Studies in Talmudic Philology (y. Ber. 9:3, 13c), HUCA 23 (1950—51), Part One: 499—514.

DAVID WEISS HALIVNI. 2 vols. to date, on 'Nashim' and the second half of 'Mo'ed', (1968, 1975). In his source-critical analysis of b. *sugyot* he systematically employs materials from y. The work makes full use of early and late rabbinic commentaries, MSS, and other literature, and especially focuses on the ways in which the history of a tradition affected its formulation and use. See ROBERT GOLDENBERG, SHAMAI KANTER, and DAVID GOODBLATT, David Weiss Halivni, Meqorot uMeśorot, in: The Formation of the Babylonian Talmud, ed. NEUSNER (Leiden, 1971), pp. 134—173.

JACOB NEUSNER, while his works are not formally an analysis of y. most, in part, if not in whole, are hermeneutically relevant: History of the Jews of Babylonia (Leiden, 1966—70), indicate how to employ Talmudic texts for historical purposes, e. g. dividing between groups of sources; Pharisees (1971) and Eliezer (1973), and Purities, 22 vols. (1974—77), demonstrate the necessity to employ first, form, tradition, and redaction criticism to analyze each discrete text and its pericopae as part of a larger redactional whole, and, secondly, exegetical plain sense to isolate the conception of each version of a text without harmonizing them or introducing absent considerations, and, thirdly, an overview to take stock of the discrete analyses.

MEYER S. FELDBLUM, Talmudic Law and Literature: Tractate Gittin (New York, 1969), includes separate exposition and analysis of y. and then its comparison with b., especially as to their interpretation of M.

I. FRANCUS, Talmud Yerushalmi Maśekhet Beṣah (New York, 1967), a sophisticated introduction to literary aspects of the tractate with notes and addenda on the text in addition to the publication of commentary, along with variants from the Leiden MS.

N. WIEDER, On an Obscure Passage in the Palestinian Talmud (y. Ber. 1 : 8, 3d = Taan. 2 : 3, 65c), Tarbiẓ 43 (1973—74), 46—52.

BOKSER (1975), includes, in English, analyses of y. pericopae, with an attempt to adopt and adapt the best from earlier research and to add considerations as to recurrent formal and literary phenomena.

D. Articles

Various journals, jubilee volumes, and special collections include materials relevant to the study of y. For representative items see the classified listings in STRACK (1931), and in M. MIELZINER, Introduction to the Talmud. With new bibliography, 1925—1967, by ALEXANDER GUTTMANN (New York, 1968[4]), pp. 397—415. For items in Hebrew in numerous fields, see the comprehensive classified index of NAHUM RAKOVER, A Bibliography of Jewish Law (Jerusalem, 1975), specifically on y., pp. 80—82.

Jubilee Volumes: JACOB MARCUS and A. BILGRAY, An Index to Jewish Festschriften (Cincinnati, 1937), to be supplemented by CHARLES BERLIN, Index to Festschriften in Jewish Studies (Cambridge and New York, 1971).

Periodical literature: 1665—1900, MOISE SCHWAB, Répertoire des articles relatifs à l'histoire et à la litterature juives (Paris, 1914—23, Repr. New York, 1970). The following periodical literature frequently have or had materials: 'HaṢofeh LeHakhmat Yisrael'; 'HeḤalus', indexed in the Jerusalem, 1969, reprint; Bet HaMidrash (Vienne, 1865), ed. I. H. WEISS; especially 'Beth Talmud' (Vienne), 1881—1896, indexed in the Jerusalem, 1965, reprint; 'Jerusalem', ed. LUNCZ (Repr. 1972), especially vols. 7—10; 'Ozar Hachaim', ed. EHRENREICH; MGWJ, indexed, in Gesamtregister 1851—1939 (Tübingen, 1966); REJ, which has an index volume following volume 100 (1936), supplemented by vol. 132 (1973); JQR, index 1—20 (1932); 'Sinai', indexed through 1947 (1948); 'Tarbiẓ'; 'Leshonenu'; 'Dine Israel'; and 'Bar Ilan Annual'. The following occasionally have items: HUCA; PAAJR, 'Journal of Jewish Studies'; 'Journal for the Study of Judaism in the Persian, Hellenistic, and Roman Period'; 'Israel Exploration Journal', indexes in vols. 11 (1961), and 26 (1976); 'Bulletin of the Institute for Jewish Studies'; and the 'AJS Review' (New York), 1ff. (1976ff.).

Kirjath Śepher contains classified and indexed listings of books, including full contents of journals and works of collected articles (citations of which were discontinued with the appearance of the next item). The more recent Index of Articles on Jewish Studies, ed. ISSACHAR JOEL, 1 (1966) ff. (Jerusalem, 1969ff.) (to date 12 vols., through 1977), provides an invaluable complete, classified, and indexed list of articles in all languages.

Addendum

(to p. 199, l. 15f.) A. LINDER, The Roman Imperial Government and the Jews under Constantine, Tarbiẓ 44 (1974—75), 95—143. — (to p. 199, l. 20f.) A. OPPENHEIMER, The Am Ha'aretz (Leiden, 1977). — (to p. 203, l. 1) ID., A Lexicon of the Verbs in the Tannaitic Hebrew (Ph.D. dissertation, Hebrew University, Jerusalem, 1972). — (to p. 203, l. 7) See M. SOKOLOFF, The Current State of Research on Galilean Aramaic, JNES 37 (1978), 161—167. — (to p. 203, l. 25) MOSHE BAR-ASHER, Palestinian Syriac Studies (Jerusalem, 1977). — (to p. 206, l. 24) See also I. VINNIKOV, Specimen of a Dictionary and Concordance of the Palestinian Literature (The Letter G), in: Palestinski Sbornik 5 (1960), 151—228. — (to p. 211, l. 38) J. PRESS, Encyclopedia of Eretz Israel, I—IV (Jerusalem, 1951—55), and P. NE'EMAN, Encyclopaedia of Talmudical Geography, I—II (Tel-Aviv, 1972) (Unreliable). — (to p. 212, l. 16) ID., Glass Utensils in Talmudic Literature (Jerusalem, 1978). — (to p. 212, l. 37) ID., et al., Ancient Synagogue Excavations at Khirbet Shema'. Upper Galilee, Israel 1970—1972 [= AOS Annual, XLII] (Durham, 1976). — (to p. 212, end) L. LEVINE, Roman Caesarea. Qedem 2 (Jerusalem, 1975). — (to p. 213, l. 18) *Donateurs et foundateurs dans les synagogues juives (Cahiers de la Revue Biblique, 7) (Paris, 1967). — (to p. 213, l. 23) See now: *On Stone and Mosaic. The Aramaic Hebrew Inscriptions from Ancient Synagogues (Jerusalem, 1978).

Errata

[Page numbers refer to pagination in the original publication]

Page	*Line*	*From*	*To*
143	18	Mavo	Mevo
	41	Shevicjt	Shevi^cit
146	38	Mavo	Mevo
151	9	tractes	tractates
155	17	LeTalmud	LaTalmud
169	9	U VaMidrash	UVaMidrash
171	18	U VaMidrash	UVaMidrash
184	34	Rabahb	Rabbah
191	30	a Zimun	Zimmun
198	20	Javitz	Jawitz
199	5	Avi Yonah	Avi-Yonah
205	41	1957	1955, 1957
216	11	Mamonot BeTalmud	HaMamonot BaTalmud
219	23	Jacob	Jakob
	36	Rozabi	Ratzaby
233	32	pp.	p.
236	29	1965	1964–1965
241	9	Shevicjt	Shevi^cit
243	4	Shedeh	Sedeh
247	40	Leshlomon	Leshlomoh
253	16a	Meir	A. M.
255	48a	Rozabi	Ratzaby
256	6	Sussman	Sussmann

Index Nominum

[Page numbers refer to pagination in the original publication.]

The index includes all entries to names of individuals and places. An asterisk (*) next to a number indicates that the item appears more than once on that page.

DARSHAN, DAVID 243
DAUBE, DAVID 183
Daud, Abraham ibn 192
David b. R. Amram of Eden 238
DAVIDSON, ISRAEL 218
DAVIS, MOSHE 197
DEVRIES, BENJAMIN 169, 171, 177, 179, 190, 221
Dimi 187
DIMITROVSKY, HAIM Z. 150, 151, 229, 234*
DINGLAS, ḤAYYIM YOSEF 157*, 208, 241
DINSTAG, JACOB 244
DONNER, H. 213
DOR, ZWI MOSHE 190
DOTAN, ARON 203, 213
DUENNER, JOSEF H. 245, 247
DZIUBAS, ABRAHAM ISAAC 220

EDELMANN, R. 171
EFRAYIM, MAYYIM 246
Egypt 226
EHRENREICH, H. Y. 233, 248, 250
EHRMAN, A. 165
EISENSTEIN 238
ELBOGEN, IṢḤAQ (ISMAR) 218
Eleazar, R. 187
Eleazar b. Judah 237
Eliezer b. Nathan of Mainz 236
Eliezer b. Yoel HaLevi 228, 236*
ELIJAH, The Gaon of Vilna 147, 179, 241, 244*, 247
Elijah of London 241
ELON, MENACHEM 215, 216, 230*
EMERTON, J. A. 207
ENELOW, H. G. 239
En Gedi 213
ENGEL, JOSEPH 245
ENGLENDER, DOV MALACHI 245
EPHRATI, JACOB N. 191
EPPENSTEIN, S. 247
EPSTEIN, A. 228
EPSTEIN, JACOB N. passim
ESH, S. 207
Estor haParḥi 211, 214

FAJGENBAUM, ISRAEL 246
FALK, ZE'EV W. 215, 216
FAUR, JOSE 236
FEINTUCH, I. Z. 153, 172
FELDBLUM, MEYER S. 176*, 177, 189*, 190, 193, 247, 249
FELDMAN, URIAH 193, 214
FELIKS, YEHUDAH 155, 214*, 223
FISCH, SOLOMON 238
FISCHEL, HENRY A. 191
FISHBANE, M. A. 212
FITZMYER, JOSEPH 203
FLEISCHER, HEINRICH L. 205
FLIESHER, EZRA 217, 219
FLOHR, P. R. 212
FLORSHEIM, J. 169, 194
FORBES, R. J. 212, 214
FOULDA, ELIJAH BEN LOEB OF WIZNICIA 243
FRAENKEL, J. 190*, 235
France 235
Franco-Germany 226
FRANCUS, ISRAEL 155, 162*, 190, 242*, 247, 249
FRANK, T. 197
FRANKEL, DAVID OF BERLIN 243
FRANKEL, Z. 146, 152*, 153, 154, 166, 167, 168, 171*, 172, 174, 177, 181, 183, 187, 188, 189, 192, 194*, 195, 196, 197, 199, 201, 204, 209*, 221, 226, 241, 245, 247
FREIMANN, A. H. 158
FREIMANN, ARON 230
FREY, JEAN B. 213
FRIEDMAN, MORDECHAI A. 158, 216, 222*
FRIEDMAN, SHAMMA 156, 170, 188, 189, 191, 208, 215, 233
FRIEDMANN, MEIR 185
FRIES-HOREB, JUDAH 220
FRIEZLER, ABRAHAM Y. 232

GALIS, YAAQOV 225
GEIGER, A. 146
GEIGER, B. 205
GERBOZ, E. Z. 157
GEREBOFF, JOEL 244
Germany 235
GILAT, ISAAC 214, 215
GINGRICH, F. WILBER 205
GINSBERG, H. L. 202
GINZBERG, LOUIS passim
GLATZER, N. 212
GOITEIN, S. D. 159, 197, 227
Golan 195
GOLDBERG, ABRAHAM 171, 177, 186, 188*, 190, 246, 248
GOLDENBERG, ESTHER 219
GOLDENBERG, ROBERT 190, 249
GOLDMAN, E. 152, 162
GOLDIN, JUDAH 186, 202
GOLDSCHMIDT, DANIEL 219, 231
GOLDSCHMIDT, LAZARUS 205
GOODBLATT, DAVID 167, 169, 170, 173, 175, 178, 180, 189, 191, 193, 195, 199*, 202*, 203, 210, 211, 225, 226, 247, 249
GOODENOUGH, ERWIN R. 212
GOREN, SHELOMOH 155, 156, 246
GOTTLIEB, ISAAC 240

Gottlieb, W. 199
Graetz, H. 191, 198
Green, William S. 170, 191, 220
Greenbaum, Aaron 238
Greenfield, Jonas 203
Greenstone, Julius 169, 171
Greenup, A. W. 165, 239*
Greenwald, Yequtiel 187
Gross, B. 205
Grossfeld, Bernard 203
Gruenhut, L. 186, 239
Gulak, Asher 215*
Guttman, Alexander 250

Haase, Wolfgang 145
Haberman, Jacob 243
Habermann, Meir 151*, 152, 167, 217, 218
Habiv, Y'aqov ibn 241
Hai, Gaon 227
Halberstam 234
Halev, Yosef 235
Halevy, E. E. 178, 215
Halevy, I. H. 181, 189, 192, 198
Halivni, David Weiss, See: Weiss Halivni
Halper 159, 160
Ḥananel, Rabbenu 149, 150, 232, 233
Ḥanokh 234
Hartmann, B. 206
Heichelheim, F. M. 197
Heide, A. van der 155
Heinemann, Joseph 169*, 177, 183, 184, 185, 218*, 219*, 248
Heller, H. 247
Herr, M. D. 184, 185, 190
Hesychius, Alexandrinus 205
Higger, Michael 174*, 175, 177, 218, 221*, 235
Hildesheimer, Ezriel 232
Hildesheimer, Hirsh 211
Hildesheimer, J. 232
Hillmann, S. I. 246
Hirschberg, A. S. 214
Hirschberg, H. Z. 214, 227, 232
Hirschenson, Yeḥiel Ṣevi 211
Hirschorn 194
Horowitz, Charles 165*
Horowitz, Eliezer 159
Horowitz, Israel S. 211
Horowitz, S. 181, 245
Hospers, J. H. 202, 203, 213
Hutner, Yehoshua 153
Hyman, Aaron 183, 196, 220*
Hyman, Arthur B. 160, 238*

Isaac Alfasi 150, 233*
Isaac b. Abba Maari 235
Isaac b. Malkiṣedeq of Siponto 240*
Isaac b. Moses of Vienna 236, 237*
Isaac Hakohen 235
Isaac ibn Giat 234*
Isaiah, The Elder of Terani 150, 237
Isaiah, The Younger of Terani 237
Israel 149, 150, 187
Israel ibn al-Nakawa 239
Israel of Shklov 244*
Italy 218, 226, 233, 237

Jackson, Bernard 215, 216
Jacob Asheri 236
Jacob David of Slotz 245
Jastrow, Marcus 206
Jawitz, Z. 191, 198
Jellinek, A. 238
Jerusalem 150
Joel, Issachar 244, 250
Joseph HaLevi ibn Migas 234
Judah of Barcelona 234
Julian the Architect of Ascalon 193, 216
Juster, Jean 198

Kaddari, M. Z. 207
Kagan, Z. 190
Kahana, Kalman 157*, 240, 241, 242, 244
Kahana, Tuviah 198, 241, 242
Kahle, P. 151, 203, 206
Kaminka, A. 231
Kanevski 220, 246*
Kanter, Shamai 171, 190, 249
Kapstein, I. 186
Karlitz, Abraham 246
Kasher, Menahem M. 146, 152, 203, 221, 229, 230
Kasowski, Chaim Joshua [See: Kosowski]
Katsh, Abraham I. 159
Kimelman, Reuven 145, 196*
Kindler, A. 197
Kirschenbaum, Aaron 216
Kisch, G. 247
Kislev, M. E. 215
Klein, Samuel 198, 211
Kochavi, Moshe 211, 212
Kohler, K. 217
Kohen, Simeon 244
Kohn, P. Jacob 146, 152, 229, 230, 241
Kohut, Alexander 205
Koningsveld, P. Sj. Van 155
Konoviș, Israel 199
Kosovsky, Biniamin 181, 196, 206*
Kosowski, Chaim Joshua 188, 203, 206*
Kotlar, David 213
Krauss, Samuel 204, 213, 214
Krochmal, Abraham 189, 192, 194, 245
Krochmal, N. 191

Krotoschin 7a, 17a, 152, 153, 173, 183
KURZWEIL, BARUCH 149, 180
KUTSCHER, E. Y. 162, 175, 201*, 202*, 203*, 204, 205*, 206* 207*, 213, 221

LACHS, SAMUEL 196
LATTE, K. 205
LAUTERBACH, JACOB 209
LEHMANN, M. 157*
LEITER, MOSHE 246
LEITER, SHMUEL 185
LERNER, M. 184
LERNER, MYRON BIALIK 183, 185, 186
LERRER 238
LEVINE, LEE I. 145, 191, 193, 195, 196, 198, 199, 250
LEVY, BARRY 203
LEVY, ISAAK 155, 165
LEVY, JACOB 205
LEWIN, B. M. 150, 171, 222, 223*, 226, 231*, 232*, 235
LEWY, ISRAEL 147, 155, 158, 181, 193, 247*
LIEBERMAN, SAUL passim
LIFSHITZ, B. 213, 250
LINDER, AMNON 250
LIPHSHITZ, ḤAYYIM 146, 152, 229
LISS, ABRAHAM 150
LOEW, I. 206, 214
LOEWINGER, D. S. 161*, 232, 235
LOF, EFRAYIM DOV HAKOHEN 245
Lud 195
LUNCZ, A. M. 152, 153, 155, 156, 211, 214, 247, 250
LURIA, B. Z. 172

Machir bar Abba Mari 239
MAIMON, YEHUDAH LEB HAKOHEN 237, 244
Maimonides 160, 192, 233*, 238, 241, 242
MALTER, H. 177
MANDELBAUM, J. B. 146, 152, 186, 229
MANN, JACOB 218*, 219, 222
MARCUS, JACOB 250
MARGALIOTH, MORDECHAI See: MARGULIES, MORDECHAI
MARGALIOTH, MOSES 243
MARGALIYOT, E. 171
MARGOLIOUTH, G. 157*, 242
MARGULIES (MARGALIOTH), MORDECHAI 149, 166, 167, 183, 184*, 196, 210, 214, 220, 222*,223, 224, 226, 231, 232*, 233*, 234*, 238, 239
MARIM, MEIR 244, 247
MARSCHALL, J. E. 206
MARX, A. 242
MAZAR, BENJAMEN 195, 199, 212*, 213
Meir, R. 236

MELAMED, E. Z. 148, 154*, 155, 156, 168 169, 170, 171*, 172, 173, 174*, 175*, 179 180*, 183, 191, 192, 194, 195, 196, 200 208, 210, 215, 226, 228, 230, 232, 233, 239 241, 242, 243*, 248
MELAMMED, E. Z. See: MELAMED, E. Z.
Menaḥem, HaMeiri 151, 234, 235*, 240
MERHAVYA, C. 240
Meshullam 151, 158, 237
MEYERS, ERIC 212, 221, 250
MIELZINER, M. 211, 250
MIESES, JOSEF 152
MILLAR, F. 213
MILLIGAN, GEORGE 205
MIRSKY, AARON 169, 217, 219
MIRSKY, S. K. 231, 235
MORAG, S. 201
MOREL, SAMUEL 231
MORESHET, MENAḤEM 177, 188, 202, 250
Moseh HaDarshon 240
Moses of Quzy 237
MOULTON, JAMES HOPE 205
MUFFS, Y. 216

Naḥmanides 228, 234*, 236
Nathan b. Yeḥiel 205, 206, 233
NAVEH, J. 213, 250
NE'EMAN, P. 250
NEUBAUER, ADOLPH 211
NEUHAUSEN, S. A. 150
NEUSNER, JACOB 145, 148, 165, 169*, 171, 172, 173, 175, 176, 177, 178, 183, 187, 189, 190, 191, 193, 196, 197, 198, 202, 209, 215, 216*, 240, 244, 247, 249*
Nissim [Gaon] of Qairawan 150*, 232*
NOAH, A. 191
NOY, DOV 169, 189

ODEBERG, H. 207
OPPENHEIM, DAVID 243
OPPENHEIMER, A. 250
ORLINSKY, HARRY M. 249
ORMAN, DAN 195, 213
ORMAN, G. L. 231

Palestine 145, 147, 150, 166, 167, 187*, 189, 197, 202, 211, 217, 221, 222*, 223, 224, 226
PETERKOV 152
PETUCHOWSKI, JAKOB 169, 217, 219*
PINELIS, HIRSCH MENDEL 244*, 247
Pirqoi ben Baboi 167, 213, 219
Piske HaRid See: Isaiah the Elder of Terani
PIZANTI, MOSEH 242
POMERANCHIK, ARYEH 246
PORTEN, BEZALEL 216
PORTON, GARY G. 169, 177

Poznanski, Samuel 150*, 164, 226, 231*, 247
Preschel, T. 248
Press, J. 250
Preuss, Julius 214
Prisman, Elijah 236

Qafiḥ, Yosef 233*
Qalonymous, Yehudah 236, 237
Qimron, E. 213
Qurqovsuv, P. 162
Rabbinovicz, R. 150, 151, 158
Rabbinowitz, Joseph 165
Rabbinowitz, Meir 236
Rabello, R. A. 198, 213
Rabin, Chaim 201*, 202, 205
Rabinovitz, A. S. 189, 198, 209
Rabinovitz, Z. M. 156, 157*, 162, 184
Rabinovitz, Z. W. 167, 172, 175*, 177, 178, 181, 189, 193, 194, 196, 207, 210, 218, 228, 245, 247
Rabinowitz, E. N. 238
Rabinowitz, Jacob J. 216
Rabinowitz, S. P. 198
Rabinowitz, Z. M. 148, 149, 208, 217, 219, 222*, 238, 239*
Rafael, Iṣḥaq 244
Rakover, Nahum 215, 230, 250
Rappaport, Soloman J. L. 211
Rashi 235*, 236, 240
Ratner, B. 151, 155, 162, 163*, 168, 189, 194, 201, 224, 226, 228*, 232, 233, 247
Raymond Martini 240*
Reif, S. C. 177
Ritter, P. 152
Rivka Ziskind 245
Röllig, W. 213
Rokeah, Moses 152
Romanoff, Paul 211
Romm 220
Rosen, H. 204
Rosen, Joseph 246
Rosenkilde 155
Rosenthal, David 191
Rosenthal, E. S. 148, 149*, 158*, 177, 180 218, 219
Roth, A. N. Z. 231, 232
Roth, Joel 236
Routenberg, Mahram 236
Rozabi, Y. 219
Rubenstein, Judah 146, 241
Saadia Gaon 218, 239
Sachs, M. 155
Sachs, Nissan 240
Sacks, M. Y. S. 241
Safrai, S. 190, 212
Saldarini, Anthony 186
Salonen, Armas 214
Samson b. Abraham of Sens 240
Samuel be Nissin from Senuth 239
Samuel b. R. Sheneur of Evreux, disciple of 237
Sarason, Richard 145, 219*
Sasoon, S. 231
Savitsky, Mordechai 246
Schachter, Jacob 189
Schachter, Melech 172
Schechter, Abraham I. 218
Schechter, S. 160, 186
Schepansky, Israel 223, 225
Schiller-Szinessy 153, 154
Schirmann, J. 218*, 220
Schlesinger, Eliyahu 246
Schlesinger, M. 207
Schlossberg, A. L. 231
Schmelzer, M. 145, 230
Schmidt, M. 205
Schreiber, Abraham 151, 152, 158*, 227, 237
Schürer, E. 213
Schwab, Moshe 164*, 250
Segal, M. H. 202
Sekles, S. 168
Sepphoris 195*, 197, 199
Sevenster, J. N. 204, 205
Shapiro, Israel 242
Shapiro, Joshua Isaak, of Slonim 245
Shaked, Shaul 159, 218, 230
Sharvit, Shimon 207
Sherry, A. P. 156
Shilone 238
Shimeon HaDarshon 238*
Shmuel b. Ḥofni 239*
Shmuel HaNagid 233, 234
Shor, Y. H. 172, 189
Shulsinger 241*
Simonsohn, Shlomo 167, 197, 205, 208, 219
Singer, A. 160
Sirillo, R. Soloman 152, 156, 157*, 158, 208, 241, 242, 243
Sivitz, M. S. 245
Smallwood, E. M. 199
Sokoloff, M. 184, 202, 208, 250
Solomon ben Adret of Barcelona 150, 151, 229, 234*
Sophocles, E, A. 205
Spain 226, 233, 234
Sperber, Daniel 197, 204, 205*
Spiegel, Shalom 167, 168, 226, 227
Spiegel, Ya'aqov 233
Spira, Y. 239
Steinsaltz 189, 238
Steinschneider, Moritz 167

Stern, Moritz 247
Stern, Tibor H. 188, 194
Stevenson, W. B. 207
Strack, Herman 148, 150, 152, 157, 168, 184, 211, 241, 250
Sussman, Y. 116*, 145, 156*, 157, 158, 159*, 162, 163, 168, 173, 184, 193, 195, 197, 208, 211, 213, 215

Tal, Abraham 203
Tam (Jacob) 233, 236
Tarshish, Perez 150
Ta-Shmah, Israel 230, 234
Taubes, Ḥayyim 231*
Taylor, C. 162
Tchernowitz, Chaim 226, 227, 230, 232, 233*, 236*, 244
Tenenblatt, M. A. 194, 198
Theodor, J. 183, 184
Tiberias 193*, 195*, 196, 209
Tobi, Y. 219
Towner, Wayne Sibley 169, 177, 183, 184
Townsend, John T. 184, 221, 240
Turner, Barton 206
Twersky, Isadore 192, 226, 229, 234, 235, 240

Ugolino, B. 164
Ulla 187
Umanski, Yosef 188, 196
Urbach, E. E. 186, 195, 224, 227, 229, 230, 235, 236*, 237*, 240, 241, 245

Valdberg, Shmuel 168
Vermes, G. 213
Viezner, Yonah Elijah 192, 194
Vilna 152
Vinnikov, I. 250
Vitto, F. 213
Vogel, Eleanor K. 212

Wacholder, Ben Zion 218, 219, 231
Weingarten, Shmuel Hakohen 167
Weiss, Abraham 148, 167, 169, 171*, 173, 176, 177, 179, 181*, 189*, 190, 248*
Weiss, Benjamin 248
Weiss, I. H. 188, 189, 190, 191, 194, 198, 250
Weiss, Raphael 207
Weiss Halivni, David 145, 148, 155, 171, 173, 176*, 177, 178, 179*, 188*, 190, 191, 194, 209, 210, 215, 235, 244, 245, 249
Wertheimer, Abraham Joseph 239
Wertheimer, Shlomo Aharon 239
White, K. D. 214
Wieder, N. 249
Wieder, Solomon 161
Wortheimer, Abraham 150
Wünsche, Aug. 164

Yadin, Yigael 212
Yalon, Henoch 201, 207
Yannai 217*, 218, 219
Yaron, Reuven 216
Yehoshua Heschel Eli Zeev 220
Yehudah b. Asher 230
Yehudai Gaon (attributed) 231
Yeivin, S. 212
Yellin, Aryeh Leib 220, 245*
Y. H. S. 231
Yoḥanan, R. 192, 194*, 196
Yose b. Yose 219
Yosef Qara 242

Zaiman, J. H. 240
Zeiri, R. 187
Zeitlin, Solomon 172
Zhitomer 152
Zimmels, H. J. 199, 227
Ziskind, Rivka 245
Zlotnick, Dov 221
Zohary, Michael 214
Zucker, Moshe 185, 239*
Zuckermandel, M. S. 177
Zulai, M. 218
Zunz, L. 183, 239
Zuri, J. S. 190, 195, 196*

The Babylonian Talmud

by DAVID GOODBLATT, Haifa

Table of Contents
[Page numbers refer to pagination in the original publication.]

I. Introduction 259
II. The Text of BT 262
   1. Introduction 264
   2. Manuscripts 265
   3. Witnesses to the Text 266
   4. Editions 267
   5. Text Criticism 268
      a) The History of Text Criticism 268
      b) Collations of Variants and Critical Editions 270
      c) The Principles of BT Text Criticism 271
III. The Languages of BT 273
   1. Introduction 276
   2. The Hebrew of BT 277
   3. Babylonian Talmudic Aramaic 278
   4. Lexicography 280
IV. Source, Form, and Redaction Criticism 281
   1. Source Criticism 285
      a) The Palestinian Sources 285
      b) The Babylonian Sources 289
         α) Variant Versions 289
         β) Quotations 289
         γ) Parallel Pericopae 290
         δ) Inconsistencies within a Pericope 290
         ε) The Anonymous Material and Early Redactions of BT 291
         ζ) Form and Subject Matter 293
         η) Post-Amoraic Sources 294
      c) Summary and Critique 296
   2. Form Criticism 297
      a) The Brief Versus the Discursive 297
      b) Other Forms 301
      c) The *Sitz im Leben* of the Forms 303
      d) Summary 303
   3. Redaction Criticism 304
      a) The Tractates 304
      b) The Traditional Theory of the Redaction of BT 307
      c) The Two Source Theories 314

V. *Hilfsbücher* and Related Works 319
1. Introductions, Methodology, Bibliographies, Encyclopediae and Special Lexica 324
a) Introductions and Methodology 324
b) Bibliographies 324
c) Encyclopediae and Special Lexica 325
2. Commentaries 326
3. Translations and Anthologies 328
4. Related Fields 329
a) History 329
b) Archaeology, Geography, Realia 330
c) Religion 330
d) Law 331

Indices 331
I. Index of Names 331
II. Index of Places 334
III. Index of Citations 335
A. Babylonian Talmud and Amoraic Midrashim 335
B. Medieval Sources 335

Abbreviations:

Archive	=	Archive of the New Dictionary of Rabbinic Literature
b.	=	ben
bh	=	Biblical Hebrew
BT	=	Babylonian Talmud
bta	=	Babylonian Talmudic Aramaic
C. E.	=	Common Era
Diq. Sof.	=	Diqduqe Soferim (RABBINOVICZ, FELDBLUM, HIRSHLER)
DTLU	=	Development of the Talmud as a Literary Unit (A. WEISS)
EJ	=	Encyclopedia Judaica
Ex. Term.	=	Die exegetische Terminologie der jüdischen Traditionsliteratur (BACHER)
GQS	=	Gemara Quotations in Sebara, JQR 43 (H. KLEIN)
GS	=	Gemara and Sebara, JQR 38 (H. KLEIN)
HUCA	=	Hebrew Union College Annual
IAL	=	Introduction to Amoraitic Literature (EPSTEIN)
ISG	=	Iggeret R. Sherira Ga'on
ITL	=	Introduction to Tannaitic Literature (EPSTEIN)
ITM	=	Introduction to the Text of the Mishnah (EPSTEIN)
JAOS	=	Journal of the American Oriental Society
JBL	=	Journal of Biblical Literature
JQR	=	Jewish Quarterly Review
JSemSt	=	Journal of Semitic Studies
MGWJ	=	Monatsschrift für die Geschichte und Wissenschaft des Judentums
mh	=	Middle ("Mishnaic") Hebrew
PAAJR	=	Proceedings of the American Academy for Jewish Research
R.	=	Rav, Rabbi
REJ	=	Revue des Études Juives
SGR	=	Some General Results of the Separation of Gemara from Sebara in the Babylonian Talmud, JSemSt 3 (H. KLEIN)
SH	=	Sarei Ha-elef (KASHER and MANDELBAUM)
SLA	=	Studies in the Literature of the Amoraim (A. WEISS)
ST	=	Sources and Traditions (HALIVNI)

STV	=	Seder Tanna'im Ve'amora'im
TD	=	The Talmud in its Development (A. WEISS)
TH	=	Tequfat Hagge'onim (ASSAF)
Trad. u. Trad.	=	Tradition und Tradenten (BACHER)
ZDMG	=	Zeitschrift der deutschen morgenländischen Gesellschaft

I. Introduction

Jewish tradition speaks of "the sea of the Talmud"[1]. The metaphor is an apt one for a document as extensive and complex as the Babylonian Talmud (hereafter: BT). It covers 2783 folio pages in the standard editions and treats almost every subject known to man. A Talmudist compiled the following list of topics encountered in BT:

> "Religion and ethics, exegesis and homiletics, jurisprudence and ceremonial laws, ritual and liturgy, philosophy and science, medicine and magic, astronomy and astrology, history and geography, commerce and trade, politics and social problems . . .."[2]

Despite the heterogeneity of its contents, BT can be characterized as a commentary on the Mishnah of Yehudah the Patriarch, a Palestinian law code published around the year 200 C.E. The Mishnah provides both the external framework and the internal continuity of the Talmud. Following the Mishnah, BT is divided into tractates and chapters. And consecutive commentary on the paragraphs of the Mishnah is the connecting link between the diverse contents of BT. That commentary is composed of pericopae. Generally each pericope relates to a paragraph, sentence, or phrase of the Mishnah. It may record the comments of several generations of masters, usually in chronological order. The earlier masters tend to comment directly on the Mishnah. Later masters may devote more attention to the words of their predecessors than to the Mishnah itself. In the course of the discussion various sources may be cited from elsewhere in the Talmud, the Mishnah, or from cognate literature. Extraneous subjects, suggested by association, are also introduced. Indeed entire pericopae may have nothing to do with the Mishnah.

BT does not contain connected commentary for all 63 tractates of the Mishnah. Only 37 tractates appear in BT. Materials from the remaining 26 are scattered throughout the text. Thus these sections of the Mishnah were studied, but they did not engender composition of separate BT tractates. The following chart summarizes the situation just described.

[1] The earliest attestation of this phrase is from the late middle ages. See E. BEN-YEHUDAH, Thesaurus totius hebraitatis (London and New York, 1960), Vol. IV, p. 2056. Cf. Midrash Psalms ad 104:25 where the sea metaphor refers to 'the tractates' or to Tannaitic collections.

[2] M. JASTROW, Dictionary of Targumim, the Talmud Babli and Yerushalmi and the Midrashic Literature (New York, 1886—1903), p. V.

Order of Mishnah	Number of Mishnah Tractates in Order	BT Tractates (with abbreviations used in article)
zera'im, 'Seeds' (agricultural laws)	11	1. Berakhot (Ber.)
mo'ed, 'Season' (festival laws)	12	1. Shabbat (Shab.)
		2. 'Eruvin ('Eruv.)
		3. Pesaḥim (Pes.)
		4. Yoma (Yom.)
		5. Sukkah (Suk.)
		6. Beṣah (Beṣ.)
		7. Rosh Hashanah (RH)
		8. Ta'anit (Ta.)
		9. Megillah (Meg.)
		10. Mo'ed Qaṭṭan (MQ)
		11. Ḥagigah (Ḥag.)
nashim, 'Women' (personal status)	7	1. Yevamot (Yev.)
		2. Ketuvot (Ket.)
		3. Nedarim (Ned.)
		4. Nazir (Naz.)
		5. Soṭah (Soṭ.)
		6. Giṭṭin (Giṭ.)
		7. Qiddushin (Qid.)
neziqin, 'Torts' (civil law)	10	1. Bava Qamma (BQ)
		2. Bava Meṣi'a' (BM)
		3. Bava Batra (BB)
		4. Sanhedrin (Sanh.)
		5. Makkot (Mak.)
		6. Shevu'ot (Shev.)
		7. 'Avodah Zarah (AZ)
		8. Horayot (Hor.)
qodashim, 'Holy Things' (sacrificial laws)	11	1. Zevaḥim (Zev.)
		2. Menaḥot (Men.)
		3. Ḥullin (Ḥul.)
		4. Bekhorot (Bekh.)
		5. 'Arakhin ('Arakh.)
		6. Temurah (Tem.)
		7. Keritot (Ker.)
		8. Me'ilah (Me'il.)
		9. Tamid (Tam.)
ṭohorot, 'Purities' (ritual purity)	12	1. Niddah (Nid.)
	123	

The masters whose comments appear in the Mishnah and cognate literature are termed *tanna'im,* from the root *tny,* 'repeat'. They flourished in late first and second century Palestine. The later masters cited in the Talmud are designated *'amora'im,* from the root *'mr* which here means 'interpret, explain'. The Amoraim were active in Palestine and in Babylonia during the third through the fifth centuries (= 'the Amoraic era'). The Mishnah commentary composed by the Amoraim is commonly called the Gemara, while Talmud refers to the combination of Mishnah and Gemara[3]. Since a *gemara* was composed in each of the aforementioned countries, we have both a Palestinian and a Babylonian Talmud. Each records views of Amoraim from both countries, but local masters tend to predominate. The sections of the Mishnah covered by each Talmud are not identical. Thus the Palestinian Talmud has tractates for all of Mishnah Order *zera'im,* but none for *qodashim.* Linguistic and stylistic features also distinguish one *gemara* from the other.

The brief description given above of the contents of BT does not hint at the role the document was to play in Jewish history. BT became the constitution of Jewish communities throughout the world. It should be noted that until modern times Jewish communities enjoyed considerable internal autonomy. Most governments did not interfere in issues of personal status and small civil claims between Jews. These matters as well as religious affairs were conducted according to the law of the Talmud. The acceptance of the authority of BT by Jews in Europe, Africa, and Asia raises two questions. First, why was the Talmud of Babylonia preferred to that of Palestine? Second, why should communities far removed from both of the latter countries submit to either Talmud? Answers to the first question can be suggested. Beginning in the eighth century the talmudic academies of Babylonia waged a vigorous campaign to establish the predominance of their Gemara. Fragments of the propaganda they disseminated have survived[4]. The success of their campaign was probably helped by Jewish connections with the Abbasid dynasty which united under its rule a large percentage of the world Jewish population. At this time the Babylonian Talmudic academies were located in Bagdad, the Abbasid capital. Perhaps another reason for the success of BT is its superior literary quality vis-a-vis the Palestinian Talmud. The second question concerns the acceptance of BT outside the Abbasid sphere of influence, for example in the communities of the Rhineland. For the present no convincing explanation exists. In any case, the place of BT in later Jewish history, when it became almost equal to the Bible in holiness and authority, lies beyond the scope of this essay.

[3] It should be stressed that in BT itself *gemara* means 'a tradition', and *talmud* means 'discussion, explication'. See Albeck, Introduction, pp. 3—7, Melammed, Introduction, pp. 323, 326, Weiss, TD, pp. 402—407, and cf. Strack, Introduction, p. 5.

[4] See S. Spiegel, Leparashat Happulmos Shel Pirqoi b. Baboi, H. A. Wolfson Jubilee Volume, Hebrew Section (Jerusalem, 1965), pp. 243—273.

My subject here is BT as a literary document. I shall concentrate on the classical philological issues of language, text-criticism, and source-, form- and redaction-criticism. Other topics relating to the contents of the document, such as law, religion, and folklore, or to its historical background will be discussed briefly in Chapter V below. Throughout I shall limit myself to the scholarship of the past fifty years. For the period before 1925 the reader is referred to H. L. STRACK's classic 'Introduction to the Talmud and Midrash' (Philadelphia, 1925; Reprint in paperback: New York, 1964). This is the English translation of a revised version of the fifth and last German edition (Munich, 1921)[5]. STRACK compiles very full bibliographies on all aspects of Talmudic literature, and I see no reason to repeat what is readily available elsewhere. Moreover, 1925 is not just an arbitrary cut-off point. In the past fifty years the centers of Talmud scholarship shifted from Eastern and Central Europe to the United States and Israel. This shift is reflected in the dominance of English and especially Hebrew in the bibliographies accompanying this essay. Separate bibliographies precede each chapter. The works listed at the head of the chapter are referred to in abbreviated form in the body of the text. A full list of abbreviations appears at the head of the essay.

II. The Text of BT

Bibliography

1. Published Manuscripts

The Babylonian Talmud. Codex Florence. 3 Vols. Jerusalem, 1972.

The Babylonian Talmud. Codex Munich 95. Reprint, Jerusalem, 1971.

The Babylonian Talmud, Seder Nezikin. Codex Hamburg. Facsimile of the Original MS and a Reprint of the Goldschmidt Edition (Berlin, 1914). Jerusalem, 1969.

The Babylonian Talmud, Tractate Hullin, Codex Hamburg 169. Jerusalem, 1972.

Manuscripts of the Babylonian Talmud from the Collection of the Vatican Library, Series A. 3 Vols. Jerusalem, 1972. Series B. 3 Vols. Jerusalem, 1974.

Talmudical Fragments in the Bodleian Library. 1. Fragment of the Talmud Babli, Tractate Keritoth of the year 1123, the oldest dated MS of this Talmud. 2. Fragment of the Talmud Jerushalmi, Tractate Berachoth. Ed. S. SCHECHTER and S. SINGER. Cambridge, 1896. Reprint, Jerusalem, 1971.

Tractate 'Abodah Zarah of the Babylonian Talmud. Ms. Jewish Theological Seminary of America. Ed. S. ABRAMSON. New York, 1957.

The Yemenite MS. of Megilla (In the Library of Columbia University). Toronto, 1916. The Yemenite MS. of Mo'ed Katon (Babylonian Talmud) in the Library of Columbia University. n.p., n.d. Ed. J. J. PRICE. Reprint, Jerusalem, 1970.

ALLONI, N., Geniza Fragments of Rabbinic Literature. Jerusalem, 1973.

HASIDAH, Y., Meginze Yehudah. Daf Gemara Ketav-Yad, Sinai 73 (1973), pp. 224—229.

[5] The bibliography in the English translation contains items as late as 1927. However it is less than complete for the period after 1920.

KATSCH, A. I., Ginze Talmud Babli. Jerusalem, 1975.
ID., Massekhet Berakhot Min Haggenizah, Zalman Shazar Jubilee Volume, Jerusalem, 1973, pp. 549—596.
ID., Unpublished Geniza Talmud Fragments, Journal of the Ancient Near Eastern Society of Columbia University 5 (1973), pp. 213—223.
ID., Unpublished Geniza Talmudic Fragments from the Antonin Collection, JQR 58 (1967—68), pp. 297—309.
ID., Unpublished Geniza Talmudic Fragments of Tractate Shabbath in the Antonin Collection in the U.S.S.R., JQR 63 (1972—73), pp. 39—47.

2. Early Witnesses to the Text

'En Ya'aqov of Ya'aqov ibn Ḥabib. p. e., Saloniki, 1516.
Haggadot Hattalmud. p. e., Constantinople, 1511. Reprint, Jerusalem, 1961.
He'arukh of Natan b. Yeḥi'el. p. e., Rome, before 1475. Crit. ed. A. KOHUT. 8 Vols. Vienna, 1878—1892.
Otzar ha-Gaonim. Thesaurus of the Gaonic Responsa and Commentaries following the order of the Talmudic Tractates. Ed. B. M. LEWIN. 13 Vols. Haifa and Jerusalem, 1928—1943.
Otzar ha-Gaonim to Tractate Sanhedrin. Ed. H. Z. TAUBES. Jerusalem, 1966.
Sefer Halachot Gedolot. Codex Paris 1402. Introduction by S. ABRAMSON. Jerusalem, 1971.
Sefer Halachot Pesuqot by Rav Yehudah Gaon. Codex Sassoon 263. Introduction by S. ABRAMSON. Jerusalem, 1971.
She'iltot of R. Ahai Gaon. p. e., Venice, 1546. Reprint, Jerusalem, 1971. Crit. ed. (incomplete) S. K. MIRSKY. 4 Vols. Jerusalem, 1960—66.
Yalqut Shim'oni. p. e., Saloniki, 1521—1527. Reprint, Jerusalem, 1968—1973.

3. Critical Editions and Collations of Variant Readings

FELDBLUM, M. S., Diḳduḳe Sopherim, Tractate Gittin. New York, 1966.
FRIEDMANN, M., Babylonischer Talmud, Tractat Makkoth. Vienna, 1888. Reprint, Jerusalem, 1970.
HIRSHLER, M., Diqduqe Sofrim Hashalem. Massekhet Ketuvot, I—II. Jerusalem, 1972—1977.
LISS, A., Diqduqe Sofrim Hashalem. Massekhet Soṭah, I. Jerusalem, 1977.
MALTER, H., The Treatise Ta'anit of the Babylonian Talmud. New York, 1930. Reprint, Jerusalem, 1973.
RABBINOVICZ, R., Diqduqe Sofrim. Variae Lectiones in Mischnam et in Talmud Babylonicum. 12 Vols. Reprint, New York, 1960.

4. Studies

ADLER, E. N., Les éditions du Talmud de Pisaro, REJ 89 (1930), pp. 98—103.
ID., Talmud incunables of Spain and Portugal, Jewish Studies in Memory of George A. Kohut, New York, 1935, pp. 1—4.
ID., Talmud manuscripts and editions, Essays in honor of J. H. Hertz, London, 1943, pp. 15—17.
ID., Talmud Printing before Bomberg, Festskrift ... David Simonsen, Kobenhavn, 1923, pp. 81—84.
APTOWITZER, V., Sous quelle forme une édition critique du Talmud est-elle possible et admissible? REJ 91 (1931), pp. 205—217.
DIMITROVSKY, H. Z., S'ridei Bavli. Spanish Incunabula Fragments of the Babylonian Talmud. New York, 1978.
KASHER, M. M., 'Al Devar Hoṣa'ah Ḥadashah Shel Talmud Bavli, Talpioth 3 (1948), pp. 475—496.

Kook, S. H., Dugma'ot Leḥaqirat Girsa'ot 'Al Pi 'Oṣar Hagge'onim, B. M. Lewin Jubilee Volume, Jerusalem, 1939, pp. 127—131.
Marx, A., Pereferkowitsch's Edition of Berakhot, JQR n. s. 2 (1910—11), pp. 279—285.
Prys (Prijs), J., Der Basler Talmuddruck, 1578—1580. Olten-Basel-Lausanne, 1960.
Rabbinovicz, R., Ma'amar 'Al Hadpasat Hattalmud. Ed. M. Haberman. Jerusalem, 1952.
Rosenthal, E. S., Hammoreh, PAAJR 31 (1963), Hebrew Section, pp. 1—71.
Id., Rav, Ben-Aḥi R. Ḥiyyah Gam Ben-Aḥoto? (Peraṭ 'Eḥad Letoldot Hannusaḥ shel Habbavli), H. Yalon Jubilee Volume, Jerusalem, 1963, pp. 281—337.
Zeitlin, S., A Critical Edition of the Talmud. An Appreciation of Malter's Text of Tractate Ta'anit, JQR n.s. 21 (1930—31), pp. 61—73.

1. Introduction

Most documents from late antiquity have come down to us in manuscripts written centuries after the original work was composed. BT is no exception, though it is impossible to pinpoint when it was 'composed'. The latest masters named flourished in the early sixth century. However, major redactional activity and substantive addition continued through the sixth and seventh centuries. Furthermore, extensive materials attributable to authorities of the eighth and ninth centuries found their way into the text. S. Assaf identifies seven such additions in the 18 folios of the first chapter of BM[6]. Glosses and comments continued to move from the margin into the body of BT throughout the middle ages[7]. Finally, the text was freely emended, on the basis of conjecture or variants in manuscripts, until modern times. The printed editions of the nineteenth century, on which all modern printings are based, contain emendations suggested by the commentaries of the sixteenth through the eighteenth centuries. Further changes in the text resulted from censorship. Both Jewish and non-Jewish censors deleted potentially offensive passages and replaced sensitive terms with more neutral ones. The earliest censorship was internal. Passages of a theosophical or magical nature ridiculed by the Qaraites and other anti-rabbinic movements were excised[8]. Later, sections offensive to Christianity were removed either voluntarily or at the insistence of government censors[9].

It turns out that BT reached its present state only in the last century. Thus the point of departure for text criticism must be sought elsewhere. The question is, when did the text achieve a form recognizable as BT, however open to accretion or emendation? According to Assaf the attitude to textual change provides a clue. He notes that through the seventh century there seems to have been no hesitation to add freely to the text. Beginning

[6] S. Assaf, Tequfat Hagge'onim Vesifrutah (Jerusalem, 1955), pp. 135ff.

[7] Writing in the sixteenth century Beṣalel Ashkenazi noted how sections of the eleventh century commentary of Rashi were incorporated into the text of BT in some manuscripts. See page 11 of the preface by S. Y. Zevin to Diqduqe Soferim Hashshalem, Ketuvot I, ed. M. Hirshler (Jerusalem, 1972).

[8] See S. Lieberman, Shkiin[2] (Jerusalem, 1970).

[9] Strack, Introduction, pp. 85f.

in the eighth century conscious substantive changes were no longer made. From then on additions were mainly the result of marginal notes finding their way into the text. Moreover, in the eighth century independent compositions by rabbinic masters began to appear. All this suggests that by the latter date BT was considered a finished work[10]. If we accept the argument of ASSAF, then BT reached its (relatively) final form by the eighth century. Further support for this view comes from the earliest tradition of a written text of BT. A tenth century Talmudist claims that a deposed Babylonian exilarch who arrived in Spain ca. 770 wrote out from memory the complete text of the Talmud[11]. Assuming that BT was 'completed' at this time, our oldest manuscripts are closer to the date when the document was composed than is usually assumed. Nonetheless several centuries separate the more complete manuscripts from the latter date, as we shall see in the following section.

2. Manuscripts

The earliest dated manuscripts extant are from the twelfth century. A Bodleian Library manuscript covering half of Ker. is dated by its colophon to 1123. Of greater importance is Codex Florence from 1177. This text includes Ber., Bekh., Tem., Ker., Me'il., BQ, BM., BB., Sanh., and Shev. (as well as Mishnah Middot and Qinnim) — about a third of BT. Only slightly later is Codex Hamburg of BQ, BM, and BB written in Gerona in 1184. From the following century we have MS JTSA of AZ written towards the end of 1290 in Ubeda, Spain[12]. The earliest manuscript of the entire BT is Codex Munich 95 written in Paris in 1343. Older texts may be found among the undated manuscripts. Most important are the BT texts from the Cairo Genizah some of which predate the year 1000. One of these manuscripts dates from the ninth century according to its editor[13]. This brings us within a century of the completion of BT. Unfortunately the Genizah manuscripts are very fragmentary, and most cover only individual

[10] ASSAF, Tequfat, p. 126.

[11] Quoted in B. M. LEWIN, Otzar ha-Geonim, Vol. I (Haifa, 1938), Responsa, p. 20 ad Ber. 8a, and cf. LEWIN's n. 1 there. See also S. ABRAMSON, Tractate 'Abodah Zarah of the Babylonian Talmud. Ms. Jewish Theological Seminary of America (New York, 1957), p. XIII, n. 1. The Talmudist is the statesman and poet Samuel ibn Nagrela Hannagid, and the deposed exilarch Natronai b. Ḥakinai/Ḥabibai/Zabinai. A passage in Sefer Rabiah, Vol. II (Berlin, 1926), ed. V. APTOWITZER, ‡462, p. 20, refers to "books" from the time of R. Ashi, ca. 400, but it is not clear what they contained. Similarly, a reference to "the Talmud and its interpretation" sent to Spain by Paltoi Gaon in the mid-ninth century need not mean a complete text of BT, cf. ABRAMSON, loc. cit.

[12] ABRAMSON, ibid., pp. XII—XIV, notes that one pericope in this manuscript reflects a *Vorlage* datable to 807! However, it is doubtful whether the *Vorlage* of the manuscript as a whole was so early.

[13] W. H. LOWE, The Fragments of the Talmud Babli Pesachim of the ninth or tenth century in the University Library, Cambridge (Cambridge, 1879).

pages (see the publications of ALLONY, FELDBLUM, HIRSHLER, and KATSCH). KASHER published a list of all extant manuscripts and fragments for each BT tractate in 1948 (Talpioth, cf. STRACK, pp. 81f.). Since then only a few additional Genizah fragments have come to light. The collation of variants for Ket. recently published by HIRSHLER illustrates the amount of material available for one of the important tractates. HIRSHLER had at his disposal seven complete manuscripts and some fifty fragments from the Genizah[14].

The manuscripts of BT are scattered throughout the world. Fortunately photographic technology facilitates textual research. Not only are photographs of the manuscripts widely available, but many of the important ones have been published in reproduction. The aforementioned Codices Munich and Hamburg were printed early in the century. Recently Makor Publishing of Jerusalem reissued them, as well as the collations of variants from the Ker. manuscript by SCHECHTER and SINGER and from a sixteenth century Yemenite manuscript of Meg. and MQ by PRICE. The same firm has also brought out Codex Florence, Codex Hamburg of Ḥul., and a series of Talmud manuscripts from the Vatican Library. The latter include MSS Vat. Ebr. 108 (Shab., MQ), 109 ('Eruv., Beṣ.), 110 (Soṭ., Ned., Naz.), 130 (Ket., Giṭ.), 134 (Yom., RH, Ta., Suk., Beṣ., Meg., Ḥag., MQ), 111 (Yev., Qid., Nid.), 112 (Ket.), 114 (Yev., BM), 118 (Zev., Men.), and 119 (Zev., Tem., 'Arakh., Bekh., Me'il., Ker.). 110 and 111 are actually a single manuscript written in 1381. The other manuscripts lack dates.

3. Witnesses to the Text

Early witnesses to the text of BT or to manuscripts no longer extant supplement the evidence reviewed in the preceding section. The oldest material is the Talmud related literature composed in Babylonia during the early Islamic era. This literature is called 'Geonic' after the heads of the Talmudic academies who bore the title *ga'on*, plural: *ge'onim*. It includes introductions to and commentaries on BT, legal compendia, and responsa to questions of Talmudic law and interpretation. The earliest of these works are the 'She'iltot' and 'Halakhot Pesuqot' from the second half of the eighth century and 'Halakhot Gedolot' from the first half of the ninth century[15]. These documents quote extensively from BT and so constitute

[14] In view of the centrality of BT in Jewish life, we should expect a larger number of manuscripts. The explanation for their relative paucity lies not only in the ravages of time, but in the hand of man. The expulsions and persecutions of Jewish communities in the Muslim and Christian worlds were not conducive to the preservation of old texts. Most serious were the burnings of the Talmud instigated by the Catholic Church. See STRACK, p. 275, n. 2, and on the whole issue of the Church's attitude toward the Talmud see CH. MERCHAVIA, The Church Versus Talmudic and Midrashic Literature, 500—1248 (Jerusalem, 1970) [Hebrew].

[15] See ASSAF, Tequfat, pp. 133—220. She'iltot (p.e., Venice 1546, reprint Jerusalem, 1971); critical edition (incomplete) by S. MIRSKY, 4 Vols. (Jerusalem, 1960—66). Sefer Halachot

a valuable early witness to the text. Frequently they seem to contain not just variant readings, but different recensions of the tractate or pericope under discussion[16]. In either case the three works mentioned are extremely important for text criticism. The Geonic commentaries and responsa are equally important. B. M. LEWIN and H. Z. TAUBES collected these materials (the commentaries are extant in fragmentary form only) and published them according to the order of the tractates. This project is still incomplete, but it does cover about two thirds of BT. Slightly later witnesses appear in the commentaries and legal epitomes of BT compiled by Spanish, North African, Franco-German, and Middle Eastern masters who flourished between the tenth and sixteenth centuries. Jewish tradition calls these authorities *rishonim*, 'the former ones', in distinction to the post-1600 masters who are designated *'aḥaronim*, 'the latter ones'. Two kinds of evidence appear in the work of the *rishonim*. First, they frequently discuss the text and refer to readings in old manuscripts at their disposal. Second, citations of BT in their writings often vary from readings in extant manuscripts and editions. The second category is problematic, for we must allow the possibility of paraphrase or inaccurate quotation from memory. The first category, though, attests to genuine variants.

Other witnesses to the text of BT may be found in compilations of aggadic or non-legal material. Most important are two epitomes of the non-legal sections of BT: 'Haggadot Hattalmud' (p. e. Constantinople, 1511) and "En Ya'aqov' (sixteenth century). The more general anthologies of aggadic material, such as the Yemenite 'Midrash Haggadol' and the thirteenth century 'Yalqut Shim'oni', may also attest variant readings. In using the latter works one must be careful not to confuse parallel but different sources with variants of the same text. Still another important witness is the "Arukh', an eleventh century dictionary of rabbinic literature. Its compiler, Natan b. Yeḥi'el of Rome, illustrates his definitions with citations from the sources including BT[17]. Finally, the early printed editions of BT, which of course were based on manuscripts, also preserve valuable variants.

4. Editions

The history of the printing of BT has already been written. R. RABBINOVICZ published an 'Essay on the Printing of the Talmud' in 1866 as an introduction to his 'Diq. Sof.' (A second edition appeared separately in Munich in 1877.) A. M. HABERMAN brought this work up to date in a revised edition which came out in 1952. Those who do not read Hebrew may con-

Pesuqot by Rav Jehudai Gaon. Codex Sassoon 263, Introduction b. S. ABRAMSON (Jerusalem, 1971). Sefer Halachot Gedolot. Codex Paris 1402, Introduction by S. ABRAMSON (Jerusalem, 1971).

[16] Cf. MELAMMED, Introduction, pp. 478—486, summarizing J. N. EPSTEIN.

[17] See ibid., pp. 487—492.

sult the summary in STRACK (pp. 83—85) and the articles by ADLER. The earliest editions appeared within fifteen years of the beginning of Hebrew printing. Incunables of individual tractates are extant from Portugal, Spain, and Italy. DIMITROVSKY has published fragments of the Spanish incunables. In the early sixteenth century tractates were published in Italy and Morocco. The first complete edition of BT was published in Venice between 1520—23 by DANIEL BOMBERG (a non-Jew). Certain features of this edition were adopted by all subsequent printings. The pagination of BOMBERG became standard. He printed the Talmud on numbered folio pages. Each side of the page contained one column of BT text. The column on the obverse side is designated 'a', that on the reverse 'b'. Since all editions follow this system, BT is cited by folio and column. Thus Ber. 33b means tractate 'Berakhot', folio 33, column b (i. e., reverse). Moreover, to this day all editions begin the BT text on page 2, for BOMBERG used page 1 as the title page. Another feature of BOMBERG's edition which became standard is the choice of commentaries printed alongside the text. On the inner edge of each side of the folio he printed the commentary of Rashi (= R. Shelomo Yiṣhaqi of France, died 1105). On the outer edge of each side he printed the Tosafot or 'Supplements'. The latter comprise commentary on BT and supercommentary on Rashi by French and German masters of the twelfth through the fourteenth centuries (including descendants of Rashi). These two commentaries appear in the same location in every subsequent edition of BT. After BOMBERG there were several more sixteenth century printings in Venice, Lublin, Constantinople, and Basel. According to RABBINOVICZ the Frankfurt a. M. edition of 1720—22 became the basis for all future editions. Most twentieth century printings reproduce the Romm edition published in Vilna between 1880—86. Critical editions will be discussed in the following section.

5. Text Criticism

a) The History of Text Criticism

Text criticism of BT is as old as the study of the document. The early commentators achieved a high degree of sophistication in this discipline. For example an eleventh century (?) authority warns of the interpolation into the text of marginal notes:

> "It is common that a reference, explanation, or variant is written in the margin or between the lines. A copyist thinks it is part of the text and writes it all together. He thus leads astray, for [his copy] will fall into the hands of a sage who will treat the matter as a unit and render decisions according to the addition[18]."

[18] Responsen der Geonim, ed. A. HARKAVY (Berlin, 1887), #272 p. 138. See p. 365 for his suggested attribution of this responsum to Hai Gaon.

Indeed it is usually information in the early commentaries which enables us to identify interpolations and late additions to BT. The *rishonim* also devoted considerable attention to variant readings. A good illustration involves a passage at Sanh. 65b. In the eleventh century the *ga'on* Hai reports four different readings of the latter text. He rejects two of them because they were not attested in "our texts". The other two, he claims, are in effect identical[19]. The allusion to "our texts" indicates that the academy of Pumbedita, of which Hai was principal, possessed texts considered authoritative, but other texts also circulated. Incidentally, Hai's contemporary Rashi attests still a fifth reading and appears to know nothing of the four cited by the former. Commentators outside Babylonia, like Rashi, did not have authoritative texts, but many of them placed a high value on Spanish manuscripts of BT. Because of the close connections between Spain and Babylonia during the Geonic period it was felt that these manuscripts contained the most accurate text[20]. We recall the tradition cited above that a deposed Babylonian exilarch wrote out a text of BT in Spain in the late eighth century. In addition to Spanish manuscripts, old manuscripts were highly prized. The *rishonim* frequently allude to "old texts on parchment" which they consulted in order to establish the correct reading[21].

The textual criticism of the early commentators was not limited to collating variants. Many were tempted to emend the text. The aforementioned Hai expressed reservations about this procedure:

> "Some of the 'emenders' (*garsanim*) report this tradition [in the following version]. Certainly this version is easier on the ear than the former [i. e., the unemended version], but it is neither our reading nor that of the early authorities. We must not change Tannaitic sources or the Talmud because of a difficulty we have [in understanding the text], for this is the accepted reading received from our masters upon whom we rely . . .[22]."

Hai thus argues that one should not emend a well attested reading on the basis of conjecture. Other commentators did not share this view. Rashi, for example, suggested many emendations in his commentary based on conjecture as well as variants[23]. In so doing he seems to have initiated a trend among the Franco-German commentators. Soon a reaction set in. A

19 'Osar Hagge'onim to Tractate Sanhedrin, ed. H. Z. Taubes (Jerusalem, 1966), p. 68, ad 65b.

20 See for example, Ramban, Novellae ad BB 134 and 137; Zeraḥyah Hallevi, Hamma'or Haggadol AZ, Chap. I, 2b; Rabad ad Ma'or, Ber. Chapter I end.

21 For example, Maimonides, Mishneh Torah, Malveh Veloveh 15:2; Ishut, 13:13. B. Ashkenazi, Shiṭṭah Mequbbeṣet ad Ket. 31b, 75b.

22 Otzar ha-Geonim, ed. B. M. Lewin, Vol. VIII (Jerusalem, 1939), Responsa, p. 207, ad Ket. 68b.

23 Cf. Melammed, Introduction, pp. 492f.

grandson of Rashi, R. Ya'aqov b. Me'ir, known as Rabbenu Tam, criticized the excesses of his own brother:

> "May his Lord forgive my brother Samuel, because for every reading R. Shelomo [Rashi] emended, he [Samuel] emended twenty. Not only this, but he erased [readings] in the books[24]."

This passage appears in a tract Ya'aqov published to correct the textual anarchy, Sefer Hayyashar. In the introduction he set forth the following principles: 1. The existence of variant readings in manuscripts does not justify emendation. 2. One must not emend on the basis of conjecture. 3. One should not emend on the basis of parallel sources[25]. The second principle repeats the opinion of Hai cited above. The third recognizes the distinction between variants of the same text and different though parallel texts. I understand the first principle to mean that variant readings may represent valid text traditions, and therefore we cannot disqualify one in favor of another. All of these principles are accepted by modern students of rabbinic literature. Indeed URBACH notes that the text critical methodology of the Tosafists (the Franco-German school of commentators of the 12th—14th century) is fully compatible with modern philological scholarship[26].

b) Collations of Variants and Critical Editions

The major contribution of modern BT text criticism consists of the systematic collation of variant readings. R. RABBINOVICZ was the pioneer in this endeavor. His 'Diqduqē Soferim' compares the readings from Codex Munich 95 with those of the standard printed text. The variants are printed in parallel columns. In the footnotes he discusses variants from other manuscripts as well as those attested in early witnesses. Unfortunately RABBINOVICZ did not live to complete his project. His Diq. Sof. does not cover the tractates of Order *nashim*, part of *qodashim*, and tractate Nid. Nor did he manage to record all the variants from Codex Munich. Finally, since the publication of this work, additional manuscript material has come to light. Despite all its shortcomings, Diq. Sof. remains a valuable tool for the study of BT. The project of RABBINOVICZ has been continued by M. S. FELDBLUM in his volume on Giṭ. An advantage in the latter volume is the addition of the standard BT page, in slightly reduced format, opposite the page containing the variants. FELDBLUM also distinguishes among the variants attested by *ge'onim* and *rishonim*. Only those witnessed by manuscripts of BT are noted among the variants. The rest appear in the footnotes. The footnotes also include 'variants' from parallel sources. Another collation of variants appears in the edition of MS JTSA of AZ by S. ABRAMSON. The most recent development is the projected 'Complete Diqduqē

24 Sefer Hayyashar, Introduction, cited from a manuscript by E. E. URBACH, The Tosaphists: Their History, Writings, and Methods² (Jerusalem, 1955), p. 528.

25 See URBACH, op. cit., pp. 80—82, 529—533.

26 Ibid., p. 532.

Soferim' announced by the Complete Israeli Talmud Institute of the Rav Herzog Foundation. This series is a by-product of plans to issue a new edition of BT and its commentaries accompanied by variant readings, full cross and source references, and additional commentaries. Since the collation of variant readings for all of BT is already complete, the editors decided to publish this material immediately rather than wait for the larger project. So far five volumes have appeared. Two contain the Mishnah of order *zera'im*, two cover BT Ket. (edited by HIRSCHLER), and one covers the first part of BT Soṭ. (edited by LISS). In the latter three volumes we find the BT text from the Vilna edition at the top of the page. Below it appear cross references and source references. Below this are variant readings from all known manuscripts, Genizah fragments, and early editions as well as those attested by the *ge'onim* and *rishonim*. Judging by the volumes which have appeared, this series promises to live up to its name and bring to a completion the endeavor initiated by RABBINOVICZ. The value of such a series for all aspects of Talmud scholarship is obvious.

Collations of variants cannot take the place of a critical edition of BT. Unfortunately, little has been done in the latter area during the past fifty years. STRACK listed only one critical edition of a single tractate in his 'Introduction': that of Ber. by N. PEREFERKOWITSCH in 1909. Some twenty years earlier M. FRIEDMANN had published a critical edition of Mak., and in 1913 S. ALBECK brought out a model edition of the first eight folios of Ber. Since STRACK the only attempt at a critical edition was that of MALTER who prepared one of Ta. which appeared posthumously in 1930. FRIEDMANN, PEREFERKOWITSCH, and MALTER all published eclectic texts. (I was unable to obtain a copy of the edition by S. ALBECK). This procedure was sharply criticised by the reviewers. MARX, for example, argues that the project of PEREFERKOWITSCH is premature. Before we can attempt to establish the correct text we must reconstruct the different text types current during the middle ages. Moreover PEREFERKOWITSCH does not establish criteria for choosing one reading over another. Finally, and most basically, MARX doubts whether there ever was a uniform text even in the academies which according to him redacted BT. This doubt is shared by APTOWIZER in his review of MALTER. APTOWITZER argues that even were the critical resources at our disposal reliable — and they are not — the eclectic method would be still inadmissible for a work like BT «*dont la valeur et l'autorité résident dans la tradition*» (p. 208). The adverse criticism had its desired effect, and after MALTER there were no further attempts to produce an eclectic text. Unfortunately no one essayed the more modest task suggested by MARX either. Thus matters stood until the recent work of ROSENTHAL which I shall discuss below.

c) The Principles of BT Text Criticism

If text criticism of BT was neglected by modern scholarship, that of other rabbinic documents was not. The researches of EPSTEIN and LIEBER-

MAN on Tannaitic sources and those of MARGULIES on a Palestinian Amoraic text are especially noteworthy. The principles established in this work should also apply, mutatis mutandis, to BT. EPSTEIN discusses in detail the prerequisites and materials for a scientific edition of the Mishnah. He stresses the difference between *Varianten* and *Versionen* (ITM, pp. 1—7). The former result from errors and changes in the course of oral or scribal transmission of the document. The latter are different versions or recensions of the text. We can legitimately decide that certain *Varianten* are incorrect, but the *Versionen* may have equal textual validity. The application of this distinction to text critical work is illustrated in the best scientific edition of a Tannaitic text we have, that of 'Tosefta' by LIEBERMAN. LIEBERMAN refrains from producing an eclectic text. One of the reasons he gives for this decision is the difficulty in deciding whether a given reading represents a scribal error or a valid alternate version[27]. Given the existence of different versions, an eclectic text would distort the unitary text traditions or text types. Finally, LIEBERMAN notes that we possess few scientific editions of rabbinic texts. Thus we cannot yet adopt the editorial procedures established by classical philology[28]. These considerations lead LIEBERMAN to choose for the body of his edition a manuscript which best represents one text type. He publishes the latter without change together with a full collation of variant readings. Parallel texts from other documents appear in the commentary, not in the critical apparatus[29]. E. S. ROSENTHAL claims that the text critical methods adopted by LIEBERMAN should apply to all of rabbinic literature (Hammoreh, p. 63). And in fact MARGULIES follows the same procedures in his edition of 'Vayyiqra Rabbah', a Palestinian Amoraic *midrash* on Leviticus. He also adds another consideration, deriving from the nature of rabbinic literature. Since these texts are compilations of discrete traditions with only a loose external framework, additions or deletions are not felt by the reader. Thus every copyist can edit the text anew if he so wishes. This makes it almost impossible to recover the *Urtext* as it left the hands of the original editor[30]. LIEBERMAN and MARGULIES thus agree that at present critical editions of rabbinic texts are not possible. For now we must be satisfied with scientific

[27] In his earlier work on the 'Tosefta' readings in the *rishonim* LIEBERMAN writes, "we must take seriously the different readings in the manuscripts and in the *rishonim*. It is not possible to decide that only one of the readings is correct, for in many instances both readings are correct — each one according to the tradition by which it was created. Each one is 'textually true' . . . each text has its own truth." See Tosefet Rishonim, Vol. IV (Jerusalem, 1939), Introduction, p. 15.

[28] ROSENTHAL notes that even some Greek texts do not permit an eclectic edition. 'Traditional' documents composed and edited by generations of savants pose the same problems as rabbinic texts. He quotes REITZENSTEIN on the problems of editing the Poimandres to illustrate this point, see Hammoreh, p. 63.

[29] See ROSENTHAL, Hammoreh, pp. 67—69 for a summary of the text-critical methods of LIEBERMAN in his edition of the 'Tosefta'.

[30] M. MARGULIES, Midrash Wayyikra Rabbah, Part V (Jerusalem, 1960), p. XL.

editions of individual recensions or text types accompanied by a collation of variant readings.

The principles discussed above are applied to BT by ROSENTHAL in the scientific edition of Pes. he is preparing. In a preliminary study of one brief pericope from this tractate he illustrates the problematic of BT text criticism. The text tradition of this passage, which ROSENTHAL believes is representative, turns out to be extremely fluid. This leads him to wonder whether we can overcome even the first hurdle of text criticism: deciding where redaction ends and text tradition begins (see 'Rav' etc.). Whatever the problem, no one is better equipped than ROSENTHAL to overcome it. His edition of Pes. should move BT scholarship beyond the collation of variants to the level of publishing recensions of tractates. However, as ROSENTHAL himself noted with regard to 'Tosefta', it is unlikely that we shall be able to move beyond recensions to the 'original text' in the foreseeable future (Hammoreh, p. 70).

III. The Languages of BT

Bibliography

1. General

BROCKELMANN, C. and BAUMSTARK, A., Aramäisch und Syrisch, Handbuch der Orientalistik, III, 2. ed. B. SPULER. Leiden, 1954.

FRAENKEL, S., Die aramäischen Fremdwörter im Arabischen. Leiden, 1866.

KUTSCHER, E. Y., Aramaic, Current Trends in Linguistics, Vol. 6, The Hague, 1970, pp. 178—183.

ID., Aramaic, Encyclopaedia Judaica, Vol. 3, Jerusalem, 1972, coll. 259—287.

ID., Mittelhebräisch und Jüdisch-Aramäisch im neuen Köhler-Baumgartner, Hebräische Wortforschung. Festschrift W. Baumgartner, Leiden, 1967, pp. 158—175 (= Supplements to Vetus Testamentum, 16).

ID., Some problems of the Lexicography of the Jewish Aramaic Dialects, Archive of the New Dictionary of Rabbinic Literature, II, Ramat Gan, 1974, pp. 96—101, English Summary, pp. XII—XIII.

ID., Studies in Galilean Aramaic. Jerusalem, 1966. = Tarbiz 21 (1951—52), pp. 192—205, 22 (1952—53), pp. 185—192, 23 (1953—54), pp. 36—60 (Hebrew; English edition in press).

ROSENTHAL, F., Die aramaistische Forschung seit Th. Nöldeke's Veröffentlichungen. Leiden, 1939.

ID., An Aramaic Handbook. 2 Vols. Wiesbaden, 1967.

2. Middle Hebrew (especially the Hebrew of BT)

ABRAMSON, S., On the Hebrew in the Babylonian Talmud, Archive of the New Dictionary of Rabbinic Literature, II, Ramat Gan, 1974, pp. 9—15, English Summary, p. V.

BENDAVID, A., Biblical Hebrew and Mishnaic Hebrew[2]. 2 Vols. Tel Aviv, 1967—71.

GINSBERG, H. L., Zu den Dialekten des Talmudisch-Hebräischen, MGWJ 77 (1933), pp. 413—429.

KUTSCHER, E. Y., Hebrew Language: Mishnaic, Encyclopaedia Judaica, Vol. 16, Jerusalem, 1972, coll. 1590—1607.

ID., The Present State of Research into Mishnaic Hebrew (Especially Lexicography) and Its Tasks, Archive of the New Dictionary of Rabbinic Literature, I, Ramat Gan, 1972, pp. 3—28, English Summary pp. III—X.

ID., Some Problems of the Lexicography of Mishnaic Hebrew and its Comparison with Biblical Hebrew, ibid., pp. 29—82, English Summary, pp. XI—XXVII.

MARGALIYOT, E., 'Ivrit Ve'aramit Batalmud Uvamidrash, Lešonenu 27/28 (1963—64), pp. 20—33.

MORESHET, M., Further Studies of the Language of the Hebrew Baraytot in the Babylonian and Palestinian Talmudim, Archive of the New Dictionary of Rabbinic Literature, II, Ramat Gan, 1974, pp. 31—73, English Summary, pp. VIII—IX.

ID., The Language of the Baraytot in the T. B. is not MHe[1], H. Yalon Memorial Volume, Jerusalem, 1974, pp. 275—314, English Summary, pp. XXI—XXII.

ID., A Lexicon of the New Verbs in the Tannaitic Hebrew. Unpublished Ph. D. Dissertation, Jerusalem, 1972. English Summary, pp. I—XIV.

ID., New and Revived Verbs in the Baraytot of the Babylonian Talmud (In Comparison with mh[2] in the Babylonian and Palestinian Talmudim), Archive of the New Dictionary of Rabbinic Literature, I, Ramat Gan, 1972, pp. 117—162, English Summary, pp. XXXVI—XXXIX.

PRIJS, L., Ergänzungen zum talmudisch-hebräischen Wörterbuch, ZDMG 120 (1970), pp. 6—29.

SOKOLOFF, M., The Hebrew of Berešit Rabba According to MS Vat. Ebr. 30, Lešonenu 33 (1968—69), pp. 25—42, 135—149, 270—279.

Midrash Bereshit Rabba. MS Vat. Ebr. 30. Introduction and Index by M. SOKOLOFF. Jerusalem, 1971.

3. Babylonian Talmudic Aramaic and Related Dialects

BEN ASHER, M., The Conjugation of the Verb in 'Halakot Pesuqot', Lešonenu 34 (1969—70), pp. 278—286, 35 (1970—71), pp. 20—35.

EPSTEIN, J. (Y.) N., Babylonisch-Aramäische Studien, Festskrift ... David Simonsen, Kobenhavn, 1923, pp. 290—310.

ID., Glosses babylo-araméennes. I. Les textes magiques araméens de Montgomery, REJ 73 (1921), pp. 27—58, 74 (1922), pp. 40—72.

ID., A Grammar of Babylonian Aramaic. Jerusalem and Tel Aviv, 1960 (Hebrew).

ID., Notes on Post-Talmudic Aramaic Lexicography. I. Linguistic Remarks to Anan's Sepher Ha-Miṣwot, JQR n.s. 5 (1914—15), pp. 233—251. II. Sheeltot, JQR n.s. 12 (1921—22), pp. 299—390.

ID., Zum magischen Text, JAOS 33 (1912), pp. 279—280.

ID., Zur Babylonisch-Aramäischen Lexicographie, Festschrift A. Schwarz, Berlin und Wien, 1917, pp. 317—327.

ID., Studies in Aramaic Philology. Selected with an Introduction and indices by DANIEL BOYARIN. New York 1978.

GINZBERG, L., Beiträge zur Lexicographie des Jüdisch-Aramäischen 1, Festschrift A. Schwarz, Berlin und Wien, 1917, pp. 329—360. 2, MGWJ 78 (1934), pp. 9—33. 3, Essays ... in Memory of Linda Miller, New York, 1938, pp. 57—108.

KAUFMAN, S. A., Akkadian and Babylonian Aramaic — New Examples of Mutual Elucidation, Lešonenu 36 (1971—72), pp. 28—33, 37 (1972—73) pp. 102—104.

ID. The Akkadian Influences on Aramaic. Chicago, 1974.

KUTSCHER, E. Y., Babylonian Aramaic, Encyclopedia Judaica, Vol. 3, Jerusalem, 1972, coll. 277—282.

ID., Babylonian Talmudic, in: An Aramaic Handbook, ed. F. ROSENTHAL, Wiesbaden, 1967, II, 1, pp. 43—45; II, 2, pp. 59—66.

ID., Lemunaḥe Shetarot Batalmud Uvesifrut Ge'onim, Tarbiz 17 (1945—46), pp. 125—127, 19 (1947—48), pp. 53—58, 125—128.

ID., Meḥqar Diqduq Ha'aramit Shel Hattalmud Habbavli, Lešonenu 26 (1962), pp. 149—183.

MALONE, J. L., Observations of Linguistic Similarity between the Babylonian Aramaic of Halakot Pesuqot and Mandaic, Lešonenu 37 (1972—73), pp. 161—164.
MORAG, S., Ha'aramit Habbavlit Bemassoret Teman: Happo'el Hashalem, H. Yalon Jubilee Volume, Jerusalem, 1963, pp. 182—220.
ID., Notes on Phonology of Babylonian Aramaic as Reflected by the Vocalization of Halakot Pesuqot, Lešonenu 32 (1967—68), pp. 67—88, English Summary, pp. IV—V.
ID., On the Yemenite Tradition of Babylonian Aramaic, Tarbiz 30 (1960—61), pp. 120—129, English Summary, p. II.
ID., Some Notes on the Grammar of Babylonian Aramaic as Reflected in the Geniza Manuscripts, Tarbiz 42 (1972—73), pp. 60—78, English Summary, pp. V—VI.
PRIJS, L., Ergänzungen zum talmudisch-aramäischen Wörterbuch, ZDMG 117 (1967), pp. 266—286.
ROSENBERG, J., Das aramäische Pronomen im babylonischen Talmud, MGWJ 77 (1933), pp. 253—265.
ROSSELL, W. H., A Handbook of Aramaic Magical Texts. Ringwood Borough, New Jersey, 1953.
SCHLESINGER, M., Satzlehre der aramäischen Sprache des babylonischen Talmuds. Leipzig, 1928.
TELEGDI, S., Essai sur la phonétique des emprunts iraniens en Araméen, Journal Asiatique 226 (1935), pp. 177—256.
VON SODEN, W., Aramäische Wörter in neuassyrischen und neu- und spätbabylonischen Texten. Ein Vorbericht, Orientalia n.s. 35 (1966), pp. 1—20.
WEISBERG, DAVID B., Some Observations on Late Babylonian Texts and Rabbinic Literature, HUCA 39 (1968), pp. 71—80.

4. Related Eastern Aramaic Dialects

a) Mandaic

DROWER, E. S. and MACUCH, R., A Mandaic Dictionary. Oxford, 1963.
MACUCH, R., Handbook of Classical and Modern Mandaic. Berlin, 1965.

b) Syriac

BROCKELMANN, C., Lexicon Syriacum[3]. Hildesheim, 1966.
ID., Syrische Grammatik, Berlin, 1899. Reprint, Leipzig, 1965.
PAYNE SMITH, R., Thesaurus Syriacus. 2 Vols. Oxford, 1879—1901. Supplement. Ed. J. P. MARGOLIOUTH, Oxford. 1927.

c) Modern Eastern Aramaic Dialects

GARBELL, I., The Jewish Neo-Aramaic Dialect of Persian Azerbaijan: Linguistic Analysis and Folkloristic Texts. The Hague, 1965.
RITTER, H., Turoyo. Die Volkssprache der Syrischen Christen des Tur 'Abdin. 2 Vols. Wiesbaden, 1967—69.
RIVLIN, Y. Y., Shirat Yehude Hattargum. Jerusalem, 1959.
SARA, S. L., A Description of Modern Chaldean. The Hague and Paris, 1971.

5. Dictionaries

BEN YEHUDA, E., Thesaurus totius Hebraitatis. 8 Vols. London and New York, 1960.
DALMAN, G., Aramäisch-neuhebräisches Wörterbuch zu Targum, Talmud und Midrasch. Frankfurt, a. M., 1901. 2nd Ed. 1922.
JASTROW, M., A Dictionary of the Targumim, the Talmud Babli and Yerushalmi, and the Midrashic Literature. 2 Vols. London and New York, 1903. Reprint New York, 1950.
KOHUT, A., Aruch Completum. 8 Vols. Vienna, 1878—92.
ID., Additamenta ad Aruch Completum. Ed. S. KRAUSS. Vienna, 1937.

KRAUSS, S., Griechische und Lateinische Lehnwörter im Talmud, Midrasch und Targum. 2 Vols. Berlin, 1898—1899. Reprint, Hildesheim, 1964.
LEVY, J., Wörterbuch über die Talmudim und Midraschim. 4 Vols. Leipzig, 1875—1889. Reprint, Darmstadt, 1963.
LÖW, I., Fauna und Mineralien der Juden. Hildesheim, 1969.
ID., Die Flora der Juden. 4 Vols. Wien und Leipzig, 1926—34.

1. Introduction

In reading BT one comes upon no less than four different dialects. They are Biblical Hebrew (bh), the Hebrew of the Tannaim (mh^1 = Middle Hebrew^1), the Hebrew of the Amoraim (mh^2 = Middle Hebrew^2), and the Aramaic of the Babylonian Amoraim (bta = Babylonian Talmudic Aramaic)[31]. Two of the four may be ignored here. bh occurs only in quotations from the Bible and mh^1 only in quotations from the Mishnah and other Tannaitic sources. Thus I shall concentrate on mh^2 and bta. Although we still do not have adequate grammars and dictionaries of these dialects, research on them has progressed considerably especially in the past 25 years. Much of that progress is connected with E. Y. KUTSCHER, whose death at 60 was a serious loss to Talmudic scholarship and semitic studies in general. In his own work, in the projects he initiated, and in the students he trained KUTSCHER laid the foundation for the recovery of the dialects of rabbinic literature. He himself stressed his dependence on the prior work of H. YALON, EPSTEIN, and LIEBERMAN. These scholars had shown that the current state of our texts severely hinders study of the latter dialects. Older manuscripts of rabbinic documents reveal linguistic features significantly different from those in the common printed texts. It could be demonstrated that during the 1500 years of transmission the original orthography, morphology, syntax, and lexica of the sources had been changed almost beyond recognition. Oral transmitters (*Tradenten*), copyists, and printers, unaware of the true character of the various linguistic strata, 'corrected' the texts in light of what they believed to be the proper forms. This process was both unconscious (especially with the *Tradenten* and coypists) and conscious (especially with the printers). And it affected all of the rabbinic dialects. Let us take bta as an example. Not only the printed texts, but also most manuscripts of BT lack a written vocalization. Nor is there a uniform traditional pronunciation. By contrast, both Biblical Aramaic and the Aramaic of the targums possess written vocalization

31 For these terms see KUTSCHER, Baumgartner-Festschr. For the last named dialect KUTSCHER uses ja^b = Jewish Aramaic, Babylonian. However, this term includes post-Talmudic Geonic Aramaic (see KUTSCHER, EJ, III), and by rights should also include the Aramaic of the Jewish incantation texts from Nippur and elsewhere. The term bta has the advantage of referring only to the Aramaic of BT.
Additional dialects of Aramaic are found in BT, e.g., in quotations from the Aramaic sections of the Mishnah, from the Bible targums, and possibly in quotations of Palestinian Amoraim. Since this material is very limited, it may be ignored here. I shall also ignore local sub-dialects of bta, the existence of which is noted by EPSTEIN, Grammar, p. 14.

systems. Consequently, bta was 'corrected' so as to conform to the former, better known dialects. Only with the recognition of this problem could the proper direction of research be determined. The study of the dialects of rabbinic literature must be based on old, linguistically reliable manuscripts, on the traditional pronunciation of the various Jewish communities, and, where available, on epigraphic material contemporary with the sources.

2. The Hebrew of BT

The Hebrew of the Tannaim, mh¹, is at present the best known of the rabbinic dialects. A summary in English of the current state of our knowledge can be found in the article by KUTSCHER in EJ, Vol. 16 (coll. 1595 to 1607 with bibliography at 1659f.; cf. KUTSCHER in: Baumgartner-Festschr. and in Archive I). The Amoraim had already recognized the distinction between bh and mh. In the latter half of the third century the Palestinian Yoḥanan b. Nappaḥa distinguished between *leshon torah*, the language of the Pentateuch, and *leshon ḥakhamim*, the language of the sages (see AZ 58b and cf. Ḥul. 137b; note also the Aramaic equivalents *lishana de'oraita* and *lishana derabbanan* at Qid. 2b). The next step was to distinguish between the mh of the Tannaim and that of the Amoraim. This was done by A. GEIGER in the last century (GEIGER, ZDMG 12 [1858], p. 148). KUTSCHER developed this distinction further, but it remained for his student M. SOKOLOFF to work out in detail the difference between mh¹ and mh². His study is based on a linguistically reliable manuscript of Bereshit Rabbah, a Palestinian Amoraic midrash on Genesis. SOKOLOFF's conclusions are as follows. mh¹ is a literary language reflecting the Hebrew spoken during the second century C.E. As is now agreed, Hebrew continued as a spoken language, at least in Judah, during the Second Temple period and into the first centuries of the Common Era. This spoken Hebrew appears beneath the surface of the bh of the later books of the Bible and of the Qumran texts, as well as in the Bar Kosiba documents. By contrast, mh² (of the Palestinian sources) is a purely literary dialect composed in the Galil during the third through the sixth centuries, at a place and in a time when Hebrew was not the spoken language. As a result, mh² was influenced much more than mh¹ by Aramaic, which was the common spoken dialect. Moreover, mh² replaced many of the forms unique to mh¹ by forms from bh (SOKOLOFF, Lešonenu, 277f., and cf. 26f.).

As noted above, SOKOLOFF details the differences between mh¹ and mh² as reflected in Palestinian sources. KUTSCHER argues that we must further distinguish the mh² of Palestinian sources (mh²p) from that appearing in BT (mh²b). Structurally the two sub-dialects are identical. The Hebrew of BT also drops mh¹ forms in favor of those from bh, and it also is colored by Aramaic. However the dialects of Aramaic involved are different. mh²p was influenced by Galilean Aramaic, mh²b by bta (KUTSCHER, Baumgartner-Festschr., pp. 164—168, cf. H. L. GINSBERG, MGWJ 77, for the distinction between Palestinian and Babylonian mh). Unfortunately we do not yet have a study of mh²b parallel to that of SOKOLOFF on mh²p. Writing in 1972 KUTSCHER noted that no linguistically reliable manuscripts of the Hebrew of BT had been identified (EJ 16, col. 1594, cf. 1607; see also Baumgartner-Festschr., pp. 165f. and Archive I, p. 16). Since then the situation has improved. The key so far has been the *baraitot* (singular: *baraita*) appearing in BT. *Baraita,* an abbreviation of *matnita baraita,* 'external Tannaitic tradition', designates all the Tannaitic sources external to the Mishnah of Yehudah the Patriarch. The term thus applies to materials in the Tannaitic collections such as the 'Tosefta' and the halakhic midrashim as well as the apparently Tannaitic sources cited in the two Talmuds. Reversing his earlier position, KUTSCHER argued that the Hebrew of the BT *baraitot* is significantly different from that found in the Tannaitic collections (Archive I, pp. 40, 45). Another one of his students, M. MORESHET studied this difference. In a series of articles MORESHET compares BT *baraitot* with their parallels in Tannaitic collections and in the Palestinian Talmud. He concludes that while the language of the latter materials is essentially identical to that of the Mishnah, that of the former is not. Thus within mh¹ also we must differentiate a Babylonian sub-dialect (mh¹b) from the Palestinian (mh¹p). What distinguishes mh¹b is the influence of mh²b. In other words, by listing the unique features of mh¹b MORESHET in effect has begun to describe mh²b. It is to be hoped that he will continue with a direct study of the latter. The identification of certain manuscripts of BT as linguistically reliable, such as MS Columbia of Pes., will facilitate such a project. In the meantime the articles of E. MARGALIYOT and ABRAMSON and the relevant chapters in BENDAVID may be consulted. Pending further research, the Hebrew of the Babylonian Amoraim remains the least known of the dialects of rabbinic literature.

3. Babylonian Talmudic Aramaic

The Amoraim recognized that Babylonian Aramaic differs from Palestinian (see, e. g., Ned. 66b). Modern semitic studies agree and locate bta, along with Syriac and Mandaic in the Eastern branch of what FITZMYER calls "late Aramaic"[32]. Modern study of bta begins in 1865 with the publication of the first grammar of the dialect. Two more grammars appeared in the period covered by STRACK's bibliography. The one grammar that has been published since, that by EPSTEIN, is by far the best. Unlike his predecessors, EPSTEIN made extensive use of manuscripts of BT as well as of cognate dialects. The latter include not only Syriac and Mandaic, but also the language of the Jewish incantation texts and of Geonic literature. In a major review (Lešonenu 26, pp. 149—183), KUTSCHER asserts that EPSTEIN's work is "the only scientific grammar of Babylonian Aramaic

[32] See J. A. FITZMYER, The Genesis Apocryphon of Qumran Cave I² (Rome, 1971), pp. 22f., n. 60.

that we have", (p. 170, cf. EJ 3, col. 279). Nevertheless, continues KUTSCHER, even this book, composed of posthumously published lecture notes, does not fill the need for a grammar of bta. He lists three major inadequacies in this book. 1. The grammar lacks both a phonology and a syntax, though for the latter we can rely on the excellent study of M. SCHLESINGER. 2. The vocalization is neither systematic nor consistent. 3. The morphology, which comprises the bulk of the book does exploit the manuscript evidence. However, EPSTEIN's use of the latter is sporadic and inconsistent (for all these points see Lešonenu, pp. 151—171). The last point is the most important. KUTSCHER argues that eclectic reliance on the manuscripts is improper. We cannot record forms now from this manuscript, now from that, and then a third time from the printed text — as EPSTEIN does. Rather, we must rely only on those few manuscripts which can be identified as linguistically reliable. This method brought excellent results in research on mh[1] and Galilean Aramaic (cf. 'Baumgartner-Festschr.'). The question is, of course, how do we determine which manuscripts are reliable. For the Palestinian dialects epigraphic evidence provided the key. We have no parallel evidence for bta, for the incantation texts reflect a different dialect. KUTSCHER believes that the solution lies in Geonic texts. These were composed shortly after BT in the same geographical location by native speakers of Aramaic. Although Geonic Aramaic is not identical with bta, it is very close. Moreover, almost all Geonic sources quote extensively from BT. Thus the first step must be to identify linguistically reliable manuscripts of Geonic texts and construct a grammar of the BT quotations appearing there. On the basis of this work we should then be able to identify linguistically reliable manuscripts of BT itself. Eventually, as our results are refined, we shall be able to distinguish bta from the Geonic dialect. Another approach involves studying the traditional pronunciation of bta by various Jewish communities. This method also produced results in the study of mh[1] and Galilean Aramaic. Both of these approaches have been followed. KUTSCHER identified two linguistically reliable manuscripts of Geonic texts. One is MS Sassoon of 'Halakhot Pesuqot'. Apparently based on a *Vorlage* copied by a native speaker of Babylonian Aramaic, it exhibits a full orthography and a grammatical accuracy (e. g. agreement in number and gender of nouns and adjectives, subjects and verbs) lacking in our common printed texts of BT. The second is MS Paris of 'Halakhot Gedolot'. Both of these manuscripts partially vocalize the BT quotations. On the basis of the linguistic picture emerging from the latter KUTSCHER notes that Codex Hamburg Neziqin and MS Columbia Pes. appear to be fairly reliable and may serve for further research. M. BEN-ASHER, another student of KUTSCHER, has begun a study of bta in MS Sassoon, and S. MORAG has begun to research the traditional pronunciation of the Yemenite community. Thus the research program outlined by KUTSCHER is being carried out. Till it is completed, the grammar of EPSTEIN may be consulted, though it should be used together with the review by KUTSCHER. The latter also contributed a short sketch of bta grammar in English in EJ 3 (coll. 279f.).

Examples of texts in bta from linguistically reliable manuscripts together with a glossary compiled by KUTSCHER can be found in ROSENTHAL's 'Aramaic Handbook'.

4. Lexicography

Lexicographical study of rabbinic dialects begins with the Amoraim and continues in the commentaries of the *ge'onim* and *rishonim*. The earliest dictionary of rabbinic literature is the "Arukh' compiled during the eleventh century by Natan b. Yeḥi'el of Rome (p. e. Rome, before 1475; this may be the oldest printed Hebrew book[33]). As KUTSCHER notes (EJ 3, col. 278), the "Arukh' set two trends followed by all later dictionaries. It treats together all the dialects and sources of rabbinic literatures, and it uses a comparative method, adducing Arabic, Persian, Greek, and Latin evidence. In the course of the following centuries several scholars contributed additions and supplements to the "Arukh'. The next independent dictionary to appear was that of LEVY. It is still the best available. A few years later A. KOHUT published a critical edition of the "Arukh' to which he added extensive complementary material. The result is, in effect, a new dictionary, but one with several drawbacks. KOHUT retained the original order of entries. Since the latter was not based on the modern concept of Hebrew grammar, it often is difficult to locate the desired root. A more serious problem results from KOHUT's attempt, in principle praiseworthy, fully to exploit Iranian evidence. Unfortunately, he wrote at a time when modern Iranology was in its early stages. Moreover KOHUT is guilty of a kind of pan-Iranism in that he seeks Iranian etymologies even for obviously semitic words. His limited knowledge of Iranian languages and his farfetched etymologies are largely corrected in the 'Additamenta' to his dictionary edited by S. KRAUSS. A highly competent Iranist, B. GEIGER, was responsible for these corrections as well as for the addition of Akkadian, Arabic, and Mandaic evidence. Shortly after the appearance of KOHUT's work M. JASTROW published his dictionary. The main deficiency in this effort is JASTROW's attempt to find semitic etymologies for words obviously of Greek or Latin origin. The corrective here is to be found in KRAUSS' 'Griechische und lateinische Lehnwörter' and in the many studies of SAUL LIEBERMAN, especially 'Greek in Jewish Palestine' (New York, 1942) and 'Hellenism in Jewish Palestine' (New York, 1950). Finally mention should be made of the specialized lexicographical studies by the brilliant semitist I. Löw[34].

The dates of publication of the dictionaries of LEVY, KOHUT, and JASTROW indicate that these works must be superseded, even were they free

[33] M. MARX, On the Date of the Apearance of the first printed Hebrew Books, A. Marx Jubilee Volume, English Section (New York, 1950), pp. 481—501. MARX dates it to 1469—72.

[34] I have not listed G. DALMAN's 'Aramäisch-neuhebräisches Handwörterbuch zu Targum, Talmud und Midrasch' (Frankfurt a. M., 1901) which is inadequate for use with BT.

from faults. In the past century the study of the dialects of rabbinic literature, of cognate dialects, and of semitic linguistics generally has made great strides. KUTSCHER estimates that the work of his predecessors and older contemporaries, DALMAN, LÖW, YALON, EPSTEIN, and LIEBERMAN, already requires the addition of over 6000 entries to the existing dictionaries. This number constitutes 20% of the lexicon of rabbinic literature according to KUTSCHER (Archive I, pp. 13, 17). The additional lexicographical material which has become available since the publication of the dictionaries may be illustrated for bta. First, many manuscripts and especially Genizah fragments of BT were not available to LEVY, KOHUT, and JASTROW. Second, most of Geonic literature with its closely related dialect has been published only in the last century. Third, while some incantation texts were published in the nineteenth century, only with the appearance of MONTGOMERY's 'Aramaic Incantation Texts from Nippur' could serious study of the language of these texts begin. Fourth, in the past fifty years many new Mandaic texts have been published, and recently a new dictionary and grammar of this closely related dialect appeared. Fifth, further work has been done in this period on modern spoken dialects of Eastern Aramaic. Sixth, Iranology has progressed considerably not only since KOHUT, but also since B. GEIGER and TELEGDI. An up to date study of Iranian influences on bta is a desideratum. Seventh, and finally, study of Akkadian has also advanced. Especially relevant is the increasing recognition of the mutual relation between Akkadian and Aramaic. In bta, spoken in what had been a center of Akkadian culture, we can expect significant Akkadian influence. Recent studies on this issue include those of VON SODEN, S. A. KAUFMAN, and D. B. WEISBERG. The latter two especially deal with bta. Research in all seven of the areas listed will require major revisions in the existing lexica of BT.

The situation described above with regard to bta applies, mutatis mutandis, to the other dialects of rabbinic literature. Clearly the existing dictionaries are out of date and inadequate. KUTSCHER initiated a project aimed at producing a new dictionary of rabbinic literature incorporating recent research and differentiated according to dialects. Completion of this project is obviously not a matter of the immediate future. Its progress and the results of recent lexicographical studies may be followed in the publication of the project, 'Archive of the New Dictionary of Rabbinic Literature'.

IV. Source, Form, and Redaction Criticism

Bibliography

ALBECK, CH. [Ḥ], Introduction to the Talmud, Babli and Yerushalmi. Tel Aviv, 1969.

ID., Le'arikhat Hattalmud Habbavli, Tarbiz 15 (1943/44), pp. 14—26. [= Introduction, Chapter 9.]

Id., Le'arikat Hattalmud Habbavli, Studies in Memory of A. Gulak and S. Klein, Jerusalem, 1942, pp. 1—12.

Id., Leḥeqer Hattalmud: 1. Sugyot Uma'amarim Shenithavu 'Al Yide Ha'ataqot Mimaqom Lemaqom, Tarbiz 3 (1931/32), pp. 1—14. [= Introduction, Chapter 7.]

Id., Leḥeqer Hattalmud: 2. Hishtamshut Bema'amare Ha'amora'im, Tarbiz 9 (1937/38), pp. 163—178.

Id., Nusḥa'ot Bammishnah Shel Ha'amora'im, Abhandlungen zur Erinnerung an H. P. Chajes, Wien, 1933, pp. 1—28.

Id., Sof Hora'ah Visiyyum Hattalmud, Sinai: Sefer Yovel, Jerusalem, 1958, pp. 73—79.

Albeck, S., Sof Hora'ah Ve'aḥarone Ha'amora'im, Sinai: Sefer Yovel, Jerusalem, 1958, pp. 57—73.

Aminoah, N., The Redaction of the Tractate Qiddushin in the Babylonian Talmud. Compilation, Redaction, Textual Readings, Parallel Sugyot. Tel Aviv, 1977.

Atlas, S., On the History of the Sugya, HUCA 24 (1952/53), pp. 1—22.

Id., Leḥeqer Hattalmud, M. Schorr Jubilee Volume, Warsaw, 1935, pp. 9—17.

Id., Some Observations on the Nature of the Amoraic Discussions, Studies in Memory of M. Schorr, New York, 1944, pp. 1—11.

Bacher, W., Die exegetische Terminologie der jüdischen Traditionsliteratur, I—II. Leipzig, 1899—1905. Reprint, Darmstadt, 1965.

Id., Tradition und Tradenten in den Schulen Palästinas und Babyloniens. Leipzig, 1914.

Bokser, B., Samuel's Commentary on the Mishnah. Its Nature, Forms, and Content. Part One: Mishnayot in the Order of Zeraim. Leiden, 1975.

De Vries, B., The form of the Ancient Sugya. (A Chapter from the Problems of the Creation of the Talmud.), Bar Ilan 4—5 (1967) pp. 67—88, English Summary, pp. XXXVII—XXXVIII. [= Studies, Part II, Chapter 1.]

Id., Hamminuaḥ Betalmud Bavli, Lešonenu 29 (1964/65), pp. 160—166. [= Studies, Part II, Chapter 4.]

Id., Literary Transfer as a Factor in the Development of Talmudic Law, Bar Ilan 1 (1963), pp. 156—164, English Summary, p. XXXV.

Id., Meqoman Hammeqori Shel Sugyot Bavliot Messuyyamot, Sinai 58 (1966), pp. 17—24. [= Studies, Part II, Chapter 6.]

Id., The Problem of the Relationship of the Two Talmuds to the Tosefta, Tarbiz 28 (1958/59), pp. 158—170, English Summary, pp. III—IV.

Id., Studies in Talmudic Literature. Jerusalem, 1968.

Id., Ṣuratan Hammeqorit Shel Sugyot Bavliot 'Aḥadot, Y. I. Herzog Memorial Volume, Jerusalem, 1962, pp. 483—492. [= Studies Part II, Chapter 7.]

Id., The Talmudic Formula wtw l' mydy, Tarbiz 37 (1967/68) pp. 30—38, English Summary, p. IV. [= Studies, Part II, Chapter 3.]

Id., The Tractate Me'ila in the Babylonian Talmud, Tarbiz 30 (1960/61), pp. 370—378, English Summary, pp. II—III. [= Studies, Part II, Chapter 5.]

Id., WeHawaynan Ba, Tarbiz 35 (1965/66), pp. 254—268, English Summary, p. IV. [= Studies, Part II, Chapter 2.]

Dor, Z., Hammeqorot Ha'ereṣyisra'eliyyim Bevet Midrasho Shel Rava, Sinai 52 (1962), pp. 128—144, 53 (1963), pp. 31—49. 55 (1964), pp. 306—316. [= Teachings, Chapter 1.]

Id., On the Sources of Gittin in the Babylonian Talmud, Bar Ilan 4—5 (1967), pp. 89—103, English Summary, pp. XXXIX—XLI.

Id., The Palestinian Sources appearing in the Tractate Gittin of the Babylonian Talmud, Bar Ilan 1 (1963), pp. 120—142, English Summary, pp. XXVII—XX. [= Teachings, Appendix II.]

Id., The Teachings of Eretz Israel in Babylon. Tel Aviv, 1971.

Ephrati, J. E., Contributions of Succeeding Generations to a Sugya in Bava Metzia, Bar Ilan 6 (1968), pp. 75—100, English Summary pp. XVII—XVIII.

Id., The Sevoraic Period and its Literature. Petach-Tikva, 1973.

Epstein, J. [Y.] N., Introduction to Amoraitic Literature. Babylonian Talmud and Yerushalmi. Jerusalem, 1962. [= IAL.]

ID., Introduction to Tannaitic Literature. Mishna, Tosephta and Halakhic Midrashim. Jerusalem, 1957. [= ITL.]

ID., Introduction to the Text of the Mishnah². Jerusalem, 1964. [= ITM.]

FELDBLUM, M. S., The Impact of the 'Anonymous Sugyah' on Halakic Concepts, PAAJR 38 (1969), pp. 19—28.

ID., Professor Abraham Weiss: His Approach and Contribution to Talmudic Scholarship, A. Weiss Jubilee Volume, New York, 1965, pp. 7—80.

ID., Talmudic Law and Literature, Tractate Gittin. New York, 1969.

FRANCUS, I., Additions and Parallels in T. B. Bava Qamma VII, Bar Ilan 12 (1974), pp. 43—63, English Summary, p. IX.

FRIEDMAN, SH., Glosses and Additions in TB Bava Qamma VIII, Tarbiz 40 (1970), pp. 418—443, English Summary, pp. III—IV.

ID., A Critical Study of Yevamot X with a Methodological Introduction, Meḥqarim Umeqorot. Measef Lemada'e Hayahadut, New York, 1978, pp. 277—441.

ID., Some Structural Patterns of Talmudic Sugyot, Proceedings of the Sixth World Congress of Jewish Studies, Vol. III, Jerusalem, 1977, pp. 389—402.

GEVIRTSMAN, M., ''Ela 'I 'Ittamar Hakhi 'Ittamar' Betalmud Bavli, Sinai 69 (1971), pp. 110—122.

ID., Ṣiṭuṭim Be'ezrat ''Ittamar', Sinai 67 (1970), pp. 43—55.

GINZBERG, L., A Commentary on the Palestinian Talmud, Vol. I. New York, 1941.

GOLDBERG, A., On the Development of the Sugya in the Babylonian Talmud, H. Albeck Jubilee Volume, Jerusalem, 1963, pp. 101—113.

ID., Palestinian Law in Babylonian Tradition as Revealed in a Study of Perek Arvei Pesahim (Trac. Pesahim Chap. X), Tarbiz, 33 (1963/64), pp. 337—348, English Summary, pp. I—II.

ID., The Sources and Development of the Sugya in the Babylonian Talmud, Tarbiz 32 (1962/63), pp. 143—152, English Summary, pp. III—V.

ID., The use of the Tosefta and the Baraitha of the School of Samuel by the Babylonian Amora Rava for the Interpretation of the Mishnah, Tarbiz 40 (1970/71), pp. 144—157, English Summary, pp. II—III.

HALIVNI (WEISS), D., Review of 'The Formation of the Babylonian Talmud', JAAR 41 (1973), pp. 260—263.

ID., Sources and Traditions. A Source Critical Commentary on Seder Nashim. Tel Aviv, 1968. [= ST.]

ID., Sources and Traditions. A Source Critical Commentary on the Talmud Seder Moed from Yoma to Hagiga. Jerusalem, 1975. [= ST.]

ID., Talmud: Source Criticism, Encyclopedia Britannica, 1963, Vol. XXI, p. 645 = 1972, Vol. XXI, p. 645.

JACOBS, L., Are There Fictitious Baraitot in the Babylonian Talmud?, HUCA 42 (1971), pp. 185—196.

ID., How Much of the Babylonian Talmud is Pseudepigraphic?, JJS 28 (1977), pp. 46—59.

KAHAN, K., Ed., Seder Tannaim we Amoraim. Frankfurt a. M., 1935.

KAHANA, I. Z., 'Rules for Decisions' Found in the Babylonian Talmud, Sinai 6 (1939/40), pp. 336—343.

KAPLAN, J., The Redaction of the Babylonian Talmud. New York, 1933.

KLEIN, H., Gemara and Sebara, JQR 38 (1947/48), pp. 67—91. [= GS.]

ID., Gemara Quotations in Sebara, JQR 43 (1952/53), pp. 341—363. [= GQS.]

ID., The Significance of the Technical Expression 'l' 'y 'ytmr hky 'ytmr in the Babylonian Talmud, Tarbiz 31 (1961), pp. 23—42.

ID., Some General Results of the Separation of Gemara from Sebara in the Babylonian Talmud, JSemSt 3 (1958), pp. 363—372. [= SGR.]

ID., Some Methods of Sebara, JQR 50 (1959/60), pp. 124—146. [= SMS.]

LEWIN, B. M., Rabbanan Savora'e Vetalmudam. Jerusalem, 1937.

LEWIN, B. M., Ed., Iggeret R. Scherira Gaon. Haifa, 1921. Reprint, Jerusalem, 1972.

LEWY, I., Interpretation des 1.—6. Abschnittes des palästinischen Talmud-tractates Nesikin, Jahresbericht des jüdisch-theologischen Seminars. Breslau, 1895—1914.

MELAMMED, E. Z., An Introduction to Talmudic Literature. Jerusalem, 1973.

MIRSKY, S. K. Types of Lectures in the Babylonian Academies, Essays and Studies on Jewish Life and Thought, New York, 1959, pp. 375—402.

NEUSNER, J., Ed., The Formation of the Babylonian Talmud. Studies in the Achievements of Late Nineteenth and Twentieth Century Historical and Literary-Critical Research. Leiden, 1970.

RABINOWITZ, Z. W., Sha'are Torath Babel. Notes and Comments on the Babylonian Talmud. Jerusalem, 1961.

REGENSBERG, H. D., 'Al 'Arikhat Hattalmudim, Gibbeath Saul: Essays ... in Honor of Saul Silber, Chicago, 1935, pp. 124—128.

ROSENTHAL, D., Pirqa De 'Abbaye (TB Rosh Ha' Shana II), Tarbiz 46 (1977), pp. 97—109, English Summary, p. III.

ROSENTHAL, E. S., Hammoreh, PAAJR 31 (1963), Hebrew Section, pp. 1—71.

ID., Leshemu'at Happetiḥah Shel Bavli Ta'anit, Y. Friedman Memorial Volume, Jerusalem, 1974, pp. 237—248.

RUBINSTEIN, S. M., Leḥeqer Siddur Hattalmud. Kovno, 1932.

SALDARINI, A. J., Form Criticism of Rabbinic Literature, JBL 96 (1977), pp. 257—274.

SCHACHTER, M., The Babylonian and Jerusalem Mishnah textually compared. Jerusalem, 1959.

ID., Babylonian-Palestinian Variations in the Mishna, JQR 42 (1951/52) pp. 1—35.

TENNENBLATT, M. A., The Formation of the Babylonian Talmud. A Historical and Textual Study. Tel Aviv, 1972.

WEINBERG, Y. J., Meḥqarim Battalmud, I. Berlin, 1938.

WEIS, P. R., The Controversies of Rab and Samuel and the Tosefta, JSemSt 3 (1958), pp. 288—297.

WEISS, A., The Development of the Talmud as a Literary Unit [Hithavut Hattalmud Bishlemuto]. New York, 1943. [= DTLU.]

ID., Hattalmud Habbavli Behithavuto Hassifrutit. I. Hemmemra. Warsaw, 1937. II. Hassugya. Warsaw, 1939.

ID., Die Herkunft und Entstehungszeit des Talmud-traktats Tamid, MGWJ 83 (1939), pp. 261—276.

ID., The Literary Activities of the Saboraim. A Lecture Held at the Hebrew University, December 31, 1952. Jerusalem, 1953.

ID., Leqorot Hithavut Habbavli. Warsaw, 1929. Reprint, Jerusalem, n. d.

ID., Meḥqarim Battalmud. Jerusalem, 1975.

ID., Meqomah Haqqadum Shel Hammemra, M. Schorr Jubilee Volume, Warsaw, 1935, pp. 39—75.

ID., Notes to Talmudic Pericopae. Bar Ilan University, n. d.

ID., Le problème de la rédaction du Talmud de Babylone par R. Aši à la lumière de la Lettre de Serîra, REJ 102 (1937), pp. 105—114.

ID., Studien zur Redaktion des babylonischen Talmuds, MGWJ 73 (1929), pp. 131—143, 184—211. [= Meḥqarim, Chapter 5.]

ID., Studies in the Literature of the Amoraim ['Al Hayyeṣirah Hassifrutit Shel Ha'amora'im]. New York, 1962. [= SLA.]

ID., The Talmud in its Development [Leḥeqer Hattalmud]. New York, 1954. [= TD.]

ZEITLIN, S., Hammishnah Shebayyerushalmi Vehammishnah Shebabbavli, Z. Shazar Jubilee Volume, Jerusalem, 1973, pp. 539—548.

ZUSSMAN, J., Babylonian Sugyot to the Order Zera'im and Tehorot. Unpublished Ph. D. Dissertation, Hebrew University, 1961. In press, Israel Academy of Sciences and Humanities.

The terms which appear in the title of this section are borrowed from classical philology and Biblical studies. They have generally not been used by students of rabbinic literature. Conscious application and adaption of these methods to rabbinic documents began only recently[35]. Nevertheless, studies which may be subsumed under these headings have been carried out since the beginning of the study of BT, even by the Amoraim within BT itself. More important, use of these categories should make what follows more accessible to those unfamiliar with Talmud studies. My attempt to impose them on scholarship organized according to different principles results in a certain amount of repetition. Hopefully the gain in clarity outweighs the loss from redundancy.

1. Source Criticism

a) The Palestinian Sources

The Babylonian Talmud, despite its name, contains a large number of sources of Palestinian provenance. These may be subdivided into Tannaitic and Amoraic materials. BT generally, though not always, introduces its Tannaitic sources with special superscriptions. Most of the latter derive from the root *tny*, such as *tenan*, *tanya*, *teno rabbanan*, etc. (see ALBECK, Introduction pp. 21—27, 28, 44—47; EPSTEIN, ITM, pp. 74—163, 803—897; MELAMMED Introduction, pp. 258f.; and cf. BACHER, Ex. Term., II, pp. 238—241). Even without superscription Tannaitic material stands out from its context in BT. It is almost entirely in Hebrew while the Amoraic material is often in Aramaic. It mentions only early masters, the Tannaim. Moreover many of the Tannaitic sources cited in BT appear in other documents. The most important of those documents is, of course, the Mishnah of Yehudah the Patriarch. As noted above, BT is primarily a commentary on the Mishnah[36]. Both the manuscripts and printed editions of BT include a complete text of the Mishnah presented chapter by chapter or paragraph by paragraph. However, the appearance of a complete text together with BT is a late phenomenon. This fact emerges from the differences between the text of the Mishnah placed before the Gemara and the

[35] J. N. EPSTEIN inaugurated the application of source criticism to Tannaitic sources and to BT. Form criticism was applied by Y. HEINEMANN to rabbinic liturgical texts and by W. S. TOWNER to one of the halakhic midrashim. The most extensive application and adaptation of these methods in rabbinic scholarship is that by J. NEUSNER, Development of a Legend. Studies on the Traditions Concerning Yoḥanan b. Zakkai (Leiden, 1970), ID., Eliezer Ben Hyrcanus, 2 Vols. (Leiden, 1973), and ID., History of the Mishnaic Law of Purities, Vols I—XXII (Leiden, 1974—78). See now the discussion of SALDARINI.

[36] For the methodology of the Amoraic commentary on the Mishnah see J. FORSHEIM, Rav Ḥisda as Exegetor of Tannaitic Sources, Tarbiz 41 (1971/72) pp. 24—48, English Summary, pp. III—IV; J. FRAENKEL, Ha Gufa Qashya. Internal Contradictions in Talmudic Literature, Tarbiz 42 (72/73), pp. 266—301, English Summary, pp. II—III; S. K. MIRSKY, The Mishnah as Viewed by the Amoraim, Leo Jung Jubilee Volume (New York, 1962), pp. 155—174; J. J. WEINBERG, Studies on Talmudic Commentaries to the Mishnah, Talpioth 6 (1955), pp. 606—636; M. ZUCKER, Ha'Ḥassore Meḥassera' Battalmud, Minḥat Bikkurim . . . leAryeh Schwarz (Vienna, 1926), pp. 47—53; MELAMMED, Introduction, pp. 330—394; and EPSTEIN, ITM, pp. 166—672.

citations and rubrics from the Mishnah cited in the body of the Gemara (see EPSTEIN, ITM, pp. 923–927). Originally BT contained only abbreviated citations of the Mishnah paragraph about to be discussed in the Gemara (ibid., pp. 827–921). In addition fuller citations appear where necessary for the discussion (ibid., pp. 771–803 and cf. 803–864; ALBECK, Chajes Mem. Vol.). The study of these rubrics and citations is important primarily for the history of the text of the Mishnah[37]. Still, establishing which text of the latter document lies behind a given pericope of Gemara is often crucial to understanding the BT, as HALIVNI stresses in his commentary. For our purposes it is sufficient to note that the Mishnah, often in a version different from what appears in the separate editions or even from what appears at the head of the Gemara, is a major source of BT.

A second set of Tannaitic sources comprises those traditions not included in the Mishnah of Yehudah the Patriarch. These are the Baraitot. Here some distinctions must be made. We possess several collections of Baraitot: the 'Tosefta', 'Mekhilta Derabbi Yishma''el', 'Mekhilta Derabbi Shim'on b. Yoḥai', 'Sifra', 'Sifre Bemidbar', 'Sifre Zuṭṭa', 'Sifre Devarim', and 'Midrash Tanna'im'[38]. Many BT Baraitot closely parallel texts appearing in these collections. Other BT Baraitot have parallels in the Palestinian Talmud. Finally, some are not paralleled elsewhere. Each group of materials poses a separate set of literary-historical problems. Regarding the first group, the problem is the relation between the BT Baraitot and the extant Tannaitic collections. Were the latter known to the Babylonian Amoraim? Or did the Amoraim cite the Baraitot from other sources? The parallels are often very close, sometimes identical. Yet frequently there are significant differences between the BT version and that in the collection. More striking, BT often ignores sources found in the collections which are relevant to discussions in the Gemara. Complicating the issue is the fact that BT mentions 'Tosefta', 'Sifra', and 'Sifre' by name (e. g., Meg. 28b, Qid. 49b, Sanh. 86a, Shev. 41b; the term *mekhilta* also appears, but not as the name of a book, see EPSTEIN, ITL, p. 545). Does BT refer here to the collections we know by these names? Scholarly opinion is divided on this issue. ALBECK argues that since BT ignores relevant sources in 'Tosefta' and the halakhic midrashim, it could not have known the latter

37 On the differences between the texts of the Mishnah in BT and in the Palestinian Talmud see EPSTEIN, ITM, pp. 921—923, 932, 1275, and cf. 706—726; M. SCHACHTER, Babylonian-Palestinian Variations in the Mishna, JQR 42 (1951/52), pp. 1—35; S. ZEITLIN, Hammishnah Shebayerushalmi Vehammishnah Shebabavli, Z. Shazar Jubilee Volume (Jerusalem, 1973), pp. 539—548.

38 Tosefta, ed. M. S. ZUCKERMANDEL, Repr. Jerusalem, 1963; ed. S. LIEBERMAN, Vols. I—V, New York, 1955—1962. Mechilta D'Rabbi Ismael, ed. H. S. HOROVITZ and I. A. RABIN, Jerusalem, 1960. Mekhilta D'Rabbi Šim'on b. Jochai, ed. J. N. EPSTEIN and E. Z. MELAMMED, Jerusalem, 1955. Sifra deve Rav, ed. I. H. WEISS, Vienna, 1862. Siphre D'Be Rab. Siphre ad Numeros adjecto Siphre zutta, ed. H. S. HOROVITZ, Repr. Jerusalem, 1966. Sifre on Deuteronomy, ed. L. FINKELSTEIN, 2nd. edition, New York, 1969. Midrash Tannaim on Deuteronomy, ed. D. S. HOFFMAN, 2 Vols., Repr. Tel Aviv, n.d.

documents. The BT Baraitot are taken from sources other than the extant collections (ALBECK, Introduction, p. 67 re Tosefta, pp. 105—129 re halakhic midrashim). EPSTEIN takes the opposite position. He notes that BT also ignores relevant sections of the Mishnah in its discussions. Obviously this does not mean that the Amoraim did not know the Mishnah. Similarly, ignoring sections of the Tannaitic collections cannot prove BT did not know them. As for the differences between the BT Baraitot and their parallels, EPSTEIN explains that the Amoraim knew the collections in slightly different, earlier recensions (EPSTEIN, ITL, p. 246 re Tosefta, and pp. 547, 609f., 615, 663, 666, 674 re halakhic midrashim; cf. MELAMMED, Introduction, pp. 262, 267). To a certain extent, the debate revolves around semantics. What is the border line between a different recension and a different collection of parallel sources? DE VRIES discusses this issue, and he finally arrives at a position closer to ALBECK than to EPSTEIN (DE VRIES, Tarbiz 30). Other scholars adopt a middle position. With regard to 'Tosefta', P. R. WEIS and A. GOLDBERG suggest that some Amoraim knew these collections and some did not (WEIS, JSemSt, argues that Rava used 'Tosefta', but Samuel did not; GOLDBERG, Tarbiz 40, claims Rava used it). A. WEISS also maintains that the authors of some pericopae knew them, and the authors of others did not (WEISS, SLA, pp. 169—171). S. LIEBERMAN, whose monumental commentary on 'Tosefta' discusses at length the BT parallels to this document, is perhaps best equipped to decide whether the Amoraim used our 'Tosefta'. However, he has yet to express his view on this question[39]. In the last analysis the issue is more relevant to the history of Tannaitic literature than to that of BT. Whether or not the Babylonian Amoraim knew the extant Tannaitic collections, they obviously had at their disposal compilations of Tannaitic sources. Some of those compilations bore the same name as the extant collections; others bore different names, e. g., *tanna deve R. Yishma''el* (cf. ALBECK, Introduction, pp. 36—43; EPSTEIN, ITM, pp. 153—163, ITL, pp. 551, 562—565, 589—597, 630, 705, 708; MELAMMED, Introduction, pp. 258—277).

The second group of BT Baraitot, those with parallels only in the Palestinian Talmud, have attracted less attention (see MELAMMED, Introduction, pp. 258—274). The parallels in the Palestinian Talmud establish the Palestinian provenance of these materials, and they are probably genuine Tannaitic sources. The BT Baraitot without parallel elsewhere are more problematic. Are they of Tannaitic origin? Or are they 'fictitious', i. e., composed by Babylonian Amoraim on the model of the genuine Baraitot? Doubts concerning their provenance arise because many of these sources appear in one place in BT with Baraita superscription and in another place as Amoraic statements (see MELAMMED, Introduction, pp. 407—412; ALBECK, Introduction, pp. 46—49). The suggestion that these Baraitot are 'fictitious' was first advanced by I. H. WEISS in the last century[40].

[39] See ROSENTHAL's attempt to ascertain the position of LIEBERMAN, Hammoreh, pp. 52—56.
[40] I. H. WEISS, Dor Dor Vedorshav (Repr. Tel Aviv, n.d.), Vol. II, pp. 242—244.

Recent opponents of this view include A. WEISS (A. WEISS, TD, pp. 35 to 63). ALBECK and MELAMMED admit that Amoraic interpolations appear in originally Tannaitic sources (ALBECK, Introduction, pp. 28, 34f.; MELAMMED, Introduction, p. 274). ALBECK is willing to go farther. He concedes that some Baraitot are 'new', i. e., post-Tannaitic — but only slightly later than the genuine Baraitot (ALBECK, pp. 47—50). L. JACOBS, after reviewing the various arguments, concludes that "occasionally the redactors [of BT] did use fictitious Baraitot for the purposes of literary device and as a pedagogic means" (JACOBS, HUCA 42, p. 196). The linguistic studies of MORESHET might solve this problem. If certain Baraitot turn out to be entirely in mh²b, rather than merely 'contaminated' by the latter dialect, then it is likely that they are of Babylonian Amoraic provenance. The present writer has argued, also on linguistic grounds, that certain BT Baraitot are not of Palestinian origin[41]. In conclusion, it seems probable that at least some of the unparalleled BT Baraitot are not Tannaitic.

BT also contains Palestinian Amoraic sources. Some of the latter are introduced by special formulae such as *'amri bama'arava*, "they say/explain in the West," *maḥakho 'alah bama'arava*, "they laughed at it in the West," and others. Other formulae refer to scholars, *nāḥotē*, "those who go down", sc. from Palestine to Babylonia. These masters travelled back and forth between the two countries, presumably on business trips, and transmitted traditions from one center to the other. The materials they brought are introduced by *ki 'ata X 'amar*, "when X came, he said". BT also reports on letters exchanged between Palestine and Babylonia (on all these see the sources collected by EPSTEIN, IAL, pp. 293—312, MELAMMED, Introduction, pp. 442—447, 559—561, and BACHER, Trad. u. Trad., pp. 506—520). The largest category of Palestinian Amoraic sources in BT is not set off by special formulae. I refer to the statements of Palestinian masters (see BACHER, Trad. u. Trad., pp. 327—331, 369—394). Finally, scholars note pericopae appearing with minor variations in both Talmuds (EPSTEIN, IAL, loc. cit., MELAMMED, pp. 447—451). The *ge'onim* and *rishonim* explained this phenomenon by asserting that BT knew and used the completed Palestinian Talmud. Today it is recognized that this claim is part of the Babylonian propaganda in favor of the hegemony of BT. Modern scholars agree that at most BT knew earlier recensions of our Palestinian Talmud (for the older claim see EPSTEIN, IAL, pp. 290f., GINZBERG, Commentary, I., pp. 84—86, and MELAMMED, pp. 556—558; in recent times only HALEVY defended this view — for the modern opinion see EPSTEIN, pp. 291f., GINZBERG, pp. 86f., and MELAMMED, pp. 558f.). Recent work concentrates on the detailed study of Palestinian Amoraic materials in BT. The research of A. GOLDBERG (Tarbiz 33) and especially Z. DOR illustrates this trend.

[41] D. GOODBLATT, Rabbinic Instruction in Sasanian Babylonia (Leiden, 1975), p. 73.

b) The Babylonian Sources

Study of the Palestinian sources in BT is facilitated by the existence of other documents containing parallel material. When we turn to the Babylonian sources, we must rely on the traditional methods of source criticism without the help of external sources. Scholars adduce various sorts of evidence indicative of Babylonian sources within BT. Almost all of this evidence derives from intensive analysis of individual pericopae. Most commonly cited are the following items.

α) Variant Versions

Frequently BT records alternate versions of Amoraic statements or pericopae. Several formulae introduce these variants. One such formula is *R. X matni hakhi . . . R. Y. matni hakhi . . .*, "R. X teaches this [version] . . . R. Y teaches this [other version] . . ." Sometimes "R. X" and "R. Y" are replaced by "you . . . we . . .", or "in town X . . . in town Y . . ." (see examples collected by LEWY, Interpretation, pp. 3—14, BACHER, Trad. u. Trad., pp. 578—589). Other formulae introducing variant versions include *'ika de'amri/dematni*, "there are those who say/teach", *lishana aḥarina*, "another version", and *ve'amri lah*, "and [some] say it [in the following version]" (see ALBECK, p. 558 and MELAMMED, pp. 455—457). It is widely agreed that these alternate versions come from sources at the disposal of the editors of the final version of the pericopae (see ALBECK and MELAMMED, loc. cit., and A. WEISS, TD, pp. 179ff., 192—260, 201—349).

β) Quotations

Certain formulae or superscriptions introduce quotations of pericopae. Two of them, *vehavēnan bah*, "and we discussed it", and *velav 'ittamar ʿalav*, "and was it not said/explained concerning it", introduce into a pericope discussions whose original context was elsewhere. The fullest study of this phenomenon is by DE VRIES. He shows that the discussions quoted usually relate to a Mishnah paragraph, sometimes to a Baraita, and least frequently to an Amoraic statement. Most of them are found elsewhere in BT, but not all. Even when found elsewhere, the parallel version frequently differs from the quoted version. The disparity between the two versions and especially those discussions not found elsewhere prove that the source of the materials quoted by these formulae is not always our BT (DE VRIES, Studies, pp. 200—214 = Tarbiz 35 [1965—66], pp. 254—268, English Summary, p. IV; cf. ALBECK, pp. 562f. and A. WEISS, DTLU, pp. 14ff.).

A similar phenomenon involves quotations from the Mishnah. While discussing one paragraph of the Mishnah, the Gemara may quote another paragraph. Often that other paragraph is quoted together with its Amoraic commentary. The formula used to introduce these citations is *tenan hatam*, "we learned there"[42]. The Mishnah so cited is frequently from a tractate which lacks Babylonian Gemara. A. WEISS states the common view that "it is almost certain that many of the pericopae introduced by the term *tenan hatam* come from a different source [i. e., other than our BT]" (DTLU, p. 142, cf. pp. 133f., 142—146). WEISS also argues that the term *'ittamar* introduces materials with a fixed literary formulation from some other source (TD, pp. 64—107; cf. GEWIRTSMAN, Sinai 67).

γ) Parallel Pericopae

Many pericopae occur at several places in BT, both in different tractates and within the same tractate. Occasionally the parallel versions are contradictory. Conflicting views are attributed to the same master or statements attributed to two masters are reversed. Sometimes the contradiction is less striking, but it is revealed by close analysis. The medieval commentators, who noticed these passages, called them "inverted" or "transposed" pericopae, *sugyot hafukhot/muḥlafot* (for the medieval sources see EPSTEIN, IAL, p. 12 and ALBECK, pp. 560f.; for examples see EPSTEIN, pp. 24—32, 45—49, 98—101, 107—115 and cf. DOR, Bar Ilan 4—5). Both EPSTEIN and ALBECK agree that the contradictory parallel pericopae evidence different sources (EPSTEIN, IAL, p. 12 and ALBECK, p. 558).

Other parallel pericopae are in effect identical. The difference between them concerns their respective contexts. In one place in BT the passage is directly related to the Mishnah section near which it appears, while in the parallel occurrence it is only peripherally related. Thus the former place seems to be the original context. In the second place the passage is a quotation. The source of the quotation is obviously our BT. Thus the question in the case of identical parallel pericopae is not so much source critical as redaction critical, viz., who is responsible for copying the pericope in its second location? This question will be considered below.

δ) Inconsistencies within a Pericope

ALBECK finds evidence for different sources within individual pericopae. For example, one part of a pericope may ignore a source cited elsewhere in the same passage. Or different sections of the pericope may contradict one another. These phenomena indicate that the pericope is composed of different sources (ALBECK, pp. 569—571). Another indication is the order in which statements of Amoraim are recorded. Usually the order is chronological: first the early masters and then the later ones. Sometimes, though, early masters are cited after later ones. ALBECK explains that the compiler of the original version of the pericope did not know the views of the early masters. The compilers of the present version were able to add the addi-

[42] It was formerly believed that this formula introduces a Mishnah from a different tractate, but EPSTEIN showed that it can introduce a Mishnah from elsewhere in the same tractate, see ITM pp. 814—817.

tional views from some other source. Rather than tamper with the existent, older pericope, they simply attached the new material at the end (ALBECK, pp. 573f.). A. WEISS rejects this second argument. He claims that divergence from the usual chronological order can be explained on logical or thematic grounds (WEISS, Meḥqarim, pp. 160—212). Still, ALBECK's first argument seems beyond question.

ε) The Anonymous Material and Early Redactions of BT

Attributed statements comprise only a part of the Gemara. Almost as numerous are comments not attributed to any named master. Frequently these anonymous materials supply connecting links between attributed statements or serve as a framework for them. Scholars see in this evidence of editing. If a named master comments on or relates to the framework, then the latter must have existed before his time. We thus have evidence of an edited pericope from before the final redaction of BT. This constitutes a fragment of an early redaction of the Gemara which served as a source for our BT. Some of the sources indicated by the evidence noted above may also come from such early editions of Gemara. Z. FRANKEL apparently was the first modern scholar to adopt this argument[43]. It was further developed by Y. I. HALEVY. The latter cited many examples of anonymous material discussed or alluded to by Amoraim. The masters involved belong to every Amoraic generation. This indicates that in every generation material was edited, i. e., given a fixed literary form and arranged according to the order of the Mishnah[44]. HALEVY adds another argument which does not involve the anonymous sections. He shows that some Amoraic comments presuppose a certain order or arrangement of attributed comments. This also indicates that early material had already been edited during the Amoraic era[45]. Finally, HALEVY maintains that in addition to the "Talmud of each generation", there were two major summarizing editions: one in the early fourth century and the second in the early fifth[46]. All of these editions constitute the sources of our BT. KAPLAN reviews the evidence adduced by FRANKEL and HALEVY, and he adds some additional proofs. While admitting that much of the evidence is inconclusive, KAPLAN concludes "enough has been brought to prove the existence of records of Amoraic opinions and discussions, arranged either by subjects or otherwise, before the [final] redaction of the Talmud" (KAPLAN, Redaction, p. 194). These 'records', in some sense early editions of the Gemara, are among the sources of BT.

The most recent proponent of this theory is ALBECK. Like HALEVY he argues that when named masters relate to anonymous sections or

43 Z. FRANKEL, Beiträge zu einer Einleitung in den Talmud, MGWJ (1861), pp. 191—192.

44 Y. I. HALEVY, Dorot Harishonim, Vol. IIa (Frankfurt a. M., 1901 = Vol. V, Jerusalem, 1966), pp. 551—556, Vol. III (Pressburg, 1897 = Vol. VI, Jerusalem, 1966), pp. 117f.

45 HALEVY, op. cit., Vol. II, pp. 557—562.

46 Ibid., p. 480, Vol. III, pp. 116, 120.

presuppose a given order in earlier materials, we have evidence of early redactions of pericopae. He generalizes that "most of the anonymous pericopae arranged in the Talmud after the Mishnah or a Baraita or the words of early Amoraim are early, and not from the time of the late editing" (ALBECK, p. 580 and cf. pp. 578—595). EPSTEIN also appears to accept this line of reasoning, though he does not discuss this issue at length. He states that "we possess fragments of a Talmud edition from the time of R. Naḥman b. Ya'aqov and his disciples, and [from the time of] Abaye and Rava . . ." (IAL, p. 12). Elsewhere he cites what he believes to be early anonymous discussions (ibid., p. 15). He also cites evidence of editorial activity on the part of Naḥman b. Yiṣḥaq (ibid., pp. 21f., 178). Thus EPSTEIN agrees that the sources of BT include early editions of the Gemara.

All of the scholars cited above base their argument on the antiquity of the anonymous sections of BT. Others, including A. WEISS, M. S. FELDBLUM, HALIVNI, and FRIEDMAN, reject the latter assumption. They claim that the anonymous sections are late. Where named masters appear to cite or discuss such sections, this is the work of later editors. Anonymous material was inserted before attributed statements, and comments relating to the former were put in the mouths of the named masters (WEISS, TD, pp. 408—412, and see 295—307 and SLA, pp. 24—58; HALIVNI, ST, II, pp. 2—6; FELDBLUM, PAAJR 38; FRIEDMAN, Critical Study, pp. 294—296, n. 42). Nevertheless, WEISS agrees that there were early editions of the Gemara which constitute sources of our BT. In effect he agrees with HALEVY that every generation, and every center of scholarship, produced its own Talmud. Some of these early editions constitute recognizable strata in our Gemara. WEISS attributes the earliest stratum to the late third century. This is the Talmud of Yehudah b. Yeḥezqel head of the Pumbedita school. This Talmud comprised formulated material from Rav and Samuel, statements of other masters of the first generation of Babylonian Amoraim, and Baraitot. This edition was limited in extent. It did not cover every tractate for which we now have Babylonian Gemara. Even for the tractates this edition did treat, it sometimes was limited to specific chapters only. The second stratum discernable in our BT dates to the early fourth century (cf. HALEVY). This edition of Gemara was equivalent in extent to our BT in the sense that it covered all the tractates for which we now have Gemara. It too originated in Pumbedita, under Abaye. When the latter died, Rava took this edition with him to Meḥoza where it was further supplemented. Later generations continued to add to this edition as it was adopted by the Naresh school under R. Papa and by the school of Sura under R. Ashi. In the latter location material from the Suran Talmud was added. Thus, according to WEISS, the main sources of our BT are the Talmuds of Yehudah b. Yeḥezqel and of Abaye and Rava as supplemented by Papa and Ashi. In addition other early editions of Gemara are cited from time to time, as the formulae discussed above indicate (DTLU, pp. 37—45). Others scholars would reject WEISS' claim that our BT comes from Pumbedita. Epstein, for example, argues that the Gemara before us is essentially that of Sura, while certain tractates come from other centers (IAL, pp. 84, 104). Yet it is almost universally agreed that older editions of the Gemara served as sources for our Talmud.

Still more evidence for an early version of the Gemara is adduced by de Vries. While agreeing that there are early anonymous sections, he asserts that most early pericopae contain attributed material. Fragments of these early sources appear in BT following the superscription *vehavēnan bah.* de Vries notes that many of the pericopae introduced by the latter phrase concern the Mishnah of Orders *zera'im* and *tohorot*. In these Orders there are no BT tractates (except Ber. and Nid.). The pericopae cited are brief and simple. The masters named in them are from the earlier generations of Amoraim. de Vries concudes that materials introduced by *vehavēnan bah* are quotations from an early *gemara* on Orders *zera'im* and *tohorot* which dates to the first half of the fourth century. Thus this early *gemara* constitutes another one of the sources of our BT (de Vries, Studies, pp. 193—202 = Tarbiz 35 [1965—66], pp. 254—268, English Summary, p. IV, and cf. Zussman, Babylonian Sugyot).

A variation on the theme of early editions of the Gemara appears in the work of Epstein. He argues persuasively that each tractate is a separate literary unit with its own redaction history. Some tractates were edited earlier than others. When we find parallel pericopae in different tractates, we can sometimes determine which version is earlier. In these cases the tractate edited earlier served as a source for the tractate edited later. In this way we can explain the 'inverted' or contradictory parallel pericopae. The later tractate modified its source in conformity to its own needs or legal conceptions.

ζ) Form and Subject Matter

A number of scholars discern sources of BT according to criteria of form or subject matter. Kaplan, Klein, Rubinstein, Halivni, Weiss, Feldblum, and Friedman propound what may be called a 'two source' theory. They hypothecate two major blocs of material, each with a unique form, of which BT is composed. However these theories may best be considered under the headings of form criticism and especially redaction criticism. Here I shall briefly treat one aspect of the work of A. Weiss. As will be seen below, Weiss isolates what he believes to be the two main forms of Talmudic literature: the brief independent statement and the discursive discussion. In addition he discovers instances of other forms such as collections of traditions, connected Bible exegesis, and 'treatises' on non-legal topics. Frequently examples of the latter three forms developed by accretion in their present context in the Gemara. That is, they do not represent distinct literary units inserted whole into BT. On the other hand, Weiss argues, in some cases these materials were added to the Gemara as finished units. In such instances we may speak of these units as sources (SLA, pp. 176—294 and cf. NEUSNER, Formation, pp. 100—102; see also FRIEDMAN, Structural Patterns, pp. 396—402).

MIRSKY suggests that the technical, legal discussions and the less technical, primarily non-legal material in the Gemara derive from different sources. The former derive from the daily lectures in the Talmudic academies. The latter originate in sermons of a popular nature delivered in the synagogues of the academies on Sabbaths and holidays. Minutes of both types of lectures were preserved. These minutes were later 'dismantled' and incorporated into the Gemara where thematically appropriate. Fragments of the technical lectures are introduced by superscriptions such as *'ittamar* and *tenan hatam*, those of the sermons by *darash*. Moreover, complete minutes of the two types of lectures survive in post-Talmudic compilations (MIRSKY, Types of Lectures, pp. 375—402). MIRSKY's hypothesis presupposes academic institutions not necessarily attested by our sources, and it thus cannot be accepted[47]. A more modest and much more acceptable theory is argued by B. BOKSER. The latter has begun a study of the Mishnah commentary of Samuel, one of the first Babylonian Amoraim. So far, one volume on material relevant to Order *zera'im* has appeared. On the basis of the evidence assembled there BOKSER believes that a commentary by Samuel circulated as a separate document. This work, and presumably others like it, constitute additional sources of our BT.

η) Post-Amoraic Sources

According to Geonic testimony the last Amoraim died around the year 500 C.E. However, BT contains considerable material from after this date. Some early sixth century masters are mentioned by name in BT. Furthermore, early commentators and some manuscripts identify both comments and entire pericopae as post-Amoraic. These materials are attributed to the 'Savoraic masters', *rabbanan savora'ē*, or the Savoraim. The latter are Babylonian scholars who flourished in the sixth and seventh centuries (see the excellent survey by EPHRATHI). Thus it is universally agreed that among the sources of our BT are Savoraic materials. The extent and nature of the latter are a matter of dispute. Behind this dispute are different theories of the redaction of BT, as we shall see.

The first stage in the research on the Savoraic sources was the collection of all the material attributed to the Savoraim by the early commentators and manuscripts. The characteristics of the material thus assembled enabled scholars to identify still more material as of Savoraic provenance. S. J. RAPAPORT, N. BRÜLL, and others in the nineteenth century and HALEVY, YAVETZ, and YUDELOWITZ in the twentieth carried this work forward[48]. This first phase of research came to a culmination with the

[47] GOODBLATT, Rabbinic Instruction, op. cit., p. 195.

[48] See S. J. RAPAPORT, 'Erekh Millin (Warsaw, 1914), pp. 18—20, cf. Kerem Chemed 6 (1841) Letter 14, pp. 249—256; N. BRÜLL, Die Entstehungsgeschichte des babylonischen Tal-

publication of B. M. LEWIN's 'Rabbanan Savora'e Vetalmudam' in 1937. Despite the extent of Savoraic material revealed by this research, there was a distinct tendency to minimize the Savoraic contribution to BT. This tendency resulted from the widely held view that BT was 'sealed' by the year 500 (see below in the discussion of redaction criticism). If the document was 'sealed', then only insignificant additions were possible. Moreover, poor manuscripts of Geonic sources on the Savoraim and their activity led scholars astray (EPHRATHI, Sevoraic Period, pp. 64—67). Thus from RAPAPORT to LEWIN scholars denied that the Savoraim made any substantive additions to BT. The contribution of the latter was limited to brief glosses, technical terms, and the like (see KAPLAN's summary of the views of RAPAPORT, GRAETZ, FRANKEL, BRÜLL, I. H. WEISS, HALEVY, and YAVETZ in Redaction, pp. 3—27; LEWIN follows the view of HALEVY). Even EPSTEIN repeats the older view. He writes that the Savoraim contributed "merely the external arrangement [sc. of BT, emphasis in the original] without changing anything except for additions and connections between statements and pericopae . . ." (IAL, p. 12, cf. MELAMMED, pp. 473—478).

New theories on the redaction of BT made possible a re-evaluation of the Savoraic contribution. KAPLAN and A. WEISS deny that BT was "sealed" ca. 500. If the Talmud was left 'open', then there is no a priori reason for limiting the Savoraic sources to brief glosses. In fact, both KAPLAN and WEISS, followed by others, assign sizeable portions of BT to the Savoraim. I shall treat the details of their theories below in the discussion of redaction criticism. Here I shall briefly summarize some of the points WEISS made in his lecture on the Savoraim. Following a clue in Geonic sources, BRÜLL had already suggested that the opening pericope of several tractates constitutes a kind of introduction to the tractate composed by the Savoraim. WEISS argues that almost every tractate and many individual chapters begin with Savoraic pericopae. Furthermore, the Savoraim were responsible for what WEISS calls the "literary and stylistic polishing" of the pericopae. This activity included not only the addition of glosses to and connecting links between arguments, but also copying out in full sources alluded to in the original pericope. Here WEISS concurs with EPSTEIN that many parallel pericopae are the result of such *Quellenbeleg* (cf. EPSTEIN, IAL, p. 12). Finally BT contains many Savoraic pericopae. Some of the latter are reworkings of Amoraic material, but others are composed entirely of Savoraic material. WEISS concludes that the Savoraic element in BT is much more extensive than previously assumed (WEISS, Literary Activities, p. 18). Detailed studies of individual chapters of BT by FRANCUS and FRIEDMAN have established the correctness of WEISS' view. Savoraic sources comprise a considerable part of our BT.

muds als Schriftwerk, Jahrbücher für jüdische Geschichte und Literatur II (1876), pp. 16—18, 17, n. 11, 66—73; Y. I. HALVEY, op. cit., Vol. III, pp. 1—63; Z. JAWITZ (YAVETZ), Toldot Yisra'el, Vol. IX (London, 1922), pp. 213—224; M. D. YUDELOWITZ (JUDELOWITZ), Yeshivat Pumbedita Bime Ha'amora' im (Tel Aviv, 1935), pp. 52—54.

c) Summary and Critique

The Palestinian sources of BT include the Mishnah, other Tannaitic materials (the Baraitot), and Palestinian traditions and pericopae. At the base of the Talmud is a recension (or recensions) of the Mishnah of Yehudah the Patriarch. This recension differs from that appearing in the separate editions of the Mishnah and even from that placed at the head of the Gemara. The sources of the Baraitot are disputed. Some come from collections no longer extant. According to EPSTEIN and WEISS others come from earlier recensions of the extant Tannaitic collections such as the 'Tosefta' and the halakhic midrashim. ALBECK and DE VRIES demur. As to the Palestinian Amoraic pericopae, it is now agreed that they do not derive from the Palestinian Talmud now before us, but from the sources thereof or from other editions of the Palestinian Gemara.

The Babylonian sources pose more problems because Babylonian Amoraic documents external to BT do not exist. Nonetheless scholars are unanimous that various Amoraic sources can be discerned within BT. Variant versions of traditions, quotation formulae, contradictory parallel pericopae, and other evidence all point to the existence of such sources. The problem is to delineate and identify the latter and determine their provenance. It is generally agreed that each center of study and each generation had its own Talmud. But which sources belong to which version, and which 'edition' is the forebear of our BT — on these issues there is little agreement. BT also contains post-Amoraic sources, and there is a growing consensus that the extent of this late material is greater than previously believed. As we shall see below, some scholars claim that the Savoraic sources of BT are almost as extensive as the Amoraic ones. Further source critical work on the Savoraic stratum will be difficult. Since this material is almost entirely anonymous, we lack the 'handle' which attribution to named masters gives us in source criticism of Tannaitic and Amoraic materials.

The central stratum of BT, the Babylonian Amoraic material, turns out to be the most problematic. Scholars agree that BT comprises various Amoraic sources and concur on some of the indications thereof. Beyond this there is little agreement. The lack of consensus raises the question, is something wrong with our methodology? A reply may be found in the caveat of E. S. ROSENTHAL regarding source criticism of Tannaitic literature. His comments apply with even greater force to study of BT where we lack the controls provided for Tannaitic literature by the existence of several documents. ROSENTHAL notes LIEBERMAN's hesitation to treat source-critical issues in his commentary on 'Tosefta'. He infers that the latter feels conditions are not yet ripe for such work. ROSENTHAL goes on to explain why. The source critical techniques of classical philology are possible only after the groundwork has been laid. First, we must firmly establish the philology, lexicography, and historical background of our sources. Once this is accomplished, we may proceed to a scientific exegesis of the latter.

Simultaneously we must carry out detailed text-critical research. Only when all this has been achieved will we be in a position to engage in source criticism (ROSENTHAL, Hammoreh, pp. 34—57). Let us see where we stand with regard to BT. As noted above, much remains to be done in the areas of philology and lexicography. We are in a much better position with respect to the historical background thanks to the recent work of NEUSNER (see below). This work and the 1500 years of traditional exegesis make a scientific exegisis of BT possible, but the latter task has yet to be carried out. As for text criticism, we are now at the stage of a full collation of variants. The real work of text criticism is just beginning. Thus LIEBERMAN's hesitation to engage in source criticism of 'Tosefta' would be all the more justified for BT. And what is true for source criticism is also true for form — and especially redaction criticism.

The nature of the task before us is illustrated by NEUSNER's work on Tannaitic sources. The latter arrived independently at the principles set forth by ROSENTHAL. In his studies on Order *ṭohorot* of 'Mishnah-Tosefta', NEUSNER insists that a detailed, scientific exegesis must precede source and form critical studies. He further demands that such work be systematic, encompassing all the material. Finally, as EPSTEIN suggests, he proceeds tractate by tractate, treating each one as a separate literary unit[49]. It is to be hoped that some of NEUSNER's students will apply his methods to the study of BT. In any event, the clarification of first principles by ROSENTHAL and NEUSNER holds promise for the future of the source criticism of the Talmud as do the detailed literary-critical studies of FRIEDMAN, to be discussed below[50].

2. Form Criticism

a) The Brief Versus the Discursive

Of the three disciplines discussed in this chapter form criticism has been the most neglected by Talmud scholarship. Still, it has not been ignored

[49] See NEUSNER, History of the Mishnaic Law of Purities, op. cit., passim.

[50] I have not discussed HALIVNI's "source critical method" here because this is primarily an exegetical tool. HALIVNI argues that the original form of a statement (= "source") was likely to be changed in the course of transmission from generation to generation and from place to place. The changed form he calls "traditions". Frequently the form of a source on which a given pericope is based differs from the form now before us in the text of the pericope. As a result questions seem pointless, answers irrelevant, discussions forced. By recovering the form which stood before the authors of the pericopae we can resolve these problems. HALIVNI's method is extremely valuable for exegesis of BT, but it does not deal with the classical issues of source criticism. In Vol. II of his 'Sources and Traditions', he does briefly deal with the latter topics and promises a full treatment in a later book. DE VRIES also stresses the changes sources were subject to in the course of transmission as well as the ramifications of these changes, see his 'Literary Transfer as a Factor in the Development of Talmudic Law', Bar Ilan I, pp. 156—164, English Summary, p. XXXV.

entirely. For example, the older work on Savoraic sources devoted considerable attention to the formal characteristics of the latter. Another example is the distinction between attributed and anonymous comments alluded to above. Both of these sets of categories have been subjects of scholarly interest since the last century. However, it is only with the work of KAPLAN and A. WEISS that form criticism, though not by this name, begins to play a major role in research on BT. KAPLAN distinguishes two major forms in the Talmudic material. In essence his distinction is between brief and discursive sources. Other scholars adopt the same formal categories, though they develop them differently. KAPLAN designates the two forms "gemara" and "talmud". "Gemara" consists of "statements of the utmost brevity and simplicity ... put in simple and concise language, in order to record the final conclusions resulting from previous, sometimes lengthy and complex discussion" (Redaction, p. 196). That discussion constitutes "talmud". In addition to being brief, "gemara" is also "essentially anonymous" (Redaction, p. 227). As noted, it sums up and crystallizes previously existing "talmud". It also gives birth to new "talmud". The "laconic, pithy, often abrupt and ambiguous style", the "vague references" to sources, and the anonymity of "gemara" provoke attempts to resolve the ambiguity, spell out the references, and identify the authors (ibid., pp. 217—227, 233f.). Thus "gemara" and "talmud" engender one another. Each form is introduced by different superscriptions in BT. Those introducing "gemara" are based on the roots *tny* or *qbʿ*; those introducing "talmud" derive from *ʾmr, drš,* and *swm* (ibid., pp. 206—216). KAPLAN stresses that these distinctions are not merely formal. Each form represents a different source. The Talmudic academies possessed "collections of gemara" arranged according to the order of the Mishnah or of the Pentateuch (ibid., pp. 235—249, 270—274). Fragments from these collections appear in BT, though our Talmud is based on one particular collection (see below under redaction criticism). The "talmud" material was added later. While "gemara" and "talmud" thus constitute separate sources, they are first of all formal categories. The former term denotes brief, anonymous material, the latter discursive, attributed material.

Essentially the same distinction appears in the work of H. KLEIN. He names the forms "gemara" and "sebara". KLEIN states that each BT pericope "consists of a central core, which was termed its Gemara, and a discursive explanatory framework termed its Sebara" (KLEIN, GQS, p. 341). There are some differences between KLEIN's categories and those of KAPLAN, aside from the replacement of the term "talmud" by "sebara". One difference stressed by KLEIN concerns the relation between the two forms. He argues that "gemara" always precedes "sebara". The former never follows upon and summarizes the latter (KLEIN, GS, p. 69, n. 7). But KAPLAN admits that the "gemara" now before us in BT preceded the "talmud" before us. More relevant to form criticism is KLEIN's assertion that "gemara" is not always anonymous, but may include attributed statements. However, brevity is not the only characteristic of this form. KLEIN adds that "gemara" is always in Hebrew, while "sebara" is in Aramaic (GS, p. 75). He agrees with KAPLAN that the two categories represent different sources as well as formal types. I shall return to this point below. A third scholar who divided Talmudic sources into brief and discursive was S. M. RUBINSTEIN. Like KAPLAN he lists anonymity as well as brevity as characteristic of the one form, together with absence of source references, proof texts, or argumentation. The second form, which includes the latter three elements, is discursive and attributed. Even more than KAPLAN and KLEIN, RUBINSTEIN stresses the source — and redaction — critical aspects of this formal distinction[51].

The formal distinction between brief and discursive material is also adopted by A. WEISS, though in different terms. WEISS is the only BT scholar who writes extensively on form critical issues. Most of his last book, 'Studies in the Literature of the Amoraim' is devoted to identifying and cataloging the literary genres found in BT. In earlier work, reviewed in the latter volume, he identifies what he believes to be the dominant literary forms used by the Amoraim: the *memra* (plural: *memrot*) and the *sugya* (plural: *sugyot*). The former is a "short Amoraic statement which contains a complete idea, without any dialectics". The *sugya*, on the other hand, is a treatment of some aspect of a topic, generally in dialectical form. In effect we have here the same two categories noted by KAPLAN, KLEIN, and RUBINSTEIN. WEISS goes on to refine and subdivide his distinctions. The *memra*, which may be in either Hebrew or Aramaic, can be "supplementary" or "independent". That is, it may explain or clarify some other source, or it may state a complete idea which stands by itself. Similarly, the *sugya* may be either "explanatory" or "independent". In the former case some older source serves as the point of departure. In the latter the *sugya* is a self-contained discussion (SLA, pp. 1—4, cf. FELDBLUM, Contribution, pp. 13—16). WEISS thus agrees with KAPLAN against KLEIN that there is no necessary connection between brevity and use of Hebrew, but with KLEIN against KAPLAN that the brief material is not always anonymous. Aside from differences in detail and degree of sophistication, all three agree that brevity and discursiveness are the most general formal categories applicable to BT. Further distinctions, such as difference in language, or anonymity versus attribution, are given different valences. Where WEISS stands apart is in his refusal to translate these formal categories into source-critical ones. He does not assert that there were separate sources composed only of *memrot* (= "gemara") or of *sugyot* (= "talmud" or "sebara"). Here WEISS' theory seems preferable, for the source constructs argued by KLEIN, KAPLAN, and RUBINSTEIN are artificial and not substantiated by the evidence.

MELAMMED contributes a detailed description of the features of the *memra* and *sugya* (MELAMMED, Introduction, pp. 395—406, 451—461). He

[51] I was not able to obtain RUBINSTEIN's book. Therefore I rely on the summary in TENNENBLATT, Formation, pp. 81—93.

also discusses at length the halakhic midrashim, i. e., the legalistic exegeses of Biblical verses, attributed to Amoraim (ibid., pp. 296—311). While MELAMMED tends to see these as a separate form, WEISS categorizes them as supplementary *memrot*. Recent research by SH. FRIEDMAN has shed additional light on the *sugya*. In his studies of Chapter X of BT Yev. FRIEDMAN discovers that a tripartite structure is frequent. Thus a statement of an early master will be followed by reactions from three Amoraim. Furthermore, the components of the tripartite *sugya* are themselves often tripartite. This indicates, FRIEDMAN concludes, the contrived literary nature of the *sugya*. This pattern appears particularly in anonymous *sugyot* (FRIEDMAN, 'Some Structural Patterns').

The most promising development in BT form criticism is the recent work of FRIEDMAN. Building on the achievements of his predecessors, especially KAPLAN, KLEIN, and WEISS, he has developed criteria for delineating the various strata in a *sugya*. On the basis of literary (or formal) considerations, FRIEDMAN distinguishes three components (or strata) in most *sugyot*: A- statements of Amoraim; B- anonymous material which provides the framework for A; and C- late glosses. A corresponds more or less to the *gemara* of KAPLAN and KLEIN and to the *memra* of WEISS, and B to the *talmud* of KAPLAN, the *sebara* of KLEIN, and the *sugya* of WEISS. As to the issues in dispute among the latter three scholars, FRIEDMAN asserts that A tends to be brief and in Hebrew, B wordy and in Aramaic, and that in most cases B is chronologically later than A. Where FRIEDMAN goes beyond his predecessors is in his detailed listing and illustration of the criteria for separating the statements of the Amoraim (A) from the anonymous framework (B), even where B has been inserted into A. He lists fourteen such criteria which are then applied in his study of BT Yev. Chapter X. They are as follows. (1) The statements of Amoraim tend to be in Hebrew, the anonymous framework in Aramaic. (2) An explanatory, dependent clause is usually editorial (i.e., from B). Further indications of anonymous 'contamination' of Amoraic statements are (3) clumsy syntax, (4) excessive sentence length, and (5) resumptive repetition. (6) Material which when excluded from the *sugya* leaves a simple, consistent text is likely to be an editorial addition. (7) References to material further on in the *sugya* are likely to be editorial. (8) The appearance of words or phrases used overwhelmingly by late Amoraim or in anonymous sections are likely to be editorial additions when they appear in statements of early Amoraim. (9) Similarly, grammatical forms common in Geonic Aramaic, but rare in BT Aramaic, are signs of editorial additions. (10) A word or phrase which witnesses to the text insert in different places in the *sugya* are likely to be editorial. (11) A clustering of variant readings in a *sugya* may indicate that the text in question is a later insertion, for the text tradition of Amoraic statements is firmer than that of the anonymous sections. (12) The absence of a phrase in the MSS or in parallel passages suggests that it is a later addition. (13) Early commentators (*rishonim*) may reflect a shorter text of the *sugya*, which suggests that the additional material is editorial. (14)

In general, authentic Amoraic statements tend to be brief. FRIEDMAN argues that the probability of separating B from A increases as more of the above criteria appear. The application of the criteria is illustrated in his study of BT Yev., Chapter X, where A and B are graphically distinguished from each other (FRIEDMAN, 'Critical Study'). While I have discussed FRIEDMAN's work under the rubric of form criticism, it obviously has important ramifications for source- and redaction-criticism.

b) Other Forms

In addition to the *memra* and the *sugya* WEISS finds other genres in BT. He groups them into three broad categories: (1) collections (*qevaṣim*, singular: *qoveṣ*), (2) *midrashim* and aggadic compilations, and (3) treatises (*massekhtot*, singular: *massekhet*; the same word means 'tractate', but I translate 'treatise' to avoid confusion). The first category is by far the largest. WEISS lists over 125 instances of this form in BT, and he admits that his catalogue is not exhaustive (SLA, p. 189). He defines a collection as an assemblage of at least three traditions with its own organizational framework. The latter may be topical or formal. The commonest type is the collection of *memrot* all attributed to one master (ibid., pp. 176—208). Occasionally the collection form is obscured by the interpolation of discussions between its components. That is, one or more of the components may have engendered the development of a *sugya*. Moreover, faulty transmission of the text may have corrupted or changed the name of the master in one of the components thereby obliterating the form. Generally, though, the collection form is easy to recognize. Some collections include questions, usually introduced by the verb *b'y*, as well as declarative sentences. Other collections are composed entirely of questions attributed to one master, to several, or unattributed (SLA, pp. 238—246). A related phenomenon is a collection of apparently contradictory sources, introduced by *rmy*, and their resolutions (ibid., pp. 222—224). In some collections the components share more than one feature. For example, the *memrot* in a collection may all be transmitted by the same *Tradent* as well as attributed to the same master, or they may all start with the same formula (ibid., pp. 209—220). Finally some collections are composed of legal decisions (*pisqē halakhah*) either attributed or anonymous (ibid., pp. 247—250). SH. FRIEDMAN notes that many collections have seven components. He calls attention to the Talmudic phrase *shev shema'ata*, 'seven traditions', and he suggests that the later is the name of a literary genre ('Some Structural Patterns').

The second category includes consecutive exegesis of sections of Biblical books and assemblages of aggadic (non-legal) material on a given theme. WEISS lists three instances of the former type involving sections of Esther, Ruth, and Job (Meg. 10b—17a, Shab. 113b—114b, and BB 13b to 17a respectively, see SLA, pp. 276—292, 256—259). Examples of aggadic compilations include units on prayer, the giving of the Torah, the mystical 'works of the chariot' (*ma'asē merkavah*), and legends concerning the destruction of the Second Temple (Ber. 31a—32b, Shab. 86b—89b, Ḥag. 13a—16a, and Giṭ. 55b—58a respectively, see SLA, pp. 251—263). The third category, treatises, includes extended treatments of subjects such as dreams, Ḥannukah, 'wonders and visions', demons, and medicine (Ber. 54a—57b, Shab. 21b—24a, BB 73a—75b, Ber. 6a + Pes. 110a, and Shab. 110a—b + Giṭ. 67b + AZ 28a respectively, see SLA pp. 264—278). The distinction between aggadic compilations and treatises is not clear. Why are units on prayer and mysticism aggadic compilations, while those on dreams and demons treatises? In any event WEISS' threefold division may be retained, for consecutive Bible exegesis should be distinguished from both aggadic compilations and treatises.

MELAMMED suggests an additional formal category: the *ba'aya* or query (MELAMMED, Introduction, pp. 429—441). WEISS prefers to include the latter, together with its answer, in the *sugya* genre (SLA, pp. 238—246). Another sub-category of the *sugya*, the sermonic or midrashic discourse, is also treated separately by MELAMMED under the heading *pirqa*, 'lecture'. This latter form is also discussed at length by MIRSKY. As noted above, MIRSKY argues that this material derives from popular sermons delivered in the synagogues of the Talmudic academies. They included both legal and aggadic topics (MIRSKY, 'Types of Lectures'). FRIEDMAN, as stated above, also discusses the collection form (both collections of *memrot* and of legal decisions), noting the frequency of units containing three or seven members. The recognition of these forms and others is facilitated by the drawing of schematic outlines of the *sugyot* (in: FRIEDMAN, Critical Study). He also treats the query form (which he refers to as the *ba'ē*). According to FRIEDMAN, all these forms are characteristic of the A stratum (statements of Amoraim), rather than the anonymous framework (B). In addition, he briefly describes another Amoraic form which was ignored by his predecessors: the story (*ma'aseh, 'ovada*). FRIEDMAN lists the following characteristics of the latter form: Aramaic language, brief sentences in asyndetic construction (i.e., without the conjunction *v*), the first sentence begins with a subject, the other sentences begin with a verb. "Contamination" by anonymous, editorial additions may also be discerned in the Amoraic story (FRIEDMAN, Critical Study, pp. 310—312). While the story form has been largely ingnored by talmudists, it has been studied by students of literature and folklore[51a].

[51a] The fullest and most recent treatment, though not devoted only to BT, is O. MEIR, The Acting Characters in the Stories of the Talmud and the Midrash (A Sample), Unpublished Doctoral Dissertation, Hebrew University, 1977. MEIR treats the stories in Tractate Ber. in BT and PT as well as those in two Palestinian midrashim. See also D. BEN-AMOS, Narrative Forms in the Haggadah: Structural Analysis, Unpublished Doctoral Dissertation, University of Indiana 1966; B. DE VRIES Studies, Part I. The Literary Genres of the Aggada; Y. FRAENKEL, Ma'aseh BeRabbi Shila, Tarbiz 40 (1971), pp. 33—40; and A. KARLIN, Darkhe Hassippur Bishne Hattalmudim, Divre Sefer (Tel Aviv, 1952), pp. 5—42.

c) The *Sitz im Leben* of the Forms

It is widely assumed that the *Sitz im Leben* of BT in general is to be found in the Talmudic academies of Babylonia. The latter institutions, which flourished in such towns as Nehardea, Sura, Pumbedita, Naresh, Meḥoza and others from the third century on, composed, preserved, edited, and transmitted the Talmudic materials. The dialectics of the pericopae transcribe or at least reflect the debates during study sessions in the academies. The scholars cited above share this assumption. Most of the forms they isolate are assigned *Sitze im Leben* in the academies. WEISS, for example, claims that the life setting of the *memra* and *sugya* was the Mishnah study of these institutions (SLA, p. 172). KAPLAN argues that the "gemara" form represents formal conclusions of the discussions in the Amoraic academies. The "talmud" before us originated in Savoraic study of the "gemara" collection compiled in the academy of Sura under R. Ashi (Redaction, pp. 235f., 306f.). MIRSKY asserts that BT contains fragments of the minutes of lectures and sermons delivered in the academies ('Types of Lectures'). All these theories presuppose a certain type of institution: the academy. However, it is far from certain that Amoraic instruction was institutionalized in this way. The present writer has argued that disciple circles and apprenticeships rather than academies were the means of instruction during the Amoraic period[52]. If so, then the *Sitze im Leben* suggested for BT in general and the forms in particular must be rejected or revised. Life settings outside the academies are also hypothecated. As noted, WEISS asserts that at least some of the collections (and other forms) are independent literary units inserted into the Gemara. The *Sitze im Leben* he suggests for these units include the collection by disciples of a master's sayings after his death, the exchange of letters or the sending of responsa, and a master's desire to assemble the traditions of an important authority (SLA, pp. 221—225). These suggestions are acceptable, but they account for only a small portion of BT. Thus the question of life settings for the mass of Amoraic sources must await further research on the institutions of the Amoraim.

d) Summary

The form critical study of BT is still at a very preliminary stage. Aside from the contribution of WEISS and of SH. FRIEDMAN, the forms isolated are extremely primitive: attributed versus anonymous, brief versus discursive, Hebrew versus Aramaic. Even WEISS' *memra* and *sugya* are very broad categories. One reason for this state of affairs is that BT scholars have ignored cognate developments in Biblical studies where form criticism has reached a high level of sophistication. Fortunately this situation is changing. NEUSNER, in his work on Tannaitic sources, adapted the achieve-

[52] GOODBLATT, op. cit., pp. 44—59, 263—285.

ment of Biblical form criticism and developed methods appropriate to rabbinic literature. And one of his students, B. BOKSER, applies these methods to the study of BT. BOKSER devotes considerable attention to form-critical issues in his study on the Mishnah commentary of Samuel (BOKSER, Chapter IV—VI). Similarly, FRIEDMAN draws not only on talmudic scholarship, but also on literary and form-critical studies in other literatures. Thus the work of BOKSER and FRIEDMAN, who combine talmudic expertise and knowledge of form-critical methodology, promises further progress in the form criticism of BT. Such progress is bound to enrich other areas of study, including the source and redaction history of BT, Aramaic philology, and the history of the Jews in Sasanian and Islamic Babylonia.

3. Redaction Criticism

a) The Tractates

Unlike form criticism, redaction criticism has received much attention in modern Talmud scholarship. Usually the focus of research is the entire BT. Some scholars also treat the redactional history of individual tractates, and I shall begin with this aspect of the problem. As mentioned, EPSTEIN stresses that each tractate is an independent unit with its own literary history. Thus the proper object of source and redaction criticism should be the tractate. The approach suggested by EPSTEIN has been followed in a few doctoral dissertations submitted by students in the Hebrew University Talmud Department where EPSTEIN taught. In addition the latter composed introductions to individual tractates which appear in his IAL. Most published work, however, concentrates on the so-called 'unusual tractates'. These are Ned., Naz., Me'il., Ker., Tam., and the materials introduced by the superscription *lishana aḥarina* in Tem. The early commentators noted that these five and a half tractates differ from the rest of BT in language and terminology. Geonic sources report that they were not studied in the Babylonian academies of the eighth century (see the sources cited in EPSTEIN, IAL, pp. 55f. and in his 'Grammar of Babylonian Aramaic' [Tel Aviv and Jerusalem, 1960], p. 15, MELAMMED, Introduction, p. 468, and DE VRIES, Studies, p. 230). The significance of the latter fact, and still more the precise nature of the peculiarities of these tractates and their explanation, are a matter of dispute.

I shall begin with the linguistic aspect of the phenomenon. The earlier grammarians of bta, LUZZATTO, LEVIAS, and MARGOLIS, all argued that the language of the 'unusual' tractates is archaic. EPSTEIN argues the opposite. He asserts that their language is closest to the post-Talmudic dialect of the Geonic writing, and it therefore is late (EPSTEIN, IAL, p. 52 and Grammar, p. 16). DE VRIES seems to say the same thing, though the formulation of his conclusion is rather opaque (Studies, p. 231). Since EPSTEIN is the greatest authority on the Geonic dialect, his assessment carries much weight. However, language is not the only, and perhaps not the most important, peculiarity of the 5½ tractates. Scholars also note differences in terminology, style, legal decisions, and even in the roster of masters quoted. Thus the phenomenon cannot be explained merely on linguistic grounds.

One of the earliest attempts at an overall explanation of the 'unusual' tractates is that of HALEVY. He argues that BT as a whole was brought to Palestine in the Savoraic period. Later, when the Babylonian academies neglected the 5½ tractates, the Palestinian schools continued to study them. The peculiarities thus result from the contamination of their text by Palestinian linguistic and terminological traits[53]. However, as RABINOWITZ and EPSTEIN point out, these supposed Palestinian traits do not appear in Palestinian sources such as the Palestinian Talmud (RABINOWITZ, Notes, pp. 299–300, EPSTEIN, IAL, p. 52). A more common view finds the explanation of this phenomenon in the redaction history of these tractates. This had already been suggested in general terms by FRANKEL and BRÜLL. In specific terms LEWY and HOROVITZ argued that the 'unusual' tractates were redacted in Pumbedita while the rest of BT comes from Sura. Thus the peculiarities of the former reflect local dialect and terminology[54]. RABINOWITZ also adopts this explanation (Notes, pp. 299–310). EPSTEIN agrees that the 5½ tractates were edited at a different time and place than the rest of BT. Specifically, they were redacted later than the other tractates, as the similarity of their language to that of the Geonim indicates. Additional evidence of their lateness derives from the comparison of pericopae from the 5½ with their parallels in other tractates. Such a comparison shows that the former depend on the latter. That is, the 'unusual' tractates quote the 'regular' ones and are therefore later (IAL, pp. 54–71 re Ned., 72–83 re Naz., and 131–144 re Tem.). As to the places of redaction, EPSTEIN suggests that Ned. comes from Meḥoza and Naz. from 'Meḥoza-Pumbedita'. The rest of BT was redacted at Sura (ibid., pp. 69f., 82, cf. MELAMMED, Introduction, pp. 468f.).

A different interpretation of the redaction history of the 'unusual' tractates is suggested by A. WEISS and DE VRIES. The school of thought summarized by EPSTEIN stresses that the 5½ differ from the rest of BT not only in external features such as language and style, but also in substantive matters such as methodology and masters cited. WEISS, on the other hand, asserts that the 'unusual' tractates are not so unusual. Their peculiarities are neither extensive nor substantive. For example, the Amoraim who appear are basically identical to those cited in the rest of BT. In essence the 5½ have the same origin as the other tractates. To be sure, some of them, such as Tam., lack the early stratum of Gemara which goes back to Yehudah b. Yeḥezqel. But they all have the middle stratum edited

[53] HALEVY, III, pp. 48f.

[54] Z. FRANKEL, Einleitung in den jerusalemischen Talmud (Leipzig 1859. Rep. Jerusalem, 1967), p. 48a; BRÜLL, Entstehungsgeschichte, op. cit., p. 185; I. LEWY, Interpretation, p. 74; H. S. HOROVITZ, Die Composition des Talmuds, MGWJ 63 (1919), p. 126.

under Abaye and Rava. What, then, is the source of their peculiarities? The answer according to WEISS lies in the post-Amoraic development of these tractates, or rather the lack thereof. Since the 5 ½ were not studied in the academies, they did not undergo the stylistic revision and supplementation that the rest of BT received in the Savoraic and Geonic era. Consequently the 'unusual' tractates preserve pericopae in their original, unpolished form (WEISS, MGWJ 83, DTLU, pp. 46—128). Thus the peculiarity of these tractates lies in the primitive state of their contents. WEISS does not respond to EPSTEIN's argument that the language of the 5 ½ is similar to the Geonic dialect. The latter fact would indicate that they were late, or at least were worked over sometime close to the Geonic period. Moreover, the Geonic sources tell us only that these tractates were not studied in the eighth century. They say nothing about the Savoraic period. Until these last two points are clarified, the theory of WEISS remains tentative.

DE VRIES arrives at conclusions similar to those of WEISS. He agrees that the 'unusual' tractates are not late. On the contrary, they preserve the short and rudimentary form of the older Talmudic material. They do so because they did not undergo the stylistic editing that other tractates did. This same fact explains their unusual terminology. In an earlier period Talmudic terminology was fluid. Later it became fixed, and editors standardized the terminology of the 'regular' tractates. This was not done for the 5 ½ because they were not studied in the academies. As to the quotations from other tractates adduced by EPSTEIN as evidence of lateness, this is not decisive. DE VRIES argues that they represent post redactional additions. In a study of Me'il. he supplies more details. On the basis of the masters named in this tractate he suggests that it was compiled in the school of R. Papa in the latter part of the fourth century. This school used a terminology different from that current in other academies (Studies, pp. 230—238 re Me'il., and 188—193, 223—229 on the problem in general, cf. Tarbiz 30 and Lešonenu 29). Here DE VRIES appears to contradict his general position that the unusual terminology reflects the fluid situation of the earlier period. Instead, in the case of Me'il., it results from the different site of redaction — a position identical to that of EPSTEIN. However, the contradiction is only partial. Had Me'il. undergone editing later, the standard terminology would have been imposed on it. More problematic is the claim that the 'unusual' tractates received post-Amoraic additions (DE VRIES speaks specifically of Ned. and Naz.). If so, then they were worked over by later editors. Why did they not receive stylistic editing at the same time? Moreover, like WEISS, DE VRIES does not respond to the linguistic argument of EPSTEIN.

To sum up, WEISS and DE VRIES agree that the redactional history of the 5 ½ tractates differs from that of the rest of BT. They did not undergo the late redactional development found in the 'regular' tractates. Instead they preserve the older, rudimentary form of the pericopae. For the rest of BT redactional activity continued in the post-Amoraic era. This activity included supplementation and stylistic polishing. In contrast to this view EPSTEIN argues that the 'unusual' tractates were redacted later than the rest of BT. Moreover, as earlier scholars had argued, and as DE VRIES himself suggests regarding Me'il., they were redacted at schools other than the one which gave us the 'regular' tractates. The linguistic argument advanced by EPSTEIN, the similarity of the language of the 5½ to the Geonic dialect, is persuasive. But so is the argument from the rudimentary state of the pericopae stressed by WEISS and DE VRIES. And the two arguments lead to mutually exclusive conclusions. As we shall see below, the latter argument is compatible with other data relevant to the redaction history of BT as a whole. However, before we can accept the view of WEISS and DE VRIES we must find an answer to the linguistic phenomenon noted by EPSTEIN. Perhaps as our knowledge of bta and of the Geonic dialect increases, this point will turn out to be less significant[54a]. In any event, study of the 'unusual' tractates suggests the complexities of the larger issue of the redaction of BT as a whole. This issue is our next topic.

b) The Traditional Theory of the Redaction of BT

Since the beginning of modern Jewish studies in the early nineteenth century both Talmudists and historians have felt obliged to present their view on the redaction history of BT. There is no point to review in detail the theories propounded prior to 1925. This has already been done by KAPLAN and in NEUSNER's Formation (see KAPLAN, Redaction, pp. 1—22, 179—194 for the views of GRAETZ, FRANKEL, RAPAPORT, BRÜLL, I. H. WEISS, HALEVY, and JAWITZ; NEUSNER, Formation, pp. 3—47 for GRAETZ, I. H. WEISS, HALEVY, JAWITZ, and ZURI; see also BACHER's view in his article 'Talmud' in the Jewish Encyclopedia, Vol. 12). Moreover, despite differences in details, all these theories are essentially identical. They all repeat the redaction history which crystallized in the middle ages. Thus we may speak of a traditional theory of the redaction of BT, canonized in the writings of the *rishonim*. This theory is based on a few enigmatic passages in BT and in Geonic sources. I shall cite these sources and show how the traditional theory emerged from them. Then I shall indicate why it must be rejected.

[54a] The most recent statement on the language of the 5½ tractates is that of S. KAUFMAN, The Akkadian Influences on Aramaic (Chicago, 1974), p. 163. Unfortunately, KAUFMAN ignores the views of WEISS and DE VRIES and asserts that "all agree" that these tractates are late. On the latter assumption, he adresses the question whether the Aramaic of the 5½ is colloquial or archaizing. The absence of Akkadian loan words, aside from those common to earlier Aramaic dialects, leads him to conclude that the language of these tractates is not colloquial. Instead, archaization "should be suspected". I wonder whether the negative conclusion of KAUFMAN vitiates the argument of EPSTEIN. If the Aramaic of the 5½ tractates is not colloquial Geonic, then perhaps it is archaic, rather than archaizing. In sum, the linguistic evidence may fit in just as well, if not better, with the view of WEISS and DE VRIES that the tractates are early.

BT contains no unequivocal reference to its redaction. Nevertheless two passages are widely believed to allude to such activity. The first appears at BM 86a. Towards the end of 85b we find a story, in bta, about how Samuel Yarḥina'ah healed an eye ailment of Rabbi (Yehudah the Patriarch). The latter sought to ordain the former, but for unexplained reasons he was unable to do so[55]. Samuel Yarḥina'ah then responds,

> "Let the master not be troubled. I myself saw the Book of the First Man, and in it was written, 'Samuel Yarḥina'ah will be called sage, but he will not be called master. And the healing of Rabbi will be by his hand'.
>
> Rabbi and R. Natan are the end of *mishnah*, R. Ashi and Ravina are the end of *hora'ah*. And your sign is, 'until I went into the sanctuary of God (*miqdashe 'ēl*); then I perceived (*'avinah*) their end' (Psalms 73 : 17)."

It is not clear whether what I have set off as a separate paragraph also is quoted from the Book of the First Man. The quotation concerning Samuel Yarḥina'ah is in Aramaic, though the text is too short and the text tradition too uncertain for us to determine which dialect. The section about Rabbi, Natan, Ashi, and Ravina is in Hebrew. As to the sign from Psalms 73, there is agreement that *'avinah* is a play on the name Ravina which is a contraction of Rav 'Avina. Most, but not all, authorities see in the word *miqdashē* an allusion to the name Ashi. Despite the agreement on the former sign, it is not clear which master is meant. Two Amoraim bore the name Ravina. One was a contemporary of Ashi; the other, Ravina b. R. Huna, died over 70 years after Ashi. More problematic are the words left untranslated, *mishnah* and *hora'ah*. The former could be the name of the book Mishnah or an abstract noun meaning '(Tannaitic) teaching'. The second word literally means 'instruction'. I shall return to these issues below. The second passage, from BB 157b, is as follows,

> "Ravina said, 'The first *mahadura* of R. Ashi said to us . . . The latter *mahadura* (of R. Ashi) said to us . . .'"

The words in parentheses are missing in several manuscripts of BT, but they are to be understood. Since Ravina does not quote Ashi directly, but only his *mahadura*, the former need not be the early Ravina. The Aramaic word *mahadura* comes from the root *hdr* which means 'to go round', or 'to return'.

These passages are cited in two important Geonic sources. The later of the two is the more widely quoted. I refer to the responsum of Sherira, *ga'on* of the academy of Pumbedita, to the Jewish community of Qairawan, North Africa from the year 986/7. This responsum is known as 'Iggeret

[55] On this story see NEUSNER, History of the Jews in Babylonia, Vol. II (Leiden, 1966), pp. 135f.

(= Epistle) of R. Sherira Ga'on (hereafter: ISG). The relevant sections are the following[56].

1. "In this way *hora'ah* was added generation after generation until Ravina, when it ceased — as Samuel Yarḥina'ah saw in the Book of the First Man: Ashi and Ravina are the end of *hora'ah*.
   And after this, though there certainly was no *hora'ah*, there were interpretations and explanations (*sevarē*) which are similar to *hora'ah*. And they (?) are called the Savoraic masters (*rabbanan savora'ē*)."

   ISG, ed. Lewin, p. 66

I note that Sherira assumes the Ashi-Ravina section to be part of the quotation from the Book of the First Man.

2. "On Wednesday, Kislev 13, in the year 811 [Selucid Era = December, 499] Ravina b. R. Huna died, and he is the end of *hora'ah*."

   ISG, ed. Lewin, p. 95

3. "In the year 787 [= 475/6] R. Sama son of Rabah died.
   After him R. Assi [Spanish recension: Yosi] presided. In his day was the end of *hora'ah*, and the Talmud *'istetēm*."

   ISG, ed. Lewin, p. 97

All manuscripts of the French recension of ISG agree the last word is from the root *stm* in the *'itpe'ēl* verb pattern. The Spanish recension manuscripts have forms from the latter root as well as from the root *swm*. The second root appears in the form *'istayyem*, meaning 'was finished/ completed'. However, the forms from *stm* which appear in all the manuscripts of the superior French recension seem to preserve the original reading. The basic meaning of this root is 'stop up, block, close'. The *'itpe'ēl* verb pattern gives the word a passive force. The question then is, what is meant by the phrase "the Talmud was stopped/blocked/closed"? Another possible interpretation connects the verb with the word *setam*, the Talmudic term for "anonymous, unattributed traditions". The passage would then mean that the Talmud "was made anonymous".

4. "R. Ashi served as principal of the academy for nearly sixty years. This is what Chapter *mi shemet* [of BB, here = 157b] refers to when it mentions the first *mahadura* of R. Ashi and the latter *mahadura* of R. Ashi. For thus the masters instituted: to teach in each semester 12 sections [sc. of BT, *metivata*] whether short or long. Thus he [Ashi] reviewed (*hadar*) his entire learning in 30 years."

   ISG, ed. Lewin, pp. 93f.

[56] I quote from the critical edition by B. M. Lewin, Haifa, 1921. Lewin printed both of the two recognized recensions, the French and the Spanish. I translate the former, following Epstein's view that the French recension is more accurate, see IAL, pp. 610—615.

The second Geonic source cited in connection with the redaction history of BT is Seder Tanna'im Ve'amora'im (hereafter: STV). This is an historical and methodological introduction to BT dated in its present form to the late ninth century[57].

1. "In the year 811 [= 499 C.E.] Ravina, the end of *hora'ah*, died. And the Talmud *nistam*."

STV, ed. KAHAN, p. 6

The Hebrew *nistam*, from the root *stm* in the *nif'al* pattern, is an exact equivalent of the Aramaic *'istetēm*. Variant readings include *nistatam* and *neḥtam*. The former, apparently a *nitaf'al* verb pattern[58], is identical in meaning to *nistam*. The word *neḥtam* means 'was sealed'. I take this to be an explanatory replacement of an original *nistam*.

2. "Rav the elder [or: the Great] was the one who began with *hora'ah*. and from Rav the elder till R. Ashi and Ravina were 204 [variant: 280] years, and they were the end of *hora'ah*."

STV, ed. KAHAN, p. 8

If "Rav the elder" is the famous Amora Rav, then the 204 or 280 years period may begin from 219. That year, when Rav settled in Babylonia according to Geonic tradition, is conventionally considered the beginning of the Amoraic era in Babylonia. 204 years would thus take us to the death of Ashi, dated by STV to 424. 280 years would bring us to 499, the date assigned to the death of Ravina b. R. Huna[59].

Let us now review how the Geonic sources understood the two BT passages quoted above. I begin with BM 86a. ISG 2 and STV 1 identify the Ravina of the latter passage with the later Ravina b. R. Huna rather than with the contemporary of Ashi. This is also implicit in ISG 1 which has the Savoraic era begin immediately after the end of *hora'ah*, and in ISG 3 where *hora'ah* ends during the principalship of Assi which began in 475/6. The reading 280 in STV 2 also suggests this identification. (Even the reading 204 does not rule it out, for the figure could refer only to Ashi.) The Geonic sources also relate to the meaning of the term *hora'ah*. ISG 3 and STV 1 assert that the end of *hora'ah* ca. 500 coincides with the closing/blocking of the Talmud. As variant readings showed, the latter event was understood in the middle ages to refer to the completion or 'sealing' of BT. The second BT passage, BB 157b, is cited only in ISG 4. SHERIRA interprets "the *mahadura* of Ashi" to mean a review of Talmudic traditions by the latter.

[57] For both ISG and STV see the excellent form- and source-critical studies by EPHRATHI, Sevoraic Period, pp. 1—32. I quote STV from the critical edition by K. KAHAN, Frankfurt a. M., 1935.

[58] For the verb pattern *nitaf'al* see H. YALON, Introduction to the Vocalization of the Mishnah (Jerusalem, 1964), pp. 127—135 = Tarbiz 1 (1930) pp. 118—122.

[59] See KAHAN's note ad loc., pp. 32f.

On the basis of the sources just discussed medieval authorities (such as Rashi, R. Nissim, and Maimonides), and after them modern scholars, derived the following conclusions. The BM passage draws a parallel between Rabbi, editor of the Mishnah, and Ashi and Ravina. The point of the parallel is that the latter two did for BT what Rabbi did for the Mishnah. Now according to the Geonic sources the Ravina mentioned is the later master of that name who died in 499, over 70 years after Ashi. Therefore the editing of BT must have been carried out in two phases. The second phase, ca. 500, was the closing or sealing of BT. Following this was the Savoraic era which saw only editorial polishing, but no substantive addition to the now closed text of the Talmud. What was the first phase of the editing in the time of Ashi? This is hinted at by BB 157b. Ashi twice reviewed all the Talmudic material which had accumulated up to his time. While doing so he 'arranged' or 'edited' this material. The great frequency with which Ashi appears in BT and the fact that many pericopae conclude with his comments were seen as confirmation for the latter assumption. The two generations of Amoraim who followed Ashi added some new material and engaged in further editing. Then, with the death of Ravina b. R. Huna in 499, BT was declared closed.

A glance at the summaries of recent scholarly opinion in KAPLAN's 'Redaction' or NEUSNER's 'Formation' will show that there are many variations on this theme. Most of them concern the two phases of editing and what happened between them. For example, the exact nature of Ashi's contribution to the redaction of BT is variously assessed: he composed only the outline or framework of the Gemara, he began the actual redaction but did not finish it, he redacted it orally but did not reduce it to writing, etc. Still the overall picture of the redaction history of BT is identical from the eleventh to the twentieth century. Our BT is the work of Ashi, supplemented by the two following generations. It was completed and 'sealed' by the end of the fifth century. This traditional theory is accepted not only by the pre-1925 scholars, but also by more recent authorities. Among the latter is EPSTEIN. Although he did not write at length on the subject, his position is clear. Thus he alludes to earlier redactions of the Gemara which continued

> "until the time of Ravina [I] and R. Ashi 'the end of hora'ah', and the 'arrangers of the Talmud', who collected all the material which preceded them, generally in its original form; they interpreted it, completed it, and 'arranged' it. But its arrangement was not finished in their day: two generations of Amoraim followed them who completed it and added to it additional interpretations and pericopae until the Savoraim came and 'sealed' it . . ."
>
> IAL, p. 12

The attribution of the 'sealing' to the Savoraim is not a departure. EPSTEIN means that they declared BT closed to substantive addition as of the death of Ravina b. R. Huna. After all, Ravina himself could not have done this. Thus his theory is identical to the traditional one described above. On the other hand ALBECK rejects the first phase of editing assumed by the theory, but he accepts the second phase. According to ALBECK BT grew by accretion generation after generation, and there was no final redaction carried out in one time and in one place. Neither BM nor BB refer to such an event. The "end of *hora'ah*" which took place in the time of Ashi and his contemporary Ravina (I) means the cessation of free interpretation of the Mishnah. After the death of these two masters the Amoraim no longer felt competent to derive new laws from the Mishnah. While ALBECK thus rejects the first part of the traditional theory, he retains the second part. He speaks of "the sealing of the Talmud which was finished (*nistayyem*) in the days of Ravina b. R. Huna" (ALBECK, Sinai Jubilee Vol., p. 79). Given the full endorsement by EPSTEIN and the partial one by ALBECK, it is not surprising that the traditional theory of the redaction of BT was then enshrined in recent textbooks and encyclopedia articles (cf. EPHRATHI, Sevoraic Period, pp. 58—62).

If we return to the original sources, we see that they cannot bear the weight of the traditional theory. The key phrases "the end of *hora'ah*" and "the Talmud was closed/blocked" are far from clear. Interpretations are as numerous as the scholars who discuss these phrases. Moreover, BM includes in the parallel it draws not only Rabbi, but also R. Natan who on no account was an editor of the Mishnah. Thus there is no reason to assume that the parallel between Rabbi and Natan on the one hand and Ashi and Ravina on the other refers to editorial activity on their part. As ALBECK stresses, the passage makes no reference to editing at all. No one interprets *hora'ah* to refer to the latter activity. Nor do BB or the Geonic sources attribute editing to Ashi. As noted, ISG explains BB 157b as alluding to Ashi's review of his learning, an activity attributed to other masters also (cf. WEISS, DTLU, p. 245, n. 9). This is certainly the most reasonable interpretation. In sum, the sources cited earlier may have given rise to the traditional theory, but they cannot support it. And aside from these sources, that theory has nothing else on which to rely.

From the methodological standpoint, the weakness of the traditional theory lies in its dependence on a very few, enigmatic passages. HALEVY stressed long ago that only extensive internal analysis could solve the problem of the redaction of BT. However, he himself could not break free of the framework canonized by the medieval commentators who were, for HALEVY, authoritative. What HALEVY could not do was accomplished almost simultaneously by KAPLAN and A. WEISS. Both rely entirely on internal evidence and follow their results through to the end. Each tests the traditional theory against the internal evidence and finds it wanting. I shall begin with the latter aspect of their work. KAPLAN analyzes at length the material attributed to Ashi. While these passages constitute a major stratum within BT, they are no more prominent than material attributed to other masters such as Ashi's older contemporary, Papa (KAPLAN,

Redaction, p. 78). Moreover, the extent of the material produced after Ashi, including reworking of traditions of the latter, "militates against the commonly accepted tradition that he [Ashi] was its [the BT's] editor", (ibid., p. 95, cf. 127 and the intervening discussion, and 192). A study of the material attributed to Ravina I and II yields similar conclusions regarding the latter (ibid., pp. 128—133, 143—147). In sum, there is no evidence in the sources from the last Amoraic century (= the fifth century) for any editing of BT. KAPLAN concludes that at the death of Ravina b. R. Huna in 499 "the editing of the Talmud was still a task to be undertaken and achieved" (ibid., p. 147).

WEISS also rejects the traditional theory. First he shows that the sources on which the latter is based do not support it. For example, he argues that BM 86a originally referred not to Ashi, but to Assi (i. e., *'śy* or *'sy* instead of *'šy*; *ś* and *š* are identical in the Hebrew alphabet). The latter was the contemporary of Ravina b. R. Huna mentioned in ISG 3 above. The passage means that in the time of Ravina II and Assi the Amoraic era came to an end. WEISS also stresses that Sherira never asserts that Ashi edited BT. In fact, the traditional theory is the creation of the *rishonim*. Nor does any internal evidence prove that the redaction of BT was the work of Ashi (WEISS, DTLU, pp. 245—254). After disposing of the traditional theory WEISS goes on to question the very terms in which the redactional issue is discussed. He asks what could we mean by a "final redaction" of BT? There are two possibilities. Either the final editor reworked the material at his disposal into the form he wanted, or he simply compiled the sources and left them in their original form, at most adding transitions and completions. On either alternative the final editing should have left some traces in BT. However we find no such traces. Certainly there is no evidence of an overall reworking of the material. On the contrary, the material is diverse and contradictory. But even signs of a "scissors and paste" editing are absent. We can discern no general principle of arrangement such as we find in the Mishnah, for example. In sum, there is not a single feature of BT attributable to a final redaction carried out at one time and in one place (ibid., pp. 243f., cf. ALBECK above).

In place of a final redaction, WEISS posits a continuous redaction. That is, the editing of Talmudic materials was simultaneous with their creation. Each generation created new Talmudic material which they added to the Talmud received from previous generations. In addition, Baraitot and Amoraic sources not previously included in the older Talmud might be inserted. The newly added material becomes an integral part of the Talmud which is then passed on to the next generation. This process took place in each center of study in Babylonia. Thus there were several local Talmuds, each of which evolved and grew layer by layer (DTLU, p. 256, SLA, pp. 117f.). The claim that BT grew by accretion from generation to generation appears to go back to Sherira. In the last century HALEVY vigorously argued this position, as ALBECK did in this century (Sinai Jub. Vol.). And as noted above in the discussion of source criticism, most modern scholars assume early redactions or editions of the Gemara. These editions are identical to the strata of BT assumed by WEISS. Where WEISS departs from other scholars is in his denial of a final editing or a 'sealing' of BT. His interpretation of the final stages of the evolution of BT will be discussed in the following section.

To sum up, the traditional theory of the redaction of BT is untenable. Neither the few Amoraic and Geonic sources on which the theory is based nor internal evidence support it. In fact, the internal evidence disproves this theory. There is no convincing evidence that either Ashi, Ravina I, or Ravina II edited BT. Nor is there any sign of a 'sealing' or closing of the document around the year 500. Rather than being closed, BT remained open to extensive addition in the post-Amoraic era. The new material includes entire pericopae indistinguishable from older sources. Thus the 'sealing' of BT in 500 is no less a will-of-the-wisp than the redaction by Ashi. Both stages of the traditional redaction history are unhistorical.

c) The Two Source Theories

The rejection of the traditional redaction history of BT is one of the important achievements in the last half-century of Talmud study. No alternate theory has achieved the wide support once enjoyed by the older view. Still it seems to me that a new consensus is emerging. While differing in terms and details, several recent theories share important structural similarities. They all maintain that BT is composed of two major blocs of material, hence my description of them as 'two source' theories. The scholars to whom this view can be attributed include KAPLAN, KLEIN, RUBINSTEIN, HALIVNI, A. WEISS, and FELDBLUM.

KAPLAN and KLEIN propose the most straightforward version of the two source theory. As explained above, each believes that the two forms they isolate, "gemara" and "talmud" or "sebara", derive from separate sources. And these sources provide the key to understanding the redaction of BT. KAPLAN approaches the latter issue by reinterpreting BM 86a. The term *hora'ah*, he argues, must be interpreted in light of a passage at Ber. 5a:

> "'to instruct them' [Exodus 24: 12, *lehorotam*, from the same root as *hora'ah*] — this is *gemara*."

The end of *hora'ah* thus means the end of Gemara. And the latter term has the technical sense of "gemara", viz., the brief summaries of "talmud" arrived at and preserved in writing in the Amoraic academies[60]. KAPLAN finds an historical explanation for the end of "gemara". A persecution towards the end of the fifth century closed the academies and put an end to

[60] KAPLAN, p. 289, n. 2, notes that Codex Munich 95 reads *talmud* instead of *gemara* at Ber. 5a. As B. COHEN points out in his review of KAPLAN, JQR 24 (1933/34), p. 264, *talmud* is clearly the correct reading. This destroys a link in KAPLAN's argument. However, his theory does not stand or fall on this point.

the process by which "gemara" was created. This development also affected "talmud". Previously no need was felt to preserve either the old "talmud" summarized by "gemara" or the new "talmud" created while studying the recently composed "gemara". The ongoing activity of the academies and the written collections of "gemara" made preservation of "talmud" unnecessary. The closing of the academies thus affected both "gemara" and "talmud" (KAPLAN, Redaction, pp. 235—296). Even the eventual reopening of the schools could not turn the clock back. KAPLAN describes the new situation as follows:

> "In the deserted halls of the academies, among the wreckage of the old system of oral instruction, the Saboraim came face to face with the danger of losing contact with posterity. They realized the need to preserve at least a minimum of the exposition necessary to compose a Talmud for the elucidation of the Mishnah and of the gemara. This stupendous undertaking was conceived and accomplished by the Saboraim."
>
> Redaction, p. 297

As the basis of their work the Savoraim took the "gemara" collection of Ashi, for "this was the standard work in the literature of gemara . . . the most authoritative . . . the most complete . . ." (ibid., p. 306). This fact explains the medieval tradition which asserted that Ashi was the redactor of BT. In fact he compiled the "gemara" upon which the Savoraim built our Talmud (ibid., p. 289). To be sure, the latter did not preserve Ashi's work intact, but rearranged it (ibid., p. 307). In addition to the "gemara" of Ashi the Savoraim drew on the "gemara" collections of other academies, treatises on special subjects, and "talmud" material which had been preserved orally (loc. cit.). Despite the role played by older material, "the Saboraim are the designers and real builders of the Talmud" (ibid., p. 301). Thus, according to KAPLAN, BT consists of two major sources: an Amoraic source (essentially the "gemara" collection of Ashi) and a Savoraic source (the "talmud" composed for Ashi's "gemara"). In KAPLAN's own words, "the gemara of R. Ashi, accompanied by the Saboraic exposition, make up the bulk of the present Talmud" (ibid., p. 306).

KLEIN arrives at a conclusion identical to that of KAPLAN, though without the historiographical superstructure of persecutions and closed academies[61]. KLEIN simply states that "the compilation of the Gemara was in fact the work of R. Ashi and Rabina [I or II?] . . . Sebara [was] added during the sixth and seventh centuries, the era of Rabbanan Saborai", (KLEIN, SGR, p. 37, cf. GQS, pp. 344f.). Here too we have two sources: the Amoraic "gemara" and the Savoraic "sebara". S. M. RUBINSTEIN also propounds a similar theory. He argues that our BT is composed of two written sources. The earlier source is a Talmud composed of brief, anony-

[61] I do not mean to imply that the persecutions and closing of the schools were not historical. They clearly were. See NEUSNER, History, Vol. V (Leiden, 1970), pp. 60—69.

mous material without source references, proof texts, or argumentation. This description, of course, recalls the "gemara" of KAPLAN and KLEIN. This early Talmud served as the basis of the second source. The latter completed and explicated the early Talmud, adding source citations, proof texts, and argumentation. These last three elements were often put in the mouths of early masters who appeared in the first source. In addition, the compilers of the later Talmud created entire 'artificial' pericopae out of materials from the early one. According to RUBINSTEIN this explains how early masters sometimes comment on the views of later ones as well as the contradictory parallel pericopae. In the latter case one of the 'inverted' pericopae is 'artificial'. The detailed working out of RUBINSTEIN's theory involves further distinctions and complications, but overall he maintains the two source scheme. He does not explicitly date the two Talmuds. So we cannot know whether his second source is of Savoraic provenance[62].

A different version of the two source theory appears in the Introduction to the second volume of HALIVNI's 'Sources and Traditions'. HALIVNI promises to develop his theory in a later book, but for the present we can rely only on the brief outline in that Introduction. He begins by pointing out that almost half of BT consists of anonymous material. Siding with WEISS against ALBECK and EPSTEIN, HALIVNI argues that most of this material is late. (The few early unattributed sources result from *Tradenten* forgetting who the authors were.) We never find named masters quoting or directly commenting upon anonymous traditions. Where they appear to do so, this is the work of later editors. HALIVNI then asserts, "We must see the *gemara* as a composition made up of two books, a book of Amoraim and a book of anonymous material, which differ from each other in language, methodology, and history" (HALIVNI, ST, Vol. II, pp. 7—8). The anonymous material includes additions interpolated into attributed traditions as well as comments deduced from the words of named masters. Here too we have two sources: the "book of Amoraim" and the "book of anonymous material". The former was apparently completed by the time of Ashi, for HALIVNI suggests that the latter dates from the period between Ashi and the Savoraim (the last 70 years of the fifth century). HALIVNI's brief summary leaves many questions unanswered. Most important, what are the differences in "language, methodology, and history" between the two sources? On what basis does he date the "book of anonymous material" to the last three quarters of the fifth century? Yet even at this preliminary stage the parallels with the theories of KAPLAN, KLEIN, and RUBINSTEIN are apparent.

The assignment of A. WEISS to the two source school is not as obvious as was the case with the four scholars just discussed. Still I believe that he belongs here. First of all, his reconstruction of the redaction of BT is, in its original form, almost identical to that of KAPLAN. As we saw, WEISS

[62] TENNENBLATT, Formation, p. 86, n. 12 infers that both of RUBINSTEIN's sources are Amoraic in provenance.

rejects the concept of a final redaction. Instead, he argues that the Gemara evolved from generation to generation as new material was created, edited, and added to the Talmud received from the preceding generation. This process continued until the close of the fifth century. At this point a worsening of the political status of the Jews in Babylonia put an end to it. The deterioration of their position also weakened their creative powers. The persecutions which marked the final decades of the fifth century caused a break in academic activity. After a few years the situation of the Jews improved, and Talmud study resumed. By the time this happened, the older material had achieved a new authority and holiness in the eyes of the people. It was seen as something that could not be created anew. Thus the evolution of Gemara characteristic of the Amoraic period did not resume. However, the received text of the Talmud was not in a finished state. Many pericopae remained without literary polish and explanation. Therefore the sages of the new period saw as their main task the explication of difficult pericopae and the facilitation of the study of the Talmud in general. Their literary activity involved adding glosses and connecting links between arguments, adducing sources, copying out parallel pericopae, and the like (DTLU, pp. 256—257). WEISS here agrees with KAPLAN that a persecution put an end to Amoraic literary activity, and that the Savoraim felt incapable of continuing the latter. He differs by limiting the contribution of the Savoraim to "literary polishing". Yet the Amoraic Talmud he posits, with its unfinished, unpolished pericopae, recalls the first member of the various two source theories discussed above.

WEISS later revised his account of the last stages of the formation of BT. In his final statement on this issue he drops the sharp historical and literary break between the Amoraic and Savoraic eras. He now asserts that the evolution of BT continued through the Savoraic period. The Talmud contains not only redactional material from the Savoraim, but entire pericopae. And "regarding literary form and presentation there is no difference between them [Savoraic sources] and the Amoraic Talmud". Moreover, BT contains more of the late pericopae than is usually assumed (SLA, p. 118). In stressing the continuity between the Amoraic and Savoraic strata WEISS somewhat overstates his case. Elsewhere he makes clear that we can often distinguish Savoraic from earlier material (see 'Literary Activities'). And he continues to maintain that the literary polishing of unfinished Amoraic pericopae was a major part of Savoraic activity. In any event, in the revised version of his theory WEISS attributes to the Savoraim a much larger role in the formation of BT. He asserts that were we able to identify all the post-Amoraic material, "we would find that the Talmud produced by the Amoraim was very different, both in quantity and in quality, from the Talmud before us" (Literary Activities, p. 18).

Implicit in WEISS' account is a distinction between the Talmud of the Amoraim and the Talmud of the Savoraim. The former was briefer, stylistically less polished, abrupt in transitions, and poor in cross references and source citations. These are precisely the traits which distinguish the "gemara" of KAPLAN and KLEIN and the early Talmud of RUBINSTEIN. One wonders whether HALIVNI's "book of Amoraim" will turn out to share these traits also. The same description calls to mind the rudimentary pericopae characteristic of the five and a half 'unusual' tractates. As noted, WEISS and DE VRIES argue that these pericopae are distinguished by the absence of Savoraic editing and supplementation. That is, in these 5½ tractates we see what the Amoraic Talmud looked like before it was supplemented by the Savoraic Talmud. Another illustration of the former may be found in the materials introduced by the formula *vehavēnan bah.* We recall that DE VRIES argued that these sources were simple pericopae which he assigned to an early edition of the Gemara. Still further illustration of the nature of the Amoraic Talmud comes from the Palestinian Talmud. Both RUBINSTEIN and GOLDBERG note that when we separate out the older stratum of BT, we find pericopae identical in form to the simpler, less polished pericopae of the Palestinian Gemara (see GOLDBERG, Tarbiz 32). In any case, WEISS concludes that the Talmud of the Savoraim remedied the deficiencies of the Amoraic Talmud — just as the "talmud" or "sebara" did for the "gemara" of KAPLAN and KLEIN, RUBINSTEIN's later Talmud for his early one, and, in a sense, HALIVNI's "book of anonymous material" for his "book of Amoraim". In connection with HALIVNI, I note that WEISS' student, M. S. FELDBLUM, identifies the anonymous element in BT as post-Amoraic (FELDBLUM, PAAJR 38). FRIEDMAN also argues that the anonymous framework is (in most cases) later than the statements of the Amoraim, though he does not explicitly attribute the later stratum to the Savoraim (FRIEDMAN, 'Critical Study').

Thus a consensus has emerged which recognizes two main sources or strata within BT. The Amoraic stratum contains material, most of it attributed to named masters, from the third through the fifth centuries. The Savoraic stratum dates from the sixth and seventh century and is mostly anonymous. The first element evolved from generation to generation and probably never underwent a final redaction — aside from the editing it received at the hands of the Savoraim. The later element both explicates and expands the older material. That is, it glossed and edited the older stratum, but it also created new material on the model of the older sources. Each stratum of Talmud is itself complex and composed of various sources. Because of its anonymity I doubt that we shall be able to say much about the formation of the Savoraic Talmud. However, more progress in the isolation and identification of this stratum can be expected. Several questions remain to be answered. What caused the change in style from attributed to anonymous traditions? Why did the Savoraic form of literary activity — anonymous additions to BT — cease in the eighth century, when separate books attributed to authors began to appear in rabbinic circles in Babylonia? Nonetheless the redactional history suggested by the new consensus, which is based on extensive internal analysis of BT, is a clear advance over the traditional theory discussed in the previous section. The emergence of this new theory is another important achievement of Talmud scholarship since 1925.

V. Hilfsbücher *and Related Works*

Bibliography

1. Introductions, Methodology, Bibliographies, Encyclopediae, Special Lexica

Albeck, H., Die Entwicklung der Talmudischen Wissenschaft seit Zacharias Frankel, Das Breslauer Seminar. Jüdisch-Theologisches Seminar (Fraenckelscher Stiftung) in Breslau, 1854—1938. Gedächtnisschrift, Tübingen, 1963, pp. 167—174.

Ashkenazi, S. and Yarden, A., Ozar Rashe Tevot. Thesaurus of Hebrew Abbreviations. Jerusalem, 1969.

Assaf, S., Tequfat Hagge'onim Vesifrutah. Jerusalem, 1955. [= TH.]

Bader, G., Cyclopedia of Hebrew Abbreviations. New York, 1951.

Berkovits, E., Talmud, Babylonian, Encyclopedia Judaica, Vol. XV, Jerusalem, 1972, coll. 755—767.

Blidstein, G. J., Method in the Study of Talmud, JAAR 39 (1971), pp. 186—192.

Chajes, Z. H., The Student's Guide through the Talmud by ... Z. H. Chajes, Translated from the Hebrew, Edited and Critically Annoted by J. Schachter. New York, 1960.

Corre, A., ed. Understanding the Talmud. New York, 1975.

De Vries, B., Mavo' Kelali Lasifrut Hattalmudit. Tel Aviv, 1966.

Goldschmidt, L., Oznayim LaTorah. Konkordansiyah leTalmud Bavli lefi Nosim, ed. R. Edelman. Copenhagen, 1959.

Gross, M. B., Oṣar Ha-agadot. 3 Vols. Jerusalem, 1954.

Guttmann, M., Mafteaḥ ha-Talmud. Songrad, Budapest, Wratislaviae, 1906—30. 3 Vols.

Id., Zur wissenschaftlichen Talmudpflege der neueren Zeit, MGWJ 74 (1930), pp. 172—184, 75 (1931), pp. 241—268, 80 (1936) pp. 425—430.

Hasidah, I. I., Oṣar Ma'amare Halakhot. 2 Vols. Jerusalem, 1959.

Hyman, A., Oṣar Divre Ḥakhamim Upitgamehem[3]. Tel Aviv, 1955.

Id., Toldot Tanna'im Ve'amora'im. 3 Vols. London, 1910. Reprint, Jerusalem, 1964.

Id., Torah Hakketuvah Vehammessurah. 3 Vols. Tel Aviv, 1960.

Jacobs, L., Studies in Talmudic Logic and Methodology. London, 1961.

Jeiteles, B., Oṣar Tanna'im Ve'amora'im. 2 Vols. Manchester, 1961—62.

Joel, I., ed., Index of Articles on Jewish Studies, Vol. 1—5. Jerusalem, 1966—1970.

Kasher, M. M., Torah Shelemah, Vols. 1—5. New York, 1953—1962.

Kasher, M. M. and Mandelbaum, J., eds. Sarei Ha-elef. A Millenium of Hebrew Authors (500—1500 C. E.). New York, 1959. [= SH.]

Kasovsky (Kosowsky), B., Thesaurus Nominum quae in Talmude Babilonico reperiuntur, Vols. 1ff. Jerusalem, 1976ff.

Kasovsky, C. J. and B., Thesaurus Talmudis: Concordantiae verborum quae in Talmude Babilonico reperiuntur. Vols. 1ff. Jerusalem, 1954ff.

Kolatch, A. J., Who's Who in the Talmud. New York, 1964.

Konovitz, Y., Ma'arkhot Ha'amora'im. Ma'amarehem Behalakhah Uva'aggadah Mesuddarim Lefi Ha'inyanim. R. Yoḥanan ve Resh Laqish. Jerusalem, 1973. Rav veShemu'el. Jerusalem, 1974.

Krengel, J., Talmud, Jüdisches Lexikon, Vol. 4, 2, Berlin, 1930, coll. 835—855.

Maged, A., Sefer Bet Aharon, Vols. 1ff. New York, 1962ff.

Maimon, Y. L., Abaye veRava. Jerusalem, 1965.

Margalioth, M., Encyclopedia of Talmudic and Geonic Literature. 2 Vols. Tel Aviv, n. d.

Mayer, R., Zum sachgemäßen Verstehen talmudischer Texte, Abraham Unser Vater. Festschrift Otto Michel, Leiden, 1963, pp. 346—355.

MEISELES, I., Talmud, Recent Research, Encyclopedia Judaica Year Book 1974, pp. 266—270.
MELAMMED, E. Z., Mavo' Lesifrut Hattalmud[3]. Jerusalem, 1961.
MIELZINER, M., Introduction to the Talmud. With a New Bibliography, 1925—1967 by A. GUTTMANN. New York, 1968.
SCHACHTER, J., Mavo' Lattalmud. Tel Aviv, 1954.
ID., 'Oṣar Hattalmud. Tel Aviv, n.d.
SCHÜRER, E., The History of the Jewish People in the Age of Jesus Christ. A New English Version Revised and Edited by G. VERMES and F. MILLAR. Vol. 1. Edinburgh, 1973.
SEVER, M., Mikhlol Hamma'amarim Vehapitgamim. 3 Vols. Jerusalem, 1961—62.
STEINBERGER, N., Bibliyografiyah Lemore Hattalmud. Jerusalem, 1970.
STEINSALTZ, A., The Essential Talmud. Trans. C. GALAI. New York, 1976.
STERN, A., Handbuch der Hebräischen Abbreviaturen. Sighetul-Marmatiei, 1929.
STRACK, H. L., Introduction to the Talmud and Midrash. Philadelphia, 1931.
TOWNSEND, J. T., Rabbinic Sources, The Study of Judaism: Bibliographical Essays, New York, 1972, pp. 35—80.
UMANSKI, Y., Ḥakhme Hattalmud. Jerusalem, 1949.
WIESENBERG, E., Observations on Method in Talmudic Studies, JSemSt 11 (1966), pp. 16—36.
ZEVIN, S. J., ed. Enṣiklopediyah Talmudit. Vols. 1ff. Jerusalem, 1949ff. English Translation by I. EPSTEIN and H. FREEDMAN, Encyclopedia Talmudica. Vol. 1. Jerusalem, 1969.

2. Commentaries

A. Texts

Abraham of Montpellier. Commentary on the Tractates Nedarim and Nazir composed by Rabenu Abraham of Montpellier. Ed. M. Y. BLAU. New York, 1962.
Abraham b. David of Posquieres. Novellae to Tractate Bava Qamma. Ed. S. ATLAS. New York, 1963.
Asher b. Yeḥi'el (Rosh). Tosfe HaRosh to Tractate Qiddushin. ed. M. S. SHAPIRA. Tel Aviv, 1969. Tosfot HaRosh: Bava Meṣi'a'. M. HIRSHLER and J. D. GORODETZKY. Jerusalem, 1959.
Ashkenazi, Beṣalei, Shiṭṭah Mequbbeṣet. 4 Vols. New York, 1966.
Isaiah the Elder of Trani (Rid). Pisqe HaRid Vepisqe HaRiaq. 2 Vols. Ed. A. J. WORTHEIMER, et al. Jerusalem, 1964—66. Teshuvot HaRid. ed. A. J. WORTHEIMER. Jerusalem, 1967. Tosafot HaRid. New York, 1955.
Me'iri, Menahem. Bet Habbeḥirah.
'Avodah Zarah. Ed. A. SOFER. Jerusalem, 1965.
Bava Batra. ed. A. SOFER, New York, 1957.
Bava Meṣi'a'. ed. K. SCHLESINGER. Jerusalem, 1959.
Bava Qamma. ed. K. SCHLESINGER. Jerusalem, 1950.
Berakhot[2]. ed. S. DICKMAN. Jerusalem, 1965.
Beṣah. ed. K. SCHLESINGER, Jerusalem, 1965.
'Eruvin. ed. B. HIRSHLER. Jerusalem, 1968.
Giṭṭin, ed. K. SCHLESINGER, Jerusalem, 1964.
Ḥagigah. ed. Y. S. LANGE. Jerusalem, 1970.
Ḥallah, Sheqalim, Tamid, Middot. ed. A. SOFER. Jerusalem, 1969.
Horayot, 'Eduyot. ed. A. SOFER, Jerusalem, 1969.
Ḥullin. ed. A. LISS. Jerusalem, 1970.
Ketuvot. ed. A. SOFER. Jerusalem, 1947.
Makkot.[2] ed. S. STERLITZ. Jerusalem, 1965.
Megillah, Mo'ed Qaṭṭan. ed. M. HIRSHLER et al. Jerusalem, 1968.
Nedarim.[2] ed. A. LISS. Jerusalem, 1970.
Niddah. ed. A. SOFER. New York, 1949.
Pesaḥim.[2] ed. Y. KLEIN. Jerusalem, 1967.

Qiddushin.[3] ed. A. SOFER. Jerusalem, 1963.
Sanhedrin.[2] ed. A. SOFER. Jerusalem, 1965. ed. Y. RALBAG. Jerusalem, 1971.
Shabbat. ed. Y. LANGE. Jerusalem, 1968.
Shevu'ot. ed. A. LISS. Jerusalem, 1968.
Sukkah. ed. A. LISS. Jerusalem, 1966.
Ta'anit. ed. A. SOFER. Jerusalem, 1967.
Yevamot. ed. S. DICKMAN. Jerusalem, 1968.
Yoma. Ed. H. B. RABITZ. Bene Beraq, 1966.
Soṭah, Nazir, ed. A. LISS. Jerusalem, 1967.

Moses b. Naḥman (Ramban). Novellae. 3 Vols. Jerusalem, 1928—29. Complete Novellae. Ed. M. HIRSHLER. Vols. 1ff. Jerusalem, 1970ff.

Pereṣ, Rabbenu. Tosafot to Tractate Pesaḥim. ed. S. VILMAN. New York, 1970. Tosafot to Tractate Bava Meṣi'a'. ed. M. HIRSHLER. Jerusalem, 1970.

Qinon, Shimshon. Sefer Keritot. ed. S. SOFER. Jerusalem, 1965.

Solomon b. Adret (Rashba). Novellae. 3 Vols. Jerusalem, 1962.

Yom-Tov b. Abraham of Seville (Ritba). Novellae. 3 Vols. New York, 1964. The New Hiddushey Ritba to Baba Metzia. ed. S. A. HALPERN. London, 1962. Commentary of the Ritva on Baba Bathra. ed. M. Y. BLAU, 2 Vols. New York, 1953—54.

A Digest of Commentaries on the Tractates Babha Kamma, Babha Mesi'a and Babha Bhatera of the Babylonian Talmud. Compiled by Zechariah Ben Judah Aghmati. Reproduced in Facsimile from the Unique Manuscript in the British Museum Or 10 013. Edited by J. LEVEEN. London, 1961.

LEWIN, B. M., ed. Otzar ha-Geonim. Thesaurus of the Gaonic Responsa and Commentaries, following the order of the Talmudic Tractates. 13 Vols. Haifa and Jerusalem, 1928—43.

TAUBES, H. S., ed. Otzar ha-Geonim to Tractate Sanhedrin. Jerusalem, 1966.

KIBLEVITZ, S., ed. Otzar Mefarshei Hatalmud. Bava Metzia. 2 Vols. Jerusalem, 1971—73. Makkoth. Jerusalem, 1975.

SCHREIBER, A., ed. Tosfoth Hachme Anglia on Tractate Betzah, Megillah, Kiddushin. Jerusalem, 1970.

B. Studies

APTOWITZER, A., Letoldot Perushe Rashi Lattalmud, B. Heller Jubilee Volume, Budapest, 1941, pp. 3—17.

FRAENKEL, Y., Darko Shel Rashi Beferusho Lattalmud Habbavli. Jerusalem, 1975.

FREIMANN, A., List of the Early Commentaries on the Talmud, L. Ginzberg Jubilee Volume, Vol. 2, New York, 1945, pp. 323—354.

FRIDMAN, S., Sefer Sha'arei Shalom. Tel Aviv, 1965.

KOHN, N. J., Sefer Osar Haggedolim 'Allufe Ya'aqov. 9 Vols. Haifa, 1966—70.

KOHN, P. J., Osar Ha-Be'urim We-Ha-Perushim. Thesaurus of Hebrew Halakhic Literature. London, 1952.

KRENGEL, J., Talmud-Kommentare, Jüdisches Lexikon, Vol. 4, 2, Berlin, 1930, coll. 858—888.

SHAQED, S., A tentative bibliography of Geniza documents. Paris, 1964.

TA-SHMAH, I., 'Hiddushei ha-Rishonim', — their Order of Publication, Kirjath Sepher 50 (1975), pp. 325—336.

URBACH, E. E., Die Entstehung und Redaktion unserer Tossafot, Jahresberichte des Jüdisch-Theologischen Seminars in Breslau, 1936.

ID., The Tosaphists: Their History, Writings, and Methods[2]. Jerusalem, 1955.

3. Translations and Anthologies

A. English

The Babylonian Talmud. Translated into English with notes, glossary, and indices. ed. I. EPSTEIN. 35 Vols. London, 1935—52.

The Talmud with English Translation and Commentary. ed. A. EHRMAN. Fascicles 1ff. Jerusalem and Tel Aviv, 1965ff.
MALTER, H., The Treatise Ta'anit of the Babylonian Talmud. Philadelphia, 1928.
COHEN, A., Everyman's Talmud. New York, 1949.
MONTEFIORE, C. G. and LOEWE, H. M., A Rabbinic Anthology. Philadelphia, 1960.
NEWMAN, L. I. and SPITZ, S., The Talmudic Anthology. New York, 1945.
NEUSNER, J., Invitation to the Talmud. New York, 1973.

B. German

Der Babylonische Talmud ... herausgegeben ... nach der Bombergschen Ausgabe ... nebst Varianten ... übersetzt und mit kurzen Anmerkungen versehen. L. GOLDSCHMIDT. 9 Vols. Berlin, Wien, The Hague, 1897—1935.
GEIS, R. R., Vom unbekannten Judentum. Freiburg, 1961.
MAYER, R., Der Babylonische Talmud (Auswahl). München, 1963.
STRACK, H. L. and BILLERBECK, P., Kommentar zum Neuen Testament aus Talmud und Midrasch. 4 Vols. München, 1922—28.

C. Hebrew

Hattalmud Habbavli. trans. and comm., E. STEINSALTZ. Vols. 1ff. Jerusalem, 1969ff.
Talmud Bavli 'Im Targum 'Ivri Uferush Ḥadash. ed. Y. N. EPSTEIN. Bava Batra. trans. and comm., S. ABRAMSON. Jerusalem, 1957. Bava Meṣi'a'. trans. and comm., M. N. ṢOVAL and H. Z. DIMITROVSKY. Jerusalem, 1960. Bava Qamma. trans. and comm., E. Z. MELAMMED. Jerusalem, 1952.

4. Related Fields

A. History

AMIR, A. S., Mossadot Veto'arim Basifrut Hattalmudit. Jerusalem, 1977.
BEER, M., The Babylonian Amoraim. Aspects of Economic Life. Ramat Gan, 1974.
ID., The Babylonian Exilarchate in the Arsacid and Sassanian Period. Tel Aviv, 1970.
DIMITROVSKY, H. Z., ed., Exploring the Talmud. Vol. 1. Education. New York, 1976.
GOODBLATT, D., Rabbinic Instruction in Sasanian Babylonia. Leiden, 1975.
NEUSNER, J., A History of the Jews in Babylonia. 5 Vols. Leiden, 1966—70.
NEUSNER, J., ed. Soviet Views of Talmudic Judaism. Five Papers by YU. A. SOLODUKHO in English Translation. Leiden, 1973.
YUDELOWITZ (JUDELOWITZ), M. D., Ha'ir Naresh (Bebavel) Bezeman Hattalmud, Sinai 14 (1943), pp. 94—99, 15 (1944) pp. 93—98, 226—229.
ID., Ha'ir Sura, Sinai 1 (1937), pp. 168—174, 268—275, 2 (1938), pp. 156—162, 317—324, 418—422, 3 (1939), pp. 130—132.
ID., Ḥayye Hayyehudim Bezeman Hattalmud. Ha'ir Pumbedita Bime Ha'amora'im. Jerusalem, 1928.
ID., Ḥayye Hayyehudim Bezeman Hattalmud. Sefer Nehardea. Vilna, 1905.
ID., Meḥoza. Miḥayye Hayyehudim Bezeman Hattalmud. Jerusalem, 1947.
ID., Yeshivat Pumbedita Bime Ha'amora'im. Tel Aviv, 1935.
ZURI, Y. S., History of Hebrew Public Law. The Reign of the Exilarchate and the Legislative Academies. Period of Rav Nachman bar Jizchak (320—355). Tel Aviv, 1938.

B. Archaeology, Geography, Realia

BEN-DAVID, A., Talmudische Ökonomie. Die Wirtschaft des jüdischen Palästina zur Zeit der Mischna und des Talmud, 1. Hildesheim und New York, 1974.

Brand, Y., Ceramics in Talmudic Literature. Jerusalem, 1953.

Goodenough, E. R., Jewish Symbols in the Greco-Roman Period, Vols. IX—XI; Symbolism in the Dura Synagogue. New York, 1965.

Kraeling, C. H., The Synagogue (= The Excavations at Dura-Europus. Final Report VIII, 1). New Haven, 1956.

Krauss, S., Talmudische Archäologie. 3 Vols. Leipzig, 1910—12.

Obermeyer, J., Die Landschaft Babylonien im Zeitalter des Talmuds und des Gaonats. Frankfurt a. M., 1929.

Montgomery, J. A., Aramaic Incantation Texts from Nippur. Philadelphia, 1913.

Ne'eman, P., Enşiklopediyah Lege'ografiyah Talmudit. 2 Vols. Tel Aviv, 1972.

Smith, M., Goodenough's Jewish Symbols in Retrospect, JBL 86 (1967), pp. 53—68.

C. Religion

Büchler, A., Studies in Sin and Atonement in Rabbinic Literature of the First Century. London, 1928.

Goldberg, A. M., Untersuchungen über die Vorstellung von der Schekhinah in der frühen rabbinischen Literatur. Talmud und Midrasch. Berlin, 1969.

Herford, R. T., Talmud and Apocrypha. New York, 1933. Reprint, New York, 1971.

Heschel, A. J., The Theology of Ancient Judaism. 2 Vols. London and New York, 1962—65.

Hirsch, W., Rabbinic Psychology. Beliefs about the Soul in Rabbinic Literature of the Talmudic Period. London, 1947.

Kadushin, M., The Rabbinic Mind². New York, 1965.

Id., Worship and Ethics. A Study in Rabbinic Judaism. Evanston, 1964.

Mach, R., Der Zaddik in Talmud und Midrasch. Leiden, 1957.

Marmorstein, A., The Doctrine of Merits in Old Rabbinic Literature. London, 1920.

Id., The Old Rabbinic Doctrine of God. 2 Vols. London, 1927—37.

Id., Studies in Jewish Theology. London, 1950.

Scholem, G., Jewish Gnosticism, Merkabah Mysticism, and Talmudic Tradition. New York, 1960.

Urbach, E. E., The Sages. Their Concepts and Beliefs. Trans. from the the Hebrew by I. Abrahams. 2 Vols. Jerusalem, 1975.

D. Law

Albeck, S., The Law of Property and Contract in the Talmud. Tel Aviv, 1976.

Cohen, B., Jewish and Roman Law. 2 Vols. New York, 1966.

Id., Law and Tradition. New York, 1959.

Elon, M., Jewish Law. History, Sources, Principles. 2 Vols. Jerusalem, 1973.

Finkelscherer, H., Zur Frage fremder Einflüsse auf das rabbinische Recht. Samuel und das sasanidische Recht, MGWJ 79 (1935), pp. 381—398, 431—442.

Gershfield, E. M., ed., Studies in Jewish Jurisprudence, I—II. New York, 1971—1972.

Gulak, A., Das Urkundenwesen im Talmud. Jerusalem, 1935.

Id., Leḥeqer Toldot Hammishpaṭ Ha'ivri Betequfat Hattalmud. Jerusalem, 1939.

Id., Toldot Hammispaṭ Beyisra'el Betequfat Hattalmud. Jerusalem, 1939.

Id., Yesode Hammispaṭ Ha'ivri. 4 Vols. Berlin, 1922.

Higger, M., Intention in Talmudic Law. New York, 1927.

Katz, S., Die Strafe im talmudischen Recht. Berlin, 1936.

Kirschenbaum, A., Self-Incrimination in Jewish Law. New York, 1970.

Levine, B. A., On the Origins of Aramaic Legal Formulary at Elephantine, Christianity, Judaism and other Greco-Roman Cults. Studies for Morton Smith at sixty, Vol. 3 (= Studies in Judaism in Late Antiquity 12), Leiden, 1975, pp. 55—71.

MUFFS, Y., Studies in the Aramaic Legal Papyri from Elephantine. Leiden, 1969.
RUBIN, S., Das talmudische Recht . . . Sachenrecht . . . Vienna, 1938.
YARON, R., Gifts in Contemplation of Death in Jewish and Roman Law. Oxford, 1960.

1. Introductions, Methodology, Bibliographies, Encyclopediae and Special Lexica

a) Introductions and Methodology

Methodological and historical introductions to BT began to appear in the Geonic period (ASSAF, TH, pp. 147—153). The oldest extant introduction is the aforementioned Seder Tanna'im Ve'amora'im from the late ninth century. Since this book is a composite of older material, we must assume that the history of BT introductions goes back still farther. Whatever its origins, this genre became a popular one in rabbinic circles. Several introductions were composed in the medieval and early modern periods (see the lists in STRACK, pp. 135—137, CHAJES-SCHACHTER, pp. xvff., and KASHER, SH, pp. 113—117). Recent introductions include the Hebrew works of EPSTEIN, ALBECK, and MELAMMED (listed in the bibliography to Chapter IV). The latter two are general, systematic introductions to both Tannaitic and Amoraic literature, not just to BT. EPSTEIN's 'Introduction to Amoraitic Literature', published posthumously from lecture notes, is both too technical and too specific to be considered a real introduction. The part devoted to BT contains introductions to nine tractates (Pes., Beṣ., Suk., Ned., Naz., Soṭ., Qid., Bekh., and Tem.) and commentaries on six chapters from three tractates (Chapters I and II of Pes., X of BM, and I—III of BB). Also available in Hebrew are several introductions designed for use in Israeli high schools. These books are of some value for the beginner who can read modern Hebrew (see the list in STEINBERGER, Bibliyographiyah, pp. 39—43; the best of these works are those by DE VRIES, MELAMMED, and SCHACHTER). The best introduction in an European language remains that by STRACK. A revised edition of this classic would be a worthwhile project. The introduction of MIELZINER was recently reprinted with the addition of a new bibliography. The section on Talmudic hermeneutics and the dictionary of technical terms make this work very useful. Further insight into Talmudic methodology may be found in JACOBS' book on the subject. Finally, CORRE anthologizes over 30 important contributions to Talmudic studies by twentieth century scholars.

b) Bibliographies

As noted above, the bibliography of STRACK is outstanding for the period up to ca. 1925. M. GUTTMANN's review of 'recent' literature is helpful for the years between 1925—1930 (Monatsschrift, 74, 75, 80), while MEISELES covers the early 1970's. The recent reprint of MIELZINER's 'Introduction' contains a bibliography for the years 1925—1967 compiled by A. GUTTMANN, STEINBERGER's 'Bibliyographiyah' contains sections on Introductions and Hilfsbücher, Textbooks, Selections, Anthologies, and Translations and includes short evaluations of each work listed. TOWNSEND lists in his 'Rabbinic Sources' bibliographies on editions, translations, and encyclopediae. He also treats targumic and midrashic literature. Exceptionally full bibliographies are found in each volume of NEUSNER's 'History of the Jews in Babylonia', though of course they are not limited to BT. Attention should also be called to his essay 'Bibliographical Reflections' which appears as Appendix II of the fourth volume of his 'History'. The revised edition of SCHÜRER's 'History' contains excellent bibliographies in the section 'Sources: Rabbinic Literature' (pp. 68—118). Finally, recent publications can be followed in 'Kirjath Sepher' and in the invaluable 'Index of Articles on Jewish Studies' edited by I. JOEL (beginning with 1966).

c) Encyclopediae and Special Lexica

I include here thesauri and compilations of various kinds. Perhaps the most important work in this category is the word concordance to BT, now nearing completion, by CH. J. and B. KASOVSKY. The latter has begun publication of a name concordance. These monumental works are based on the standard printed text of BT, an unavoidable decision given the current state of text criticism. In any case, the KASOVSKYS' project is of inestimable value to all aspects of Talmud scholarship. Subject concordances have been compiled by GOLDSCHMIDT and M. GUTTMANN. The entries in that by GOLDSCHMIDT are brief phrases in Hebrew-Aramaic keyed both to his German translation and to the standard pagination of the original text. The 'Mafteaḥ' of GUTTMANN is an alphabetical list of subjects and terms from all of rabbinic literature, not just BT. It covers only the first half of the Hebrew alphabet. The fullest name and subject index appears in the final volume of the English translation of BT edited by I. EPSTEIN. Unfortunately this is keyed only to the pages of the translation.

The 'Encyclopedia Talmudica' appearing under the editorship of ZEVIN is devoted exclusively to legal matters. It includes as much medieval as Talmudic material. An English translation of the first volume has appeared. Another encyclopedia devoted to legal topics is HASIDAH's 'Oṣar', a compilation of rules from rabbinic literature. The two volumes published so far reach the letter m. Several encyclopediae collect sayings of the Talmudic masters. GROSS (''Oṣar'), HYMAN (''Oṣar'), and SEVER ('Mikhlol') arrange the sayings alphabetically. JEITELES (''Oṣar'), KONOVITZ ('Ma'erkhot'), and MAIMON do so by author. HYMAN ('Torah') and KASHER ('Torah Shelemah') collect rabbinic exegesis according to the order of the Bible. The former merely lists the references in rabbinic literature, the latter cites the comments in full. Biographical encyclopediae of the Talmudic masters include the works of HYMAN ('Toldot'), KOLATCH ('Who's Who'), and MARGALIOTH ('Encyclopedia'). The best list, though the most sparse in biographical detail, appears in ALBECK's 'Introduction'. UMANSKI ('Ḥakhme') lists the masters and the pages in BT where they are mentioned. MAGED ('Sefer') has begun an encyclopedia of 'Talmudic principles and personalities'. Two older special lexica remain useful. They are BACHER's 'Exegetische Terminologie' and the glossary of hermeneutics in MIELZINER's 'Introduction'. Among more recent publications, the ''Oṣar Hattalmud' by SCHACHTER is a handy dictionary of technical terms of great help to the beginner. Several dictionaries of abbreviations, which are so common in rabbinic literature, are available. Those of ASHKENAZI, BADER, and STERN, listed above, are full and reliable.

2. Commentaries

Exegetical work on BT begins within the document itself. Later masters explicate the work of earlier ones, and one source explains another. The Savoraic material, as Geonic sources stressed, frequently takes the form of commentary. Commentaries external to BT begin to appear in the Geonic era, in the form of books, responsa, and legal compendia. Many of these works, especially the books of commentaries, are lost or extant only in fragments, though the Cairo Geniza continues to disclose new material (see the bibliography of SHAQED). A full description of the BT related literature of the Geonim appears in ASSAF's 'Tequfat Hagge'onim' (pp. 137—146 for commentaries, 154—210 for legal compendia, and 211—220 for responsa; cf. KASHER, SH, pp. 246—248). B. M. LEWIN published a thesaurus of this material, arranged according the order of BT, in his 'Otzar ha-Geonim'. LEWIN's work covers Ber., Orders *mo'ed* and *nashim*, BQ, and the first third of BM. A similar work on tractate Sanh. was recently published by H. Z. TAUBES.

The post-Geonic commentaries (I include legal epitomes of BT) are divided by Jewish tradition into those of the *rishonim*, ca. 1000—1600, and those of the *aḥaronim*, ca. 1600 to the present. STRACK publishes a list of the major commentaries composed through the nineteenth century (Introduction, pp. 149—154, cf. BACHER, Talmud Commentaries, Jewish Encyclopedia, 12, pp. 27—30 and J. KRENGEL, Talmud-Kommentare, Jüdisches Lexikon, Vol. 4, 2 [Berlin, 1930], coll. 858—888). A fuller list, but covering only the *rishonim*, was compiled by FREIMAN. He records, tractate by tractate, all known commentaries, both published and unpublished (Marx Jub. Vol.; this is an expanded version of the article cited by STRACK, p. 149). The published commentaries of the *rishonim* are also listed by KASHER (SH, pp. 117—245, and see 248—255 for responsa and 255—279 for legal compendia). TA-SHMAH contributes a history of the publication of the early commentaries (Kirjath Sepher 50). For commentaries published since the appearance of KASHER's list the bibliographical journal 'Kirjath Sepher' may be consulted. Many of the major commentaries appear in the standard editions of BT. As mentioned above, the Complete Israeli

Talmud Institute plans a new edition with improved texts of the classical commentaries together with variant readings from manuscripts thereof. Pending completion of this project, the major achievement of the past half century has been the publication of the commentaries of Menaḥem b. Shelomo Hamme'iri of Perpignan (died 1306). Previously this work was available in manuscript only, and when STRACK wrote only the commentary on Suk. and Mishnah Avot had been published. Another recent project seeks to publish selected commentaries of the *aḥaronim*. So far three volumes have appeared under the general editorship of KIBLEVITZ. My bibliography at the head of this chapter lists the most recent editions of the major commentaries, especially those not printed together with BT. Biographical and bibliographical data on the *rishonim* appear in the encyclopedia of KOHN. Similar information on the Tosafists, the Franco-German commentators of the twelfth through the fourteenth centuries, can be found in the works of FRIDMAN and URBACH. The latter also discusses the methodology of these authorities. The history of the greatest BT commentary, that of Rashi, is sketched by APTOWITZER, while FRAENKEL studies its methodology.

All of the commentaries alluded to above are traditionalist in outlook. They all accept the authority of BT. Moreover, they all assume a consistency of religious and legal principles throughout the document. Within the limitations imposed by these assumptions they achieve a high degree of exegetical sophistication. For example, I have already mentioned that the text-critical work of the *rishonim* is compatible with modern philological method. Thus in areas of 'lower criticism' and in exegesis of individual pericopae the traditionalist commentaries have much to teach the modern student of BT (cf. the remarks of HALIVNI in the Introduction to ST, Vol. 1). However, in questions of 'higher criticism', of source, form, and redaction history, they are inadequate. Indeed these issues hardly exist in the ahistorical world view of the medieval commentators. Moreover, even those few commentators with an interest in realia and the historical background of BT were very poorly informed on these subjects. Thus the traditionalist commentaries, which continue to be composed, leave much for the scientific exegete to accomplish.

Oddly enough, modern Talmud scholarship has neglected the task of exegesis. A systematic, modern commentary on BT does not exist. To be sure, hundreds of pericopae have been explicated in the course of recent literary and historical studies. But we have nothing for BT equivalent to LIEBERMAN's commentary on the 'Tosefta' or that of NEUSNER on 'Mishnah-Tosefta' *ṭohorot*. Aside from annotated translations (to be considered below), the only scientific exegetical studies of BT are EPSTEIN's commentary on six chapters (IAL, pp. 145—270), that of HALIVNI on Orders *mo'ed* and *nashim*, RABINOWITZ' 'Notes', and the articles by WEISS collected in 'Notes' (see bibliography to Chapter IV). The work of HALIVNI, which is projected to cover all of BT, is the fullest. But even he does not claim to supply a complete, systematic commentary, The absence of a full, scientific exegesis of BT is one of the failures of modern Talmud scholarship, especially if such an exegesis must precede other literary studies as ROSENTHAL and NEUSNER argue.

3. Translations and Anthologies

The oldest translations of Aramaic sections of BT appear in a ninth century Hebrew recension of Halakhot Pesuqot known as 'Hilkhot Re'u' (see MELAMMED, Introduction, pp. 482f.). Subsequent translations up till 1925 are listed by STRACK (pp. 144f., 154—159). Translations of the entire BT are available in German and English. Both the German version, by GOLDSCHMIDT, and the English one, by several scholars under the editorship of I. EPSTEIN, are generally reliable. The latter has fuller notes. In addition to these works, translations of individual tractates have appeared since 1925 in English, German, Italian, Spanish, Arabic, and modern Hebrew (see STEINBERGER, Bibliyographiyah, pp. 59—74 and TOWNSEND, Rabbinic Sources, pp. 61f.). Among the English translations, the best is MALTER's fully annotated rendition of Ta. However, he does not translate the standard printed text, but an eclectic text which he prepared. A vocalized edition of BT with English translation and commentary began to appear in 1965, edited by EHRMAN. So far only a few fascicles, covering parts of Ber., Qid., and BM, have come out. The strictures of NEUSNER on this project should be consulted (Invitation, pp. 250f.). Most recent translations have been into Hebrew. The highest scholarly level was achieved in an abortive project initiated by EPSTEIN. Only three tractates appeared: BQ, BB, and BM. They include the original text and Hebrew translation in parallel columns with variant readings, cross references, and brief commentary. The translation is too literal and the commentary too brief for these volumes to be of much help to the beginner. The more advanced student will benefit from the fact that these volumes are the work of such outstanding Talmudists as ABRAMSON, DIMITROVSKY, and MELAMMED. A project of greater benefit to the beginner is the Hebrew translation and commentary by A. STEINSALTZ. The latter has already completed about a third of BT. STEINSALTZ succeeds in bringing the Talmud within reach of anyone who reads modern Hebrew. However, the author's outlook is traditionalist.

Selected BT texts in translation have also appeared in several languages. My bibliography above lists works of this kind which have appeared since 1925 in German and English (for Hebrew anthologies and selections see STEINBERGER, pp. 48—58). Generally these anthologies are organized thematically and include sources from all of rabbinic literature. They also exhibit a tendency to prefer non-legal texts. All these factors prevent the reader from gaining an accurate impression of the character of BT. The major exception is NEUSNER's 'Invitation'. This work contains related legal sections from the Mishnah, Tosefta, Palestinian Talmud, and BT in English translation with a detailed commentary and analysis together with a very instructive introduction and a bibliographical supplement. The commentary and analysis enable the reader to follow the mode of Talmudic argument. This book provides the best entry into Talmudic literature for the English reader.

4. Related Fields

a) History

One of the major achievements of recent Talmud scholarship is J. NEUSNER's 'History of the Jews in Babylonia'. This work supersedes all previous histories. NEUSNER summarizes all modern scholarship on the Sasanian background as well as that on the Jewish community of Babylonia itself. More important, he achieves significant breakthroughs in several areas of research. I shall mention just two which are relevant to the study of BT. NEUSNER is the first to define the socio-political role of the masters cited in BT. Previously scholars viewed the masters as "popular leaders" and "part of the people". NEUSNER proves that they constituted a distinct "estate" often in conflict with the masses. Their influence over the people derived from two sources. In civil law and certain areas of ritual they were able to impose their views because of their status as functionaries of the autonomous Jewish administration headed by the exilarch. In other areas they were limited to moral persuasion based on their reputation as "holy men", a reputation they seem to have cultivated. This distinction results in part from NEUSNER's insight that we must distinguish between actual court cases reported in BT and purely academic discussions. A second breakthrough concerns the religion of the Talmudic masters. For our purposes the most important point is NEUSNER's discovery of the ritualistic aspect of their academic activity, a part of what he calls "the ritual of being a rabbi". Both of these points enrich our understanding of BT passages, and they are only examples. A scientific exegesis of BT will have routinely to consult the source index of NEUSNER's 'History'.

M. BEER has contributed two valuable monographs. His 'Exilarchate' complements NEUSNER's study of the relations between the masters and the exilarchs. The detailed study of the economic status of the masters in his 'Babylonian Amoraim' reinforces NEUSNER's discovery of their class status. BEER's work supersedes the inadequate pamphlet on 'The Commercial Life of the Jews in Babylonia' by J. NEWMAN. The latter's 'The Agricultural Life of the Jews in Babylonia', 200—500 (London, 1932) is at best a preliminary collection of relevant sources. Further contributions to the economic history of the Jews in Babylonia appear in the provocative essays by Y. SOLODUKHO, edited in English translation by NEUSNER (Soviet Views). They are written from the standpoint of an orthodox Marxism-Leninism. A. BEN-DAVID's 'Talmudische Ökonomie' is limited to Palestine as its subtitle indicates: Die Wirtschaft des jüdischen Palästina zur Zeit der Mischna und des Talmud (Band I, Hildesheim and New York, 1974). Still this book is helpful for comparative research. YUDELOWITZ' studies on the various Jewish towns in Babylonia also contain data relevant to economic history. Finally, the academic institutions of the Talmudic masters are studied in YUDELOWITZ' monograph on the Pumbedita academy (Yeshivat Pumbedita) and in the present writer's 'Rabbinic Instruction in Sasanian Babylonia'.

b) Archaeology, Geography and Realia

The only archaeological remains of the Jews in Babylonia from Talmudic times are the incantation texts published by MONTGOMERY and others. These texts are important both for the study of Jewish Babylonian Aramaic and for the history of Judaism in Babylonia. The Dura Europos Synagogue is several hundred kilometers from Babylonia. Nevertheless KRAELING uses Talmudic sources to explicate the synagogue frescoes. GOODENOUGH vigorously rejects this approach (see M. SMITH, JBL 76, for the current state of the question). At the very least, the Dura Europos discovery reveals a Mesopotamian Jewish community contemporary with the early Amoraic era in Babylonia. The dearth of Jewish remains from the latter country is symptomatic of a larger problem. In general the archaeological evidence from the Sasanian sphere is less than that available from the Roman world. While considerable progress has been made during the past 50 years in Sasanian archaeology, it still lags behind that of the Roman empire. And in the Jewish sphere the situation has not improved at all. Iraq remains closed to students of Jewish history. Thus both in general topics and in specifically Jewish ones we must often rely on comparative evidence from outside Babylonia. And specialized monographs, such as BEN-DAVID's 'Ökonomie' and BRAND's 'Ceramics in Talmudic Literature', understandably concentrate on Palestine. The only synthetic study available is S. KRAUSS' 'Talmudische Archaeologie'. Published at the beginning of the century, this work is clearly outdated from the archaeological standpoint. Moreover, KRAUSS fails to differentiate the various chronological strata within rabbinic literature. However, as a collection of the literary evidence from Talmudic sources the work still has value. Until Talmudic scholars are allowed into Iraq, OBERMEYER's 'Landschaft' remains the definitive study of the geography of Jewish Babylonia. For the flora, fauna, and minerals mentioned in BT, the studies of I. Löw, cited in the bibliography to Chapter III (above, p. 276) are invaluable.

c) Religion

The only study devoted entirely to the religion of Babylonian Jews appears in the relevant chapters of NEUSNER's 'History'. All other scholars take as their subject 'rabbinic Judaism', a term which covers both Palestine and Babylonia, both Tannaim and Amoraim. NEUSNER himself finds little in the thought of the Babylonian Amoraim not attested in Tannaitic or Palestinian Amoraic sources, so the common approach may be justified. In any case, the general studies of rabbinic Judaism do treat topics and personalities found in BT. BÜCHLER and MOORE claim to treat an earlier period, but many of their sources are from BT. The fullest compendium of rabbinic religious thought is URBACH's 'The Sages', though here too Babylonian Judaism receives limited attention. In the realm of theosophy (I include magic and mysticism) we do have evidence unique to Babylonia. I refer to the incantation texts from late Sasanian times. The implications of this material for Babylonian Judaism are discussed at length by NEUSNER in his 'History'. Jewish theosophy of the Talmudic period in general is studied by SCHOLEM (especially in 'Jewish Gnosticism'), but he concentrates on Palestine.

d) Law

In this area also little differentiation is made between Palestine and Babylonia. This approach is justifiable, for BT is based on a Palestinian law code, the Mishnah. Most recent work is comparative. A. GULAK pioneered the comparative study of Jewish and Roman law (including that of the papyri). Further contributions were made by B. COHEN. R. YARON also exploits the Elephantine documents in his model study on 'Gifts in Contemplation of Death'. His stress on the development of the law enables him to delineate the contribution of specific Babylonian masters. A recent trend in legal research seeks continuities with the Akkadian legal tradition. MUFFS found such continuities both at Elephantine and in BT. B. LEVINE briefly summarizes the current state of research on this question ('Smith Festschrift'). Since BT comes from what had been a center of Akkadian culture, and since bta is much influenced by Akkadian, we can expect to find many such continuities in BT law. Clearly this topic is a promising one for future research. Treatment of the influence of Iranian legal traditions may be found in the article by FINKELSCHERER (MGWJ 79) and in NEUSNER's 'History'.

Indices

[Page numbers refer to pagination in the original publication.]

I. Index of Names

Ashi 292, 303, 308—316
Ashkenazi, Beṣalel 264, n. 7, 269, n. 21
ASHKENAZI, S. 326
ASSAF, S. 264f., 266, n. 15, 324, 326
Assi/Yosi 309f., 313

BACHER, W. 285, 288f., 307, 326
BADER, G. 326
Bar Kosiba 277
BEN-AMOS, D. 302, n. 51a
BEN ASHER, M. 279
BENDAVID, ABBA 278
BEN-DAVID, ARYE 329
BEN YEHUDAH, E. 259, n. 1
BEER, M. 329
BOKSER, B. 294, 304
BOMBERG, D. 268
BRAND, Y. 330
BRÜLL, N. 294f., 305, 307
BÜCHLER, A. 331

CHAJES, Z. H. 324
COHEN, B. 314, n. 60, 331
CORRE, A. 324

DALMAN, G. 280, n. 34, 281
DE VRIES, B. 287, 289, 293, 296, 297, n. 50, 302, n. 51a, 305—307, 318, 324
DIMITROVSKY, H. Z. 268, 328
DOR, Z. 288, 290

EHRMAN, A. 328
EPHRATHI, J. 294f., 310, n. 57, 312
EPSTEIN, I. 325, 328
EPSTEIN, J. (Y.) N. 267, n. 15, 271f., 276—278, 285, n. 35, 286—288, 290, 292f., 295—297, 304—307, 309, n. 56, 311f., 316, 324, 327f.

FELDBLUM, M. S. 266, 270, 292f., 299, 314, 318
FINKELSCHERER, H. 331
FINKELSTEIN, L. 286, n. 38
FITZMYER, J. A. 278, n. 32
FORSHEIM, J. 285, n. 36
FRAENKEL, J. 285, n. 36, 302, n. 51a, 327
FRANCUS, I. 295
FRANKEL, Z. 291, 295, 305, 307
FREIMANN, A. 326
FRIDMAN, S. 327
FRIEDMAN, SH. 292—295, 297, 300—304
FRIEDMANN, M. 271

GEIGER, A. 277
GEIGER, B. 280f.
GEWIRTSMAN, B. 290
GINSBERG, H. L. 277
GINZBERG, L. 288
GOLDBERG, A. 287f., 318
GOLDSCHMIDT, L. 325, 328
GOODBLATT, D. 288, n. 41, 294, n. 47, 303, n. 52
GOODENOUGH, E. R. 330
GRAETZ, H. 295, 307
GROSS, M. B. 325
GULAK, A. 331
GUTTMANN, A. 325
GUTTMANN, M. 324f.

HABERMAN, M. 267
Hai Ga'on 268, n. 18, 269f.
HALEVY, Y. I. 288, 291f., 294f., 305, 307, 312f.
HALIVNI (WEISS), D. 286, 292f., 297, n. 50, 314, 316, 318, 327
HARKAVY, A. 268, n. 18
HASIDAH, I. I. 325
HEINEMANN, Y. 285, n. 35
HIRSHLER, M. 264, n. 7, 266, 271
Ḥisda 285, n. 36
HOFFMANN, D. S. 286, n. 36
HOROVITZ, H. S. 286, n. 36, 305
HYMAN, A. 325

JACOBS, L. 288, 324
JASTROW, M. 259, n. 2, 280
JAWITZ, W. See YAVETZ, Z.
JEITELES, B. 325
JOEL, I. 325

KAHAN, K. 310, nn. 57, 59
KAPLAN, J. 291, 293, 295, 298—300, 303, 307, 311—318
KARLIN, A. 302, n. 51a
KASHER, M. M. 266, 324, 326
KASOVSKY (KOSOWSKY), B. 325
KASOVSKY (KOSOWSKY), CH. J. 325
KATSCH, A. I. 266
KAUFMAN, S. A. 281, 307, n. 54a
KIBLEVITZ, S. 327
KLEIN, H. 293, 298f., 314—316, 318
KOHN, N. J. 327

KOHUT, A. 280f.
KOLATCH, A. J. 325
KONOVITZ, Y. 325
KRAELING, C. H. 330
KRAUSS, S. 280, 330
KRENGEL, J. 326
KUTSCHER, E. Y. 276—281

LEVIAS, C. 304
LEVINE, B. 331
LEVY, J. 280f.
LEWIN, B. M. 265, n. 11, 267, 269, n. 22, 295, 309, n. 56, 326
LEWY, I. 289, 305
LIEBERMAN, S. 264, n. 8, 271f., 276, 280f., 286, n. 38, 287, 296f., 327
LISS, A. 271
LÖW, I. 280f., 330
LOWE, W. H. 265, n. 13
LUZZATTO, S. D. 304

MAGED, A. 326
MAIMON, Y. L. 325
Maimonides See Moses b. Maimon
MALTER, H. 271, 328
MARGALIOTH (MARGULIES), M. 272, 325
MARGALIYOT, E. 278
MARGOLIS, M. L. 304
MARGULIES, M. See MARGALIOTH, M.
MARX, A. 271
MARX, M. 280, n. 33
MEIR, O. 302, n. 51a
MEISELES, I. 324
MELAMMED, E. Z. 261, n. 3, 267, n. 16, 269, n. 23, 285, 286, n. 38, 287—289, 295, 299f., 302, 304, 324, 328
Menaḥem b. Shelomoh Hamme'iri 327
MERCHAVIA, CH. 266, n. 14
MIELZINER, M. 324
MIRSKY, S. K. 266, n. 15, 285, n. 36, 294, 302
MONTGOMERY, J. A. 281, 330
MOORE, G. F. 331
MORAG, S. 279
MORESHET, M. 278, 288
Moses b. Maimon (Maimonides, Rambam) 269, n. 21, 311
Moses b. Naḥman (Ramban) 269, n. 20
MUFFS, Y. 331

Naḥman b. Ya'aqov 292
Naḥman b. Yiṣḥaq 292
Natan 308, 312
Natan b. Yeḥi'el of Rome 267, 280
Natronai b. Ḥakinai 265, n. 11
NEUSNER, J. 285, n. 35, 294, 297, 303, 307, 308, n. 55, 311, 315, n. 61, 328—331
NEWMAN, J. 329
Nissim Ga'on 311

OBERMEYER, J. 330

Paltoi Ga'on 265, n. 11
Papa 292, 306, 312
PEREFERKOWITSCH, N. 271
PRICE, J. J. 266

Rabad See Abraham b. David
Rabbi See Yehudah the Patriarch
RABBINOVICZ, R. 267f., 270f.
RABIN, I. A. 286, n. 38
RABINOWITZ, Z. W. 305
Rambam See Moses b. Maimon
Ramban See Moses b. Naḥman
RAPAPORT, S. J. 294f., 307
Rashi See Shelomoh b. Yiṣḥaq
Rav 287, 292, 310
Rava 287, 292, 306
Ravina (I or II?) 308, 315
Ravina I 308, 311—314
Ravina II b. R. Huna 308—314
REITZENSTEIN, R. 272, n. 28
ROSENTHAL, E. S. 271—273, 296f., 328
ROSENTHAL, F. 280
RUBINSTEIN, S. M. 293, 299, 314—316, 318

SALDARINI, A. J. 285, n. 35
Sama b. Rabah 309
Samuel 287, 292, 294, 304
Samuel b. Me'ir 270
Samuel ibn Nagrela Hannagid 265, n. 11
Samuel Yarḥina'ah 308f.
SCHACHTER, J. 324, 326
SCHACHTER, M. 286, n. 37
SCHECHTER, S. 266
SCHLESINGER, M. 279
SCHOLEM, G. 331
SCHÜRER, E. 325
SEVER, M. 325
SHAQED, S. 326
Shelomoh b. Yiṣḥaq (Rashi) 264, n. 7, 286f., 311, 327
Sherira Ga'on 308—310, 313
SINGER, S. 266
SMITH, M. 330
SOKOLOFF, M. 277f.

Solodukho, Yu. 329
Spiegel, S. 261, n. 4
Stern, A. 326
Steinberger, N. 324f., 328
Steinsaltz, A. 328
Strack, H. L. 262, 264, n. 9, 266, 268, 271, 278, 324, 326—328

Ta-Shmah, I. 326
Taubes, H. Z. 267, 269, n. 19, 326
Telegdi, S. 281
Tennenblatt, M. A. 299, n. 51, 316, n. 62
Towner, W. S. 285, n. 35
Townsend, J. T. 324, 328

Umanski, Y. 326
Urbach, E. E. 270, 327, 331

Von Soden, W. 281

Weinberg, J. J. 285, n. 36
Weis, P. R. 287
Weisberg, D. B. 281
Weiss, A. 271, n. 3, 287—293, 295f., 298—303, 305—307, 312—314, 316—318, 327
Weiss, I. H. 286, n. 36, 287, 295, 307

Ya'aqov b. Me'ir (Rabbenu Tam) 270, 281
Yalon, Ḥ. 276, 281, 310, n. 58
Yaron, R. 331
Yavetz (Jawitz), Z. 295, 307
Yehudah b. Yeḥezqel 292, 305
Yehudah the Patriarch (Rabbi) 259, 278, 285f., 296, 308, 311
Yehudai (Jehudai) Ga'on 267, n. 15
Yoḥanan b. Nappaḥa 277
Yudelowitz, M. D. 294f., 330

Zeitlin, S. 286, n. 37
Zeraḥyah Hallevi 269, n. 20
Zevin, S. Y. 264, n. 7, 325
Zucker, M. 285, n. 36
Zuckermandel, M. S. 286, n. 38
Zuri, J. S. 307
Zussman, Y. 293

II. Index of Places

Babylon, Babylonia 259, 261, 265f., 269, 276, 278f., 285—290, 292, 294, 296, 303—305, 310, 317f., 329—331
Bagdad 261
Basel 268

Cairo 265, 326
Constantinople 267f.

Dura Europos 330

France 268
Frankfurt a. M. 268

Galil, Galilean 277, 279
Gerona 265

Iran, Iranian 280f., 331
Iraq 330
Italy 268

Judah 277

Lublin 268

Meḥoza 292, 303, 305
Mesopotamia 330
Morocco 268

Naresh 292, 303
Nehardea 303
Nippur 276, n. 31, 281

Palestine, Palestinian 259, 261, 276, n. 31, 277—280, 285—289, 296, 305, 318, 329—331
Paris 265
Perpignan 327
Portugal 268
Pumbedita 269, 292f., 303, 305, 308, 330

Qairawan 308
Qumran 277

Rhineland 261
Rome 267, 280

Spain 265, 268f.
Sura 292, 303f., 305

Ubeda (Spain) 265

Venice 268
Vilna 268

III. Index of Citations

A. Babylonian Talmud and Amoraic Midrashim

Berakhot
5a 314
6a 302
31a—32b 302
54a—57b 302

Shabbat
21b—24a 302
86b—89b 302
110a—b 302
113b—114b 301

Pesaḥim
110a 302

Megillah
10b—17a 301
28b 286

Ḥagigah
13a—16a 302

Giṭṭin
55b—58a 302
67b 302

Qiddushin
2b 277
49b 286

Bava Meṣi'a'
85b 308
86a 308, 310, 312f.

Bava Batra
13b—17a 301
73a—75b 302
157b 308—312

Sanhedrin
65b 269
86a 286

Shevu'ot
41b 286

'Avodah Zarah
28a 302
58b 277

Ḥullin
137b 277

Midrash Tehillim (Psalms)
ad 104:25 259, n. 1

B. Medieval Sources

Hamma'or Haggadol
ad Alfasi, AZ, Chap. I, p. 2b 269, n. 20
Hassagot of Rabad
ad Hamma'or Haqqatan, Ber., Chap. I, end 269, n. 20

Iggeret of Sherira Ga'on, ed. Lewin, pp. 66, 93f., 95, 97 309
Mishneh Torah of Rambam
Malveh Veloveh 15:2 269, n. 20
Ishut 13:13 269, n. 20

Novellae of Ramban
ad BB 134, 137 269, n. 20

Otzar Hagge'onim, ed. Lewin
ad Ber. 8a, Resp., p. 20 265, n. 11
ad Ket. 68b, Resp. p. 207 269, n. 21

Otzar Hagge'onim, ed. Taubes
ad Sanh. 65b, p. 68 269, n. 19

Responsa of Ge'onim, ed. Harkavy
p. 138 268, n. 18

Seder Tanna'im Ve'amora'im, ed. Kahan
pp. 6, 8 310

Sefer Hayyashar
Introduction 270

Sefer Rabiah, ed. Aptowitzer
Vol. II, p. 20 265, n. 11

Shiṭṭah Mequbbeṣet
ad Ket. 31b 269, n. 20

Aufstieg und Niedergang der römischen Welt

Geschichte und Kultur Roms im Spiegel der neueren Forschung

3 Teile in mehreren Einzelbänden und Gesamtregister. Lexikon-Oktav. Ganzleinen

---

Teil II: Principat

Herausgegeben von Hildegard Temporini und Wolfgang Haase

Band 19: Religion (Judentum: Allgemeines; Palästinisches Judentum)

Herausgegeben von Wolfgang Haase

19.1: XVI, 875 Seiten. Mit 5 Textabbildungen, 14 Kunstdrucktafeln und 2 Faltkarten. 1979. DM 380,– ISBN 3 11 007968 2

19.2: VIII, 688 Seiten. Mit 2 Kunstdrucktafeln. 1979. DM 275,– ISBN 3 11 007969 0

Band 19.1:
Sacchi, P.: Da Qohelet al tempo di Gesù. Alcune linee del pensiero giudaico (3–32) · Jackson, B. S.: The Concept of Religious Law in Judaism (33–52) · Charlesworth, J. H.: A History of Pseudepigrapha Research: The Re-emerging Importance of the Pseudepigrapha (54–88) · Gruenwald, I.: Jewish Apocalyptic Literature (89–118) · Kraft, R. A.: „Ezra" Materials in Judaism and Christianity (119–136) · Rubinkiewicz, R.: La vision de l'histoire dans l'Apocalypse d'Abraham (137–151) · Holm-Nielsen, S.: Religiöse Poesie des Spätjudentums (152–186) · Charlesworth, J. H.: The Concept of the Messiah in the Pseudepigrapha (188–218) · Baumgarten, J. M.: The Heavenly Tribunal and the Personification of Ṣedeq in Jewish Apocalyptic (219–239) · Cavallin, H. C. C.: Leben nach dem Tode im Spätjudentum und im frühen Christentum I. Spätjudentum (240–345) · Maier, J.: Die Sonne im religiösen Denken des antiken Judentums (346–412) · Goldenberg, R.: The Jewish Sabbath in the Roman World up to the Time of Constantine the Great (414–447) · Hoenig, S. B.: The Ancient City-Square: The Forerunner of the Synagogue (448–476) · Kraabel, A. Th.: The Diaspora Synagogue: Archaeological and Epigraphic Evidence since Sukenik (477–510) · Hultgård, A.: Das Judentum in der hellenistisch-römischen Zeit und die iranische Religion – ein religionsgeschichtliches Problem (512–590) · Wardy, B.: Jewish Religion in Pagan Literature during the Late Republic and Early Empire (592–644) · Strange, J. F.: Archaeology and the Religion of Judaism in Palestine (646–685) · Meyers, E. M.: The Cultural Setting of Galilee: The Case of Regionalism and Early Judaism (686–702) · Bietenhard, H.: Die Handschriftenfunde vom Toten Meer (Ḥirbet Qumran) und die Essener-Frage. Die Funde in der Wüste Juda (704–778) · Gabrion, H.: L'interprétation de l'Ecriture dans la littérature de Qumrān (779–848) · Hollenbach, P.: Social Aspects of John the Baptizer's Preaching Mission in the Context of Palestinian Judaism (850–875).
Band 19.2:
Neusner, J.: The Formation of Rabbinic Judaism: Yavneh (Jamnia) from A. D. 70 to 100 (3–42) · Schäfer, P.: Die Flucht Joḥanan b. Zakkais aus Jerusalem und die Gründung des 'Lehrhauses' in Jabne (43–101) · Porton, G.: Midrash: Palestinian Jews and the Hebrew Bible in the Greco-Roman Period (103–138) · Bokser, B. M.: An Annotated Bibliographical Guide to the Study of the Palestinian Talmud (139–256) · Goodblatt, D.: The Babylonian Talmud (257–336) · Stemberger, G.: Die Beurteilung Roms in der rabbinischen Literatur (338–396) · Hadas-Lebel, M.: Le paganisme à travers les sources rabbiniques

▶

Walter de Gruyter — W DE G — Berlin New York

200 Saw Mill River Road — Hawthorne, N. Y. 10532/USA

des IIe et IIIe siècles. Contribution à l'étude du syncrétisme dans l'empire romain (397–485) · Stiegman, E.: Rabbinic Anthropology (487–579) · Bietenhard, H.: Logos-Theologie im Rabbinat. Ein Beitrag zur Lehre vom Worte Gottes im rabbinischen Schrifttum (580–618) · Green, W. S.: Palestinian Holy Men: Charismatic Leadership and Rabbinic Tradition (619–647) · Levine, L. I.: The Jewish Patriarch (Nasi) in Third Century Palestine (649–688).

Band 20: Religion (Hellenistisches Judentum in römischer Zeit: Allgemeines)

Inhalt:

Delling, G.: Die Begegnung zwischen Hellenismus und Judentum · Walter, N.: Jüdisch-hellenistische Literatur vor Philon von Alexandrien (unter Ausschluß der Historiker) · Doran, R.: The Jewish-Hellenistic Historians before Josephus · Hadas-Lebel, M.: L'évolution de l'image de Rome auprès des Juifs en deux siècles de relations judéo-romaines, 164 avant –66 après J. C. · Lease, G.: Jewish Mystery Cults since Goodenough · Hay, D. M.: The Psychology of Faith in Hellenistic Judaism · Charlesworth, J. H.: Jewish Interest in Astrology during the Hellenistic and Roman Period · De Jonge, M.: The Testaments of the Twelfe Patriarchs: Central Problems and Essential Viewpoints · Collins, J. J.: The Development of the Sibylline Tradition · Nikiprowetzky, V.: La Sibylle Juive et le IIIe livre des pseudo-oracles sibyllins depuis Ch. Alexandre · Charlesworth, J. H.: The Treatise of Shem: Introduction, Text and Translation · Strugnell, J.: The Testament of Orpheus. Edition, Translation, and Commentary · Riaud, J.: Les Thérapeutes d'Alexandrie dans la tradition et dans la recherche critique jusqu'aux découvertes de Qumran.

Band 21: Religion (Hellenistisches Judentum in römischer Zeit: Philon und Josephus)

Inhalt:

Sandmel, S.: Philo Judaeus: An Introduction to the Man, his Writings, and his Significance · Hilgert, E.: Bibliographia Philoniana 1935–1980 · Borgen, P.: Philo of Alexandria. A critical and synthetical survey of research since World War II · Cazeaux, J.: Philon d'Alexandrie exégète · Mack, B. L.: Philo Judaeus and Exegetical Traditions in Alexandria · Terian, A.: A Critical Introduction to Philo's Dialogues · Hecht, R. D.: Philo's Interpretation of the Sacrificial Laws · Reister, W.: Philons Einfluß auf die frühchristliche Exegese · Trisoglio, F.: Filone Alessandrino e la fioritura della cultura cappadocica. Contributo alla conoscenza dell'influsso esercitato da Filone sul IV secolo, specificatamente in Gregorio di Nazianzo · Savon, H.: Saint Ambroise et Saint Jérôme, lecteurs de Philon · Pearson, B. A.: Philo and Gnosticism · Conley, T. M.: Philo's Rhetoric. Argumentation and Style · Spoerri, W.: Die Kosmogonie Philons von Alexandrien: Präexistente Materie oder 'creatio ex nihilo'? · Winston, D.: Philo's Ethical Theory and its Metaphysical Presuppositions · Sills, D. R.: Politics and Allegory in Philo · Kraus Reggiani, C.: I rapporti fra l'impero romano e il mondo ebraico al tempo di Caligola secondo la 'Legatio ad Gaium' di Filone Alessandrino · Feldman, L. H.: Flavius Josephus: An Introduction to the Man, his Writings, and his Significance · Moehring, H. R.: Joseph Ben Matthia and Flavius Josephus. The Jewish Prophet and Roman Historian · Michel, O.: Die Rettung Israels und die Rolle Roms nach den Reden im ‚Bellum Iudaicum' des Josephus.

Nachtrag zu Bd. II 19: Rabello, A. M.: L'observance des fêtes juives dans l'Empire romain · Gutmann, J.: Early Synagogue and Jewish Catacomb Art and its Relation to Christian Art.

Walter de Gruyter · Berlin · New York
200 Saw Mill River Road · Hawthorne, N. Y. 10532/USA